A-Z NOTTINGHAM

Key to Map Pages	2-3
Large Scale City Centre	4-5
Map Pages	6-81
Postcode Map	82-83

Ro
In
Vil
an

REFERE

Motorway	**M1**
A Road	**A46**
B Road	**B682**
Dual Carriageway	
One-way Street Traffic flow on A Roads is also indicated by a heavy line on the driver's left.	
Road Under Construction Opening dates are correct at the time of publication.	
Proposed Road	
Restricted Access	
Pedestrianized Road	
Track / Footpath	
Residential Walkway	
Railway	Heritage Station / Station / Level Crossing / Tunnel
Nottingham Express Transit (NET) The boarding of NET trams at stops maybe limited to a single direction, indicated by the arrow	Stop
Built-up Area	MILL RD.
Local Authority Boundary	
Postcode Boundary	
Map Continuation	**40** / Large Scale City Centre **4**

Ca	
Church or Chapel	†
Cycleway (selected)	
Fire Station	■
Hospital	**H**
House Numbers (A & B Roads only)	37 44
Information Centre	**i**
National Grid Reference	³45
Park and Ride	Lace market **P+R**
Police Station	▲
Post Office	★
Toilet	▽
Educational Establishment	
Hospital or Healthcare Building	
Industrial Building	
Leisure or Recreational Facility	
Place of Interest	
Public Building	
Shopping Centre or Market	
Other Selected Buildings	

SCALE

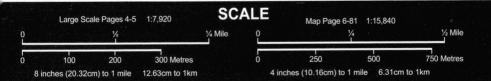

Large Scale Pages 4-5   1:7,920

0   ⅛   ¼ Mile

0   100   200   300 Metres

8 inches (20.32cm) to 1 mile   12.63cm to 1km

Map Page 6-81   1:15,840

0   ¼   ½ Mile

0   250   500   750 Metres

4 inches (10.16cm) to 1 mile   6.31cm to 1km

EDITION 9   2021

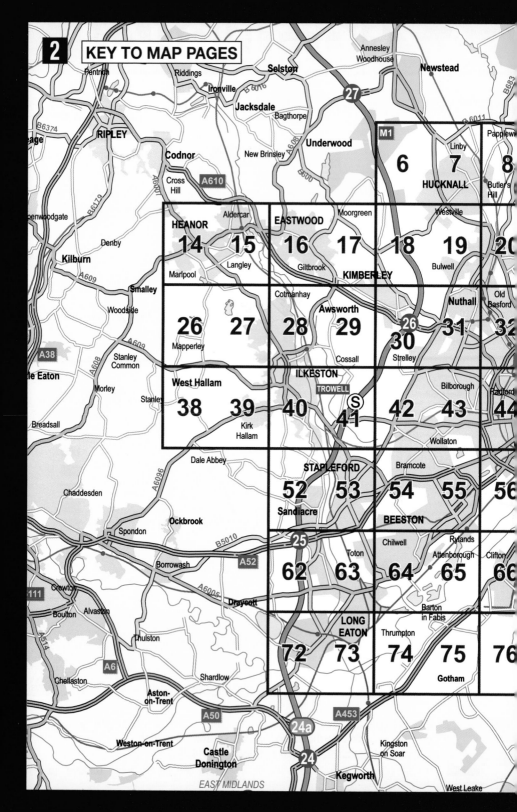

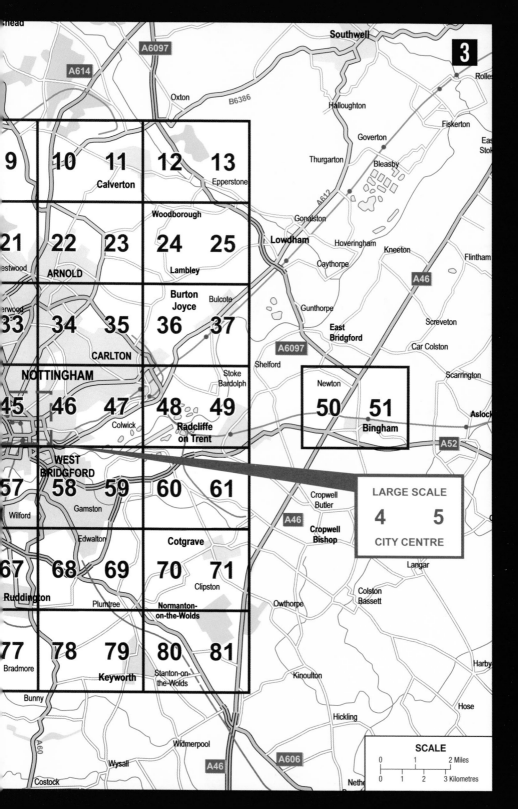

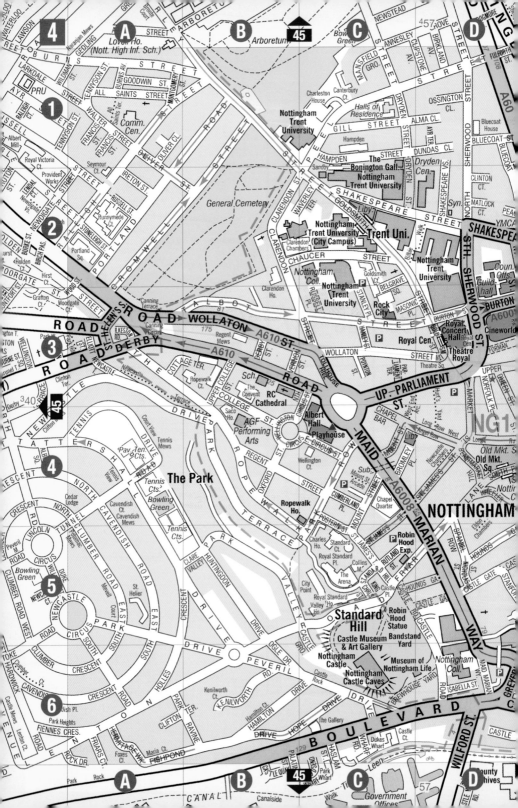

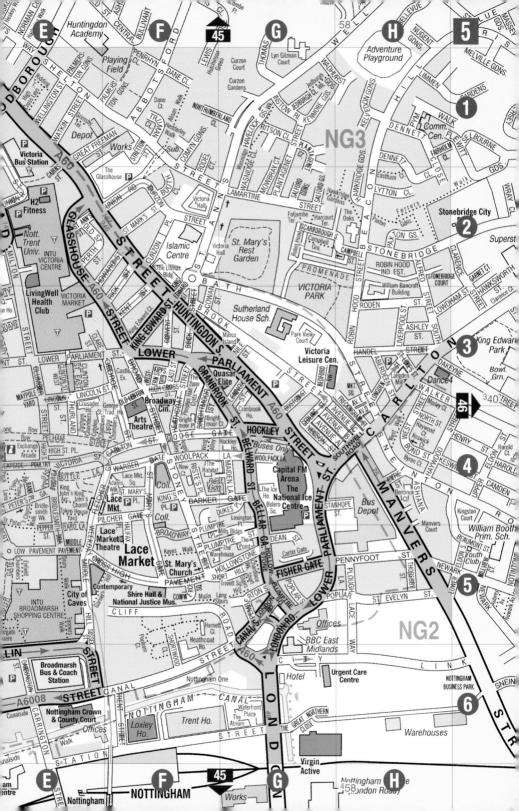

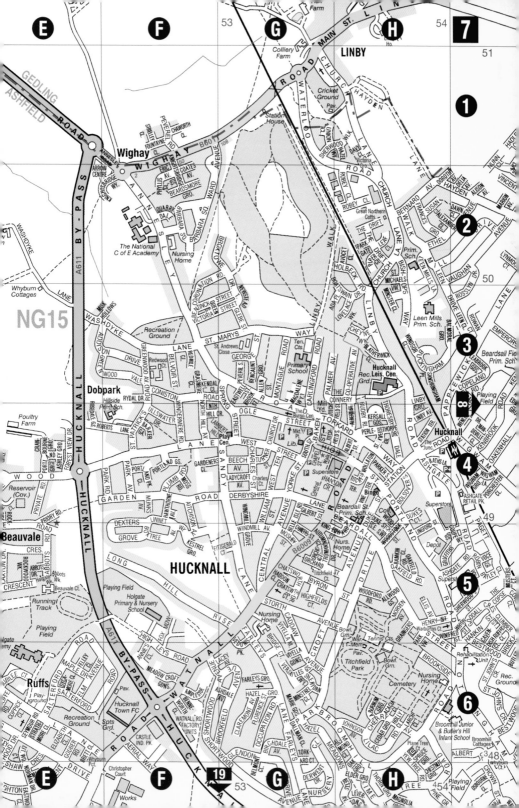

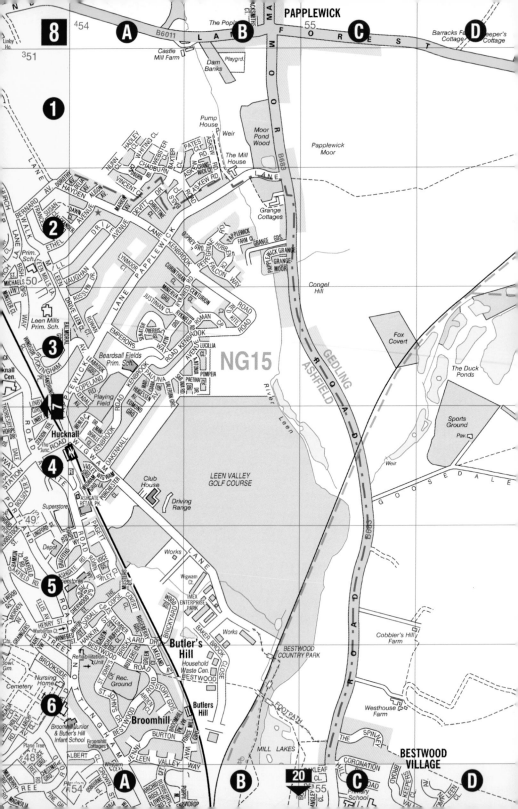

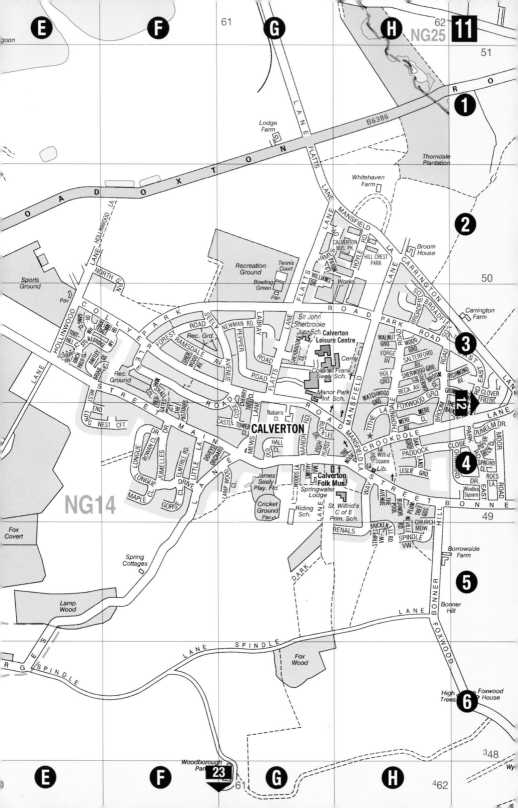

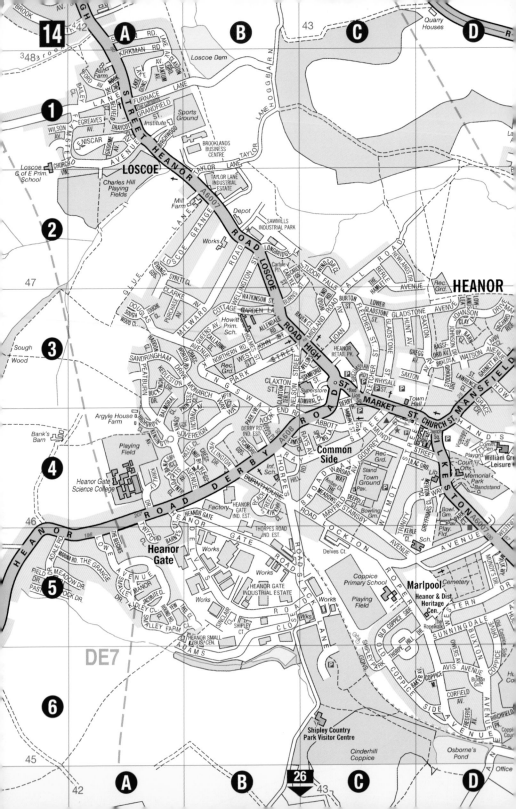

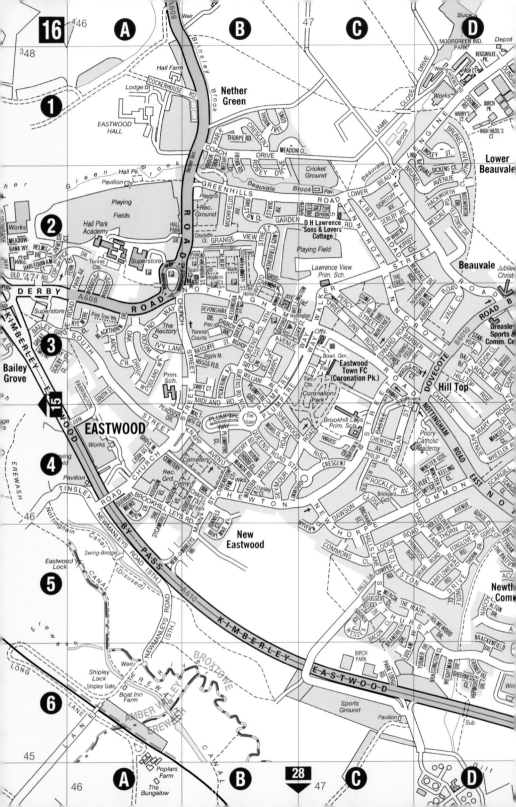

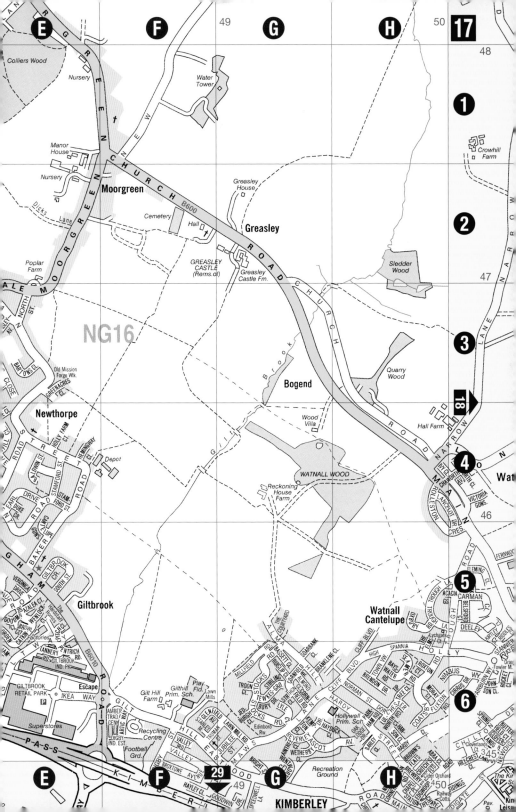

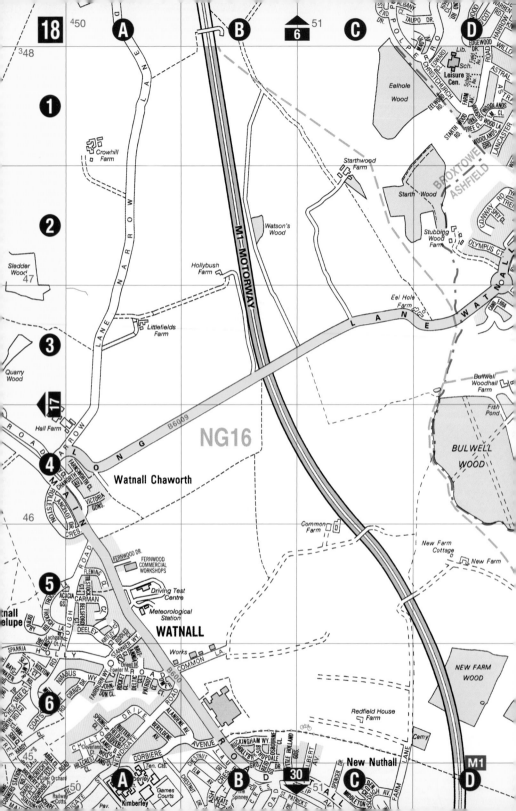

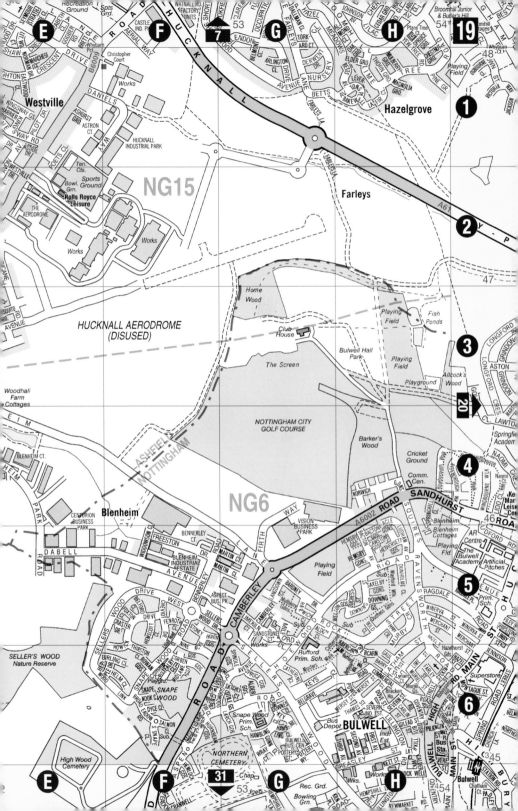

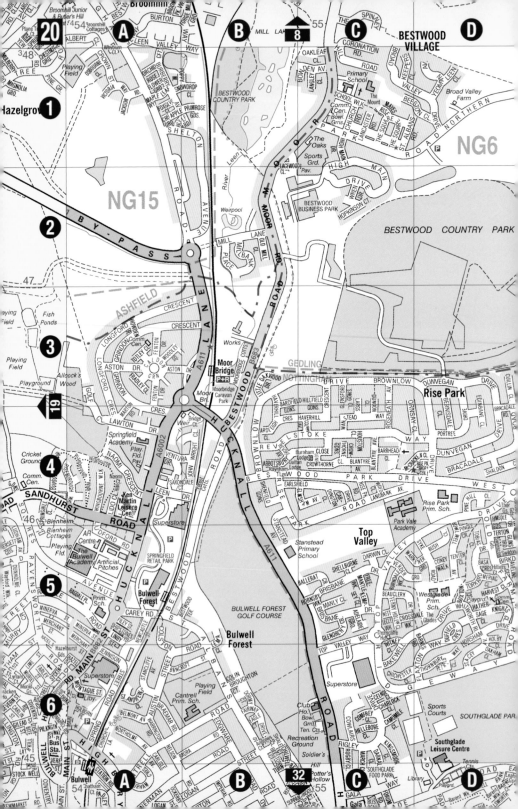

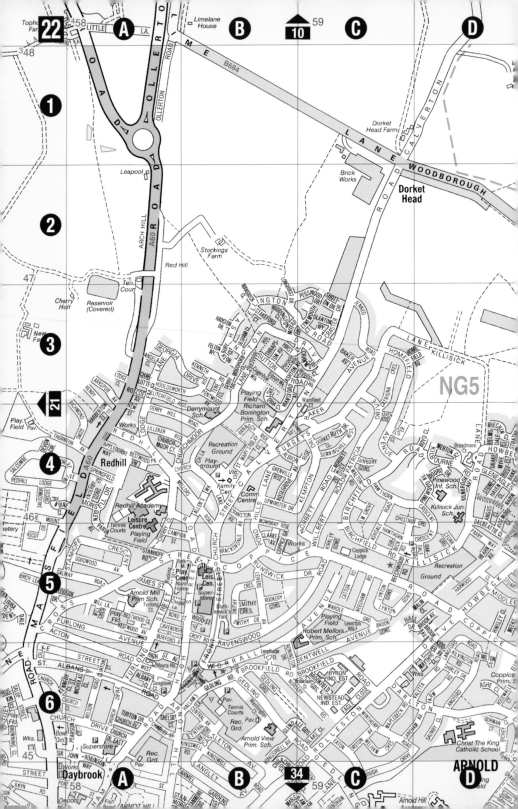

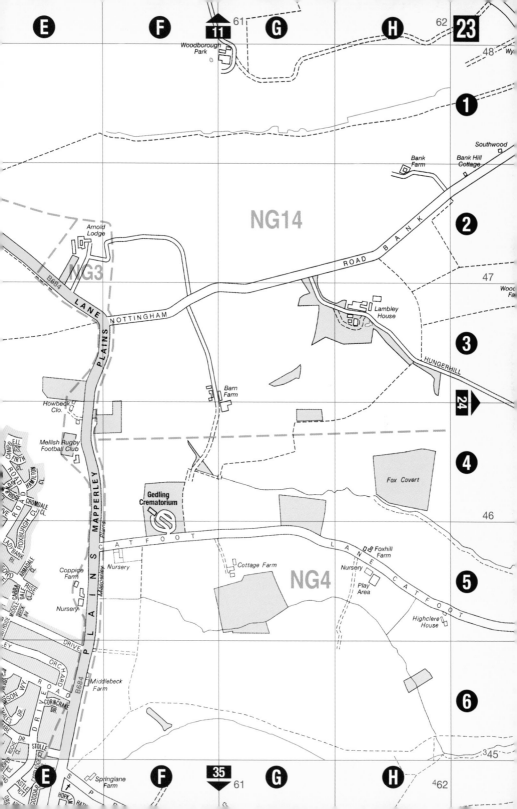

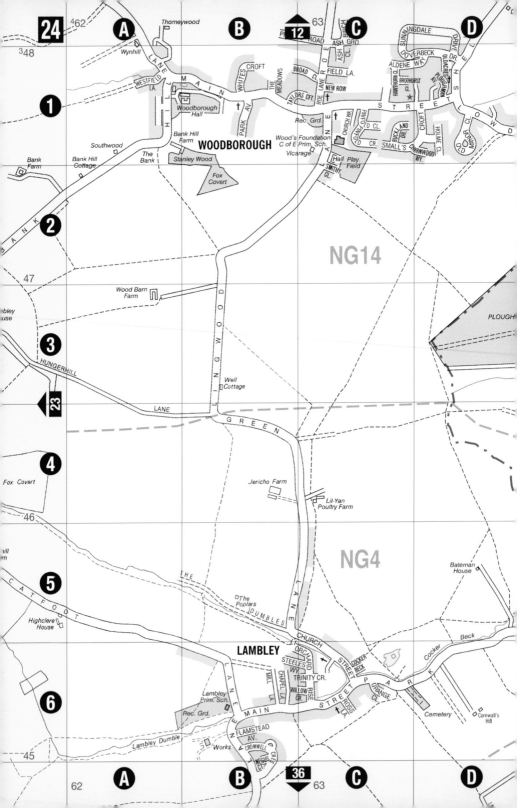

E F 13 65 G Village Hall / Pav. H 66 25 48

Epperstone Playing Field

ONNALSTON

BY-PASS A6097 EPPERSTONE Wash Bridge Beck

1 The Old Mill House

Nursery EPPERSTONE ROA A60

OLD Woodlands Hunters Cotts.

Nurseries

Eliment Hill Farm 2 st End illas

Th

GRANGE FM. COTTS Lowdham Grange 47

Cemetery

WOOD HMP LOWDHAM GRANGE THE GREEN HILL SYKE LONG MEADOW HILL 3 Greenacres

ROCKLEYS VIEW The Beck House

Beck Nursery

4

Hunters Hill Low Meadow

Cocker 46

NEWARK and SHERWOOD GEDLING Lowinds Farm

Park Lane Nurseries Hywinds Farm LANE LAMBLEY 5 Lowdham Lodge

Harlow Wood Farm

Works

6

Broughton Park

Bulcote Wood Sunny Bank Sibthorpe House Bee 345 Fari

Stockhill Farm Mumby House

E F 37 65 G Hill Farm H Tall Trees Nurseries

466

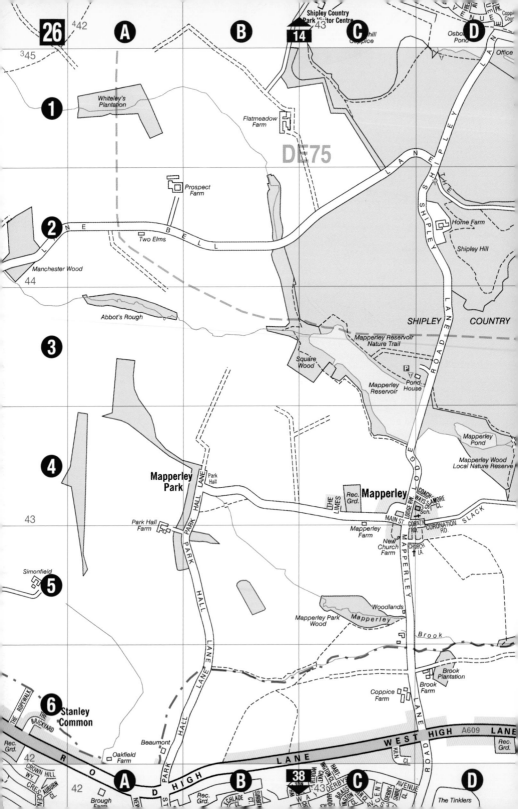

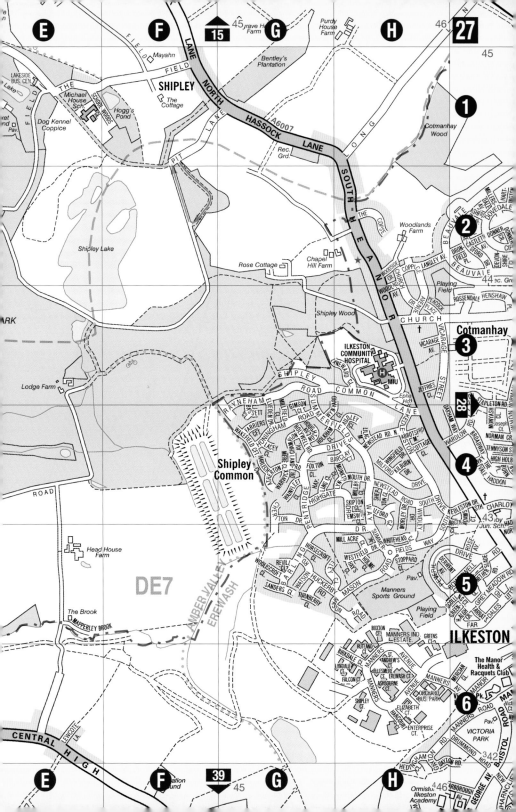

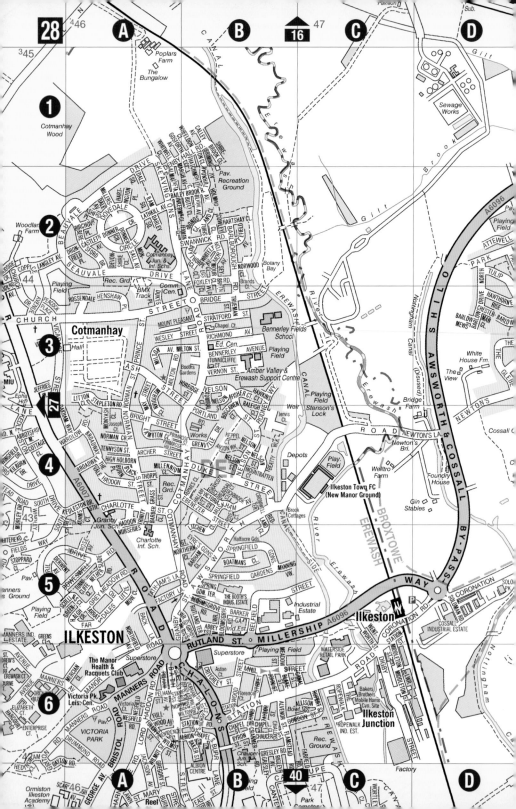

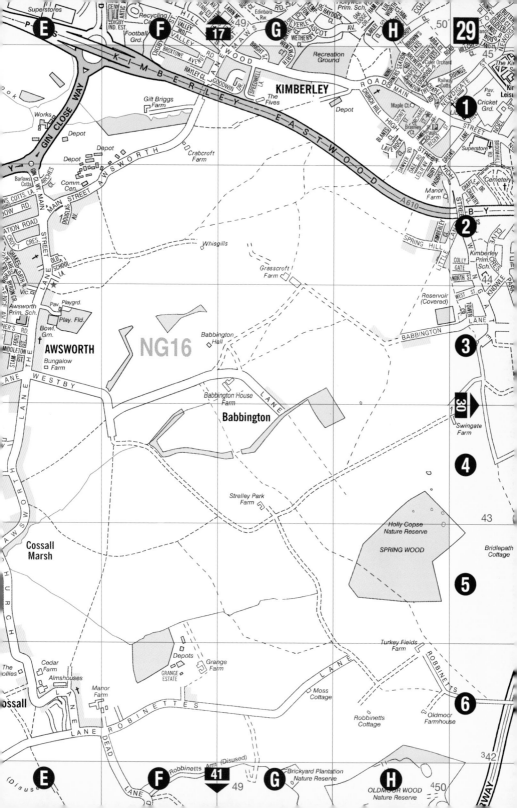

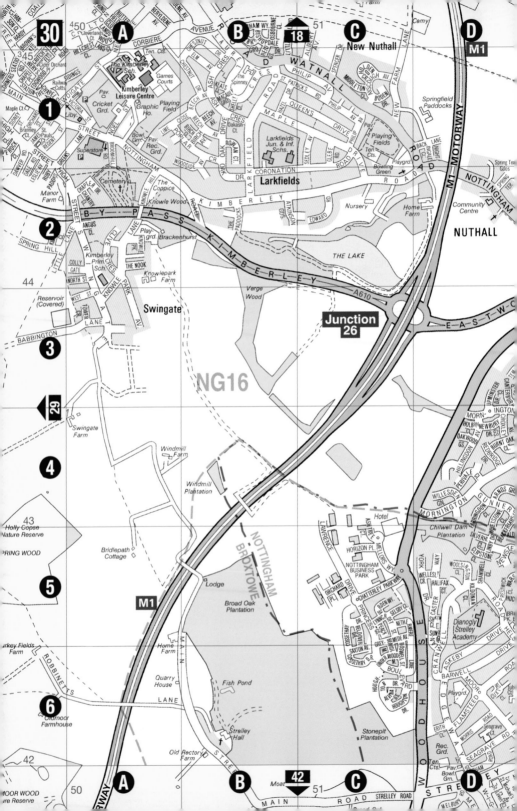

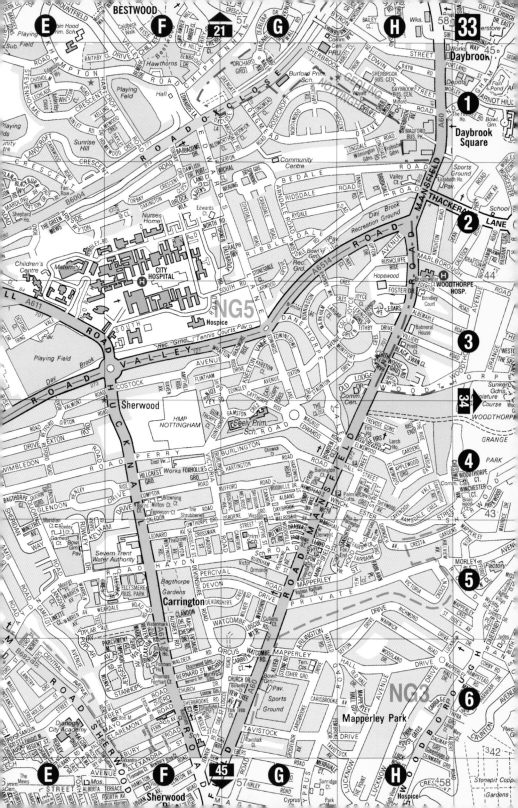

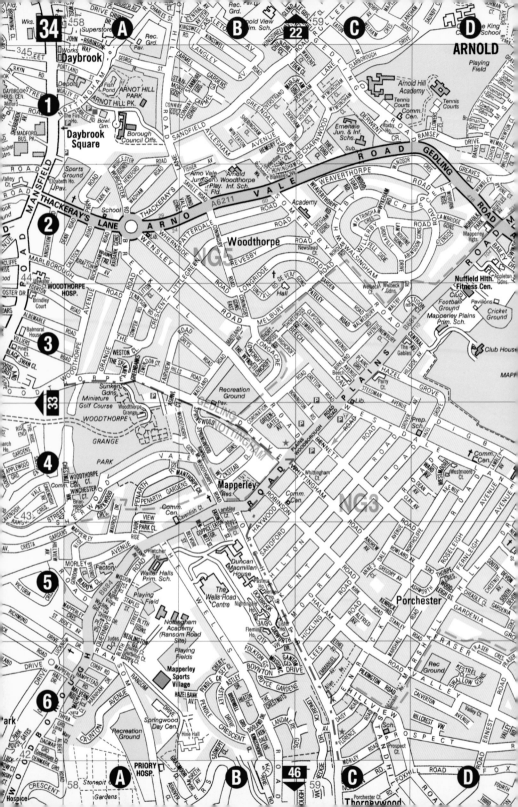

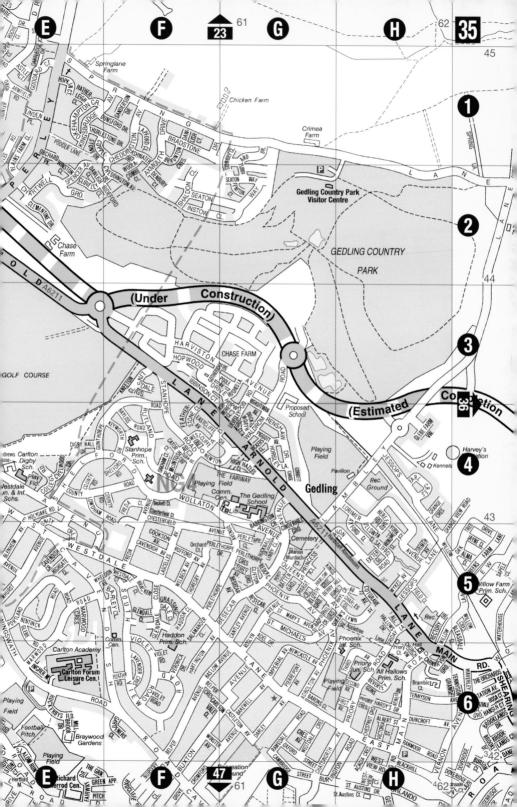

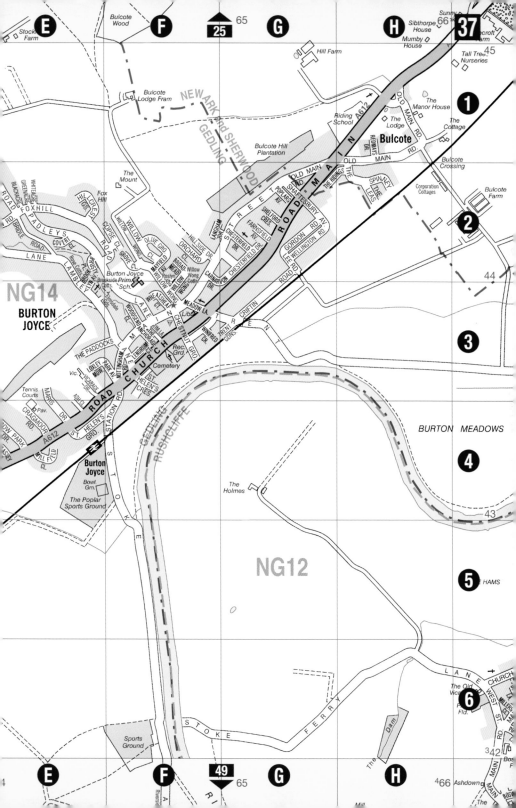

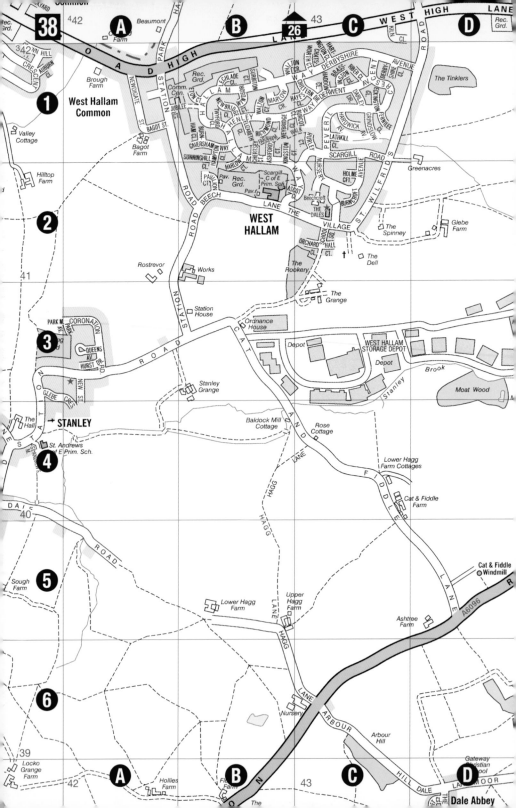

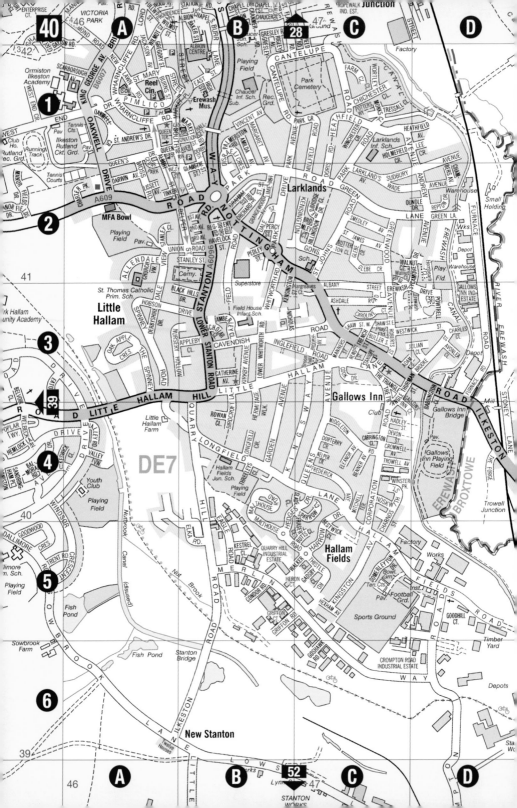

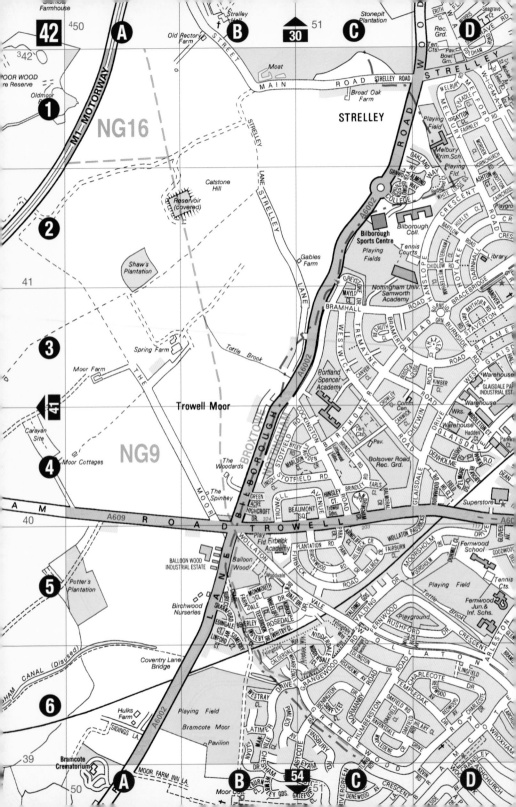

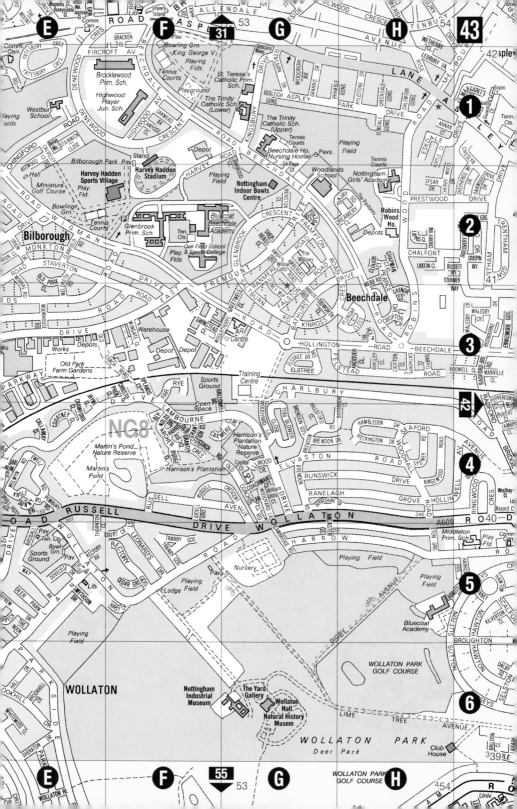

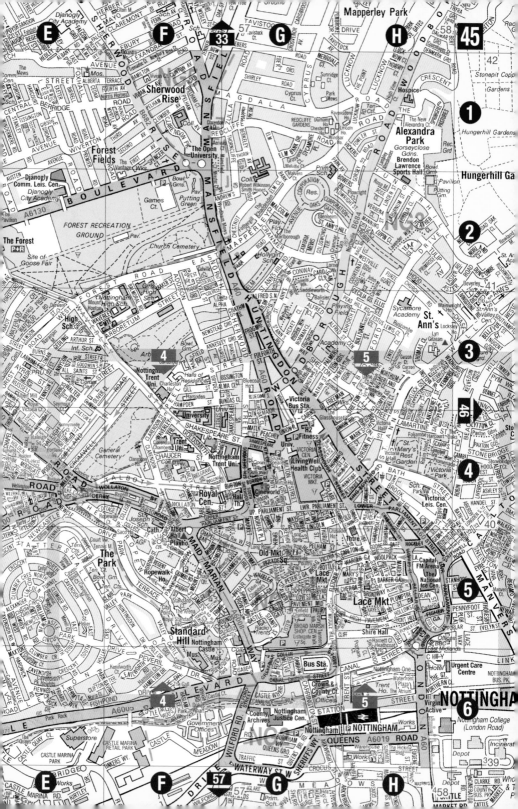

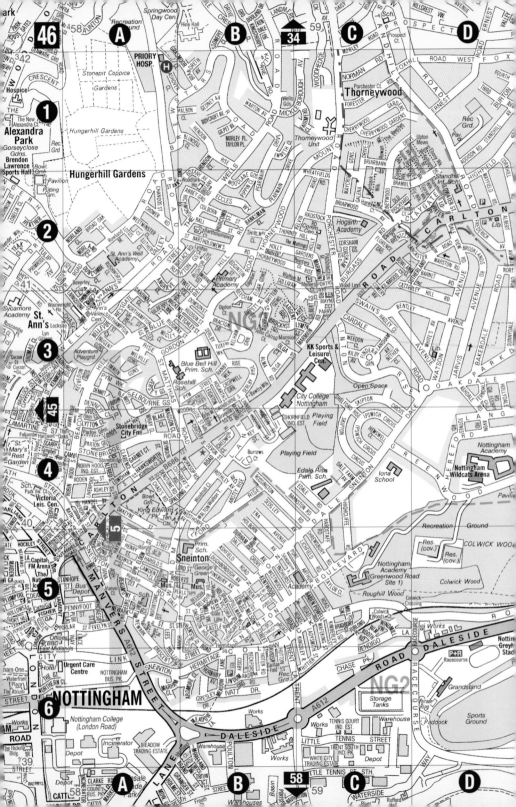

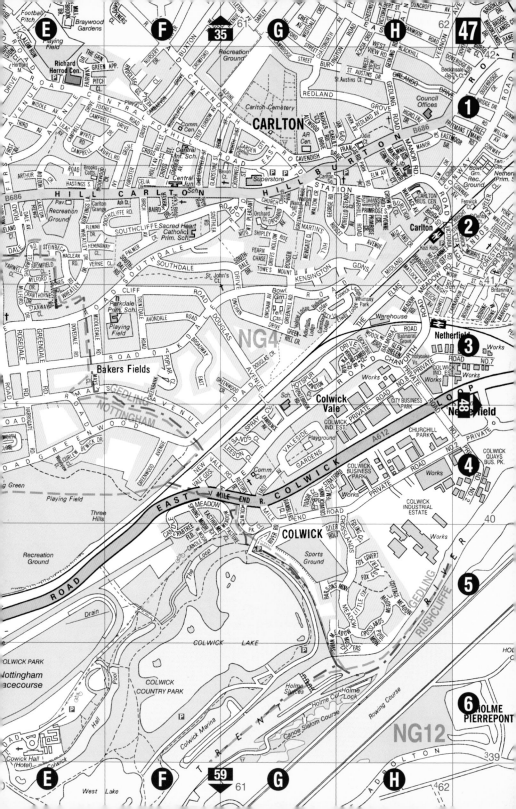

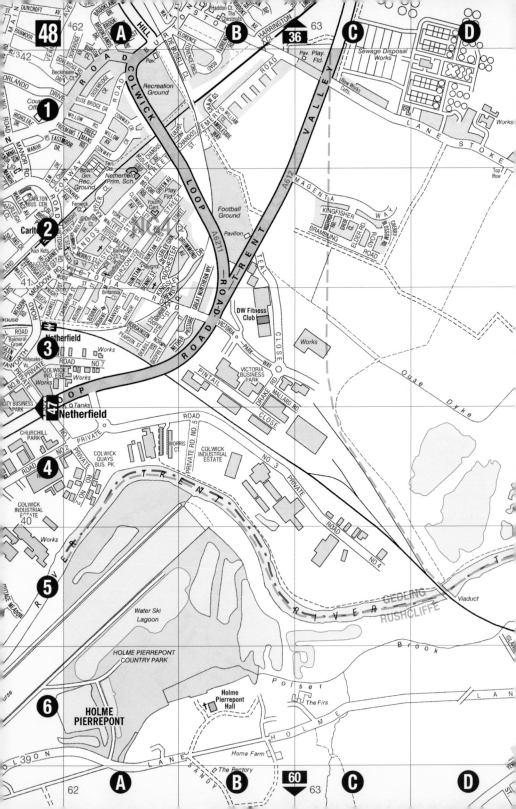

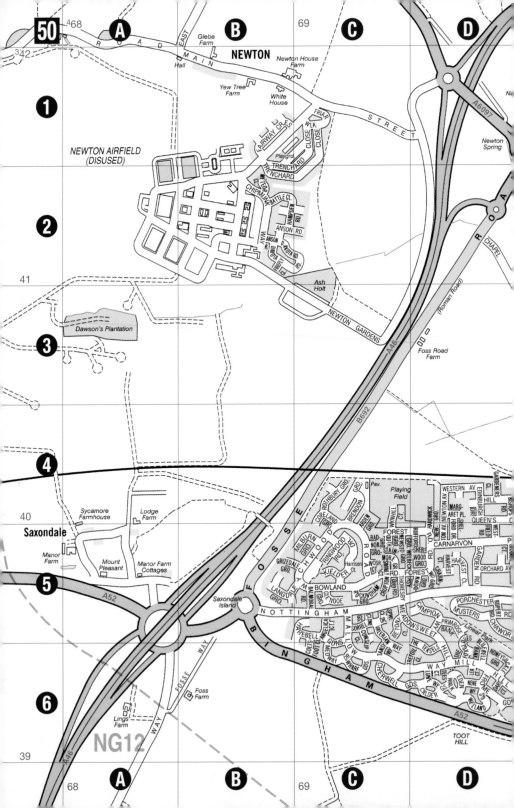

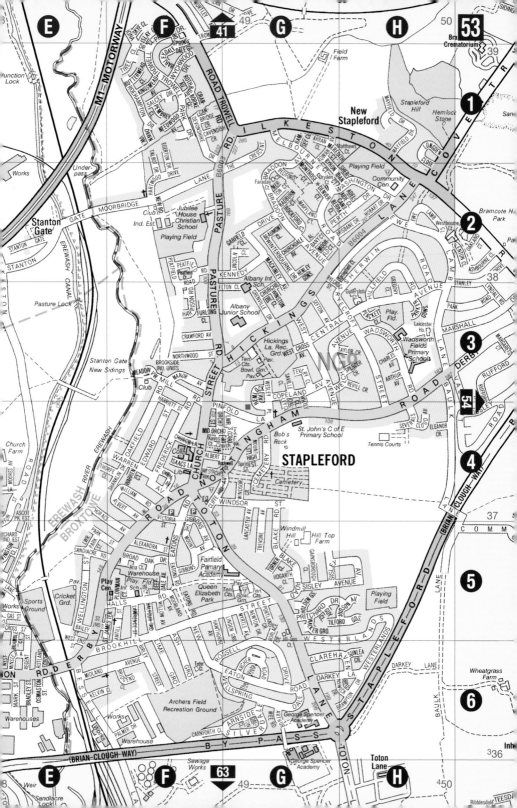

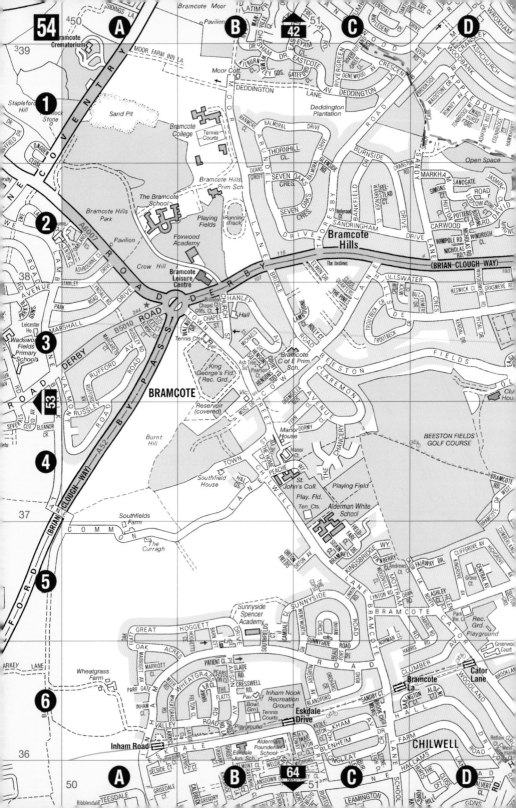

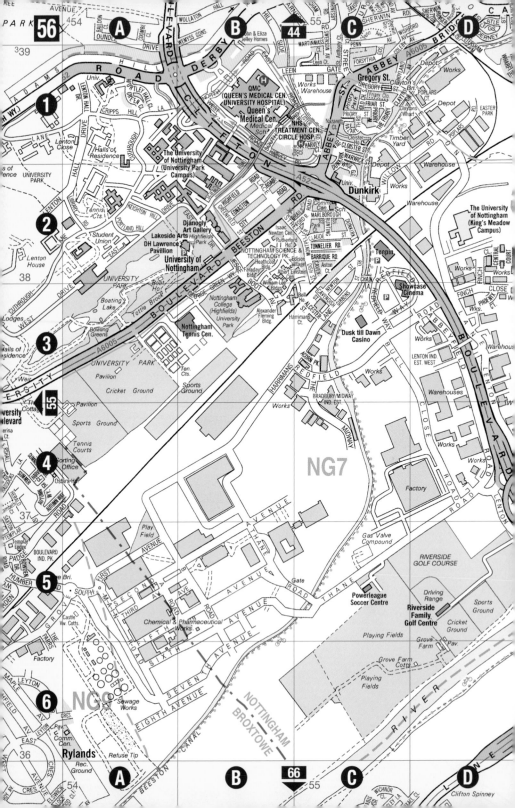

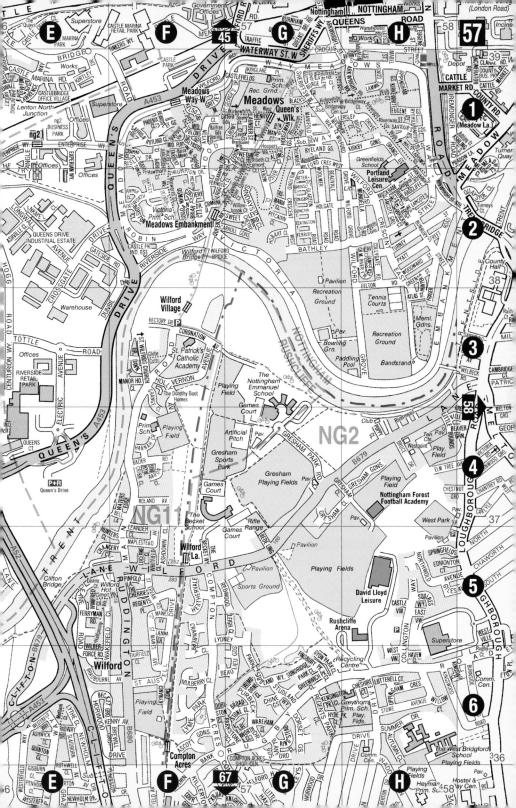

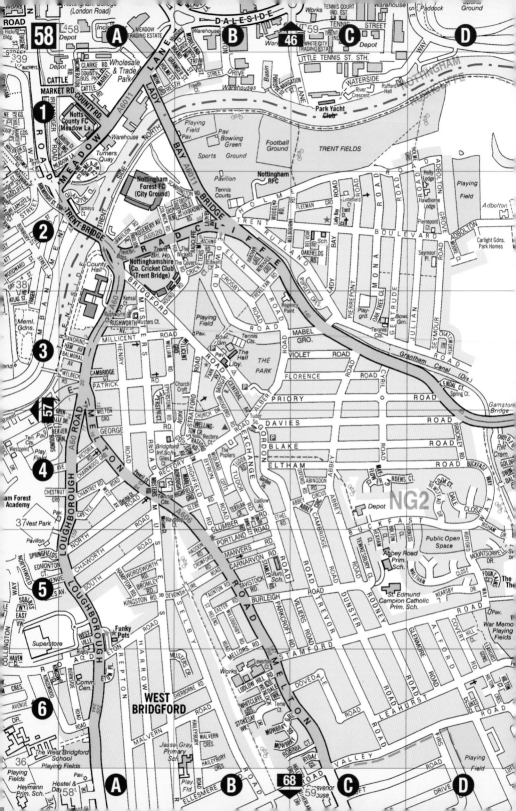

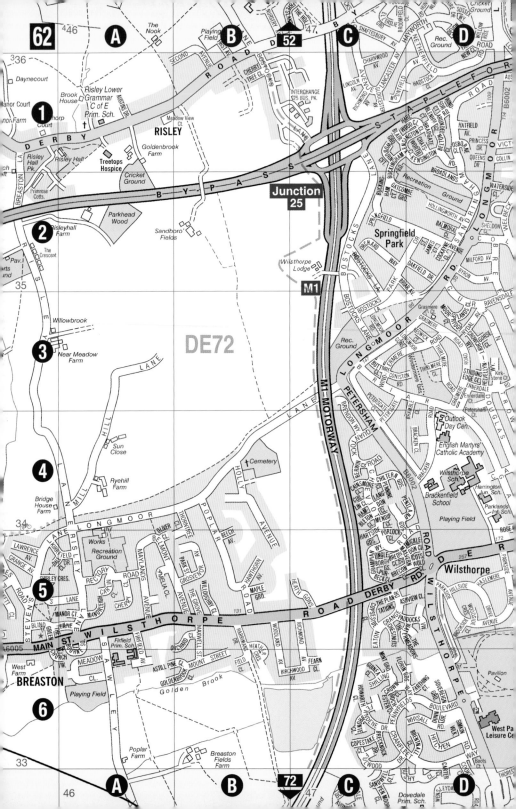

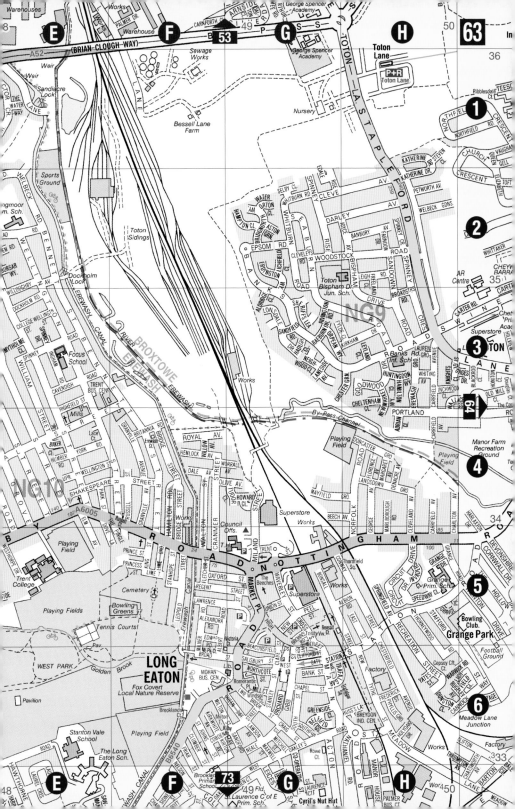

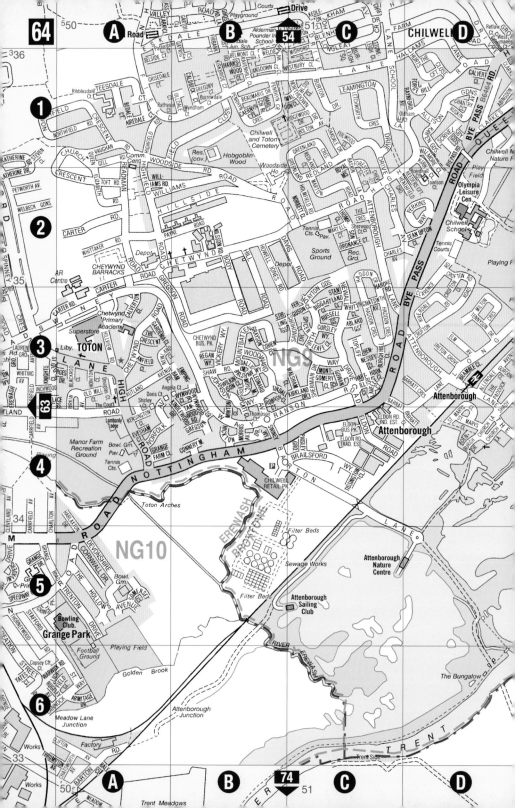

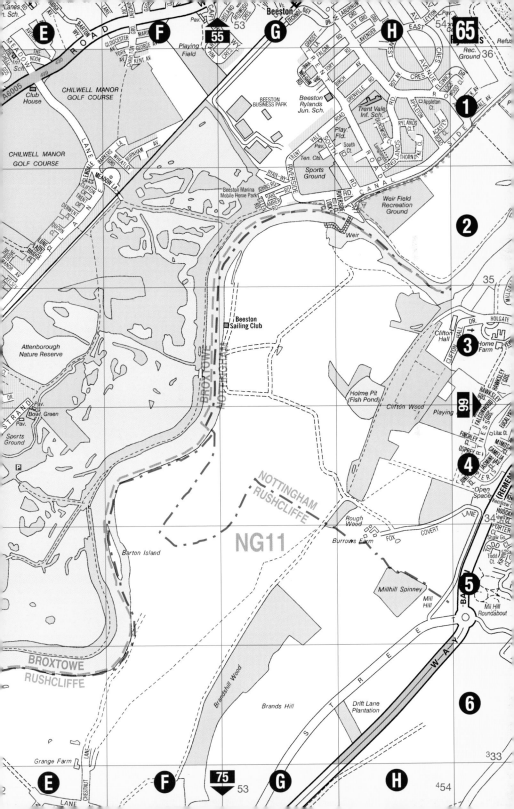

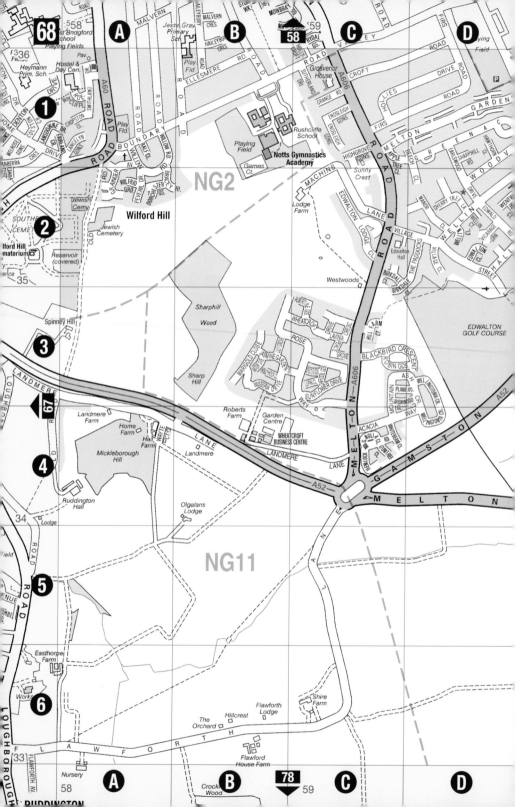

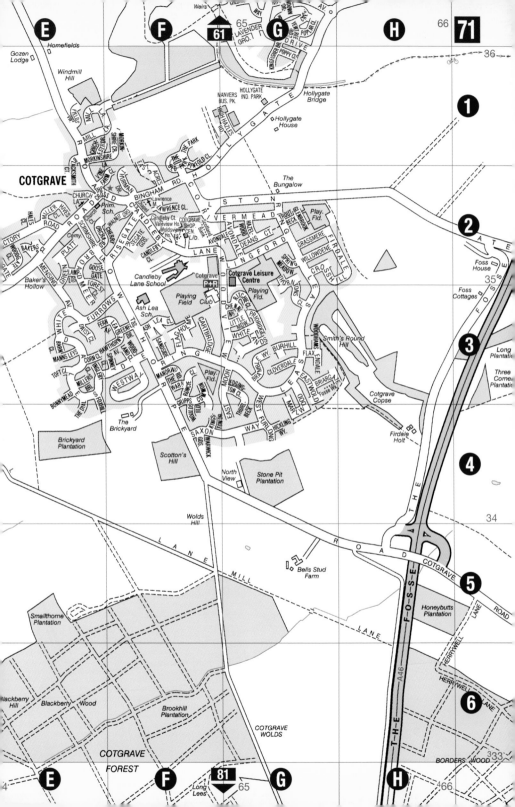

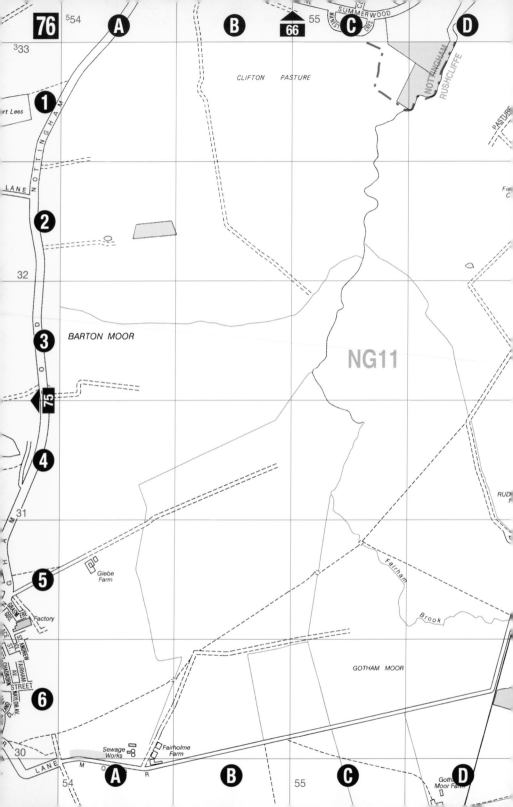

E COTGRAVE
FOREST
F 65 **71** COTGRAVE WOLDS **G** **H** 68 **81** BORDERS WOOD
33

Long Lees

1

Newark Gate

Wolds Farm

OWTHORPE WOLDS

Garston's Hill

Newfield Farm

2

Wynnstay Lodge

Clipston Wolds

G A P

ds m

32

3

Wynnstay Cottage

L A N E

Wynnstay Wood

NG12

Owthorpe Lodge

4

LANE

Hill Farm

Lodge on the Wolds

Kinoulton Gorse

31

Hillcrest

Roundhill Spinney

Bank Farm

Woodlands

5

L A N E

A606

The Wolds Nurseries

R O A D

Kinoulton Wolds

Brook

Kinross

6

LANE

Roehoe

Roehoe Wood

Fossways

330

E 64 **F** 65 **G** **H** 66 KINGSTON LANE

Woods Farm

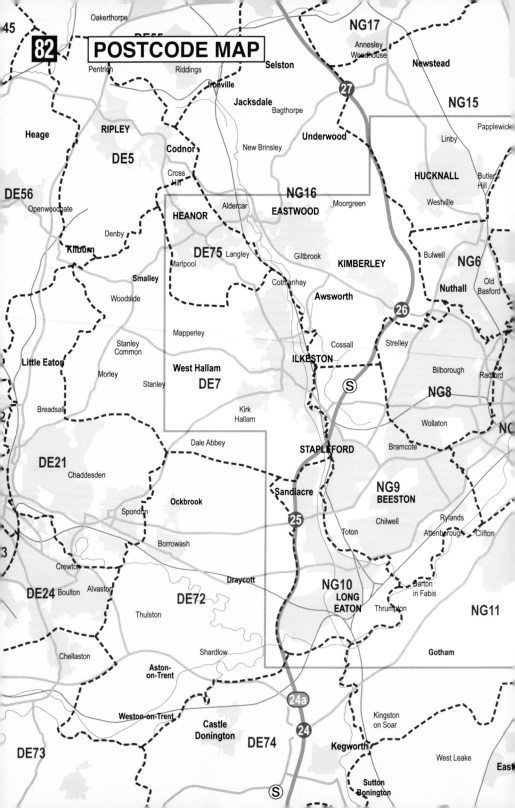

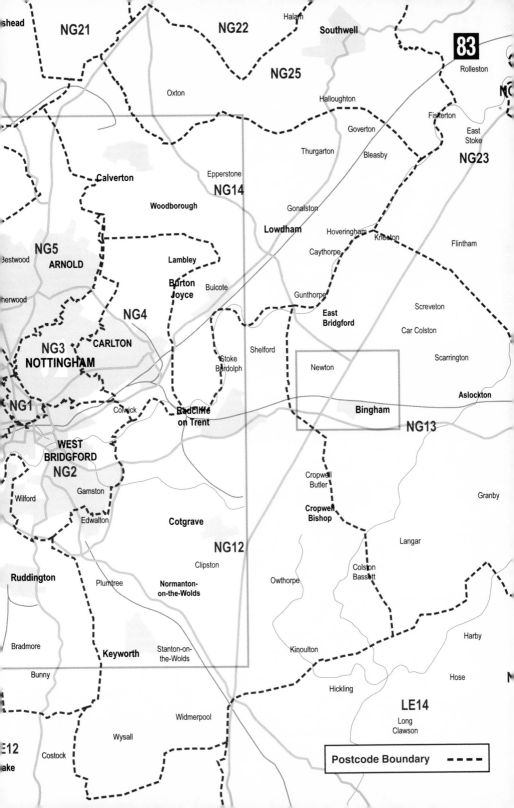

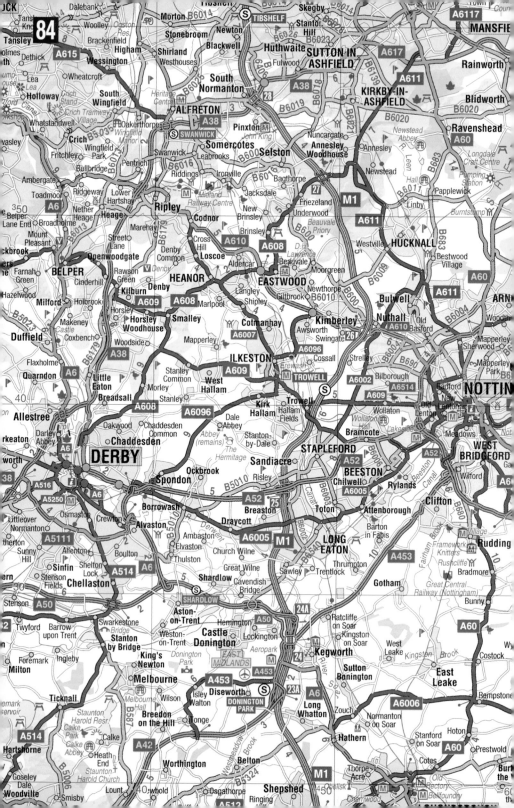

INDEX

Including Streets, Places & Areas, Hospitals etc., Industrial Estates,
Selected Flats & Walkways, Service Areas, Stations and Selected Places of Interest.

HOW TO USE THIS INDEX

1. Each street name is followed by its Postcode District, then by its Locality abbreviation(s) and then by its map reference; e.g. **Abbey Rd.** NG2: West Br..........4C **58** is in the NG2 Postcode District and the West Bridgford Locality and is to be found in square 4C on page **58**. The page number is shown in bold type.

2. A strict alphabetical order is followed in which Av., Rd., St., etc. (though abbreviated) are read in full and as part of the street name; e.g. **Apple Tree Cl.** appears after **Appleton Rd.** but before **Appletree La.**

3. Streets and a selection of flats and walkways that cannot be shown on the mapping, appear in the index with the thoroughfare to which they are connected shown in brackets; e.g. **Albion Terr.** DE7: Ilk..........6B **28** *(off Northgate St.)*

4. Addresses that are in more than one part are referred to as not continuous.

5. Places and areas are shown in the index in BLUE TYPE and the map reference is to the actual map square in which the town centre or area is located and not to the place name shown on the map; e.g. ALDERCAR..........1F **15**

6. An example of a selected place of interest is **Acorn Cen.**..........2G **15**

7. An example of a station is **Attenborough Station (Rail)**..........3D **64**

8. An example of a junction name or service area is **TROWELL SERVICE AREA**..........3G **41**

9. An example of a Hospital, Hospice or selected Healthcare facility is **CIRCLE NOTTINGHAM HOSPITAL**..........1C **56**

10. Map references for entries that appear on large scale page **4** & **5** are shown first, with small scale map references shown in brackets; e.g. **Abbotsford Dr.** NG3: Nott..........1F **5** (3H **45**)

GENERAL ABBREVIATIONS

App. : Approach	**Dr.** : Drive	**La.** : Lane	**Rdbt.** : Roundabout
Arc. : Arcade	**E.** : East	**Lit.** : Little	**Shop.** : Shopping
Av. : Avenue	**Ent.** : Enterprise	**Lwr.** : Lower	**Sth.** : South
Blvd. : Boulevard	**Est.** : Estate	**Mnr.** : Manor	**Sq.** : Square
Bri. : Bridge	**Fld.** : Field	**Mkt.** : Market	**St.** : Street
Bldgs. : Buildings	**Flds.** : Fields	**Mdw.** : Meadow	**Ter.** : Terrace
Bus. : Business	**Gdn.** : Garden	**Mdws.** : Meadows	**Trad.** : Trading
Cvn. : Caravan	**Gdns.** : Gardens	**M.** : Mews	**Up.** : Upper
Cen. : Centre	**Gth.** : Garth	**Mt.** : Mount	**Vw.** : View
Circ. : Circle	**Ga.** : Gate	**Mus.** : Museum	**Vs.** : Villas
Cl. : Close	**Gt.** : Great	**Nth.** : North	**Vis.** : Visitors
Cnr. : Corner	**Grn.** : Green	**Pde.** : Parade	**Wlk.** : Walk
Cott. : Cottage	**Gro.** : Grove	**Pk.** : Park	**W.** : West
Cotts. : Cottages	**Hgts.** : Heights	**Pas.** : Passage	**Yd.** : Yard
Ct. : Court	**Ho.** : House	**Pl.** : Place	
Cres. : Crescent	**Ind.** : Industrial	**Ri.** : Rise	
Cft. : Croft	**Info.** : Information	**Rd.** : Road	

LOCALITY ABBREVIATIONS

Arnold: NG3, NG5..........Arn
Aslockton: NG13..........Aslo
Aspley: NG8..........Aspl
Attenborough: NG9..........Atten
Awsworth: NG16..........Aws
Babbington: NG16..........Babb
Barton in Fabis: NG11..........Bart F
Basford: NG5, NG6, NG7, NG8..........Bas
Beeston: NG9..........Bee
Bestwood Village: NG6, NG15..........Bestw V
Bestwood: NG5, NG6..........Bestw
Bilborough: NG8..........Bilb
Bingham: NG13..........Bing
Bramcote: NG9..........Bram
Breaston: DE72..........Brea
Broxtowe: NG8..........Brox
Bulcote: NG14..........Bulc
Bulwell: NG6..........Bulw
Bunny: NG11..........Bunny
Burton Joyce: NG14..........Bur J
Calverton: NG5, NG14..........Calv
Carlton: NG4..........Car
Car Colston: NG13..........Car C
Chilwell: NG9..........Chil
Cinderhill: NG6, NG8, NG16..........Cin
Clifton: NG11..........Cliftn
Clipston: NG12..........C'ton
Colwick: NG2, NG4..........Colw
Cossall: NG16..........Coss

Cotgrave: NG12..........Cotg
Cropwell Bishop: NG12..........Crop Bi
Dale Abbey: DE7..........D Ab
Draycott: DE72..........Dray
East Bridgford: NG13..........East B
Eastwood: NG16..........Eastw
Edwalton: NG12..........Edwal
Epperstone: NG14..........Epp
Gamston: NG2..........Gam
Gedling: NG3, NG4..........Ged
Giltbrook: NG16..........Gilt
Gonalston: NG14..........Gon
Gotham: NG11..........Goth
Greasley: NG16..........Grea
Heanor: DE7, DE75..........Hea
Holme Pierrepont: NG12..........Hol P
Hoveringham: NG14..........Hove
Hucknall: NG15..........Huck
Hyson Green: NG7, NG8..........Hys G
Ilkeston: DE7..........Ilk
Keyworth: NG12..........Key
Kimberley: NG16..........Kimb
Kingston on Soar: NG11..........King
Kirk Hallam: DE7..........Kirk H
Kneeton: NG13..........Knee
Lambley: NG4..........Lamb
Langar: NG13..........Lang
Langley Mill: NG16..........Lang M
Lenton Abbey: NG9..........Lent A

Lenton: NG7, NG8, NG9..........Lent
Linby: NG15..........Lin
Long Eaton: NG10..........Long E
Loscoe: DE75..........Los
Lowdham: NG14..........Lowd
Mapperley Park: NG3..........Mapp P
Mapperley: DE7, NG3..........Mapp
Netherfield: NG4..........Neth
Newthorpe: NG16..........Newth
Newton: NG13..........Newt
Normanton-on-the-Wolds: NG12..........Norm W
Nottingham: NG1, NG2, NG3, NG7, NG9..........Nott
Nuthall: NG16..........Nuth
Owthorpe: NG12..........Owt
Oxton: NG25..........Oxton
Papplewick: NG15..........Pap
Plumtree: NG12..........Plum
Radcliffe on Trent: NG12..........Rad T
Radford: NG7, NG8..........Radf
Ratcliffe on Soar: NG11..........Rat
Redhill: NG5..........Redh
Risley: DE72..........Ris
Ruddington: NG11..........Rudd
Sandiacre: NG10..........Sand
Saxondale: NG13..........Saxon
Screveton: NG13..........Scre
Shardlow: DE72..........Shar
Shelford: NG12..........S'frd

Sherwood: NG5, NG7..........Sher
Shipley: DE75..........Ship
Smalley: DE7..........Smal
Southwell: NG25..........S'well
Stanley Common: DE7..........Stan C
Stanley: DE7..........Stly
Stanton-by-Dale: DE7..........Stant D
Stanton-on-the-Wolds: NG12..........Stant W
Stapleford: NG9..........Stfrd
Stoke Bardolph: NG4, NG14..........Stoke B
Strelley: NG8..........Stre
Thrumpton: NG11..........Thru
Tithby: NG13..........Tith
Tollerton: NG12..........Toll
Top Valley: NG5..........Top V
Toton: NG9..........Toton
Trowell: NG9..........Trow
Watnall: NG16..........Want
West Bridgford: NG2, NG11..........West Br
West Hallam: DE7..........West H
Whatton: NG13..........What
Widmerpool: NG12..........Widm
Wilford: NG11..........Wilf
Wollaton: NG8..........Woll
Woodborough: NG5, NG14..........Woodbo
Woodthorpe: NG5..........Woodt

A

Aaron Cl. NG11: Wilf..........4F **57**
Abba Cl. NG16: Kimb..........6H **17**
Abbey Bri. NG7: Lent..........1C **56**
Abbey Cir. NG2: West Br..........4C **58**
Abbey Cl. NG15: Huck..........4E **7**
Abbey Cl. NG9: Bee..........3F **55**
Abbey Dr. NG9: Bee..........4F **55**
Abbeyfield Rd. NG7: Lent..........3D **56**
Abbey Gro. NG3: Nott..........2B **46**
Abbey Rd. NG13: Bing..........4G **51**
Abbey Rd. NG16: Eastw..........3D **16**

Abbey Rd. NG2: West Br..........4C **58**
Abbey Rd. NG9: Bee..........3F **55**
Abbey St. DE7: Ilk..........5B **28**
Abbey St. NG7: Lent..........1C **56**
Abbot Cl. NG12: Key..........3G **79**
Abbot Rd. DE7: Kirk H..........3G **39**
Abbotsbury Cl. NG5: Top V..........4B **20**
Abbots Cl. NG5: Arn..........1H **33**
Abbots Dr. NG15: Huck..........5E **7**
Abbotsford Dr. NG3: Nott..........1F **5** (3H **45**)
Abbotsford M. DE7: Ilk..........4H **27**
Abbots Rd. NG15: Huck..........5E **7**
Abbot St. NG16: Aws..........3E **29**

Abbots Wlk. NG15: Huck..........5E **7**
Abbots Way NG8: Woll..........5H **43**
Abbott St. DE75: Hea..........4C **14**
Abbott St. NG10: Long E..........1F **73**
Abercarn Cl. NG6: Bulw..........6H **19**
Abercarn M. NG6: Bulw..........6H **19**
Aberdeen St. NG3: Nott..........3H **5** (4A **46**)
Aberford Av. NG8: Bas..........1B **44**
Abingdon Dr. NG11: Rudd..........5H **67**
Abingdon Gdns. NG5: Woodt..........2C **34**
Abingdon Gdns. NG9: Chil..........1D **64**
Abingdon Rd. NG2: West Br..........4C **58**
Abingdon Sq. NG8: Aspl..........6H **31**

Ablard Gdns. NG9: Chil..........3C **64**
Acacia Cl. NG15: Huck..........6H **7**
Acacia Cres. NG4: Car..........1H **47**
Acacia Gdns. NG16: Want..........5H **17**
Acacia Wlk. NG9: Bee..........5F **55**
Acacia Way NG12: Edwal..........4C **68**
Academy Cl. NG6: Bas..........4C **32**
Acaster Cl. NG9: Bee..........1H **65**
Access 26 Bus. Pk.
..........NG16: Lang M..........2G **15**
Acle Gdns. NG6: Bulw..........4H **19**
Acorn Av. NG16: Gilt..........5D **16**
..........(not continuous)

Acorn Bank NG2: West Br 1F **67**
Acorn Cen. 2G **15**
Acorn Av. NG4: Ged 4A **36**
Acorn Pk. NG7: Lent 3C **56**
A'court St. NG7: Hys G 3D **44**
Acre Cl. NG2: West Br................2E **59**
Acton Av. NG10: Long E..............1G **73**
Acton Av. NG6: Bas.....................3B **32**
Acton Cl. NG10: Long E 1G **73**
Acton Gro. NG10: Long E 1G **73**
Acton Rd. NG10: Long E 6G **63**
Acton Rd. NG5: Arn 5H **21**
Acton Rd. Ind. Est.
    NG10: Long E 1G **73**
    .... (not continuous)
Acton St. NG10: Long E 1G **73**
Adale Rd. DE7: Smal..................5A **14**
Adams Cl. DE75: Hea.................6B **14**
Adams Ct. DE7: Ilk 4A **28**
Adams Hill NG12: Key 4H **79**
Adams Hill NG7: Nott..................1H **55**
Adam St. DE7: Ilk 3C **40**
Adams Wlk. NG1: Nott.... 4F **5** (5H **45**)
    .... (off Fletcher Ga.)
Ada Pl. NG15: Huck.......................3G **7**
Adbolton Av. NG4: Ged 6G **35**
Adbolton Gro. NG2: West Br.. 1D **58**
Adbolton La. NG12: Hol P...........1H **59**
Adbolton La. NG2: West Br 2D **58**
Adbolton Lodge NG4: Car............3G **47**
Adderley Cl. NG5: Bestw............1E **33**
Addington Ct. NG12: Rad T 5G **49**
Addington Rd. NG7: Radf 3D **44**
Addison Dr. NG15: Huck..............3E **7**
Addison Rd. NG4: Car..................1D **46**
Addison St. NG1: Nott.................2F **45**
Addison Vs. NG16: Eastw............4A **16**
    .... (not continuous)
Adelaide Cl. NG9: Stfrd...............2H **53**
Adelaide Gro. NG5: Top V.............5C **20**
Adel Dr. NG4: Ged 5C **34**
Adenburgh Dr. NG9: Atten 4D **64**
Admiral Cl. DE75: Hea................3C **14**
Admiral Ct. DE7: Ilk 3B **28**
Adrian Cl. NG9: Toton 4H **63**
Aeneas Ct. NG5: Sher 1F **45**
Aerial Way NG15: Huck.................6F **7**
Aerodrome, The NG15: Huck......2E **19**
Agnes Vs. NG3: Mapp.................5A **34**
Aidan Gdns. NG5: Top V 3E **21**
Ainsdale Cres. NG8: Cin 4G **31**
Ainsley Rd. NG8: Aspl................3B **44**
Ainsworth Dr. NG2: Nott............2E **57**
Aintree Cl. NG16: Kimb...............6G **17**
Aira Cl. NG2: Gam.......................5F **59**
Airedale Cl. NG10: Long E...........1C **72**
Airedale Ct. NG9: Chil................1A **64**
Airedale Wlk. NG8: Woll...............6C **42**
Aitchison Av. NG15: Huck............4F **7**
Alandene Av. NG16: Want............6A **18**
Albany Cl. NG15: Huck................6C **6**
Albany Cl. NG5: Arn....................6A **22**
Albany Ct. NG9: Stfrd.................2G **53**
Albany Rd. NG7: Bas...................1E **45**
Albany St. DE7: Ilk......................3C **40**
Albemarle Rd. NG5: Woodt.........3H **33**
Alberta Ter. NG7: Hys G..............1E **45**
Albert Av. NG15: Huck.................6C **18**
Albert Av. NG4: Car....................2D **46**
Albert Av. NG8: Aspl...................1B **44**
Albert Av. NG9: Stfrd..................5G **53**
Albert Ball Cl. NG5: Top V 5D **20**
Albert Ball Ho. NG5: Top V 5E **21**
Albert Cl. NG15: Huck..................6A **8**
Albert Einstein Cen. NG7: Nott....2B **56**
Albert Gro. NG7: Lent 4D **44**
Albert Gro. NG7: Radf.................4D **44**
Albert Hall Nottingham.... 4C **4** (5F **45**)
Albertine Gdns. NG12: Edwal......3C **68**

Albert Mill NG7: Radf................3E **45**
Albert Rd. NG10: Long E.............5F **63**
Albert Rd. NG10: Sand................5D **52**
Albert Rd. NG11: Bunny..............6A **78**
Albert Rd. NG2: West Br.............3B **58**
Albert Rd. NG3: Nott...................6H **33**
Albert Rd. NG9: Bee 3G **55**
Albert Sq. NG7: Lent..................6C **44**
Albert St. DE7: Ilk......................1A **40**
Albert St. NG1: Nott........ 5E **5** (5G **45**)
Albert St. NG12: Rad T...............6F **49**
Albert St. NG15: Huck..................4H **7**
    .... (not continuous)
Albert St. NG16: Eastw...............2B **16**
Albert St. NG4: Ged....................6H **35**
Albert St. NG9: Stfrd..................4F **53**
Albion Cen. 1B **40**
Albion Ri. NG5: Arn.....................4B **22**
Albion Rd. NG10: Long E 5H **63**
Albion St. DE7: Ilk......................6B **28**
Albion St. NG1: Nott....6D **4** (6G **45**)
Albion St. NG9: Bee 4F **55**
Albion Ter. DE7: Ilk....................6B **28**
    .... (off Northgate St.)
Albury Dr. NG8: Aspl...................6H **31**
Albury Sq. NG7: Nott...... 4A **4** (5E **45**)
Alcester St. NG7: Lent.................3C **56**
Aldene Ct. NG9: Chil...................6D **54**
Aldene Way NG14: Woodbo.........1C **24**
ALDERCAR 1F **15**
Alder Gdns. NG6: Bulw................6G **19**
Alderman Cl. NG9: Bee................3F **55**
Aldermens Cl. NG2: Nott............1G **57**
Alderney St. NG7: Lent...............6D **44**
Alderton Rd. NG5: Bestw............1G **33**
Alder Way NG12: Key.................5A **80**
Aldgate Cl. NG6: Bulw................5G **19**
Aldred's La. NG16: Lang M...........3F **15**
Aldreds La. DE75: Hea................4E **15**
Aldridge Cl. NG9: Toton..............3G **63**
Aldrin Cl. NG6: Bulw...................2F **31**
Aldworth Cl. NG5: Bestw.............1F **33**
Aldwych Cl. NG16: Nuth..............5D **30**
Aldwych Cl. NG5: Arn..................4E **21**
Alexander Cl. NG15: Huck............2H **7**
Alexander Fleming Bldg.
    NG7: Nott...............................3B **56**
Alexander Rd. NG7: Nott............5E **45**
Alexandra Cres. NG9: Bee...........5G **55**
Alexandra Gdns. NG5: Sher.........6F **33**
Alexandra M. NG5: Sher.............1F **45**
ALEXANDRA PARK 1H **45**
Alexandra Rd. NG10: Long E........5F **63**
Alexandra St. NG16: Eastw..........3B **16**
Alexandra St. NG5: Sher..............1F **45**
Alexandra St. NG9: Stfrd.............5F **53**
Alford Cl. NG9: Bee 6G **55**
Alford Rd. NG12: Edwal...............1E **69**
Alford Rd. NG2: West Br.............5D **58**
Alfred Av. NG3: Mapp.................5C **34**
Alfred Cl. NG3: Nott...................3G **45**
Alfred St. Central NG3: Nott........3G **45**
Alfred St. Nth. NG3: Nott.............3G **45**
Alfred St. Sth. NG3: Nott... 2H **5** (4A **46**)
Alfreton Rd. NG7: Hys G.............2C **44**
Alfreton Rd. NG7: Nott................2C **44**
Alfreton Rd. NG7: Radf................2C **44**
Alison Av. NG15: Huck.................2A **8**
Alison Wlk. NG3: Nott..... 1F **5** (3H **45**)
Allen Av. NG3: Mapp...................6C **34**
Allendale DE7: Ilk.......................2A **40**
Allendale Av. NG8: Aspl...............6F **31**
Allendale Av. NG9: Atten............3D **64**
Allendale Rd. DE75: Hea..............3B **14**
Allen Fld. Ct. NG7: Lent..............6D **44**
Allen St. NG15: Huck...................3G **7**
All Hallows Dr. NG4: Ged.............5H **35**

Allington Av. NG7: Lent 6D **44**
Allison Gdns. DE7: Ilk.................6C **28**
Allison Gdns. NG9: Chil...............1D **64**
All Saints St. NG7: Radf 1A **4** (3E **45**)
All Saints Ter. NG7: Radf.. 1A **4** (3E **45**)
Allwood Dr. NG4: Car..................1G **47**
Allwood Gdns. NG15: Huck..........5H **7**
Alma Cl. DE7: Ilk........................2A **28**
Alma Cl. NG1: Nott.........1D **4** (3G **45**)
Alma Cl. NG4: Ged......................5A **36**
Alma Hill NG16: Kimb..................5G **17**
Alma Rd. NG3: Nott.....................3B **46**
Alma St. NG7: Bas......................1E **45**
Almond Cl. NG15: Huck................6H **7**
Almond Cl. NG16: Kimb...............6G **17**
Almond Ct. NG2: Nott.................1G **57**
Almond Wlk. NG4: Ged...............5A **36**
Almond Way NG8: Bilb.................2D **42**
Alnwick Cl. NG6: Bulw................1B **32**
Alpha Ter. NG1: Nott...................3F **45**
Alpine Cres. NG4: Car.................4C **34**
Alpine St. NG6: Bas.....................5C **32**
Althea Ct. NG7: Bas....................6E **33**
    .... (off Poyser Cl.)
Althorpe St. NG7: Radf................4E **45**
Alton Av. NG11: Wilf....................1F **67**
Alton Cl. NG2: West Br...............2G **67**
Alton Dr. NG16: Gilt....................5D **16**
Alum Ct. NG5: Top V...................5D **20**
Alverstone Rd. NG3: Mapp P......6G **33**
Alvey Ter. NG7: Radf...................4C **44**
Alvina Gdns. NG8: Stre...............6C **30**
Alwood Gro. NG11: Cliftn............2B **66**
Alwyn Ct. NG9: Bee 6F **55**
Alwyn Rd. NG8: Brox...................5F **31**
Alyth Ct. NG6: Bas......................4D **32**
Amber Cl. NG5: Bestw.................6F **21**
Amber Ct. NG15: Huck..................4C **14**
Amber Dr. NG16: Lang M..............3F **15**
Ambergate Rd. NG8: Bilb.............2G **43**
    .... (not continuous)
Amber Hill NG5: Bestw................6F **21**
Amberley Cl. DE7: Ilk..................3B **40**
Amber Rd. NG9: Bee 2G **65**
Amber Trad. Cen. NG16: Kimb......6F **17**
Ambleside NG15: Huck..................6F **7**
Ambleside NG2: Gam...................4E **59**
Ambleside Dr. NG16: Eastw.........2H **15**
Ambleside Rd. NG8: Aspl.............6G **31**
Ambleside Way NG4: Ged............1B **48**
Amelia Cl. DE72: Brea.................5A **62**
Amersham Rd. NG8: Aspl............6H **31**
Amilda Av. DE7: Ilk.....................1B **40**
Ampthill Ri. NG5: Sher................3F **33**
Ancaster Gdns. NG8: Woll...........4G **43**
Anchorage, The NG14: Bur J.......3F **37**
Anchor Cl. NG8: Aspl...................5H **31**
Anchor Ct. NG5: Bestw................6F **21**
Anchor Rd. NG16: Eastw..............2G **15**
Anders Dr. NG6: Bulw.................2F **31**
Anderson Cl. NG5: Top V.............5E **21**
Anderson Cres. NG9: Bee............3E **55**
Andover Cl. NG8: Bilb.................3H **43**
Andover Rd. NG5: Bestw.............1C **32**
Andrew Av. DE7: Ilk....................2D **40**
Andrew Av. NG3: Mapp...............5C **34**
Andrews Cl. NG9: Chil.................5C **54**
Andrews Dr. NG16: Lang M..........1E **15**
Anfield Cl. NG9: Toton.................3A **64**
Anford Cl. NG6: Bulw...................2H **31**
Angela Cl. NG5: Arn.....................3A **22**
Angela Ct. NG9: Toton.................3A **64**
Angel All. NG1: Nott......... 4F **5** (5H **45**)
Angelica Ct. NG13: Bing..............5C **50**
Angell Grn. NG11: Cliftn...............5A **66**
Angel Row NG1: Nott..... 4D **4** (5G **45**)
Angletarn Cl. NG2: West Br.........5E **59**

Angrave Cl. NG3: Nott.................2A **46**
Angus Cl. NG16: Kimb.................2A **30**
Angus Cl. NG5: Arn.....................4D **22**
Anmer Cl. NG2: Nott...................2F **57**
Annan Ct. NG8: Aspl...................1H **43**
Anne's Cl. NG3: Mapp.................6C **34**
Annesley Gro. NG1: Nott... 1C **4** (3F **45**)
Annesley Rd. NG2: West Br.........4B **58**
Annies Cl. NG15: Huck.................6F **7**
Anslow Av. NG9: Lent A...............3G **55**
Anson Rd. NG13: Newt................2B **50**
Anson Wlk. DE7: Ilk....................4B **28**
Anstee Rd. NG10: Long E............2E **73**
Anstey Ri. NG3: Nott...................4B **46**
Anthony Wharton Ct.
    NG11: Cliftn...........................2C **66**
Antill St. NG9: Stfrd....................5F **53**
Antonia Dr. NG15: Huck..............3B **8**
Apollo Dr. NG6: Bulw...................2F **31**
Appleby Cl. DE7: Ilk....................3B **40**
Appledore Av. NG8: Woll.............1D **54**
Appledorne Way NG5: Arn...........4A **22**
Appleton Cl. NG11: Cliftn.............4A **66**
Appleton Ct. NG9: Bee................1H **65**
Appleton Gdns. NG3: Mapp.........2D **34**
Appleton Rd. NG9: Bee................1H **65**
Apple Tree Cl. NG12: Edwal.........1C **68**
Appletree La. NG4: Ged...............5H **35**
Apple Wlk. NG3: Nott..................1C **46**
Applewood Gro. NG5: Sher..........4H **33**
Approach, The NG11: Rudd..........5G **67**
Arboretum St. NG1: Nott.. 1B **4** (3F **45**)
Arbour Hill DE7: D Ab.................6C **38**
Arbrook Dr. NG8: Aspl.................3B **44**
Arbutus Cl. NG11: Cliftn..............4A **66**
Archdale Rd. NG5: Bestw............1G **33**
Archer Cres. NG8: Woll...............4F **43**
Archer Rd. NG9: Stfrd.................6G **53**
Archer St. DE7: Ilk......................4A **28**
Arches Cl. NG16: Aws..................2E **29**
Arch Hill NG5: Redh.....................2A **22**
Archway Ct. NG7: Radf................3D **44**
    .... (off Limpenny St.)
Arden Cl. NG15: Huck...................6A **8**
Arden Cl. NG9: Lent A.................3G **55**
Arden Gro. NG13: Bing................4C **50**
Ardleigh Cl. NG5: Top V..............4B **20**
Ardmore Cl. NG2: Nott................6B **46**
Ardsley Cl. DE75: Hea.................3E **15**
Arena, The NG1: Nott..... 5C **4** (5F **45**)
Argyle Cl. NG7: Radf...................4D **44**
Argyle M. NG16: Eastw................3B **16**
Argyle St. NG16: Lang M..............1F **15**
Argyle St. NG7: Radf...................4D **44**
Aria Ct. NG9: Stfrd......................5F **53**
Ariel Cl. NG6: Bas.......................2D **32**
Arkers Cl. NG8: Aspl...................5G **31**
Arklow Cl. NG8: Aspl...................5G **31**
Arkwright Cl. NG2: Nott
    Queens Rd...............................6G **45**
Arkwright Cl. NG2: Nott
    Radcliffe St..............................2H **57**
Arkwright St. Sth. NG2: Nott.......2H **57**
Arkwright Wlk. NG2: Nott............1H **57**
    .... (not continuous)
Arleston Dr. NG8: Woll................6D **42**
Arlington Cl. NG15: Huck..............1G **19**
Arlington Dr. NG3: Mapp P..........6G **33**
Armadale Cl. NG5: Arn................5E **23**
Armes Cl. DE7: Ilk......................4B **28**
Armfield Rd. NG5: Arn.................1E **35**
Armitage Dr. NG10: Long E..........6A **64**
Armstrong Rd. NG6: Bulw............2F **31**
Armstrong Way NG7: Bas............6C **32**
Arncliff Cl. NG8: Woll..................5C **42**
Arndale Rd. NG5: Sher.................2G **33**
Arne Ct. NG2: Nott......................2G **57**
Arnesby Rd. NG7: Lent................6B **44**
Arno Av. NG7: Hys G...................1F **45**

ARNOLD......6B 22
Arnold Av. NG10: Long E......3C 72
Arnold Cres. NG10: Long E......3C 72
Arnold La. NG3: Ged......2D 34
Arnold La. NG3: Mapp......2D 34
Arnold La. NG4: Ged......4G 35
Arnold Leisure Cen.......5B 22
Arnold Rd. NG5: Bestw......2D 32
Arnold Rd. NG6: Bas......3C 32
Arnold Rd. NG6: Bestw......3C 32
Arnos Gro. NG16: Nuth......4D 30
Arnot Hill Pk. NG5: Arn......1A 34
Arnot Hill Pk.......1A 34
Arnot Hill Rd. NG5: Arn......6A 22
Arnot Ho. NG4: Car......1G 47
......(off Foxhill Rd. E.)
Arno Vale Gdns. NG5: Woodt......2B 34
Arno Vale Rd. NG5: Woodt......2A 34
Arnside NG9: Stfrd......6G 53
Arnside Cl. NG5: Bestw......2F 33
Arnside Rd. NG5: Bestw......2E 33
A Rd. NG7: Nott......5A 56
Arran Cl. NG9: Stfrd......1G 53
Arrow Cen. NG15: Huck......2E 7
Arthur Av. NG7: Lent......5D 44
Arthur Av. NG9: Stfrd......3H 53
Arthur Cres. NG4: Car......2E 47
Arthur Mee Rd. NG9: Stfrd......6G 53
Arthur St. NG4: Neth......3A 48
Arthur St. NG7: Radf......1A 4 (3E 45)
Artic Way NG16: Kimb......6F 17
Arundel Cl. NG10: Sand......1D 62
Arundel Dr. NG9: Bram......1B 54
Arundel St. NG7: Lent......4E 45
Ascot Av. NG16: Kimb......6G 17
Ascot Cl. DE7: West H......2B 38
Ascot Dr. NG15: Huck......6D 6
Ascot Dr. NG5: Redh......5H 21
Ascot Pk. Est. NG10: Sand......4E 53
Ascot Rd. NG8: Aspl......2B 44
Ascott Gdns. NG2: West Br......6F 57
Ashbourne Cl. NG9: Bram......2A 54
Ashbourne Ct. DE7: Ilk......6H 27
Ashbourne Ct. NG6: Bulw......1F 31
Ashbourne St. NG7: Lent......4E 45
Ashburnham Av. NG7: Lent......5D 44
Ashchurch Dr. NG8: Woll......1D 54
Ash Cl. NG13: Bing......5G 51
Ash Cl. NG14: Bur J......3E 37
Ash Cl. NG14: Woodbo......1C 24
Ash Cl. NG15: Huck......6C 6
Ash Ct. NG5: Newth......1D 16
Ash Ct. NG4: Car......2F 47
Ash Cres. NG16: Nuth......1B 30
Ashdale Av. NG15: Huck......6G 7
Ashdale Rd. DE7: Ilk......3C 40
Ashdale Rd. NG3: Nott......3D 46
Ashdale Rd. NG5: Arn......5C 22
Ashdown Cl. NG11: Wilf......5F 57
Ashdown Gro. NG13: Bing......5D 50
Ashe Cl. NG5: Arn......6D 22
Asher La. NG11: Rudd......1G 77
Ashfield Av. NG9: Bee......6H 55
Ashfield Rd. NG2: Nott......5B 46
Ashford Ct. DE7: West H......1B 38
Ashford Pl. DE7: Ilk......2A 28
Ashford Ri. NG8: Woll......1D 54
Ashforth Av. DE75: Hea......4E 15
Ashforth Bus. Cen. NG3: Nott......3H 45
......(off Ashforth St.)
Ashforth St. NG3: Nott......1F 5 (3H 45)
Ashgate Retail Pk.......4A 8
Ashgate Rd. NG15: Huck......4H 7
Ash Gro. NG10: Long E......1E 73
Ash Gro. NG10: Sand......4C 52
Ash Gro. NG12: Key......5H 79
Ash Gro. NG14: Woodbo......6C 12
Ash Gro. NG9: Stfrd......6F 53

Ashiana NG2: Nott......4H 5 (5A 46)
Ashington Dr. NG5: Arn......3B 22
Ash La. NG15: Pap......1H 9
Ash Lea Cl. NG12: Cotg......3F 71
Ashley Cl. NG9: Chil......5D 54
Ashley Cres. NG12: Key......4H 79
Ashley Gro. NG15: Huck......4E 7
Ashley Rd. NG12: Key......4G 79
Ashley St. NG3: Nott......3H 5 (4A 46)
Ashling Ct. NG2: Nott......1A 58
Ashling St. NG2: Nott......1A 58
Ashmore Cl. NG4: Ged......4G 35
Ash Mount Rd. NG16: Lang M......2F 15
Ashness Cl. NG2: Gam......5E 59
Ashover Cl. NG3: Nott......1A 46
Ashridge Way NG12: Edwal......1E 69
Ash St. DE7: Ilk......3A 28
Ashton Av. NG5: Arn......3B 22
Ashton Ct. NG8: Bilb......2D 42
Ash Tree Ct. NG8: Stre......4C 30
Ash Tree Sq. NG9: Bram......3B 54
Ashurst Gro. NG15: Huck......1E 19
Ash Vw. NG7: Radf......3D 44
Ashview Cl. NG10: Long E......5D 62
Ash Vs. NG5: Sher......6F 33
Ashville Cl. NG2: Nott......2E 57
Ashwater Dr. NG3: Mapp......1F 35
Ashwell Ct. NG5: Woodt......3A 34
Ashwell Gdns. NG7: Hys G......1C 44
Ashwell St. NG4: Neth......3H 47
Ashwick Cl. NG11: Wilf......6E 57
Ashworth Av. NG11: Rudd......5G 67
Ashworth Cl. NG3: Nott......4E 47
Ashworth Cres. NG3: Mapp......5D 34
Askeby Dr. NG8: Stre......6D 30
Askew Rd. NG15: Huck......2B 8
Askham Ct. NG2: Gam......4E 59
......(off Radcliffe Rd.)
Aslockton Dr. NG8: Aspl......5B 32
Aspect Bus. Pk. NG6: Bulw......5F 19
Aspen Cl. NG13: Bing......5G 51
Aspen Rd. NG6: Bulw......1F 31
Asper St. NG4: Neth......2A 48
Aspinall Ct. NG8: Woll......4A 44
Aspley La. NG8: Aspl......6F 31
Aspley La. NG8: Bilb......6F 31
Aspley Pk. Dr. NG8: Bilb......1G 43
Aspley Pl. NG7: Radf......3D 44
Assarts Rd. NG16: Nuth......3E 31
Astcote Cl. DE75: Hea......4E 15
Aster Gro. NG12: Edwal......3C 68
Aster Rd. NG3: Nott......2H 45
Astill Pine Cl. DE72: Brea......6A 62
Astle Ct. NG5: Arn......1E 35
Astley Dr. NG3: Nott......6B 34
Aston Av. NG9: Lent A......3G 55
Aston Ct. DE7: Ilk......6B 28
Aston Ct. NG7: Lent......2C 56
Aston Dr. NG6: Bulw......3A 20
Aston Grn. NG9: Toton......2G 63
Astral Dr. NG15: Huck......1E 19
Astral Gro. NG15: Huck......1D 18
Astrid Gdns. NG5: Bestw......1D 32
Astron Ct. NG15: Huck......1E 19
Astwood Cl. NG8: Bilb......2E 43
Atherfield Gdns. NG16: Eastw......2B 16
Atherton Ri. NG8: Aspl......4H 31
Atherton Rd. DE7: Ilk......4G 27
Athorpe Gro. NG6: Bas......4C 32
Atkinson Gdns. NG16: Nuth......2B 30
Atlas St. NG2: Nott......3H 57
Atrium, The NG2: Nott......6G 5 (6H 45)
ATTENBOROUGH......3D 64
Attenborough Cl.
  NG10: Long E......2B 72
Attenborough La. NG9: Atten......2C 64
......(not continuous)

Attenborough La. NG9: Chil......2C 64
......(not continuous)
Attenborough Nature Cen.......5C 64
Attenborough Nature Reserve...3E 65
Attenborough Station (Rail)......3D 64
Attercliffe Ter. NG2: Nott......2G 57
Attewell Rd. NG16: Aws......2D 28
Aubrey Av. NG2: Nott......5H 5 (5A 46)
Aubrey Rd. NG5: Sher......5F 33
Auburn Cl. DE7: Stan C......1A 38
Auckland Cl. NG7: Radf......4C 44
Auckland Rd. NG15: Huck......6D 6
Audley Cl. DE7: Ilk......4H 27
Audley Dr. NG9: Lent A......2F 55
Audon Av. NG9: Chil......6E 55
Augustine Gdns. NG5: Top V......4E 21
Austen Av. NG10: Long E......2E 73
Austen Av. NG7: Hys G......2E 45
Austin's Dr. DE72: Ris......1A 62
Austins Dr. NG10: Sand......1D 62
Austin St. NG6: Bulw......6A 20
Austrey Av. NG9: Lent A......3G 55
Autumn Cl. NG2: West Br......6H 57
Autumn Ct. NG15: Huck......5G 7
Autumn Rd. NG12: Cotg......6G 61
Autumn Way NG9: Bee......4H 55
Avalon Cl. NG6: Bulw......1C 32
Avebury Cl. NG11: Clftn......5B 66
Aveline Cl. NG5: Top V......5D 20
Avenue, The NG11: Rudd......2H 77
Avenue, The NG12: Rad T......5F 49
Avenue, The NG14: Calv......4H 11
Avenue A NG1: Nott......4G 5 (5H 45)
Avenue B NG1: Nott......4G 5 (5H 45)
Avenue C NG1: Nott......4H 5 (5A 46)
Avenue D NG1: Nott......4H 5 (5A 46)
Avenue E NG1: Nott......3H 5 (4A 46)
Averton Sq. NG8: Woll......6B 44
Aviemore Cl. NG5: Arn......4D 22
Avis Av. DE75: Hea......6D 14
Avocet Cl. DE75: Hea......4F 15
Avocet Cl. NG13: Bing......6G 51
Avocet Cl. NG15: Huck......2H 7
Avocet Wharf NG7: Lent......1E 57
Avon Av. NG15: Huck......2E 19
Avonbridge Cl. NG5: Arn......4E 23
Avondale NG12: Cotg......2G 71
Avondale Cl. NG10: Long E......1C 72
Avondale Rd. DE7: Kirk H......4G 39
Avondale Rd. NG4: Car......3F 47
Avon Gdns. NG2: West Br......4B 58
Avonlea Cl. DE7: Ilk......3D 40
Avon Pl. NG9: Bee......4G 55
Avon Rd. NG3: Nott......4D 46
Avon Rd. NG4: Ged......5H 35
Awsworth & Cossall By-Pass
  NG16: Aws......3D 28
Awsworth La. NG16: Coss......5E 29
Awsworth La. NG16: Kimb......2F 29
Axford Cl. NG4: Ged......5H 35
Axmouth Dr. NG3: Mapp......2F 35
Aylesham Av. NG5: Arn......1B 34
Aylestone Dr. NG8: Bilb......1H 43
Ayr St. NG7: Radf......3E 45
Ayscough Av. NG16: Nuth......1C 30
Ayton Cl. NG2: Nott......1F 57
Ayton Gdns. NG9: Chil......3C 64
Azalea Ct. NG16: Gilt......5E 17

B

Babbacombe Dr. NG5: Bestw......1F 33
Babbacombe Way NG15: Huck......5D 6
BABBINGTON......3G 29
Babbington Cl. DE7: Ilk......3D 40
Babbington Cres. NG4: Ged......5G 35
Babbington Dr. NG6: Cin......3H 31
Babbington La. NG16: Kimb......3H 29
Babington Ct. NG9: Chil......6C 54
Back La. DE7: Ilk......5A 28
Back La. NG12: Norm W......1A 80
Back La. NG16: Nuth......1D 30
Bacon Cl. NG16: Gilt......5C 16
Bacon Av. NG6: Bulw......5H 19
Bacon Gdns. NG6: Bulw......5H 19
Baden Powell Rd. NG2: Nott......5C 46
Bader Rd. NG11: Wilf......4F 57
Badger Cl. NG15: Huck......5C 6
Badger Dr. NG4: Car......1G 47
Bagnall Av. NG5: Arn......1G 33
Bagnall Cotts. NG6: Bulw......2H 31
Bagnall Rd. NG6: Bas......3H 31
Bagnall Rd. NG6: Cin......3H 31
Bagot St. DE7: West H......1A 38
Bagthorpe Cl. NG5: Sher......4E 33
Baildon Cl. NG8: Woll......6A 44
Bailey Brook Cres.
  NG16: Lang M......2E 15
Bailey Brook Dr.
  NG16: Lang M......2D 14
Bailey Brook Ind. Est.
  NG16: Lang M......3F 15
Bailey Brook Rd. DE7: Ilk......2A 28
Bailey Brook Wlk.
  NG16: Lang M......2E 15
Bailey Cl. DE75: Los......1A 14
Bailey Cl. NG5: Arn......6H 21
Bailey Ct. NG12: Rad T......1E 61
Bailey Ct. NG4: Neth......2A 48
Bailey Dr. NG3: Mapp......2D 34
BAILEY GROVE......3H 15
Bailey Gro. Rd. NG16: Eastw......3H 15
Bailey La. NG12: Rad T......1E 61
Bailey St. NG4: Neth......2A 48
Bailey St. NG9: Stfrd......5E 53
Bainbridge, The NG14: Calv......4A 12
Bainton Gro. NG11: Clftn......4D 66
Baird-Parker Dr. NG4: Car......2F 47
Baker Av. DE75: Hea......6D 14
Baker Av. NG5: Arn......4C 22
Baker Brook Cl. NG15: Huck......5B 8
Baker Cl. NG10: Long E......4E 63
Bakerdale Rd. NG3: Nott......3D 46
Baker Rd. NG16: Gilt......5E 17
Baker Rd. NG6: Newth......5E 17
Bakers Brothers Mobile Home
  Cvn. Site DE7: Ilk......6C 28
Bakers Cl. NG12: Cotg......2C 68
Bakers Ct. NG7: Radf......3C 44
BAKERS FIELDS......3D 46
Baker St. DE7: Ilk......6B 28
Baker St. NG1: Nott......2F 45
Baker St. NG15: Huck......4G 7
Bakewell Av. NG4: Car......6G 35
Bakewell Dr. NG5: Top V......6C 20
Bakewell La. NG15: Huck......1H 19
Bakewell Rd. NG10: Long E......2G 73
Bala Dr. NG5: Bestw......6E 21
Baldwin Ct. NG7: Radf......4D 44
Baldwin St. NG16: Newth......4E 17
Baldwin St. NG7: Radf......4E 45
Bale Cl. NG10: Long E......1A 74
Balfour Rd. NG7: Lent......4D 44
Balfour Rd. NG7: Radf......4D 44
Balfour Rd. NG9: Stfrd......5F 53
Balfron Gdns. NG2: Nott......1F 57
Balisier Ct. NG3: Nott......3G 45
Ballantrae Cl. NG5: Arn......5D 22
Ballerat Cres. NG5: Top V......5C 20
Balloon Wood Ind. Est.

Balmoral Cl. – Bennett St.

Balmoral Cl. NG10: Sand............2D 62
Balmoral Cres. NG8: Woll............4C 42
Balmoral Dr. NG9: Bram..............1B 54
Balmoral Gro. NG15: Huck...........3H 7
Balmoral Gro. NG4: Colw............3H 47
Balmoral Ho. NG5: Woodt............3H 33
Balmoral Rd. DE7: Kirk H...........4H 39
Balmoral Rd. NG1: Nott...............3F 45
Balmoral Rd. NG13: Bing.............5C 50
Balmoral Rd. NG4: Colw..............3H 47
Balshaw Way NG9: Chil...............3B 64
Bamkin Cl. NG15: Huck...............5H 7
Bampton Ct. NG2: Gam................4E 59
Banbury Av. NG9: Toton..............2H 63
Bancroft St. NG6: Bulw...............6A 20
Bandstand Yard...............5C 4 (6G 45)
.................................(off Castle Rd.)
Banes Rd. NG13: Bing................5H 51
Bangor Wlk. NG3: Nott................2G 45
Bankfield Dr. DE7: Kirk H............3F 39
Bankfield Dr. NG9: Bram.............2C 54
Bank Hill NG14: Woodbo............2H 23
Bank Pl. NG1: Nott............4E 5 (5G 45)
Banks, The NG13: Bing................5E 51
Banksburn Cl. DE75: Hea............4A 14
Banks Cl. NG5: Arn......................1D 34
Banks Cres. NG13: Bing..............5E 51
Banksman Cl. NG3: Nott..............2B 46
Banks Paddock NG13: Bing.........5F 51
Banks Rd. NG9: Toton.................2G 63
Bank St. NG10: Long E................6G 63
Bank St. NG16: Lang M...............1G 15
Banks Yd. NG6: Bulw..................6H 19
....(off Main St.)
Bankwood Cl. NG8: Aspl.............6G 31
Bannerman Rd. NG6: Bulw..........1A 32
Barbara Sq. NG15: Huck...............2F 7
Barber Cl. DE7: Ilk.......................4A 28
Barber St. NG16: Eastw................3C 16
Barbrook Cl. NG8: Woll................4H 43
Barbury Dr. NG11: Clftn...............6B 66
Barclay Ct. DE7: Ilk......................4H 27
Barden Rd. NG3: Mapp.................2C 34
Bardfield Gdns. NG5: Top V..........3B 20
Bardney Dr. NG6: Bulw.................5G 19
Bardsey Gdns. NG5: Bestw...........6E 21
Barent Cl. NG5: Bestw..................1D 32
Barent Wlk. NG5: Bestw...............1D 32
Barker Av. E. NG10: Sand.............5D 52
Barker Av. Nth. NG10: Sand..........5C 52
Barker Ga. DE7: Ilk.......................5B 28
Barker Ga. NG1: Nott.........4F 5 (5H 45)
Barker Ga. NG15: Huck..................4F 7
Barkers La. NG9: Chil....................1F 65
Barkla Cl. NG11: Clftn..................5A 66
Bar La. NG6: Bas..........................5A 32
Bar La. NG8: Aspl.........................5A 32
Bar La. Ind. Pk. NG6: Bas..............5B 32
Barlborough Rd. DE7: Ilk...............2B 28
Barley Cl. NG16: Kimb...................6H 17
Barley Cl. NG4: Car........................5F 35
Barley Cft. NG2: West Br...............1G 67
Barleydale Dr. NG9: Trow..............1F 53
Barleylands NG11: Rudd...............1G 77
Barling Dr. DE7: Ilk........................5G 27
Barlock Rd. NG6: Bas.....................3C 32
Barlow Dr. Nth. NG16: Aws............3D 28
Barlow Dr. Sth. NG16: Aws.............3D 28
Barlows Cotts. NG16: Aws..............2E 29
Barlows Cotts. La. NG16: Aws.........2E 29
Barnby Wlk. NG5: Sher....................2G 33
Barn Cl. NG10: Long E....................2E 73
Barn Cl. NG12: Cotg........................3E 71
Barn Cl. NG6: Bulw..........................2F 31
Barn Cft. NG9: Chil..........................5B 54
Barndale Cl. NG2: West Br...............2G 67
Barnes Cl. NG11: Wilf.......................1F 67
Barnes Cft. DE75: Hea......................5A 14
Barnes Rd. NG5: Top V.....................5D 20
Barnet Rd. NG3: Nott.......................2D 46
Barnett Ct. NG12: Key.....................4G 79
Barnfield NG11: Wilf........................1F 67
Barnsley Cl. NG6: Bestw V...............5F 9
Barnsley Ter. NG2: Nott....................2G 57
Barnston Rd. NG2: Nott....................4B 46
Barnum Cl. NG8: Woll.......................4E 43
Barons Cl. NG4: Ged........................6G 35
Barrack La. NG7: Nott.......................5D 44
Barra M. NG2: Nott...........................1F 57
Barratt Cl. NG9: Atten.......................4D 64
Barratt Cres. NG9: Atten...................3D 64
Barratt La. NG9: Atten.......................3C 64
Barrhead Cl. NG5: Top V...................4C 20
Barrington Cl. NG12: Rad T...............1E 61
Barrique Rd. NG7: Lent......................2C 56
Barrow Slade NG12: Key....................5G 79
Barrydale Av. NG9: Bee......................6F 55
Barry St. NG6: Bulw...........................6H 19
Bartholomew Cl. NG12: Edwal............2C 68
Bartley Gdns. NG14: Calv...................3E 11
Bartlow Rd. NG8: Bilb........................2D 42
Barton Cl. NG11: Rudd.......................1F 77
BARTON IN FABIS..............................1E 75
Barton La. NG11: Bart F.....................1G 75
Barton La. NG11: Clftn.......................5A 66
Barton La. NG11: Rat..........................6C 74
Barton La. NG11: Thru........................6C 74
Barton La. NG9: Atten.........................4B 64
Barton La. NG9: Chil............................4B 64
Barton Rd. NG10: Long E.....................1A 74
Bartons Cl. NG16: Newth.....................3E 17
Barton St. NG9: Bee.............................6G 55
Barton Way NG9: Chil..........................6E 55
Barwell Dr. NG8: Stre...........................6D 30
Basa Cres. NG5: Top V.........................5D 20
Basford Rd. NG6: Bas...........................6B 32
Basford Stop (NET)...............................4C 32
Baskin La. NG9: Chil..............................1C 64
Baslow Av. NG4: Car..............................6F 35
Baslow Cl. NG10: Long E........................2C 72
Baslow Dr. NG9: Lent A..........................2G 55
Bass Cl. NG15: Huck...............................2A 8
Bassett Cl. DE7: Ilk.................................4G 27
Bassett Cl. NG16: Kimb...........................6G 17
Bassford Av. DE75: Hea...........................3D 14
BASSINGFIELD.......................................4H 59
Bassingfield La. NG12: Rad T..................3H 59
Bassingfield La. NG2: Gam......................4F 59
....(not continuous)
Bastion St. NG7: Radf...............................4C 44
Bateman Gdns. NG7: Hys G......................2D 44
Bathley St. NG2: Nott.................................2G 57
Baths La. NG15: Huck.................................4H 7
Bath St. DE7: Ilk..6A 28
Bath St. NG1: Nott..........................2F 5 (4H 45)
Bathurst Dr. NG8: Bilb..................................3G 43
Battle Cl. NG13: Newt....................................2B 50
Baulk La. NG9: Stfrd......................................3H 53
Bawtry Wlk. NG3: Nott....................................3B 46
Baxter Cl. NG15: Huck.....................................1A 8
Bayard Ct. NG8: Woll.......................................4A 44
Bayliss Rd. NG4: Ged.......................................4F 35
Bayswater Rd. NG16: Kimb...............................6H 17
Baythorn Rd. NG8: Bilb......................................3D 42
Beacon Flatts NG9: Bee.....................................5H 55
Beacon Hill Dr. NG15: Huck................................6C 6
Beacon Hill Ri.
NG3: Nott..2H 5 (4A 46)
Beacon Rd. NG9: Bee..5H 55
Beaconsfield St. NG10: Long E............................6G 63
Beaconsfield St. NG7: Hys G................................1D 44
Beaconsfield Street Stop (NET)...........................1D 44
Bean Cl. NG6: Bulw...2F 31
Beardall St. NG15: Huck...4H 7
Beardsall Ho. NG7: Lent...5C 44
....(off Faraday Rd.)
Beardsall M. NG8: Stre..5C 30
Beardsley Gdns. NG2: Nott......................................1F 57
Beardsmore Gro. NG15: Huck....................................2F 7
Beastmarket Hill
NG1: Nott..4D 4 (5G 45)
Beatty Wlk. DE7: Ilk..4B 28
Beauclerk Dr. NG5: Top V...5C 20
Beaufort Ct. NG2: West Br..2G 67
Beaufort Dr. NG9: Chil..6C 54
Beaulieu Gdns. NG2: West Br..6G 57
Beaumaris Dr. NG4: Ged...6B 36
Beaumaris Dr. NG9: Chil..1B 64
Beaumont Cl. NG12: Key..3G 79
Beaumont Cl. NG9: Stfrd..2G 53
Beaumont Gdns. NG2: West Br......................................1H 67
Beaumont Sq. NG8: Woll...4B 42
Beaumont St. NG2: Nott..............................5H 5 (5A 46)
BEAUVALE...5E 7
Beauvale NG16: Newth...3D 16
BEAUVALE...2D 16
Beauvale Ct. NG15: Huck..5E 7
Beauvale Cres. NG15: Huck...5D 6
Beauvale Dr. DE7: Ilk..2H 27
Beauvale Ri. NG16: Eastw..2D 16
Beauvale Rd. NG15: Huck...5D 6
Beauvale Rd. NG2: Nott..2G 57
Beaver Grn. NG2: West Br..4H 57
Beck Av. NG14: Calv..3H 11
Beckenham Rd. NG7: Radf..3D 44
Becket Gro. NG11: Wilf...6E 57
Beckett Ct. NG4: Ged...4F 35
Becket Way, The NG2: West Br...5F 57
Beckford Rd. NG2: Nott...6B 46
Beckhampton Rd. NG5: Bestw...5F 21
Beckinsale Ct. NG4: Car..1A 48
Beckley Rd. NG8: Brox...5F 31
Beckside NG2: West Br...1E 69
Beck St. NG1: Nott..................................3F 5 (4H 45)
Beck St. NG4: Car..1F 47
Bedale Ct. NG9: Chil...1A 64
Bedale Rd. NG5: Sher...2G 33
Bedarra Gro. NG7: Lent..5C 44
Bede Ling NG2: West Br...5G 57
Bedford Ct. NG7: Hys G..1D 44
Bedford Ct. NG9: Stfrd..2G 53
Bedford Gro. NG6: Bulw..2B 32
Bedford Row NG1: Nott...........................3G 5 (4H 45)
Bedlington Gdns. NG3: Mapp..5A 34
Beecham Av. NG3: Nott..3B 46
Beech Av. DE72: Brea..5B 62
Beech Av. NG10: Long E..4G 63
Beech Av. NG10: Sand...4D 52
Beech Av. NG12: Key...5H 79
Beech Av. NG13: Bing..5G 51
Beech Av. NG15: Huck..4G 7
Beech Av. NG16: Nuth..1B 30
Beech Av. NG3: Mapp...3B 34
Beech Av. NG4: Neth...3H 47
Beech Av. NG7: Bas...1E 45
Beech Av. NG9: Bee...6H 55
Beech Cl. NG12: Edwal...1D 68
Beech Cl. NG12: Rad T..1F 61
Beech Cl. NG2: West Br...2F 59
Beech Cl. NG6: Cin..3A 32
Beech Ct. NG3: Mapp...3C 34
Beechcroft DE7: West H...2C 38
BEECHDALE..3G 43
Beechdale Rd. NG8: Aspl..1F 43
Beechdale Rd. NG8: Bilb...1F 43
Beeches, The DE7: Smal...5A 14
Beeches, The NG10: Long E..5G 63
Beeches, The NG3: Nott..1C 46
Beech La. DE7: West H..2B 38
Beech Lodge NG13: Bing...5G 51
Beechwood Rd. NG5: Arn..5C 22
BEESTON...4G 55
Beeston Bus & Tram
Interchange...5F 55
Beeston Bus. Pk. NG9: Bee..1G 65
Beeston Centre Stop (NET)...5F 55
Beeston Cl. NG6: Bestw V..1C 20
Beeston Ct. NG6: Bulw...6B 20
Beeston Flds. Dr. NG9: Bee..3C 54
Beeston Flds. Dr. NG9: Bram..3C 54
Beeston Fields Golf Course...3D 54
Beeston La. NG7: Nott...2H 55
Beeston Marina Mobile
Home Pk. NG9: Atten..2G 65
Beeston Rd. NG7: Nott...2B 56
Beeston Sailing Club..3G 65
Beeston Station (Rail)...6G 55
Beetham Cl. NG13: Bing...5F 51
Beggarlee Pk. NG16: Newth...1D 16
Bel-Air Res. Homes NG2: Gam..4F 59
Belconnen Rd. NG5: Bestw...2D 32
Beldover Dr. NG8: Stre...5C 30
Beldover Ho. NG7: Lent..5C 44
....(off Faraday Rd.)
Belfield Ct. DE75: Los...1A 14
Belfield Gdns. NG10: Long E..6G 63
Belfield St. DE7: Ilk...5B 28
Belford Cl. NG6: Bulw..5F 19
Belfry Way NG12: Edwal..1E 69
Belgrave M. NG2: West Br...2G 67
Belgrave Rd. NG6: Bulw...6G 19
Belgrave Sq. NG1: Nott..............................3C 4 (4F 45)
Bella Cl. NG16: Lang M...1F 15
Bellar Ga. NG1: Nott...................................4G 5 (5H 45)
Belle Isle Rd. NG15: Huck..5G 7
Belleville Dr. NG5: Bestw...6F 21
Bellevue Ct. NG3: Nott.................................1H 5 (3A 46)
Bell Ho. NG7: Nott...3C 56
Bell La. DE75: Ship..2B 26
Bell La. NG11: Wilf...4F 57
Bells La. NG8: Cin..5G 31
Bell St. NG4: Car..1F 47
Belmont Av. DE72: Brea...5A 62
Belmont Av. NG6: Bulw..6A 20
Belmont Cl. NG15: Huck...1G 19
Belmont Cl. NG9: Chil...1B 64
Belmore Gdns. NG8: Bilb..4D 42
Belper Av. NG4: Car...6F 35
Belper Cres. NG4: Car..6F 35
Belper Rd. NG7: Hys G...2D 44
Belper St. DE7: Ilk..2B 40
Belsay Rd. NG5: Bestw...6E 21
Belsford Ct. NG16: Want...5A 18
Belton Cl. NG10: Sand..1D 62
Belton Dr. NG2: West Br...1F 67
Belton St. NG7: Hys G..1D 44
Belvedere Av. NG7: Hys G...1D 44
Belvedere Cl. NG12: Key...3G 79
Belvoir Cl. DE7: Kirk H...3H 39
Belvoir Cl. NG10: Long E...2G 73
Belvoir Hill NG2: Nott...5B 46
Belvoir Lodge NG4: Car...3G 47
Belvoir Rd. NG2: West Br..2C 58
Belvoir Rd. NG4: Neth...2A 48
Belvoir St. NG15: Huck..3F 7
Belvoir St. NG3: Mapp..5B 34
Belvoir Ter. NG2: Nott...5B 46
Belvoir Va. Gro. NG13: Bing...5F 51
Belward St. NG1: Nott...............................4G 5 (5H 45)
Belwood Cl. NG11: Clftn...3D 66
Bembridge Ct. NG9: Bram...3A 54
Bembridge Dr. NG5: Bestw..1F 33
....(not continuous)
Bencaunt Gro. NG15: Huck..3G 7
Bendigo La. NG2: Nott...6C 46
Benedict Ct. NG5: Top V..4E 21
Benington Dr. NG8: Woll...6C 42
Ben Mayo Ct. NG7: Radf...3D 44
Benner Av. DE7: Ilk...4C 40
Bennerley Av. DE7: Ilk...3B 28
Bennerley Ct. NG6: Bulw..5F 19
Bennerley Rd. NG6: Bulw..5F 19
Bennett Rd. NG3: Mapp..4C 34
Bennett St. NG10: Long E..2E 63
Bennett St. NG10: Sand...6D 52
Bennett St. NG3: Mapp..5B 34

Benneworth Cl. – Bourne Dr.

Benneworth Cl. NG15: Huck 6F 7
Ben St. NG7: Radf 3D 44
Bentinck Av. NG12: Toll 4F 69
Bentinck Ct. NG2: Nott 4H 5 (5A 46)
(off Manvers St.)
Bentinck Rd. NG4: Car 5E 35
Bentinck Rd. NG7: Hys G 3D 44
Bentinck Rd. NG7: Radf 3D 44
Bentinck St. NG15: Huck 3F 7
Bentley Av. NG3: Nott 3C 46
Bentwell Av. NG5: Arn 6C 22
Beresford Dr. DE7: Ilk 2A 28
Beresford Rd. NG10: Long E 2C 72
Beresford St. NG7: Radf 4C 44
Berkeley Av. NG10: Long E 1E 73
Berkeley Av. NG3: Mapp P 1G 45
Berkeley Ct. NG5: Sher 6G 33
Berle Av. DE75: Hea 2C 14
Ber Mar Anda Res. Mobile Home Pk. NG16: Lang M 1F 15
Bernard Av. NG15: Huck 2H 7
Bernard St. NG5: Sher 6F 33
Bernard Ter. NG5: Sher 6F 33
Bernisdale Cl. NG5: Top V 4D 20
Berridge Rd. NG7: Hys G 1E 45
Berridge Rd. Central NG7: Hys G 1D 44
Berridge Rd. W. NG7: Hys G 2C 44
Berriedale Cl. NG5: Arn 4D 22
Berrydown Cl. NG8: Aspl 6A 32
Berry Hill Gro. NG4: Ged 5G 35
Berwick Cl. NG5: Bestw 1G 33
Berwin Cl. NG10: Long E 4C 62
Beryldene Av. NG16: Want 6A 18
Besecar Av. NG4: Ged 5G 35
Besecar Cl. NG4: Ged 5G 35
Bessell La. NG9: Stfrd 6E 53
Bestwick Av. DE75: Hea 4F 15
Bestwick Cl. DE7: Ilk 5C 40
BESTWOOD 6F 21
Bestwood Av. NG5: Arn 5A 22
Bestwood Bus. Pk. NG6: Bestw V 2C 20
Bestwood Cl. NG5: Arn 5A 22
Bestwood Country Pk. Mill Lakes 1B 20
Bestwood Country Pk. Mill Lakes 6B 8
Bestwood Country Pk. 2C 20
Bestwood Footpath NG15: Bestw V 6B 8
Bestwood Footpath NG15: Huck 6B 8
Bestwood Lodge Dr. NG5: Arn 4G 21
Bestwood Lodge Stables NG5: Arn 3F 21
Bestwood Pk. NG5: Arn 3F 21
Bestwood Pk. Dr. NG5: Top V 4F 21
Bestwood Pk. Dr. W. NG5: Top V 4B 20
Bestwood Pk. Vw. NG5: Arn 4A 22
Bestwood Rd. NG15: Huck 6A 8
Bestwood Rd. NG6: Bulw 5A 20
Bestwood Ter. NG6: Bulw 5B 20
BESTWOOD VILLAGE 1C 20
Bethel Gdns. NG15: Huck 6C 6
Bethnal Wlk. NG6: Bulw 6H 19
Betony Cl. NG13: Bing 5C 50
Bettison Ct. NG3: Mapp 3C 34
Betts Av. NG15: Huck 1G 19
Betula Cl. NG11: Clftn 4A 66
Bevel St. NG7: Hys G 2D 44
Beverley Cl. NG8: Woll 5B 42
Beverley Dr. NG16: Kimb 6G 17
Beverley Gdns. NG4: Ged 6H 35
Beverley Sq. NG3: Nott 2A 46
Bewcastle Rd. NG5: Arn 4E 21
Bewcastle Rd. NG5: Top V 4E 21
Bewick Dr. NG3: Nott 4E 47
Bexhill Ct. NG9: Bee 2E 55
Bexleigh Gdns. NG8: Bilb 1G 43
Bexon Ct. NG4: Car 2G 47
Bexwell Cl. NG11: Clftn 5C 66
Biant Cl. NG8: Cin 4H 31
Bideford Cl. NG3: Mapp 2F 35
Bidford Rd. NG8: Brox 6F 31
Bidwell Cres. NG11: Goth 5H 75
Biggart Cl. NG9: Chil 3C 64
Biko Sq. NG7: Hys G 1D 44
Bilberry Wlk. NG3: Nott 3A 46
Bilbie Wlk. NG1: Nott 2C 4 (4F 45)
BILBOROUGH 2E 43
Bilborough Rd. NG8: Bilb 4B 42
Bilborough Rd. NG8: Stre 4B 42
Bilborough Sports Cen. 2C 42
Bilby Gdns. NG3: Nott 4B 46
Billesdon Dr. NG5: Sher 3D 32
Binch Fld. Cl. NG14: Calv 3E 11
Binding Cl. NG5: Sher 6F 33
Binding Ho. NG5: Sher 6F 33
BINGHAM 5E 51
Bingham By-Pass NG13: Bing 5B 50
Bingham Ind. Pk. NG13: Bing 4E 51
Bingham Leisure Cen. 5F 51
Bingham Rd. NG12: Cotg 2F 71
Bingham Rd. NG12: Rad T 6F 49
Bingham Rd. NG5: Sher 5G 33
Bingham Station (Rail) 4F 51
Bingley Cl. NG8: Bilb 3H 43
Birch Av. DE7: Ilk 2C 40
Birch Av. NG16: Nuth 1B 30
Birch Av. NG4: Car 2F 47
Birch Av. NG9: Bee 1H 65
Birch Cl. NG16: Nuth 1B 30
Birchdale Av. NG15: Huck 6G 7
Birchfield Pk. DE75: Hea 6D 14
Birchfield Rd. NG5: Arn 4C 22
Birch Lea NG5: Redh 5H 21
Birchover Pl. DE7: Ilk 2A 28
Birchover Rd. NG8: Bilb 4C 42
Birch Pk. NG16: Gilt 6C 16
Birch Pk. NG16: Newth 1D 16
Birch Pas. NG7: Radf 2A 4 (4E 45)
Birch Ri. NG14: Woodbo 6C 12
Birch Wlk. NG5: Sher 4H 33
Birchwood DE75: Los 1A 14
Birchwood Av. DE72: Brea 6B 62
Birchwood Av. NG10: Long E 1E 73
Birchwood Rd. NG8: Woll 5C 42
Bircumshaw Rd. DE75: Hea 3C 14
Birdcroft La. DE7: Ilk 4B 40
Birdsall Av. NG8: Woll 5E 43
Birkdale Cl. DE7: Ilk 6H 27
Birkdale Cl. NG12: Edwal 2C 68
Birkdale Way NG5: Top V 5D 20
Birkin Av. NG11: Rudd 5G 67
Birkin Av. NG12: Rad T 5G 49
Birkin Av. NG7: Hys G 2D 44
Birkin Av. NG9: Toton 3A 64
Birkland Av. NG1: Nott 1D 4 (3G 45)
Birkland Av. NG3: Mapp 3C 34
Birley St. NG9: Stfrd 6F 53
Birling Cl. NG6: Bulw 6F 19
Birrell Rd. NG7: Hys G 1E 45
Bisham Dr. NG2: West Br 4D 58
Bishopdale Cl. NG10: Long E 1C 72
Bishopdale Dr. NG16: Want 6B 18
Bishops Cl. NG12: Key 3G 79
Bishops Rd. NG13: Bing 4D 50
Bishop St. NG16: Eastw 3B 16
Bishops Way NG15: Huck 2H 7
Bispham Dr. NG9: Toton 2H 63
Blackacre NG14: Bur J 2E 37
Blackbird Cres. NG12: Edwal 3C 68
Blackburn Pl. DE7: Ilk 4A 28
Blackburn Way NG5: Bestw 2E 33
Blackcliffe Farm M. NG11: Rudd 4A 78
Blackett's Wlk. NG11: Clftn 5A 66
Blackfriars Cl. NG16: Nuth 5D 30
Blackhill Dr. NG4: Car 1H 47
Black Hills Dr. DE7: Ilk 3A 40
Blackrod Cl. NG9: Toton 3A 64
Blacksmith Ct. NG12: Cotg 1E 71
Blacksmiths Ct. NG15: Pap 1B 8
Blackstone Wlk. NG2: Nott 1G 57
Black Swan Cl. NG5: Sher 3H 33
Blackthorn Cl. NG13: Bing 5G 51
Blackthorn Cl. NG4: Ged 5A 36
Blackthorn Dr. NG16: Eastw 3A 16
Blackthorne Dr. NG6: Cin 4H 31
Blackwell Av. DE7: Ilk 2B 28
Bladon Cl. NG3: Mapp 5A 34
Bladon Rd. NG11: Rudd 6F 67
Blair Ct. NG2: Nott 2G 57
Blair Gro. NG10: Sand 1C 62
Blaise Cl. NG11: Clftn 5C 66
Blake Cl. NG3: Nott 4A 46
Blake Cl. NG5: Arn 6C 22
Blake Ct. NG10: Long E 2D 72
Blakeney Ho. NG7: Hys G 2D 44
(off St Paul's Av.)
Blakeney Rd. NG12: Rad T 6H 49
Blakeney Wlk. NG5: Arn 2B 34
Blake Rd. NG2: West Br 4B 58
Blake Rd. NG9: Stfrd 5G 53
Blake St. DE7: Ilk 6B 28
Blandford Av. NG10: Long E 1D 72
Blandford Rd. NG9: Chil 6C 54
Bland La. NG14: Epp 6G 13
Blanford Gdns. NG2: West Br 6G 57
Blankney St. NG6: Bas 3C 32
Blants Cl. NG16: Kimb 1H 29
Blantyre Av. NG5: Top V 4C 20
Blatherwick Cl. NG15: Huck 3H 7
Blatherwick's Yd. NG5: Arn 5B 22
Bleaberry Cl. NG2: West Br 6E 59
Bleachers Yd. NG7: Bas 6C 32
Bleasby St. NG2: Nott 5B 46
Bleasdale Cl. NG4: Ged 5A 36
Blencathra Cl. NG2: West Br 6E 59
Blenheim NG3: Nott 2G 45
BLENHEIM 4F 19
Blenheim Av. NG3: Mapp 5E 35
Blenheim Cl. NG11: Rudd 6F 67
Blenheim Ct. NG10: Sand 1D 62
Blenheim Ct. NG6: Bulw 4E 19
Blenheim Dr. NG9: Chil 6C 54
Blenheim Ind. Est. NG6: Bulw 5F 19
Blenheim La. NG6: Bulw 3D 18
Blenheim Pk. Rd. NG6: Bulw 4E 19
Blidworth Cl. NG8: Stre 5E 31
Blind La. DE72: Brea 5A 62
Blind La. NG12: Key 5G 79
Bloomsbury Ct. NG1: Nott 3F 5 (4H 45)
(off Beck St.)
Bloomsbury Dr. NG16: Nuth 4E 31
Bloomsgrove Ind. Est. NG7: Radf 4D 44
Bloomsgrove Rd. DE7: Ilk 5B 28
Bloomsgrove Rd. NG7: Radf 4D 44
Bloomsgrove St. NG7: Radf 4D 44
Bluebell Av. NG12: Cotg 6G 61
Bluebell Bank NG13: Bing 6D 50
Bluebell Cl. NG15: Huck 5C 6
Blue Bell Hill Rd. NG3: Nott 1H 5 (3A 46)
Bluebell Way DE75: Hea 4F 15
Bluecoat Cl. NG1: Nott 1D 4 (3G 45)
Bluecoat Ho. NG1: Nott 1D 4 (3G 45)
Bluecoat St. NG1: Nott 1D 4 (3G 45)
Blundell Cl. NG3: Nott 1B 46
Blyth Gdns. NG3: Mapp 5A 34
Blyth St. NG3: Mapp 6A 34
Blyton Wlk. NG5: Bestw 6F 21
BMI THE PARK HOSPITAL 1H 9
Boatmans Cl. DE7: Ilk 5B 28
Boatswain Dr. NG15: Huck 3H 7
Bobbers Mill NG8: Hys G 2C 44
Bobbers Mill Bri. NG7: Hys G 2B 44
Bobbers Mill Bri. NG8: Hys G 2B 44
Bobbers Mill Rd. NG7: Hys G 2C 44
Boden Dr. NG16: Nuth 1C 30
Boden St. NG7: Radf 4D 44
Bodill Gdns. NG15: Huck 5A 8
Bodmin Av. NG15: Huck 6C 6
Bodmin Dr. NG8: Aspl 5A 32
Body Rd. NG9: Chil 2B 64
BOGEND 3G 17
Bohem Rd. NG10: Long E 2E 63
Bold Cl. NG6: Bulw 5H 19
Bolero Cl. NG8: Woll 4E 43
Bolero Sq. NG1: Nott 4G 5 (5H 45)
(off Bellar Ga.)
Bolingey Way NG15: Huck 6C 6
Bolsover St. NG15: Huck 4H 7
Bolton Av. NG9: Chil 1C 64
Bolton Cl. NG2: West Br 5C 58
Bolton Ter. NG12: Rad T 6F 49
Bond Ho. NG5: Arn 5A 22
(off Bond St.)
Bonds Cl. DE7: Ilk 2B 28
Bond St. NG2: Nott 4H 5 (5A 46)
Bond St. NG5: Arn 5A 22
Bonetti Cl. NG5: Arn 2D 34
Boniface Gdns. NG5: Top V 4E 21
Bonington Cl. NG6: Bulw 1G 31
Bonington Dr. NG5: Arn 6B 22
Bonington Gallery, The 1C 4 (3F 45)
(off Hampden St.)
Bonington Rd. NG3: Mapp 3B 34
Bonington Theatre 5B 22
Bonner Hill NG14: Calv 5H 11
Bonner La. NG14: Calv 4A 12
Bonner's Rd. NG16: Aws 3E 29
Bonnington Cres. NG5: Sher 3G 33
Bonnymead NG12: Cotg 3E 71
Bonsall Ct. NG10: Long E 5G 63
Bonsall St. NG10: Long E 5G 63
Bonser Cl. NG4: Car 2G 47
Bonser Hedge Ct. NG10: Long E 3D 72
Booth Cl. NG3: Nott 2F 5 (4H 45)
Booths Gdns. DE7: Ilk 3B 28
Booth's Ind. Est., The DE7: Ilk 5B 28
Boots Ct. NG10: Long E 6D 62
Borlace Cres. NG9: Stfrd 5G 53
Borman Cl. NG6: Bulw 2F 31
Borrowdale Cl. NG2: Gam 5F 59
Borrowdale Ct. NG9: Chil 1B 64
Borrowdale Dr. NG10: Long E 1C 72
Boscawen Ct. DE7: Ilk 4B 28
Bosden Cl. NG8: Bilb 3C 42
Bosley Sq. NG9: Lent A 3G 55
Bostock's La. DE72: Ris 1B 62
Bostocks La. NG10: Sand 2C 62
Boston M. NG5: Sher 4D 32
Boston St. NG1: Nott 3G 5 (4H 45)
Boswell St. NG7: Radf 4C 44
Boswell St. NG8: Stre 6C 30
Bosworth Cl. NG12: S'frd 1H 49
Bosworth Dr. NG16: Newth 2D 16
Bosworth Wlk. NG2: Nott 2F 57
Bosworth Way NG10: Long E 2F 73
Botany Av. NG3: Nott 2B 46
Botany Cl. NG2: West Br 2G 67
Botany Rd. NG3: Nott 2B 46
Bothe Cl. NG10: Long E 1E 73
Bottle La. NG1: Nott 4E 5 (5G 45)
Boulevard Ind. Pk. NG9: Bee 5H 55
Boundary Cres. NG9: Bee 2F 55
Boundary La. NG16: Lang M 2G 15
Boundary Rd. NG2: West Br 1A 68
Boundary Rd. NG9: Bee 2F 55
Bourne Cl. NG9: Bram 2D 54
Bourne Dr. NG16: Lang M 2F 15

90 A-Z Nottingham

Bourne M. – Brook Chase M.

Bourne M. NG4: Neth....3A **48**
Bourne Sq. DE72: Brea....5A **62**
Bourne St. NG4: Neth....3A **48**
Bournmoor Av. NG11: Clftn....4C **66**
Bovill St. NG7: Radf....3D **44**
Bowden Av. NG6: Bestw V....1C **20**
Bowden Cl. NG5: Arn....5H **21**
Bowden Cl. NG5: Sher....4G **33**
Bowden Dr. NG9: Bee....5H **55**
Bowers Av. NG3: Mapp P....2H **45**
Boweswell Rd. DE7: Ilk....5A **28**
Bowland Cl. NG3: Nott....2C **46**
Bowland Rd. NG13: Bing....5C **50**
Bowling Cl. DE7: Stant D....3A **52**
Bowlwell Av. NG5: Top V....5D **20**
Bowness Av. NG6: Bas....5A **32**
Bowness Cl. NG2: Gam....4E **59**
Bowscale Cl. NG2: West Br....6E **59**
Boxley Dr. NG2: West Br....1G **67**
Boxtree Av. NG15: Huck....5F **7**
Boyce Gdns. NG3: Mapp....6B **34**
Boycroft Av. NG3: Nott....1B **46**
Boyd Cl. NG5: Arn....4D **22**
Boynton Dr. NG3: Mapp....6B **34**
Boythorpe Cl. DE7: Ilk....2B **28**
Bracadale Rd. NG5: Top V....4D **20**
Bracebridge Dr. NG8: Bilb....3D **42**
Bracey Ri. NG2: West Br....2A **68**
Bracken Cl. NG10: Long E....4D **62**
Bracken Cl. NG4: Car....5F **35**
Bracken Cl. NG8: Bilb....6F **31**
Brackendale Av. NG5: Arn....5B **22**
Brackendale Cl. NG13: Bing....6E **51**
Brackenfield Dr. NG16: Gilt....5D **16**
Bracken Ho. NG6: Bulw....6H **19**
Bracken Rd. NG10: Long E....4D **62**
Bracknell Cres. NG8: Bas....6B **32**
Bracton Dr. NG3: Nott....3B **46**
Bradbourne Av. NG11: Wilf....6E **57**
Bradbury Gdns. NG11: Rudd....6F **67**
Bradbury/Midway Ind. Est.
NG7: Lent....3C **56**
Bradbury St. NG2: Nott....5C **46**
Braddock Cl. NG7: Lent....5C **44**
Braddon Av. NG9: Stfrd....2G **53**
Bradfield Rd. NG8: Brox....6F **31**
Bradford Ct. NG6: Bulw....1G **31**
Bradford Way NG6: Bestw V....5F **9**
Bradgate Cl. NG10: Sand....1D **62**
Bradgate Rd. NG7: Hys G....1E **45**
Bradley Ct. NG9: Bee....5G **55**
Bradley St. NG10: Sand....6E **53**
Bradleys Yd. NG12: Plum....6G **69**
Bradley Wlk. NG11: Clftn....5D **66**
Bradman Gdns. NG5: Arn....1D **34**
BRADMORE....4B **78**
Bradmore Av. NG11: Rudd....5G **67**
Bradmore Bus. Pk.
NG11: Bunny....5A **78**
Bradmore La. NG12: Plum....3E **79**
Bradmore Ri. NG5: Sher....3G **33**
Bradshaw St. NG10: Long E....2D **72**
Bradstone Dr. NG3: Ged....1F **35**
Bradstone Dr. NG3: Mapp....1F **35**
Bradwell Cl. NG16: Gilt....5E **17**
Bradwell Dr. NG5: Top V....5D **20**
Braefell Cl. NG2: West Br....6F **59**
Braefield Cl. DE7: Kirk H....4G **39**
Braemar Av. NG16: Eastw....5B **16**
Braemar Dr. NG4: Ged....6B **36**
Braemar Rd. NG6: Bulw....6A **20**
Braidwood Ct. NG7: Hys G....2D **44**
Brailsford Rd. NG7: Lent....2C **56**
Brailsford Way NG9: Chil....4C **64**
Bramber Gro. NG11: Clftn....6C **66**
Bramble Cl. NG10: Long E....4D **62**
Bramble Cl. NG6: Bas....4B **32**
Bramble Cl. NG9: Atten....3D **64**
Bramble Ct. NG10: Sand....6E **53**
Bramble Ct. NG4: Ged....6H **35**
Bramble Dr. NG3: Nott....2C **46**
Bramble Gdns. NG8: Bilb....1G **43**
Bramble Way NG12: Cotg....3G **71**
Brambling Rd. NG4: Neth....2C **48**
Brambling Rd. NG4: Stoke B....2C **48**
BRAMCOTE....3A **54**
Bramcote Av. NG9: Chil....5C **54**
Bramcote Crematorium....6A **42**
Bramcote Dr. NG8: Woll....6D **42**
Bramcote Dr. NG9: Bee....4E **55**
Bramcote Dr. W. NG9: Bee....5D **54**
BRAMCOTE HILLS....2C **54**
Bramcote La. NG8: Woll....1D **54**
Bramcote La. NG9: Chil....5C **54**
Bramcote Lane Stop (NET)....6C **54**
Bramcote Leisure Cen.....2B **54**
Bramcote Rd. NG9: Bee....4D **54**
Bramcote St. NG7: Radf....4C **44**
Bramcote Wlk. NG7: Radf....4C **44**
Bramerton Rd. NG8: Bilb....3C **42**
Bramhall Rd. NG8: Bilb....3C **42**
Bramley Ct. NG16: Kimb....1H **29**
Bramley Grn. NG8: Brox....6E **31**
Bramley Rd. NG10: Long E....2D **72**
Bramley Rd. NG8: Brox....6E **31**
Brampton Av. DE75: Hea....3E **15**
Brampton Cl. DE7: Ilk....2B **28**
Brampton Dr. NG9: Stfrd....6H **53**
Bramwell Dr. NG9: Bram....5C **54**
Brancaster Cl. NG6: Cin....3H **31**
Brandish Cres. NG11: Clftn....4B **66**
Brandreth Av. NG3: Nott....1B **46**
Brandreth Dr. NG16: Gilt....5C **16**
Brands Cl. DE7: Ilk....2B **28**
Brand St. NG2: Nott....1B **58**
Brangwen Ho. NG7: Lent....5C **44**
....*(off Faraday Rd.)*
Branklene Cl. NG16: Kimb....6G **17**
Branksome Wlk. NG2: Nott....1G **57**
Bransdale Cl. NG10: Long E....1D **72**
Bransdale Rd. NG11: Clftn....4B **66**
Branston Gdns. NG2: West Br....1H **67**
Branston Wlk. NG5: Sher....3G **33**
Brantford Av. NG11: Clftn....4D **66**
Brassington Cl. DE7: West H....1C **38**
Brassington Cl. NG16: Gilt....6D **16**
Bratton Dr. NG5: Bestw....2E **33**
Braunton Cl. NG15: Huck....5D **6**
Braunton Cres. NG3: Mapp....1F **35**
Brayton Cres. NG6: Bulw....2B **32**
Breach Ho. NG7: Lent....5C **44**
....*(off Faraday Rd.)*
Breach Rd. DE75: Hea....5E **15**
Breadsall Ct. DE7: Ilk....4B **28**
BREASTON....5A **62**
Breaston Ct. NG5: Top V....5E **21**
....*(off Erewash Gdns.)*
Breaston La. DE72: Ris....2A **62**
Brechin Cl. NG5: Arn....4D **22**
Breckhill Rd. NG3: Mapp....3B **34**
Breckhill Rd. NG5: Woodt....2A **34**
Brecknock Dr. NG10: Long E....6C **62**
Breckswood Dr. NG11: Clftn....6C **66**
Brecon Cl. NG10: Long E....5C **62**
Brecon Cl. NG8: Cin....4G **31**
Breconshire Gdns. NG6: Bas....3C **32**
Bredon Cl. NG10: Long E....5C **62**
Breedon St. NG10: Long E....2D **62**
Brendon Ct. NG9: Bram....3B **54**
Brendon Dr. NG16: Kimb....6H **17**
Brendon Dr. NG8: Woll....4G **43**
Brendon Gdns. NG8: Woll....4G **43**
Brendon Gro. NG13: Bing....4C **50**
Brendon Lawrence
Sports Hall....1H **45**
Brendon Rd. NG8: Woll....4G **43**
Brendon Way NG10: Long E....3C **62**
Brentcliffe Av. NG3: Nott....2C **46**
Brentnall Cl. NG10: Long E....6D **62**
Brentnall Ct. NG9: Chil....2D **64**
Bressingham Dr.
NG2: West Br....2G **67**
Brett Cl. NG15: Huck....6E **7**
Brettsil Dr. NG11: Rudd....6F **67**
Brewery St. NG16: Kimb....1H **29**
Brewhouse Yd.
NG1: Nott....6C **4** (6F **45**)
Brewill Gro. NG11: Wilf....6F **57**
Brewsters Cl. NG13: Bing....5E **51**
Brewsters Rd. NG3: Nott....1A **46**
Breydon Ind. Cen.
NG10: Long E....6H **63**
Brian Clough Way NG7: Lent....1H **55**
....(not continuous)
Brian Clough Way NG7: Nott....1H **55**
....(not continuous)
Brian Clough Way NG9: Bram....6E **53**
....(not continuous)
Brian Clough Way NG9: Stfrd....6E **53**
....(not continuous)
Briar Av. NG10: Sand....2C **62**
Briarbank Av. NG3: Nott....1C **46**
Briarbank Wlk. NG3: Nott....2C **46**
Briar Cl. NG12: Key....3H **79**
Briar Cl. NG15: Huck....6D **6**
Briar Cl. NG9: Bram....2E **55**
Briar Ct. NG2: Nott....2F **57**
Briar Gdns. NG14: Calv....3E **11**
Briar Ga. NG10: Long E....3C **62**
Briargate NG12: Cotg....3G **71**
Briar Rd. NG16: Newth....5D **16**
Briarwood Av. NG3: Nott....2C **46**
Briarwood Ct. NG5: Sher....4A **34**
Brickenell Rd. NG14: Calv....5H **11**
Brickyard NG15: Huck....5A **8**
Brickyard, The DE7: Stan C....6A **26**
Brickyard Cotts. NG16: Newth....4C **16**
Brickyard Dr. NG15: Huck....6A **8**
Brickyard La. NG12: Rad T....6H **49**
Brickyard Plantation Nature
Reserve....1G **41**
Bridge Av. NG9: Chil....6E **55**
Bridge Ct. NG15: Huck....5G **7**
Bridge Ct. NG6: Bulw....4B **20**
Bridge Ct. NG9: Bee....4H **55**
Bridge Farm La. NG11: Clftn....3C **66**
Bridge Grn. NG8: Brox....6E **31**
Bridge Grn. Wlk. NG8: Brox....6E **31**
Bridge Gro. NG2: West Br....3A **58**
Bridgend Cl. NG9: Stfrd....6F **53**
Bridge Rd. NG8: Woll....4D **42**
Bridge St. DE7: Ilk....3B **28**
Bridge St. NG10: Long E....4F **63**
Bridge St. NG10: Sand....6E **53**
Bridge St. NG16: Lang M....2G **15**
Bridgewater Ct. NG5: Woodt....2H **33**
Bridgeway Cen. NG2: Nott....1G **57**
Bridgeway Ct. NG2: Nott....1H **57**
Bridgford Rd. NG2: West Br....2A **58**
Bridgnorth Dr. NG11: Clftn....3C **66**
Bridgnorth Way NG9: Toton....2G **63**
Bridle Rd. NG14: Bur J....1D **36**
Bridle Rd. NG9: Bram....2B **54**
Bridlesmith Ga.
NG1: Nott....4E **5** (5G **45**)
Bridlesmith Wlk.
NG1: Nott....4E **5** (5G **45**)
....*(off Bridlesmith Ga.)*
Bridlington St. NG7: Hys G....2C **44**
Bridport Av. NG8: Radf....4B **44**
Brielen Ct. NG12: Rad T....6G **49**
Brielen Rd. NG12: Rad T....6G **49**
Brierfield Av. NG11: Wilf....1F **67**
Brierley Grn. NG4: Neth....2A **48**
Brightmoor Ct.
NG1: Nott....4F **5** (5H **45**)
....*(off Brightmoor St.)*
Brightmoor Pl.
NG1: Nott....4F **5** (5H **45**)
....*(off Brightmoor St.)*
Brightmoor St.
NG1: Nott....4F **5** (5H **45**)
Bright St. DE7: Ilk....4A **28**
Bright St. NG16: Kimb....1G **29**
Bright St. NG7: Lent....4C **44**
Brimington Cl. DE7: Ilk....1B **28**
Brindley Ct. NG5: Woodt....3H **33**
Brindley Rd. NG8: Bilb....4C **42**
Brinkhill Cres. NG11: Clftn....2D **66**
Brinsley Cl. NG8: Aspl....6G **31**
Brisbane Dr. NG5: Top V....5C **20**
Brisbane Dr. NG9: Stfrd....2H **53**
Bristol Rd. DE7: Ilk....6A **28**
Britannia Av. NG6: Bas....2C **32**
Britannia Cl. NG16: Want....6A **18**
Britannia Ct. NG4: Neth....3A **48**
Britannia Rd. NG10: Long E....4F **63**
Britten Gdns. NG3: Nott....3B **46**
Brixham Rd. NG15: Huck....6D **6**
Brixton Rd. NG7: Radf....4C **44**
B Rd. NG7: Nott....5B **56**
Broad Cl. NG14: Woodbo....1C **24**
Broad Eadow Rd. NG6: Bulw....6F **19**
Broadfields NG14: Calv....3H **11**
Broadgate NG9: Bee....4G **55**
Broadgate Av. NG9: Bee....4G **55**
Broadgate La. NG9: Bee....4G **55**
Broadgate Pk. NG9: Bee....3G **55**
Broadgate Pk. Student Village
NG9: Bee....3G **55**
....*(off Salthouse La.)*
Broadholme St. NG7: Lent....6D **44**
Broadhurst Av. NG6: Bas....5B **32**
Broadlands NG10: Sand....2D **62**
Broadleigh Cl. NG2: West Br....2G **67**
Broadmarsh Bus &
Coach Station....6E **5** (6G **45**)
Broadmead NG14: Bur J....2F **37**
Broadmeer NG12: Cotg....2E **71**
Broadmere Ct. NG5: Arn....4D **22**
Broad Oak Cl. NG3: Nott....2A **46**
Broad Oak Dr. NG9: Stfrd....5F **53**
Broadstairs Rd. NG9: Toton....3H **63**
Broadstone Cl. NG2: West Br....6G **57**
Broad St. NG1: Nott....3F **5** (4H **45**)
Broad St. NG10: Long E....6F **63**
Broad Valley Dr. NG6: Bestw V....1C **20**
Broad Wlk. NG6: Bas....4A **32**
Broadway DE7: Ilk....4A **28**
Broadway DE75: Hea....4C **14**
Broadway NG1: Nott....5F **5** (5H **45**)
Broadway Cinema
Nottingham....3F **5** (4H **45**)
....*(off Broad St.)*
Broadway E. NG4: Car....3F **47**
Broadwood Ct. NG9: Bee....3G **55**
Broadwood Rd. NG5: Bestw....5F **21**
Brockdale Gdns. NG12: Key....3G **79**
Brockenhurst Gdns. NG3: Nott....3B **46**
Brockhall Ri. DE75: Hea....4E **15**
Brockhole Cl. NG2: West Br....6F **59**
Brockley Rd. NG2: West Br....4D **58**
Brockwood Cres. NG12: Key....3G **79**
Brodhurst Cl. NG14: Woodbo....1C **24**
Brodwell Gro. NG3: Nott....6B **34**
Bromfield Cl. NG3: Nott....2E **47**
Bromley Cl. NG6: Bulw....1H **31**
Bromley Ct. DE7: Ilk....2C **40**
Bromley Pl. NG1: Nott....4C **4** (5F **45**)
Bromley Rd. NG2: West Br....5A **58**
Brompton Cl. NG5: Arn....3E **21**
Brompton Way NG2: West Br....2G **67**
Bronte Cl. NG10: Long E....6C **62**
Bronte Ct. NG7: Radf....3E **45**
Brook Av. NG5: Arn....5D **22**
Brook Chase M. NG9: Chil....6C **54**

A-Z Nottingham 91

Brook Cl. NG10: Long E 2G 73
Brook Cl. NG16: Newth............... 4D 16
Brook Cl. NG6: Bulw 1H 31
Brook Cotts. DE7: Ilk 4B 28
Brook Ct. NG16: Lang M 3F 15
Brook Ct. NG7: Radf 3D 44
Brookdale Ct. NG5: Sher 2H 33
Brooke St. DE7: Ilk 3D 40
Brooke St. NG10: Sand...............6D 52
Brookfield Av. NG15: Huck...........6G 7
Brookfield Cl. NG12: Rad T 6F 49
Brookfield Ct. NG2: Nott...............1G 57
Brookfield Ct. NG5: Arn 6C 22
Brookfield Gdns. NG5: Arn..........6C 22
Brookfield M. NG10: Sand...........5E 53
Brookfield Rd. NG5: Arn 6B 22
Brookfield Way DE75: Hea 4F 15
Brook Gdns. NG5: Arn 5C 22
BROOK HILL 5E 67
Brookhill Cres. NG8: Woll..............6E 43
Brookhill Dr. NG8: Woll..............6E 43
Brookhill Leys Rd.
NG16: Eastw 4A 16
Brookhill St. NG9: Stfrd..............6E 53
Brookland Dr. NG9: Chil 6D 54
Brooklands Av. DE75: Hea 3D 14
Brooklands Bus. Cen.
DE75: Los...............1B 14
Brooklands Ct. NG10: Long E......6F 63
Brooklands Cres. NG4: Ged 6A 36
Brooklands Rd. NG4: Ged 6A 36
Brooklands Rd. NG3: Nott...........2D 46
Brook La. NG12: Stant W 4D 80
Brooklyn Av. NG14: Bur J...........2E 37
Brooklyn Cl. NG6: Bulw.............2B 32
Brooklyn Rd. NG6: Bulw.............1B 32
Brook Rd. NG9: Bee...............3F 55
Brooksby La. NG11: Clftn 1D 66
Brooks Cotts. NG4: Car 2E 47
Brookside NG15: Huck...............6H 7
Brookside NG16: Eastw...........1B 16
Brookside Av. NG8: Woll.............1D 54
Brookside Cl. NG10: Long E 5D 62
Brookside Cotts. NG14: Bur J......2E 37
Brookside Gdns. NG11: Rudd......5F 67
Brookside Ind. Units
NG9: Stfrd 3F 53
Brookside Rd. NG11: Rudd..........5F 67
Brook St. NG1: Nott 3F 5 (4H 45)
Brook St. NG15: Huck...............3G 7
Brookthorpe Way NG11: Wilf 1E 67
Brookvale Rd. NG16: Lang M 3G 15
Brook Vw. Ct. NG12: Key...........5G 79
Brook Vw. Dr. NG12: Key...........5G 79
Brookwood Cres. NG4: Car 2E 47
Broom Cl. NG14: Calv 3H 11
Broomfield Cl. NG10: Sand.........6C 52
BROOMHILL 6A 8
Broomhill Av. DE7: Ilk...............3C 40
.... (not continuous)
Broomhill Cotts. NG15: Huck 6A 8
Broomhill Pk. Vw. NG15: Huck.....6A 8
Broomhill Rd. NG15: Huck...........6G 7
Broomhill Rd. NG16: Kimb 1A 30
Broomhill Rd. NG6: Bulw.............1A 32
Broom Rd. NG14: Calv...............4H 11
Broom Wlk. NG3: Nott 1D 46
Brora Rd. NG6: Bulw...............6B 20
Broughton Cl. DE7: Ilk...............4A 28
Broughton Dr. NG8: Woll 5A 44
Broughton St. NG9: Bee 4E 55
Brownes Rd. NG13: Bing.............4G 51
Browning Cl. NG5: Arn...............6H 21
Browning Ct. NG5: Sher 4F 33
Brown La. NG11: Bart F...............1E 75
Brownlow Pl. NG5: Top V...........4B 20
Browns Cft. NG6: Bas..............4B 32
Brown's Flats NG16: Kimb 6H 17
Browns La. NG12: Stant W 6B 80

Browns La. Bus. Pk.
NG12: Stant W....................6C 80
Brown's Rd. NG10: Long E 5G 63
Brown St. NG7: Hys G...............2D 44
BROXTOWE 5G 31
Broxtowe Av. NG16: Kimb 1F 29
Broxtowe Av. NG8: Aspl.............5A 32
Broxtowe Country Pk. 5E 31
Broxtowe Dr. NG15: Huck............ 2G 7
Broxtowe Hall Cl. NG8: Brox 5G 31
Broxtowe La. NG8: Aspl..............6F 31
Broxtowe La. NG8: Brox..............6F 31
Broxtowe Pk. Bus. Cen.
NG8: Stre 5D 30
Broxtowe Ri. NG8: Cin...............4H 31
Broxtowe St. NG5: Sher 5G 33
Bruce Cl. NG2: Nott 1H 57
Bruce Dr. NG2: West Br 4H 57
Brunel Av. NG16: Newth 1D 16
Brunel Ter. NG7: Radf...............4E 45
Brushfield St. NG7: Hys G...........2C 44
Brussells Ter. DE7: Ilk...............6A 28
Brusty Pl. NG14: Bur J...............2E 37
Bryan Ct. NG8: Aspl...............1A 44
Buckfast Way NG2: West Br.........4C 58
Buckingham Av. NG15: Huck 3H 7
Buckingham Ct. NG10: Sand........2C 62
Buckingham Dr. DE75: Hea.........3A 14
Buckingham Rd. NG10: Sand.......1C 62
Buckingham Rd. NG5: Woodt.......2A 34
Buckingham Way NG16: Want......6B 18
Buckland Dr. NG14: Woodbo 1C 24
Buckley Dr. NG14: Calv 4G 11
Bucklow Cl. NG8: Bas...............6B 32
Buckminster Rd. DE7: Kirk H 5G 39
Budby Ri. NG15: Huck 4H 7
Buildings, The NG11: Thru..........4C 74
BULCOTE 1H 37
Bulcote Dr. NG14: Bur J 4D 36
Bulcote Ho. NG4: Car...............1G 47
.... (off Garden City)
Bulcote Rd. NG11: Clftn 2D 66
Bullace Rd. NG3: Nott...............2B 46
Bull Cl. Rd. NG7: Lent 3C 56
Buller St. DE7: Ilk...............3C 40
Buller Ter. NG5: Sher 4H 33
Bullfinch Rd. NG6: Bas...............3B 32
Bullins Cl. NG5: Arn...............4G 21
Bullivant St. NG3: Nott 1F 5 (3H 45)
Bull Mdw. NG14: Calv...............3F 11
Bunbury St. NG2: Nott...............2H 57
Bunny La. NG11: Bunny.............5D 78
Bunny La. NG12: Key...............5E 79
Bunting Cl. DE7: Kirk H 3G 39
Buntings La. NG4: Car...............2E 47
Bunting St. NG7: Lent...............2C 56
Burcot Cl. DE7: West H...............1C 38
Burford Rd. NG7: Hys G.............1D 44
Burgass Rd. NG3: Nott...............2C 46
Burge Cl. NG2: Nott 1G 57
Burgh Hall Cl. NG9: Chil.............3C 64
Burhill NG12: Cotg...............3G 71
Burke St. NG7: Radf 2A 4 (4E 45)
Burleigh Cl. NG4: Car...............2H 47

Burleigh Rd. NG2: West Br 5B 58
Burleigh Sq. NG9: Chil...............1C 64
Burleigh St. DE7: Ilk...............6B 28
Burlington Av. NG5: Sher 4F 33
Burlington Ct. NG5: Sher 4G 33
Burlington Rd. NG4: Car.............1G 47
Burlington Rd. NG5: Sher 4G 33
Burnaby St. NG6: Bas...............3B 32
Burnbank Cl. NG2: West Br 6F 59
Burnbreck Gdns. NG8: Woll 5E 43
Burncroft DE7: West H...............2C 38
Burndale Wlk. NG5: Top V..........5C 20
Burnham Av. NG9: Chil...............1F 65
Burnham Cl. DE7: West H............1B 38
Burnham Lodge NG5: Top V........4C 20
Burnham St. NG5: Sher 5G 33
Burnham Way NG2: Nott.............6G 45
Burnor Pool NG14: Calv.............4H 11
Burns Av. NG7: Radf 1A 4 (3E 45)
Burns Ct. NG5: Sher 4F 33
Burnside Dr. NG9: Bram.............1C 54
Burnside Grn. NG8: Bilb 3D 42
Burnside Gro. NG12: Toll.............4E 69
Burnside Rd. NG2: West Br 6A 58
Burnside Rd. NG8: Bilb...............3D 42
Burns St. DE7: Ilk...............1A 40
Burns St. DE75: Hea...............3B 14
Burns St. NG7: Radf........1A 4 (3E 45)
Burnthouse Rd. DE75: Hea..........4B 14
Burnt Oak Cl. NG16: Nuth...........4D 30
Burntstump Country Pk.............1H 9
Burntstump Hill NG5: Arn...........1G 9
Burnwood Dr. NG8: Woll.............4D 42
Burr La. DE7: Ilk...............6B 28
Burrows Av. NG9: Bee...............2F 55
Burrows Ct. NG3: Nott...............4B 46
Burrows Cres. NG9: Bee 2F 55
Bursar Way NG10: Long E...........2E 63
Burtness Rd. NG11: Clftn.............4C 66
Burton Av. NG4: Car 1D 46
Burton Cl. NG4: Car...............6A 36
Burton Dr. NG9: Chil...............1C 64
Burton Joyce Station (Rail) 4E 37
Burton Manderfield Ct.
NG2: Nott 1G 57
Burton Rd. NG14: Bur J 5C 36
.... (not continuous)
Burton Rd. NG2: Car...............2G 47
Burton Rd. NG4: Ged...............2G 47
Burton St. DE75: Hea...............3C 14
Burton St. NG1: Nott.......3D 4 (4G 45)
Burwell St. NG7: Hys G.............3D 44
Bush Cl. NG5: Top V...............5D 20
Bushy Cl. NG10: Long E.............1C 62
Bute Av. NG7: Lent...............5D 44
Butler Av. NG12: Rad T 5G 49
Butlers Cl. NG15: Huck...............6A 8
BUTLER'S HILL 5A 8
Butterfield Cl. NG16: Want..........6A 18
Butterley Cl. DE7: Ilk...............2B 28
Buttermead Cl. NG9: Trow 1F 53
Buttermere Cl. NG10: Long E......3C 62
Buttermere Cl. NG2: Gam...........4E 59
Buttermere Ct. NG5: Sher 5G 33
Buttermere Dr. NG9: Bram 3D 54
Butterton Cl. DE7: Ilk...............2C 40
Buttery Gdns. NG11: Rudd..........1G 77
Butt Ho's. NG7: Lent...............5C 44
Butt Rd. NG13: Bing...............5G 51
Butts Cl. DE7: Ilk...............5C 40
Butt St. NG10: Sand...............6D 52
Buxton Av. DE75: Hea...............5D 14
Buxton Av. NG4: Car...............6F 35
Buxton Cl. NG5: Top V...............5D 20
Buxton Ct. DE7: Ilk...............5H 27
Buxton Grn. DE75: Hea...............6D 14
Byard La. NG1: Nott.........5E 5 (5G 45)

Bye Pass Rd. NG9: Chil 3D 64
Byfield Cl. NG7: Radf...............3D 44
Byford Cl. NG3: Mapp...............5A 34
Byley Rd. NG8: Bilb...............4B 42
Byrne Ct. NG5: Arn...............2D 34
Byron Cl. NG10: Long E...............2D 62
Byron Cen., The NG15: Huck 4G 7
Byron Ct. NG2: Nott 4H 5 (5A 46)
Byron Ct. NG9: Stfrd...............2G 53
Byron Cres. NG16: Aws...............3E 29
Byron Gro. NG5: Sher...............4G 33
Byron Ind. Est. NG5: Arn.............6C 22
Byron Pl. NG7: Lent...............4C 44
.... (off Wragby Rd.)
Byron Rd. NG2: West Br.............4B 58
Byron Sq. NG15: Huck...............4G 7
.... (off Baker St.)
Byron St. DE7: Ilk...............6B 28
Byron St. NG15: Huck...............5G 7
Byron St. NG5: Arn...............6H 21

C

Caddaw Av. NG15: Huck............. 5G 7
Cadlan Cl. NG5: Bestw...............6E 21
Cadlan Ct. NG5: Bestw...............6E 21
Caernarvon Pl. NG9: Chil.............1B 64
Caincross Rd. NG8: Bilb 2D 42
Cairngorm Dr. NG5: Arn.............3F 21
Cairns Cl. NG5: Bestw...............2E 33
Cairnsmore Cl. NG10: Long E......4C 62
Cairns St. NG1: Nott 2E 5 (4G 45)
Cairo St. NG7: Bas...............6D 32
Caister Rd. NG11: Clftn...............5C 66
Caithness Ct. NG5: Sher.............6F 33
Calcroft Cl. NG8: Aspl...............5A 32
Caldbeck Cl. NG2: Gam...............4E 59
Caldbeck Ct. NG9: Chil...............1B 64
Caldbeck Wlk. NG5: Bestw..........6F 21
Caldedale NG8: Woll...............6B 42
Calderdale Dr. NG10: Long E.......1C 72
Calder Gdns. NG13: Bing............6D 50
Calderhall Gdns. NG5: Bestw......5G 21
Calder Wlk. NG6: Bulw...............6H 19
Caldon Grn. NG6: Bulw...............3A 20
Caledon Rd. NG5: Sher...............4F 33
Calladine Cl. DE75: Hea...............3B 14
Calladine Cl. NG6: Bulw 1G 31
Callaway Cl. NG8: Woll...............4E 43
Calley Av. DE7: Ilk...............1B 28
Calstock Rd. NG5: Woodt...........2A 34
Calveley Rd. NG8: Bilb...............1E 43
Calver Cl. NG8: Woll...............5A 44
Calvert Cl. NG16: Lang M...........2F 15
Calverton Av. NG4: Car...............1D 64
CALVERTON 4H 11
Calverton Av. NG4: Car...............6D 34
Calverton Bus. Pk. NG14: Calv....2H 11
Calverton Cl. NG9: Toton...........3A 64
Calverton Dr. NG8: Stre 5D 30
Calverton Folk Mus...............4G 11
CALVERTON HILL 5C 10
Calverton Leisure Cen...............4H 11
Calverton Rd. NG5: Arn...............4B 22
Camberley Ct. NG6: Bulw...........5G 19
Camberley Rd. NG6: Bulw...........5G 19
Camborne Dr. NG8: Aspl.............5A 32
Cambria M. NG3: Nott...............2G 45
Cambridge Cres. NG9: Stfrd........1F 53
Cambridge Gdns. NG5: Woodt.....2D 34
Cambridge Rd. NG2: West Br 4C 58
Cambridge Rd. NG8: Woll...........5G 43
Cambridge St. NG4: Car...............6G 35
Camdale Cl. NG9: Chil...............1B 64
Camden Cl. NG2: Nott.......4H 5 (5A 46)
Camelia Av. NG11: Clftn...............4A 66
Camelot Av. NG5: Sher...............5E 33

Camelot Cres. – Chandos St.

Camelot Cres. NG11: Rudd..........5F **67**
Camelot St. NG11: Rudd..............5F **67**
Cameo Cl. NG4: Colw.................. 3H **47**
Camer Ct. NG9: Bee..................... 5G **55**
................................*(off Waverley Av.)*
Cameron St. NG5: Sher 5G **33**
Camish Ho. NG10: Sand 6D **52**
.................................*(off Bennett St.)*
Camomile Cl. NG5: Top V............6C **20**
Camomile Gdns. NG7: Hys G.......2C **44**
Campbell Cl. NG8: Brox............. 6G **31**
Campbell Dr. NG4: Car 1E **47**
Campbell Gdns. NG5: Arn.............4E **23**
Campbell Gro. NG3: Nott ...2G **5** (4H **45**)
Campbell St. NG16: Lang M........ 1G **15**
Campbell St. NG3: Nott 2H **5** (4A **46**)
Campden Grn. NG11: Clftn 3C **66**
Campion St. NG5: Arn 5A **22**
Campion Way NG13: Bing 5D **50**
Camrose Cl. NG8: Bilb 1F **43**
Canal Side DE7: Ilk.........................4B **28**
Canal Side NG9: Bee 2H **65**
Canalside NG1: Nott 6E **5** (6G **45**)
Canalside Wlk.
NG1: Nott 6B **4** (6G **45**)
Canal St. DE7: Ilk..........................6C **28**
Canal St. NG1: Nott...........6D **4** (6G **45**)
Canal St. NG10: Long E 4D **62**
Canal St. NG10: Sand 6D **52**
Canberra Cl. NG9: Stfrd.............. 2G **53**
Canberra Cres. NG15: Huck 3D **18**
Canberra Cres. NG2: West Br...... 1H **67**
Canberra Gdns. NG2: West Br..... 2H **67**
Candleby Cl. NG12: Cotg 2F **71**
Candleby Ct. NG12: Cotg..............2F **71**
Candleby La. NG12: Cotg 2F **71**
Candle Mdw. NG2: Colw...............5F **47**
Canning Cir. NG7: Nott 3A **4** (4E **45**)
Canning Ter. NG7: Nott...... 3A **4** (4E **45**)
Cannock Way NG10: Long E........ 6H **63**
Cannon St. NG5: Sher.................. 4G **33**
Canonbie Cl. NG5: Arn................. 4D **22**
Cantabury Av. NG7: Hys G.......... 1D **44**
Cantelupe Gdns. NG16: Gilt..........5E **17**
Cantelupe Rd. DE7: Ilk 1B **40**
Canterbury Cl. NG16: Nuth.......... 3D **30**
Canterbury Ct. NG1: Nott .. 1C **4** (3F **45**)
Canterbury Rd. NG8: Radf...........4B **44**
Cantley Av. NG4: Ged 5G **35**
Cantrell Rd. NG6: Bulw.................1A **32**
Canver Cl. NG8: Bilb 3C **42**
Canwick Cl. NG8: Bilb 4C **42**
Capenwray Gdns. NG5: Bestw 5G **21**
Capital FM Arena 4G **5** (5H **45**)
Capitol Ct. NG8: Woll 4G **43**
Caporn Cl. NG6: Bulw..................2A **32**
Cardale Rd. NG3: Nott 3C **46**
Cardiff St. NG3: Nott.....................4B **46**
Cardigan Cl. NG3: Nott 2G **45**
Cardinal Cl. NG3: Nott 3A **46**
Cardington Cl. NG5: Top V 4C **20**
Cardwell St. NG7: Hys G.............. 1D **44**
Carew Rd. NG11: Clftn...................3C **66**
Carey Rd. NG6: Bulw 5A **20**
Carisbrooke Av. NG3: Mapp P 6G **33**
Carisbrooke Av. NG4: Ged............6B **36**
Carisbrooke Av. NG9: Bee............ 3G **55**
Carisbrooke Dr. NG3: Mapp P 6G **33**
Carlight Gdns. Pk. Homes
NG2: West Br............................ 2D **58**
Carlile Rd. NG4: Car 1G **47**
Carlin Cl. DE72: Brea.....................5A **62**
Carlingford Rd. NG15: Huck.......... 3G **7**
Carlin St. NG6: Bulw.................... 6H **19**
Carlisle Av. NG6: Bulw..................6A **20**
Carlswark Gdns. NG5: Top V....... 4D **20**
CARLTON 2H **47**
Carlton Bus. Cen. NG4: Car......... 2H **47**
Carlton Cl. DE75: Hea...................2E **15**
Carlton Fold NG2: Nott 6B **46**
Carlton Forum Leisure Cen. 6E **35**
Carlton Grange NG4: Car..............2E **47**
Carlton Hgts. NG4: Car 2E **47**
Carlton Hill NG4: Car 2D **46**
Carlton M. NG4: Car 2E **47**
Carlton Rd. NG10: Long E........... 2D **72**
Carlton Rd. NG3: Nott....... 4H **5** (5A **46**)
Carlton Sq. NG4: Car 2G **47**
Carlton Station (Rail).....................2H **47**
Carlton St. NG1: Nott......... 4F **5** (5H **45**)
Carlton Va. Cl. NG4: Car 6F **35**
Carlyle Gdns. DE75: Hea 2B **14**
Carlyle Pl. DE75: Hea 2B **14**
Carlyle Rd. NG2: West Br.............4A **58**
Carlyle St. DE75: Hea 2B **14**
Carman Cl. NG16: Want.................5A **18**
Carmel Gdns. NG5: Arn 1B **34**
Carnarvon Cl. NG13: Bing 4E **51**
Carnarvon Dr. NG14: Bur J...........2F **37**
Carnarvon Gro. NG4: Car..............1F **47**
Carnarvon Gro. NG4: Ged............ 6H **35**
Carnarvon Pl. NG13: Bing............ 5D **50**
Carnarvon Rd. NG2: West Br........5B **58**
Carnarvon St. NG4: Neth...............3A **48**
Carnforth Cl. NG9: Stfrd 6F **53**
Carnforth Ct. NG5: Bestw............. 5G **21**
Carnwood Rd. NG5: Bestw............1E **33**
Caroline Ct. DE7: Ilk 3C **40**
Caroline Wlk. NG3: Nott 3H **45**
Carradale Cl. NG5: Arn 5E **23**
Carrfield Av. NG10: Long E.......... 5H **63**
Carrfield Av. NG9: Toton.............. 4H **63**
Carriage Cl. NG3: Nott................. 6H **33**
CARRINGTON 5F **33**
Carrington Cl. DE7: Ilk..................4C **40**
Carrington Ct. NG5: Sher............ 6G **33**
Carrington La. NG14: Calv........... 2H **11**
Carrington St. NG1: Nott ... 6E **5** (6G **45**)
Carrington St. NG2: Nott 6G **45**
Carrock Av. DE75: Hea 4F **15**
Carroll Gdns. NG2: Nott............... 2G **57**
Carr Rd. NG13: Bing 4H **51**
Cartbridge NG12: Cotg...................3F **71**
Carter Av. NG11: Rudd.................. 1G **77**
Carter Av. NG12: Rad T................. 6H **49**
Carter Cl. NG10: Long E................ 1D **72**
Carter Ga. NG1: Nott..........5G **5** (5H **45**)
Carter Rd. NG9: Chil 3A **64**
...................................(not continuous)
Carterswood Dr. NG16: Nuth........4F **31**
Cartledge Dr. NG3: Arn.................1E **35**
Cartwright Way NG9: Bee 6F **55**
Carver St. NG7: Hys G 1D **44**
Carwood Rd. NG9: Bram 2D **54**
Casper Ct. NG5: Top V...................5E **21**
................................*(off Birkdale Way)*
Castellan Ri. NG5: Bestw............. 5G **21**
Casterton Rd. NG5: Bestw.............5F **21**
Castle Blvd. NG7: Lent 6D **44**
Castle Blvd. NG7: Nott.................. 6D **44**
Castlebridge Office Village
NG7: Lent..................................1E **57**
Castle Bri. Rd. NG7: Lent..............6E **45**
Castle Cl. NG14: Calv.................... 4G **11**
Castle Ct. DE75: Hea 4E **15**
Castle Ct. NG7: Nott........... 6C **4** (6F **45**)
Castle Exchange
NG1: Nott 3F **5** (4H **45**)
..............................*(off Old Lenton St.)*
Castlefields NG2: Nott 1G **57**
Castle Gdns. NG7: Lent 6D **44**
Castle Ga. NG1: Nott..........5D **4** (5G **45**)
Castle Gro. NG7: Nott 5C **4** (5F **45**)
Castle Ind. Pk. NG15: Huck 6F **7**
Castle Marina Pk. NG7: Lent........6E **45**
Castle Marina Retail Pk..............6F **45**
Castle Marina Rd. NG7: Lent........1E **57**
Castle Mdw. Rd. NG2: Nott...........6F **45**
Castle M. NG7: Nott.......................6E **45**
Castle Museum & Art Gallery
Nottingham 5C **4** (6F **45**)
Castle Pk. NG2: Nott
Castle Mdw. Rd. 1F **57**
Castle Pk. Ind. Est. NG2: Nott
Robin Hood Way..........................2F **57**
Castle Pl. NG1: Nott........... 5C **4** (5F **45**)
Castle Quay NG7: Nott....... 6B **4** (6F **45**)
Castle Quay Cl. NG7: Lent 6E **45**
Castle Retail Pk. 3C **44**
Castlerigg Cl. NG2: West Br 6E **59**
Castle Rd. NG1: Nott.......... 5C **4** (5F **45**)
Castle Rock NG7: Nott........ 6C **4** (6F **45**)
Castle St. NG16: Eastw.................4C **16**
Castle St. NG2: Nott......................5B **46**
Castleton Av. DE7: Ilk...................2A **28**
Castleton Av. NG4: Car................ 6G **35**
Castleton Av. NG5: Arn.................6B **22**
Castleton Cl. NG15: Huck............. 5D **6**
Castleton Cl. NG2: Nott.................1F **57**
Castleton Ct. NG6: Bulw................1F **31**
Castle Vw. NG16: Lang M..............1E **15**
Castle Vw. NG2: West Br 5H **57**
Castle Vw. Cotts. NG9: Bee 5A **56**
Castle Vs. NG2: Nott 5B **46**
....*(off Castle St.)*
Castle Wlk. NG7: Hys G 2D **44**
Castle Wharf NG1: Nott 6D **4** (6G **45**)
Cat & Fiddle La. DE7: West H.......3B **38**
Cat & Fiddle Windmill..................5D **38**
Caterham Cl. NG8: Bilb................ 2D **42**
Catfoot La. NG4: Lamb 5F **23**
Catherine Av. DE7: Ilk...................3B **40**
Catherine Cl. NG6: Bulw............... 6G **19**
Catherine St. NG6: Bulw............... 6G **19**
Catkin Dr. NG16: Gilt......................5E **17**
Catlow Wlk. NG5: Bestw............... 5G **21**
Cator Cl. NG4: Ged.........................4F **35**
Cator La. NG9: Chil 5D **54**
Cator La. Nth. NG9: Chil 5D **54**
Cator Lane Stop (NET) 6D **54**
Catriona Cres. NG5: Arn 3C **22**
Catt Cl. NG9: Chil 4B **64**
Catterley Hill Rd. NG3: Nott..........2C **46**
Cattle Mkt. Rd. NG2: Nott.............. 1H **57**
Catton Rd. NG5: Arn 5C **22**
Caudale Ct. NG2: Gam....................4E **59**
Caulton St. NG7: Hys G................. 3D **44**
....(not continuous)
Caunton Av. NG3: Nott...................6A **34**
Causeway M. NG2: Nott 1F **57**
Cavan Ct. NG2: Nott...................... 2G **57**
Cavell Cl. NG11: Clftn 3B **66**
Cavendish Av. NG4: Ged................5F **35**
Cavendish Av. NG5: Sher............ 4H **33**
Cavendish Cl. NG15: Huck 5A **8**
Cavendish Ct. NG3: Mapp 4B **34**
Cavendish Ct. NG7: Nott.... 4A **4** (5E **45**)
Cavendish Cres. NG4: Car 5E **35**
Cavendish Cres. NG9: Stfrd..........1F **53**
Cavendish Cres. Nth.
NG7: Nott 5E **45**
Cavendish Cres. Sth.
NG7: Nott 6A **4** (6E **45**)
Cavendish Dr. NG4: Car................ 1G **47**
Cavendish Ho. NG4: Car............... 1G **47**
.....................................*(off Garden City)*
Cavendish M. NG12: Cotg 3F **71**
....*(off Daleside)*
Cavendish M. NG7: Nott.... 4A **4** (5E **45**)
Cavendish Pl. NG7: Nott.... 6A **4** (6E **45**)
Cavendish Pl. NG9: Bee...................5F **55**
Cavendish Rd. DE7: Ilk...................3B **40**
Cavendish Rd. NG10: Long E........3E **63**
Cavendish Rd. NG4: Car 5E **35**
Cavendish Rd. E.
NG7: Nott 4A **4** (5E **45**)
Cavendish Rd. W. NG7: Nott 5E **45**
Cavendish St. NG5: Arn.................5A **22**
Cavendish St. NG7: Lent 2C **56**
.................................(not continuous)
Cavendish Va. NG5: Sher 4H **33**
Caversham Way DE7: West H.......1B **38**
Cawdron Wlk. NG11: Clftn............3C **66**
Cawston Gdns. NG6: Bulw 5H **19**
Caxmere Dr. NG8: Woll..................4F **43**
Caxton Cl. NG4: Neth.....................2A **48**
Caxton Rd. NG5: Sher....................6F **33**
Caythorpe Cres. NG5: Sher 3G **33**
Caythorpe Ri. NG5: Sher 3G **33**
Cecil St. NG7: Lent 6D **44**
Cedar Av. NG10: Long E.................2E **73**
Cedar Av. NG16: Nuth....................3F **31**
Cedar Av. NG9: Bee 4G **55**
Cedar Cl. NG10: Sand 4D **52**
Cedar Cl. NG13: Bing.................... 5G **51**
Cedar Ct. NG9: Bee........................ 4G **55**
Cedar Dr. NG12: Key...................... 5G **79**
Cedar Gro. NG15: Huck.................. 6H **7**
Cedar Gro. NG5: Arn...................... 5D **22**
Cedar Gro. NG8: Woll......................5F **43**
Cedarland Cres. NG16: Nuth 3F **31**
Cedar Lodge NG7: Nott...... 4A **4** (5E **45**)
Cedar Lodge Cvn. Pk.
NG12: Hol P...................................1C **60**
Cedar Pk. DE7: Ilk...........................1A **40**
Cedar Rd. NG7: Hys G....................1E **45**
Cedar Rd. NG9: Chil 6E **55**
Cedars, The NG5: Sher 3H **33**
Cedar Tree Rd. NG5: Arn 4F **21**
Celandine Cl. NG5: Top V 6C **20**
Celandine Gdns. NG13: Bing 5C **50**
Celia Dr. NG4: Car 2F **47**
Cemetery Rd. NG9: Stfrd 4G **53**
Cemetery Wlk. NG16: Eastw 4A **16**
Central Av. NG10: Sand 5D **52**
Central Av. NG15: Huck 5G **7**
Central Av. NG2: West Br...............3B **58**
Central Av. NG3: Mapp 3D **34**
Central Av. NG5: Arn.......................6B **22**
Central Av. NG7: Bas 6E **33**
Central Av. NG9: Bee 2E **55**
Central Av. NG9: Chil 5D **54**
Central Av. NG9: Stfrd................... 3G **53**
Central Av. Sth. NG5: Arn 6B **22**
Central Ct. NG7: Lent.................... 2D **56**
Central St. NG3: Nott 3A **46**
Central Wlk. NG15: Huck............... 4G **7**
Centre Way NG12: Rad T................5E **49**
Centurion Bus. Pk. NG6: Bulw......4E **19**
Centurion Cl. NG15: Huck...............3B **8**
Centurion Way NG2: Nott 3E **57**
Century Ct. NG1: Nott 2F **45**
..........................*(off Nth. Sherwood St.)*
Cernan Ct. NG6: Bulw.....................2F **31**
Cerne Cl. NG11: Clftn.................... 5D **66**
Chaceley Way NG11: Wilf...............2E **67**
Chadborn Av. NG11: Goth.............. 6H **75**
Chadburn Rd. NG15: Huck 1A **8**
Chaddesden, The NG3: Mapp P... 2G **45**
Chad Gdns. NG5: Top V..................3E **21**
Chadwick Rd. NG7: Hys G..............2C **44**
Chain La. NG7: Lent..........................2C **56**
Chalfield Cl. NG11: Clftn................4B **66**
Chalfont Dr. NG8: Aspl.................. 2H **43**
Challond Ct. NG5: Bestw 6G **21**
Chalons Cl. DE7: Ilk........................6B **28**
Chalons Way DE7: Ilk 6B **28**
Chamberlain Cl. NG11: Clftn 4A **66**
Chambers Av. DE7: Ilk.................. 2D **40**
Chambers Ct. NG5: Bestw 2D **32**
Champion Av. DE7: Ilk.................. 4G **27**
Chancery, The NG9: Bram 4C **54**
Chancery Ct. NG11: Wilf.................5E **57**
Chandos Av. NG4: Neth 1A **48**
Chandos St. NG3: Nott....................2A **46**
Chandos St. NG4: Neth...................2A **48**

A-Z Nottingham 93

Chantrey Rd. NG2: West Br 4A 58
Chantry Cl. NG10: Long E............3C 72
Chantry Cl. NG16: Kimb............2A 30
Chantry Cl. NG9: Chil....................1D 64
Chapel Bar NG1: Nott 4C 4 (5F 45)
Chapel Cl. NG11: Goth................6H 75
Chapel Ct. DE7: Ilk.....................3B 28
Chapelfield Gro. NG13: Bing 6E 51
Chapel La. NG12: Cotg 2F 71
Chapel La. NG13: Bing.................2D 50
Chapel La. NG14: Epp..................5G 13
Chapel La. NG4: Lamb.................6B 24
Chapel La. NG5: Arn 5A 22
Chapel Mews Ct. NG9: Bram.......3B 54
Chapel Pl. NG16: Kimb 1H 29
Chapel Quarter
NG1: Nott 4C 4 (5F 45)
Chapel St. DE7: Ilk.....................6B 28
.... (not continuous)
Chapel St. DE75: Hea 5E 15
Chapel St. NG10: Long E 6G 63
Chapel St. NG11: Rudd 1G 77
Chapel St. NG15: Huck..................4G 7
Chapel St. NG16: Eastw..............4B 16
Chapel St. NG16: Kimb 1H 29
Chapel St. NG7: Radf...................4E 45
Chapel St. NG9: Bram.................3B 54
Chapel Yd. NG12: Norm W...........6A 70
Chapman Ct. NG8: Bilb................2H 43
Chapmans Wlk. NG6: Bestw V......5F 9
Chapter Dr. NG16: Kimb 2A 30
Chardlace Wlk.
NG1: Nott 5G 5 (5H 45)
.... (off Hollowstone)
Chard St. NG2: Bas......................5D 32
Chard Ter. NG7: Bas....................5D 32
Charlbury Ct. NG9: Bram.............5B 42
Charlbury Rd. NG8: Woll 3G 43
Charlecote Dr. NG8: Woll 6D 42
Charlecote Pk. Dr.
NG2: West Br 1G 67
Charles Av. NG10: Sand...............5D 52
Charles Av. NG16: Eastw.............3D 16
Charles Av. NG9: Chil...................2C 64
Charles Av. NG9: Lent A 2G 55
Charles Av. NG9: Stfrd.................3H 53
Charles Cl. DE7: Ilk.....................3D 40
Charles Cl. NG4: Ged 5H 35
Charles Ct. NG15: Huck..................4G 7
Charles Ho. NG1: Nott..........5C 4 (5F 45)
.... (off Park Row)
Charles St. NG10: Long E 1F 73
Charles St. NG11: Rudd 6G 67
Charles St. NG15: Huck..................4G 7
Charles St. NG5: Arn....................6A 22
Charleston Ho.
NG1: Nott 1C 4 (3F 45)
Charles Way NG6: Bulw................2H 31
Charles Way Bus. Pk.
NG6: Bulw 2A 32
Charlesworth Av. NG7: Bas...........1C 44
Charlock Cl. NG5: Top V...............6C 20
Charlock Gdns. NG13: Bing 6D 50
Charlotte Cl. NG5: Arn 3A 22
Charlotte Cl. NG16: Eastw............2B 16
Charlotte Gro. NG9: Bram............2D 54
Charlotte St. DE7: Ilk..................4A 28
Charlton Av. NG10: Long E 4H 63
Charlton Gro. NG9: Bee................1F 65
Charnock Av. NG8: Woll 6B 44
Charnos St. DE7: Ilk....................5C 40
Charnwood Av. NG10: Long E 3D 72
Charnwood Av. NG10: Sand...........1C 62
Charnwood Av. NG12: Key.............5G 79
Charnwood Av. NG9: Bee..............5D 54
Charnwood Gdns. NG5: Sher 6B 20
Charnwood Gro. NG13: Bing 5D 50
Charnwood Gro. NG15: Huck 4E 7
Charnwood Gro. NG2: West Br 4A 58

Charnwood La. NG5: Arn..............1C 34
Charnwood Way
NG14: Woodbo 1D 24
Charter Pk. DE7: Ilk...................2A 40
Chartwell Av. NG11: Rudd............6F 67
Chartwell Gro. NG3: Mapp 2E 35
Chase Farm NG4: Ged 3G 35
Chase Pk. NG2: Nott...................6C 46
Chatham Cl. NG6: Bulw...............1A 32
Chatham St. NG1: Nott 3G 45
Chatsworth Av. NG10: Long E 1A 74
Chatsworth Av. NG12: Rad T........5G 49
Chatsworth Av. NG4: Car 1G 47
Chatsworth Av. NG7: Bas 5D 32
Chatsworth Av. NG9: Chil.............3C 64
Chatsworth Cl. NG10: Sand..........1D 62
Chatsworth Ct. DE7: West H 1C 38
Chatsworth Ct. NG15: Huck 5G 7
Chatsworth Dr. NG15: Huck 5G 7
Chatsworth Pl. DE7: Kirk H 4F 39
Chatsworth Rd. NG2: West Br 3D 58
Chatsworth Way DE75: Hea 3A 14
Chatterley Ct. NG7: Lent..............4C 44
.... (off Wragby Rd.)
Chatterley Parkway NG8: Stre 5C 30
Chaucer St. DE7: Ilk 6B 28
Chaucer St. NG1: Nott 2C 4 (4F 45)
Chaworth Av. NG16: Want.............4H 17
Chaworth Cl. NG15: Huck...............1F 7
Chaworth Rd. NG13: Bing 5D 50
Chaworth Rd. NG2: West Br 5A 58
Chaworth Rd. NG4: Colw................3H 47
Cheadle Cl. NG3: Mapp................5D 34
Cheadle Cl. NG8: Bilb 1D 42
Cheapside NG1: Nott 4E 5 (5G 45)
Cheddar Rd. NG11: Cliftn.............5C 66
Chedington Av. NG3: Mapp 1F 35
Chediston Va. NG5: Bestw..............5F 21
Chedworth Cl. NG3: Nott..............4B 46
Chelmsford Rd. NG7: Bas.............5D 32
Chelmsford Ter. NG7: Bas 5D 32
.... (off Zulu Rd.)
Chelsbury Ct. NG5: Arn.................6A 22
Chelsea Cl. NG16: Nuth................4E 31
Chelsea St. NG7: Bas...................6D 32
Cheltenham Cl. NG9: Toton 3H 63
Cheltenham St. NG6: Bas.............3C 32
Chelwood Dr. NG3: Mapp 4E 35
Chennel Nook NG12: Cotg............3G 71
Chepstow Rd. NG11: Cliftn...........5C 66
Cherhill Cl. NG11: Cliftn...............6B 66
Cheriton Dr. DE7: Ilk 4G 27
Cherries, The NG11: Wilf..............5F 57
Cherry Av. NG15: Huck 6H 7
Cherry Blossom Rd.
NG14: Stoke B..........................2C 48
Cherry Cl. DE72: Brea..................5A 62
Cherry Cl. NG2: West Br 2E 59
Cherry Cl. NG5: Arn 5A 22
Cherry Cl. NG5: Bestw..................1F 33
Cherry Hill NG12: Key..................4H 79
Cherry Orchard NG12: Cotg 2F 71
Cherry Orchard Mt.
NG5: Bestw 1F 33
Cherry Vw. NG8: Aspl 2H 43
Cherry Wood Dr. NG8: Aspl 2H 43
Cherrywood Gdns. NG3: Nott........1C 46
Chertsey Cl. NG3: Nott.................6B 34
Chertsey Ct. DE7: West H 1B 38
Cherwell Ct. NG6: Bulw................1F 31
Cherwell Gdns. NG13: Bing..........6C 50

Chesham Dr. NG5: Sher................5F 33
Chesham Dr. NG9: Bram...............6B 42
Cheshire Ct. NG2: West Br............6H 57
Chesil Av. NG8: Radf...................4B 44
Chesil Cotts. NG8: Radf...............4B 44
.... (off Chesil Av.)
Cheslyn Dr. NG8: Aspl..................1A 44
Chesnuts, The NG4: Ged 6B 36
Chesterfield Av. NG10: Long E 6H 63
Chesterfield Av. NG13: Bing 5E 51
Chesterfield Av. NG4: Ged.............4F 35
Chesterfield Cl. NG4: Ged 4F 35
Chesterfield Dr. NG14: Bur J 2G 37
Chesterfield St. NG4: Car 2F 47
Chester Grn. NG10: Long E 3G 63
Chester Ho. NG3: Mapp P 1G 45
Chesterman Cl. NG16: Aws............3D 28
Chester Rd. NG3: Nott 4E 47
Chestnut Av. NG13: Bing...............5E 51
Chestnut Av. NG3: Mapp 5D 34
Chestnut Av. NG9: Bee 5F 55
Chestnut Bank DE75: Hea.............4B 14
Chestnut Cl. NG12: Key................4G 79
Chestnut Cl. NG14: Calv................5C 12
Chestnut Dr. NG12: Cotg 6G 61
Chestnut Dr. NG16: Nuth 6B 18
Chestnut Gro. NG10: Sand............4C 52
Chestnut Gro. NG12: Rad T...........5F 49
Chestnut Gro. NG14: Bur J 3F 37
Chestnut Gro. NG15: Huck 1H 19
Chestnut Gro. NG2: West Br 4H 57
Chestnut Gro. NG3: Mapp P 2G 45
Chestnut Gro. NG4: Ged 6H 35
Chestnut Gro. NG5: Arn................4C 22
Chestnut La. NG11: Bart F..............1E 75
Chestnut M. NG12: Toll 1H 69
Chestnut Rd. NG16: Lang M..........2E 15
Chestnuts, The NG10: Long E.........5C 62
Chestnuts, The NG12: Rad T.........6E 49
Chestnuts, The NG3: Nott..............6B 34
Chestnut Wlk. NG5: Sher..............4A 34
Chettles Ind. Est. NG7: Radf..........4B 44
Chettles Trade Pk. NG7: Radf........4B 44
Chetwin Rd. NG8: Bilb.................4D 42
Chetwynd Bus. Pk. NG9: Chil........3B 64
Chetwynd Cl. NG9: Chil................2A 64
Chetwynd Rd. NG9: Toton.............3A 64
Chevin Gdns. NG5: Top V..............4E 21
Cheviot Cl. NG5: Arn 3F 21
Cheviot Ct. NG9: Chil...................2C 64
Cheviot Dr. NG6: Bulw..................5F 19
Cheviot Rd. NG10: Long E 4C 62
Chewton Av. NG16: Eastw.............4C 16
Chewton St. NG16: Eastw.............4B 16
Cheyne Wlk. NG15: Huck 3H 7
Cheyny Cl. NG2: Nott 2G 57
Chichester Cl. DE7: Ilk..................1C 40
Chichester Cl. NG5: Top V.............6C 20
Chichester Dr. NG12: Cotg 1E 71
Chidlow Rd. NG8: Bilb..................2D 42
Chigwell Cl. NG16: Nuth...............4E 31
Chillon Way NG15: Huck................5D 6
Chiltern Cl. NG5: Arn 3F 21
Chiltern Dr. DE7: West H...............1C 38
Chiltern Gdns. NG10: Long E.........4C 62
Chiltern Way NG5: Bestw 1F 33
Chilton Dr. NG16: Want.................6A 18
Chilvers Cl. NG5: Bestw................6E 21
CHILWELL 5C 54
Chilwell Cl. NG6: Bulw..................6B 20
Chilwell La. NG9: Bram 6B 54
Chilwell Manor Golf Course 1E 65
Chilwell Meadow
Nature Reserve 1D 64
Chilwell Olympia Leisure Cen. 2D 64
Chilwell Retail Pk. 4B 64
Chilwell Rd. NG9: Bee..................6F 55
Chilwell Road Stop (NET) 6F 55
Chilwell St. NG7: Lent 6D 44

Chine Gdns. NG2: West Br 6G 57
Chingford Rd. NG8: Bilb 1E 43
Chipmunk Way NG13: Newt...........2B 50
Chippendale St. NG7: Lent............6D 44
Chippenham Rd. NG5: Bestw 1F 33
Chisbury Grn. NG11: Cliftn............6B 66
Chisholm Way NG5: Bestw............1E 33
Chiswick Ct. NG5: Sher 4G 33
Christchurch Rd. NG15: Huck 1D 18
Christina Av. NG6: Cin 3A 32
Christina Cres. NG6: Cin 3A 32
Christine Cl. NG15: Huck...............2A 8
Christine Ct. NG3: Nott................2C 46
Christopher Cl. NG8: Woll.............3F 43
Christopher Ct. NG15: Huck 1F 19
Chrysalis Way NG16: Eastw..........2G 15
Chrysalis Way Ind. Pk.
NG16: Eastw 2G 15
Church Av. NG10: Long E 3C 72
Church Av. NG5: Arn 6A 22
Church Av. NG7: Lent...................6D 44
Church Cl. NG12: Rad T................6E 49
Church Cl. NG13: Bing..................4F 51
Church Cl. NG5: Arn 6A 22
Church Cl. NG9: Trow...................5E 41
Church Ct. NG12: Cotg 2E 71
Church Cres. NG5: Arn 6H 21
Church Cres. NG9: Chil................1A 64
Churchdale Av. NG9: Stfrd............2G 53
Church Dr. DE7: Ilk......................2H 27
Church Dr. NG10: Sand.................4D 52
Church Dr. NG12: Key...................4G 79
Church Dr. NG15: Huck..................4G 7
Church Dr. NG2: West Br...............4B 58
Church Dr. NG5: Arn 6H 21
Church Dr. NG5: Sher...................6F 33
Church Dr. E. NG5: Arn.................6A 22
Churchfield La. NG7: Radf.............2C 44
Churchfield Ter. NG6: Bas 5C 32
Churchfield Way NG5: Top V..........4E 21
Church Ga. NG12: C'ton................5C 70
Church Gro. NG7: Lent..................6C 44
Church Hill NG12: Plum................1G 79
Church Hill NG16: Kimb................1H 29
Churchill Cl. NG5: Arn..................1B 34
Churchill Dr. NG11: Rudd 6F 67
Churchill Dr. NG9: Stfrd...............3G 53
Churchill Pk. NG4: Colw................4H 47
Church La. DE7: Mapp..................5C 26
Church La. DE7: Stant D................2B 52
Church La. NG11: Bart F................1E 75
Church La. NG11: Thru..................4B 74
Church La. NG12: Cotg 2E 71
Church La. NG12: Plum.................6G 69
Church La. NG13: Bing..................5F 51
Church La. NG14: Epp...................5G 13
Church La. NG15: Lin.....................1G 7
Church La. NG16: Coss..................5E 29
Church La. NG5: Arn.....................4B 22
Church La. NG6: Bulw...................6A 20
Church La. NG8: Atten..................4D 64
Church La. NG9: Stfrd...................4F 53
Church Mdw. NG14: Calv..............5H 11
Church M. NG2: Nott....................2H 57
Churchmoor Ct. NG5: Arn.............4A 22
Churchmoor La. NG5: Arn.............4A 22
Church Rd. NG14: Bur J 3F 37
Church Rd. NG16: Grea.................2F 17
Church Rd. NG16: Want.................2F 17
Church Rd. NG3: Nott...................2H 45
Church Rd. NG6: Bestw V..............1C 20
Churchside Gdns. NG7: Hys G........1C 44
Church Sq. DE75: Hea 4D 14
Church St. DE7: Ilk......................3H 27
Church St. DE75: Hea...................4D 14
Church St. NG10: Sand.................4D 52
Church St. NG11: Goth 6H 75

Church St. NG11: Rudd 6G 67
Church St. NG12: S'frd 6H 37
Church St. NG13: Bing............5F 51
Church St. NG16: Eastw 3A 16
Church St. NG4: Car 2G 47
Church St. NG4: Lamb 5C 24
Church St. NG5: Arn 5B 22
Church St. NG6: Bas 5C 32
Church St. NG7: Lent.............6C 44
Church St. NG9: Bee.............5F 55
Church St. NG9: Bram 3B 54
Church St. NG9: Stfrd 4F 53
Church Vw. DE7: Ilk..............2A 40
Church Vw. DE72: Brea........6A 62
Church Vw. DE75: Los..........1A 14
Church Vw. NG4: Ged 6H 35
Church Vw. Cl. NG5: Arn 4F 21
Church Wlk. NG14: Woodbo 1C 24
Church Wlk. NG16: Eastw 3B 16
Church Wlk. NG4: Car 2G 47
Church Wlk. NG9: Stfrd 4G 53
Churnet Cl. NG11: Clftn..........1C 66
Churston Ct. NG9: Bee 5G 55
Cider Orchard Pl. NG16: Kimb..... 1H 29
Cigar Factory, The
  NG7: Nott 3A 4 (4E 45)
  ....(off Derby Rd.)
CINDERHILL.............................3H 31
Cinderhill Footway NG6: Bulw ...3B 32
Cinderhill Gro. NG4: Ged 5G 35
Cinderhill Gym 4H 31
Cinderhill Rd. NG6: Bulw 3H 31
Cinderhill Rd. NG6: Cin.......... 3H 31
Cinderhill Stop (NET) 3H 31
Cinderhill Wlk. NG6: Bulw 1H 31
Cineworld Cinema
  Nottingham 3D 4 (4G 45)
CIRCLE NOTTINGHAM
  HOSPITAL 1C 56
Circuit Dr. NG10: Long E.............. 5H 63
Cirrus Dr. NG16: Want 6A 18
Citadel St. NG7: Radf............4C 44
City, The NG9: Bee.................. 5G 55
  ....(not continuous)
City Bus. Pk. NG4: Colw 3H 47
City Ground 2A 58
CITY HOSPITAL (NOTTINGHAM
  UNIVERSITY).....................2F 33
City Link NG2: Nott.......6G 5 (6H 45)
City of Caves 5E 5 (5G 45)
  ....(off Middle Hill)
City Point NG1: Nott... 5C 4 (5F 45)
City Rd. NG7: Nott....................2B 56
City Rd. NG9: Bee 4G 55
City Vw. NG3: Mapp.................5B 34
Clandon Dr. NG5: Sher.............5F 33
Clanfield Rd. NG8: Bilb.............2E 43
Clapham St. NG7: Radf...........4C 44
Claramount Rd. DE75: Hea 4E 15
Clarborough Dr. NG5: Arn........1C 34
Clare Cl. NG6: Bas 3C 32
Clarehaven NG9: Stfrd 6G 53
Claremont Av. NG15: Huck....... 6G 7
Claremont Av. NG9: Bram 3C 54
Claremont Dr. NG2: West Br 2G 67
Claremont Gdns. NG5: Sher 6F 33
Claremont Rd. NG5: Sher........6F 33
Clarence Ct. NG3: Nott 3H 5 (4A 46)
Clarence Rd. NG10: Long E........1E 73
Clarence St. NG3: Nott 2H 5 (4A 46)
Clarendon Chambers
  NG1: Nott 2B 4 (4F 45)
Clarendon Ct. NG5: Sher 1F 45
Clarendon Ho. NG1: Nott... 3B 4 (4F 45)
Clarendon Pk. NG5: Sher 1F 45
Clarendon St. NG1: Nott... 2B 4 (4F 45)
Clare St. NG1: Nott 3E 5 (4G 45)
Clare Valley NG7: Nott....... 5B 4 (5F 45)

Clarewood Gro. NG11: Clftn 6C 66
Clarges St. NG6: Bulw 1A 32
Clarke Av. DE75: Los..............3A 14
Clarke Av. NG5: Arn 5B 22
Clarke Dr. NG10: Long E.............3C 72
Clarke Rd. NG7: Nott 1A 58
Clarke's La. NG9: Chil............... 1D 64
Clarkson Dr. NG9: Bee............. 5H 55
Claude St. NG7: Lent.................2C 56
Claxton St. DE75: Hea 3B 14
Claxton Ter. DE75: Hea............3B 14
Clay Av. NG3: Mapp.................4C 34
Claye St. NG10: Long E............ 6G 63
Clayfield Cl. NG6: Bulw 1G 31
Claygate NG3: Nott 2D 46
Clay La. DE75: Hea.................. 3D 14
Claypit Wlk. NG11: Wilf.............5E 57
Claypole Rd. NG7: Hys G 2D 44
Clayton Ct. NG7: Radf...............4D 44
Clayton Ct. NG9: Bee............... 6G 55
Clayton Gro. DE75: Los 1A 14
Claytons Dr. NG7: Lent 1C 56
Claytons Wharf NG7: Lent........1C 56
Clement Dr. NG3: Mapp...........2E 35
Clether Rd. NG8: Bilb...............3D 42
Cleve Av. NG9: Toton 2G 63
Clevedon Dr. NG5: Arn.............4E 23
Cleveland Av. NG10: Long E...... 4H 63
Cleveland Cl. NG7: Radf 4C 44
Cleveley's Rd. NG9: Toton 2G 63
Clevely Way NG11: Clftn...........2C 66
Cliff, The NG6: Bulw 3H 31
Cliff Blvd. NG16: Kimb............. 6H 17
Cliff Cres. NG12: Rad T..............5F 49
Cliff Dr. NG12: Rad T................ 4G 49
Cliffe Hill Av. NG9: Stfrd 4F 53
Cliffgrove Av. NG9: Chil.............5D 54
Cliffmere Wlk. NG11: Clftn 4B 66
Clifford Av. NG9: Bee................3E 55
Clifford Cl. NG10: Long E...........3C 72
Clifford Cl. NG12: Key...............3H 79
Clifford Cl. NG10: Long E........... 6G 63
Clifford St. NG7: Radf 3D 44
Cliff Rd. NG1: Nott 5F 5 (5H 45)
Cliff Rd. NG12: Rad T................5E 49
Cliff Rd. NG4: Car 3F 47
Cliffs, The NG12: Rad T 4G 49
Cliff Way NG12: Rad T...............5F 49
CLIFTON...................................4D 66
Clifton Av. NG10: Long E............6A 64
Clifton Av. NG11: Rudd 5G 67
Clifton Blvd. NG11: Rudd...........6E 57
Clifton Blvd. NG11: Wilf.............6E 57
Clifton Blvd. NG7: Lent.............1B 56
Clifton Blvd. NG7: Nott 1B 56
Clifton Centre Stop (NET) 4C 66
Clifton Cres. NG9: Atten 2E 65
Clifton Grn. NG11: Clftn............3B 66
Clifton Gro. NG4: Ged 5G 35
Clifton Hall Dr. NG11: Clftn........3H 65
Clifton La. NG11: Clftn..............5B 66
Clifton La. NG11: Rudd 5E 67
Clifton La. NG11: Wilf................5B 66
Clifton Leisure Cen....................4D 66
Clifton M. NG7: Nott 4A 4 (5E 45)
Clifton Pastures NG11: Goth 6A 66
Clifton Rd. NG11: Rudd.............6F 67
Clifton South Park & Ride 6A 66
Clifton St. NG9: Bee................. 5G 55
Clifton Ter. NG7: Nott... 6A 4 (6E 45)
Clinton Av. NG5: Sher............... 1F 45
Clinton Ct. NG1: Nott...2D 4 (4G 45)
Clinton St. NG5: Arn.................6A 22
Clinton St. NG9: Bee................4E 55
Clinton St. E. NG1: Nott... 3E 5 (4G 45)
Clinton St. W. NG1: Nott... 3E 5 (4G 45)
Clinton Ter. NG7: Nott... 3A 4 (4E 45)
CLIPSTON 4D 70
Clipstone Av. NG1: Nott... 1C 4 (3F 45)

Clipstone Av. NG3: Mapp...........3C 34
Clipstone Cl. NG8: Stre.............5D 30
Clipston La. NG12: Norm W........ 6H 69
Clive Cres. NG16: Kimb 2A 30
Cliveden Grn. NG11: Clftn..........4B 66
Cloister Ho. NG7: Lent..............1C 56
Cloisters, The NG9: Bee 3G 55
Cloister St. NG7: Lent...............1C 56
Close, The NG5: Sher............... 4G 33
Close, The NG9: Chil................ 1D 64
Close Quarters NG9: Bram 3C 54
Cloud Av. NG9: Stfrd 4H 53
Clouds Hill NG11: Clftn.............5C 66
Cloudside Ct. NG10: Sand 4D 52
Cloudside Rd. NG10: Sand 4D 52
Clough Ct. NG8: Bilb................. 2H 43
Clovelly Dr. NG3: Mapp.............2E 35
Cloverdale NG12: Cotg 3G 71
Clover Flds. NG14: Calv.............3A 12
Clover Grn. NG6: Bas................4B 32
Cloverlands NG2: West Br 2G 67
Cloverlands Cl. NG16: Want.......6A 18
Cloverlands Dr. NG16: Want.......6A 18
Clover Ri. NG16: Newth 4D 16
Clumber Av. NG3: Mapp...........3C 34
Clumber Av. NG4: Neth.............2A 48
Clumber Av. NG5: Sher............. 1F 45
Clumber Av. NG9: Chil.............. 6D 54
Clumber Ct. NG7: Nott... 6A 4 (6E 45)
Clumber Cres. Nth.
  NG7: Nott 5E 45
Clumber Cres. Sth.
  NG7: Nott 6A 4 (6E 45)
Clumber Dr. NG12: Rad T 4G 49
Clumber Rd. NG2: West Br 4B 58
Clumber Rd. E.
  NG7: Nott 5A 4 (5E 45)
Clumber Rd. W. NG7: Nott... 5A 4 (5E 45)
Clumber St. NG1: Nott ... 3E 5 (4G 45)
Clumber St. NG10: Long E.........6F 63
Clumber St. NG15: Huck............5A 8
Coach Dr. NG16: Eastw.............1B 16
Coachmans Cft. NG8: Woll 4G 43
Coachways DE7: Mapp.............. 4D 26
Coates Av. NG15: Huck..............2F 7
Coatsby Rd. NG16: Kimb 6H 17
Cobden Chambers
  NG1: Nott 4E 5 (5H 45)
  ....(off Pelham St.)
Cobden St. NG10: Long E..........6F 63
Cobden St. NG7: Lent...............4C 44
Cockayne Cl. NG10: Sand..........2D 62
Cocker Beck NG4: Lamb............6C 24
Cockerhouse Rd. NG16: Eastw 1A 16
Cockington Rd. NG8: Bilb..........4C 42
Cockleys NG10: Long E.............1E 73
Codnor Gdns. NG5: Bestw.........5G 21
Cogenhoe Wlk. NG5: Arn 3B 22
Coggan Wlk. NG14: Calv 3E 11
Cogley La. NG13: Bing.............. 5G 51
Cohen Cl. NG5: Arn..................1D 34
Cohen Cl. NG9: Chil..................3B 64
Cokefield Av. NG16: Nuth 4F 31
Colborn St. NG3: Nott...............2B 46
Colbrook Pl. NG4: Car 2H 47
Colchester Rd. NG8: Brox..........6E 31
Coleby Av. NG7: Lent................1C 56
Coleby Rd. NG8: Brox................5F 31
Coledale NG2: West Br 5E 59
Coleridge Cres. NG5: Arn 6H 21
Coleridge St. NG7: Radf.............3C 44
Colesbourne Pl. NG11: Clftn...... 3D 66
Colesbourne Rd. NG11: Clftn..... 3D 66
Colin Broughton Cl. NG6: Bulw...6B 20
Colindale Gdns. NG16: Nuth......4E 31
Colinwood Av. NG5: Top V.........4C 20
College Dr. NG11: Clftn.............3B 66
  ....(not continuous)
College Rd. NG3: Mapp.............4E 35

College Rd. NG9: Chil 6E 55
College St. NG1: Nott...... 3B 4 (4F 45)
College St. NG10: Long E 2D 62
College Way NG8: Bilb...............2C 42
Colleymoor Leys La.
  NG11: Clftn 3D 66
Colliers Bus. Pk. NG12: Cotg...... 6G 61
Colliers Way NG12: Cotg 6G 61
Colliers Way NG8: Cin 3G 31
Colliery Cl. NG2: Nott...............2F 57
Collin Av. NG10: Sand............... 1D 62
Collin Grn. NG5: Sher 3H 33
Collington St. NG9: Bee.............5E 55
Collington Way NG2: West Br...... 6H 57
Collingwood Cl. NG11: Clftn.......1C 66
Collingwood Rd. NG10: Long E....1F 73
Collins Cl. NG6: Bulw.................2F 31
Collins Homes NG9: Bee............2E 55
Collin St. NG1: Nott........ 6E 5 (6G 45)
Collin St. NG9: Bee...................5F 55
Collyer Rd. NG14: Calv 3E 11
Colly Ga. NG16: Kimb 2A 30
Collygate Rd. NG2: Nott............2H 57
Colmon Cl. NG5: Bestw 6E 21
Colmon Wlk. NG5: Bestw 6E 21
Colonsay Cl. NG9: Trow.............6F 41
Colston Cres. NG2: West Br....... 1H 67
Colston Ga. NG12: Cotg.............2F 71
Colston Ga. NG12: Crop Bi.........2F 71
Colston Rd. NG6: Bas................5A 20
Coltsfoot Cl. NG13: Bing...........6C 50
Colville St. NG1: Nott................2F 45
Colville St. NG1: Nott................3F 45
Colville Ter. NG1: Nott...............3F 45
Colville Vs. NG1: Nott................2F 45
COLWICK..................................4G 47
Colwick Bus. Pk. NG4: Colw 4H 47
Colwick Country Pk. 6F 47
Colwick Crossing NG2: Nott.......5C 46
Colwick Ind. Est. NG4: Colw
  Private Rd. No. 2 .... 4H 47
Colwick Ind. Est. NG4: Colw
  Private Rd. No. 5 ....4B 48
Colwick Ind. Est. NG4: Colw
  Private Rd. No. 8 .... 4G 47
Colwick Lodge NG4: Car 3H 47
Colwick Loop Rd. NG4: Car........1A 48
Colwick Loop Rd. NG4: Colw 1A 48
Colwick Loop Rd. NG4: Neth......1A 48
Colwick Mnr. Farm NG4: Colw 4G 47
Colwick Pk. Cl. NG4: Colw 4G 47
Colwick Quays Bus. Pk.
  NG4: Colw 4A 48
Colwick Rd. NG2: Nott...............6B 46
Colwick Rd. NG2: West Br..........2A 58
COLWICK VALE 3G 47
Colwick Woods Ct. NG2: Nott.....5C 46
Comery Av. NG3: Nott...............3C 46
Comet Dr. NG16: Eastw 3C 16
Comfrey Cl. NG5: Top V.............6C 20
Commerce Sq.
  NG1: Nott 5F 5 (5H 45)
Commercial Av. NG9: Bee..........5F 55
Commercial Rd. NG12: Key.........5G 79
Commercial Rd. NG6: Bulw........ 6H 19
Commodore Cl. NG8: Aspl.........5A 32
Commodore Gdns. NG8: Aspl......5A 32
Common, The NG15: Huck..........5C 6
Common La. NG15: Huck............ 5D 6
Common La. NG16: Want............6B 18
Common La. NG9: Bram.............5A 54
Commons Cl. NG16: Newth........5C 16
COMMON SIDE..........................4B 14
Compton Acres NG2: West Br 5F 57
Compton Acres Shop. Cen.........6G 57
Compton Rd. NG5: Sher............4F 33
Comyn Gdns. NG3: Nott... 1F 5 (3H 45)
Condor Rd. DE7: Ilk..................5B 40

Conduit Cl. NG2: Nott 1G 57
Coney Wlk. NG5: Top V 5D 20
Conifer Cres. NG11: Clftn 6C 66
Conifer Wlk. NG3: Nott 2C 46
Coningsby Gdns. E.
NG5: Woodt.................3B 34
Coningsby Rd. NG5: Woodt 2B 34
Coningswath Rd. NG4: Car 5E 35
Conisborough Ter. NG2: Nott 2G 57
Conisbrough Av. NG4: Ged 6B 36
Coniston Av. NG6: Bas....5A 32
Coniston Cl. NG2: Gam.......4E 59
Coniston Dr. DE7: Kirk H.......4H 39
Coniston Rd. NG10: Long E 3C 62
Coniston Rd. NG15: Huck....3F 7
Coniston Rd. NG9: Bram....2D 54
Connelly Cl. NG5: Arn 1E 35
Connelly Ct. NG6: Bulw 1A 32
Connery, The NG15: Huck.... 3H 7
Conrad Cl. NG6: Bulw.........2F 31
Constance St. NG7: Bas 6E 33
Convent, The NG1: Nott..... 3B 4 (4F 45)
...........(off College St.)
Convent St. NG1: Nott...... 3F 5 (4H 45)
Conway Av. NG4: Car 2A 48
Conway Cl. NG3: Nott........ 2G 45
Conway Cres. NG4: Car.......1A 48
Conway Gdns. NG5: Arn 1A 34
Conway Rd. NG15: Huck......2D 18
Conway Rd. NG4: Car 2H 47
Conway St. NG10: Long E.... 5G 63
Conway Wlk. NG3: Nott....... 2G 45
Cook Dr. DE7: Ilk...........3C 40
Cooke Cl. NG10: Long E........ 1D 72
Cookson Av. NG4: Ged.......5F 35
Coombe Cl. NG8: Woll........6A 44
Coombe Rd. NG6: Newth......1D 16
Co-operative Av. NG15: Huck.... 3H 7
Co-operative St. NG10: Long E... 6G 63
Cooper Cl. NG5: Arn..........1E 35
Cooper Cl. NG6: Bulw.........1F 31
Cooper Gdns. NG11: Rudd........6F 67
Coopers Grn. NG8: Woll.........1E 55
Cooper St. NG4: Neth 3A 48
Copeland Av. NG9: Stfrd 3G 53
Copeland Gro. NG13: Bing......4C 50
Copeland Rd. NG15: Huck......3A 8
Copenhagen Ct. NG3: Nott 6H 33
Copestake Cl. NG10: Long E 6C 62
Cope St. NG7: Hys G 3D 44
Coppice Av. DE7: Ilk 2H 27
Coppice Cl. NG15: Huck........6E 7
Coppice Ct. DE75: Hea.........6D 14
Coppice Dr. DE75: Hea.........6D 14
Coppice Dr. NG16: Eastw......2H 15
Coppice Ga. NG5: Arn..........5B 22
Coppice Gro. NG3: Mapp.......5B 34
Coppice Lodge NG5: Arn.......5C 22
Coppice M. DE75: Hea.........6D 14
Coppice Rd. NG5: Arn..........5B 22
Copplestone Dr. NG3: Mapp......1E 35
Copse, The DE7: Ilk 2H 27
Copse, The NG15: Huck.......5A 8
Copse, The NG9: Chil 5C 54
Copse Cl. NG14: Bur J........2F 37
Copseside Cl. NG10: Long E.... 6H 63
Copsey Cft. Ct. NG10: Long E.... 6H 63
Corben Gdns. NG6: Bulw........6F 19
Corbett Chase NG4: Ged 4G 35
Corbiere Av. NG16: Want........6A 18
Corby Rd. NG3: Nott 6A 34
Corfield Av. DE75: Hea 6D 14
Coriander Dr. NG6: Bas 4B 32
Corinthian Cl. NG15: Huck.....2A 8
Corinth Rd. NG11: Clftn......3C 66
Corke Ho. NG7: Lent..........5C 44
.............(off Faraday Rd.)
Corn Cl. NG12: Cotg........3E 71

Corncrake Av. NG6: Bas........4B 32
Corncrake Dr. NG5: Arn...........6E 23
Corn Cft. NG11: Clftn.........4D 66
Cornell Dr. NG5: Arn...........5D 22
Cornfield Rd. NG16: Kimb.....6G 17
Cornfields, The NG5: Bestw....5F 21
Cornhill Rd. NG4: Car 1D 46
Cornwall Av. NG9: Bee 1A 66
Cornwall Cl. NG16: Lang E.....5A 64
Cornwallis Cl. NG10: Long E.....1F 73
Cornwall Rd. NG5: Arn 6G 21
Cornwall's Hill NG4: Lamb......6D 24
Coronation Av. NG10: Sand.....4C 52
Coronation Av. NG11: Wilf......3F 57
Coronation Pk. Eastwood.......3C 16
Coronation Rd. DE7: Ilk.......5C 28
Coronation Rd. DE7: Mapp......4C 26
..................(not continuous)
Coronation Rd. DE7: Stly........3A 38
Coronation Rd. NG15: Huck......3F 7
Coronation Rd. NG16: Coss......5D 28
Coronation Rd. NG16: Nuth......2B 30
Coronation Rd. NG3: Mapp......4B 34
Coronation Rd. NG6: Bestw V....6C 8
Coronation St. DE7: Ilk........1B 40
Coronation Wlk. NG4: Ged......6A 36
Corporation Cotts. NG14: Bulc....2H 37
Corporation Oaks NG3: Nott......2G 45
Corporation Rd. DE7: Ilk........4C 40
Corsham Gdns. NG3: Nott......2C 46
Corve Dale Wlk. NG2: West Br....6B 58
Cosby Rd. NG2: Nott............6B 46
COSSALL......................6E 29
Cossall Ind. Est. DE7: Ilk......5D 28
COSSALL MARSH..............5E 29
Cossall Rd. NG16: Coss........2E 41
Cossall Rd. NG9: Trow..........2E 41
Costhorpe Dr. NG8: Stre........6C 30
Costock Av. NG5: Sher.........3F 33
Cotgrave Av. NG4: Ged.........5H 35
Cotgrave Cl. NG8: Stre.........5E 31
Cotgrave Country Pk. 5F 61
Cotgrave La. NG12: Toll........2G 69
Cotgrave Leisure Cen. 2F 71
Cotgrave Park & Ride 2F 71
Cotgrave Rd. NG12: C'ton......6H 69
Cotgrave Rd. NG12: Crop Bi....5H 71
Cotgrave Rd. NG12: Owt........5H 71
Cotgrave Rd. NG12: Plum.......6H 69
Cotgrave Shop. Cen. 2F 71
COTMANHAY..................3A 28
Cotmanhay Rd. DE7: Ilk........4A 28
Coton Cl. NG11: Wilf..........2E 67
Cotswold Cl. NG10: Long E......5D 62
Cotswold Ct. NG9: Bram.........2D 54
Cotswold Rd. NG8: Stre........6E 31
Cottage Cl. DE7: Ilk............4H 27
Cottage Gdn. La. DE75: Hea.....3B 14
Cottage Grn. NG2: West Br......2E 59
Cottage Mdw. NG4: Colw........5H 47
Cottage Ter. NG1: Nott..... 3A 4 (4E 45)
Cottage Wlk. NG8: Woll........4E 43
Cottam Dr. NG5: Top V.........5D 20
Cottam Gdns. NG5: Top V.......5E 21
Cottesmore Rd. NG7: Lent......5D 44
Cotton Ho. NG7: Radf..........3C 44
.............(off Radford Blvd.)
County Archives...........6D 4 (6G 45)
County Bus. Pk. NG2: Nott......1A 58
County Cl. NG9: Bee...........6G 55
County Court
Nottingham............6E 5 (6G 45)
County Rd. NG2: Nott...........1A 58
County Rd. NG4: Ged...........4E 35
County Rd. NG15: Huck.........5A 8
Court, The NG9: Toton..........3A 64
Court Cres. NG8: Woll..........5F 43
Courtenay Gdns. NG3: Nott.....2H 45

Court Gdns. NG2: West Br.......1F 67
Courtleet Way NG6: Bulw.......2H 31
Courtney Cl. NG8: Woll.........4E 43
Court St. NG7: Hys G 2D 44
Court Vw. NG7: Nott..... 4A 4 (5E 45)
Court Yd. NG9: Bram............3B 54
Courtyard, The NG16: Kimb......5G 17
Covedale Rd. NG5: Sher 2G 33
Coventry Cl. NG6: Bulw.........2H 31
Coventry La. NG9: Bram.........2H 53
Coventry Rd. NG6: Bulw
Gilead St. 6H 19
Coventry Rd. NG6: Bulw
Main St. 1H 31
Coventry Rd. NG9: Bee..........4G 55
Covers, The NG2: West Br......2B 58
Covert Cl. NG12: Key...........3H 79
Covert Cl. NG14: Bur J.........2E 37
Covert Cl. NG15: Huck..........5A 8
Covert Cres. NG12: Rad T......6H 49
Covert Rd. NG2: West Br........5D 58
Cowan St. NG1: Nott..... 3F 5 (4H 45)
Cowdrey Gdns. NG5: Arn........1D 34
Cowlairs NG5: Top V...........6C 20
Cow La. NG9: Bram..............3B 54
Cowley Cl. DE7: Ilk............2B 28
Cowley St. NG6: Bas...........4B 32
Cowper Rd. NG5: Newth.........5C 16
Cowper Rd. NG5: Woodt.........3A 34
Cowslip Cl. NG13: Bing.........5C 50
Coxmoor Cl. NG12: Edwal......1E 69
Coxmoor Ct. NG5: Top V........4E 21
Crabapple Dr. NG16: Lang M....1G 15
Crab Apple Gro. NG15: Huck....1A 20
Crabtree Fld. NG2: Colw........5F 47
Crabtree Rd. NG6: Bulw.........1G 31
Cragdale Rd. NG5: Sher 2G 33
Cragmoor Rd. NG14: Bur J......4E 37
Craig Moray NG12: Rad T........5G 49
Craig St. NG10: Long E.........6G 63
Crammond Cl. NG2: Nott........1F 57
Crampton Ct. NG5: Top V.......5E 21
Cramworth Gro. NG5: Sher 4H 33
Cranberry Cl. NG2: West Br.....5F 57
Cranborne Cl. NG9: Trow.......1F 53
Cranbourne Gro. NG15: Huck....4E 7
Cranbrook Ho. NG1: Nott..4G 5 (4H 45)
.............(off Cranbrook St.)
Cranbrook St. NG1: Nott.. 3F 5 (4H 45)
Cranfield Wlk. NG11: Clftn......5A 66
.............(off Southchurch Dr.)
Cranfleet Way NG10: Long E.....6C 62
Cranford Gdns. NG2: West Br....1G 67
Cranmer Gro. NG3: Nott........2G 45
Cranmer St. DE7: Ilk...........6B 28
Cranmer St. NG10: Long E......5F 63
Cranmer St. NG3: Nott.........2G 45
Cranmer Wlk. NG3: Nott........2G 45
Cranmore Cl. NG5: Arn.........3C 22
Cransley Av. NG8: Woll.........1D 54
Cranston Av. NG5: Arn.........4B 22
Cranston Rd. NG9: Bram........2C 54
Cranswick Cl. NG15: Huck......1B 8
Cranthorne Dr. NG3: Nott......3E 47
Crantock Gdns. NG12: Key......4H 79
Cranwell Ct. NG6: Bulw.........1F 31
Cranwell Rd. NG8: Stre........6D 30
Craster Dr. NG5: Arn..........3C 22
Craster Dr. NG6: Bulw..........5F 19
Craven Rd. NG7: Hys G.........2C 44
Crawford Av. NG9: Stfrd........3F 53
Crawford Cl. NG8: Woll.........4E 43
Crawford Ri. NG5: Arn..........5E 23
Crawford Wlk. NG11: Clftn......3D 66
Creamery Cl. NG8: Bilb.........2H 43
Creeton Grn. NG11: Clftn......5D 66
Cremorne Dr. NG2: Nott........2F 57
Crescent, The DE72: Ris........2A 62
Crescent, The NG12: Rad T......6G 49

Crescent, The NG16: Eastw.......2C 16
Crescent, The NG3: Nott.........1H 45
Crescent, The NG5: Woodt 3A 34
Crescent, The NG9: Chil 2C 66
Crescent, The NG9: Stfrd........2G 53
Crescent, The NG9: Toton........3A 64
Crescent Av. NG4: Car 6G 35
Cresswell Rd. NG9: Chil 6B 54
Cressy Rd. NG11: Clftn.........3D 66
Cresta Gdns. NG3: Mapp........5F 33
Crest Vw. NG5: Sher............4F 33
Crewe Cl. NG7: Radf............3D 44
Cribb Cl. NG11: Wilf............4F 57
Crich Vw. NG5: Sher............5G 33
Cricketers Ct. NG2: West Br....2B 58
Criftin Ent. Cen. NG14: Epp.....3D 12
Criftin Rd. NG14: Bur J.........3G 37
Cripps Hill NG7: Nott..........1A 56
Crispin Way NG8: Aspl..........2A 44
Critchley St. DE7: Ilk..........6B 28
Critch's Flats NG16: Kimb......1H 29
Crocus Gdns. NG12: Edwal......3C 68
Crocus St. NG2: Nott...........1G 57
Croft Av. NG15: Huck...........6G 7
Croft Cres. NG16: Aws..........2E 29
Crofton Cl. NG8: Bilb...........3H 43
Crofton Cl. NG9: Chil 3D 64
Crofton Rd. NG9: Chil 2D 64
Croft Rd. NG12: Edwal..........1C 68
Croft Rd. NG12: Key............4F 79
Croft Rd. NG5: Arn.............5B 22
Crofts, The NG13: Bing.........5E 51
Cromdale Cl. NG5: Arn.........4E 23
Cromer Rd. NG3: Nott..........2A 46
Cromford Av. NG4: Car 1F 47
Cromford Cl. NG10: Long E......2C 72
Cromford Cl. NG16: Lang M......1F 15
Cromford Rd. NG2: West Br.....5B 58
Cromford Rd. Ind. Est.
NG16: Lang M..................1F 15
Crompton Rd. DE7: Ilk..........1D 52
Crompton Rd. DE7: Stant D......1D 52
Crompton Rd. Ind. Est. DE7: Ilk...6C 40
Cromwell Av. DE7: Ilk...........4C 40
Cromwell Cres. NG4: Lamb......6B 24
Cromwell Rd. NG9: Bee.........4E 55
Cromwell St. NG16: Gilt........5D 16
Cromwell St. NG4: Car 2G 47
Cromwell Ter. NG7: Radf.. 2A 4 (4E 45)
Crookdale La. NG14: Calv.......4H 11
Cropston Cl. NG2: West Br......1A 68
Cropton Cres. NG8: Bilb........3H 43
Cropton Gro. NG13: Bing........5C 50
Cropwell Gdns. NG12: Rad T.....1G 61
Cropwell Grn. NG3: Nott........3B 46
Cropwell Rd. NG12: Rad T.......6F 49
Crosby Rd. NG2: West Br........2B 58
Cross, The NG12: Cotg..........2E 71
Crossdale Dr. NG12: Key........3G 79
Crossdale Wlk. NG5: Top V......5C 20
Crossfield Dr. NG5: Top V......5E 21
Crossfield Dr. NG5: Top V......5E 21
Crossgate Dr. NG2: Nott........3E 57
Crosshill NG12: Cotg...........2G 71
Crosshill Dr. DE7: Kirk H.......4F 39
Crossland Rd. NG5: Bestw......2E 33
Crosslands Mdw. NG4: Colw.....5H 47
Crossley St. NG5: Sher.........5F 33
Crossman St. NG5: Sher........5F 33
Cross St. NG10: Long E.........5G 63
Cross St. NG10: Sand...........5E 53
Cross St. NG16: Eastw..........3C 16
Cross St. NG4: Car.............1F 47
Cross St. NG4: Neth............2A 48
Cross St. NG5: Arn.............5H 21
Cross St. NG9: Bee.............4F 55
Crowborough Av. NG8: Woll.....1E 55
Crow Ct. NG13: Bing............5G 51

Crowcroft Way – DH Lawrence Craft Cen.

Crowcroft Way NG10: Long E...... 3D **62**
Crow Hill Rd. NG4: Car................ 2H **47**
Crowley Cl. NG8: Bilb...................3C **42**
Crown Cl. NG10: Long E..............6C **62**
Crown Court
Nottingham....................... 6E **5** (6G **45**)
Crown Hill Way DE7: Stan C.........1A **38**
Crown St. NG15: Huck..................1A **20**
Crown Way NG16: Lang M 1F **15**
Crow Pk. Dr. NG14: Bur J.............4E **37**
Crowthorne Cl. NG5: Top V 4C **20**
Crowthorne Gdns. NG5: Top V 4C **20**
Croxall Cl. NG11: Clftn..................1C **66**
Croxley Gdns. NG16: Nuth.......... 4D **30**
Croyde Gdns. NG2: Gam.............. 4D **58**
Croydon Rd. NG7: Radf.................4C **44**
Crummock Cl. NG9: Bram 3C **54**
Crusader Ct. NG11: Clftn 4A **66**
Crusader Ho. NG1: Nott..... 3E **5** (5G **45**)
Cudworth Dr. NG3: Mapp 5B **34**
Cuillin Cl. NG10: Long E 4C **62**
Cuillin Cl. NG5: Top V 3D **20**
Culbert Lodge NG7: Bas............. 6D **32**
Culbert Pl. NG7: Bas.................... 6D **32**
Cullens Ct. NG5: Sher.................. 5G **33**
Cultivation Rd. NG16: Eastw 4C **16**
Cumberland Av. NG9: Bee........... 5D **54**
Cumberland Cl. NG11: Rudd 6G **67**
Cumberland Pl.
NG1: Nott 4C **4** (5F **45**)
Cumbria Grange NG2: Gam..........4E **59**
Curie Ct. NG7: Nott 1C **56**
Curlew Cl. NG3: Nott......................4E **47**
Curlew Wharf NG7: Lent 1E **57**
Cursley Way NG9: Chil..................3C **64**
Curtis St. NG15: Huck.................... 5G **7**
Curzon Av. NG4: Car..................... 2D **46**
Curzon Ct. NG3: Nott 1G **5** (3H **45**)
Curzon Gdns. NG3: Nott 1G **5** (3H **45**)
Curzon Pl. NG3: Nott.......... 2F **5** (4H **45**)
Curzon St. NG10: Long E............. 3D **62**
Curzon St. NG11: Goth.................. 6H **75**
Curzon St. NG3: Nott 2F **5** (4H **45**)
Curzon St. NG4: Neth.....................2A **48**
Cuthrough La. NG7: Nott............. 3H **55**
Cutlers Ct. NG12: Rad T 6E **49**
Cuxton Cl. NG8: Stre...................... 6D **30**
Cycle Rd. NG7: Lent.......................5C **44**
CYGNET HOSPITAL 3B **66**
Cypress Ct. NG15: Huck.................6C **6**
Cyprus Av. NG9: Bee 4F **55**
Cyprus Ct. NG3: Mapp P............. 1G **45**
Cyprus Dr. NG9: Bee.......................4F **55**
Cyprus Rd. NG3: Mapp P............. 1G **45**
Cyril Av. NG8: Aspl.........................1B **44**
Cyril Av. NG9: Bee 4E **55**
Cyril Av. NG9: Stfrd.........................4F **53**
Cyril Cotts. NG8: Aspl.....................1B **44**
Cyril Rd. NG2: West Br....................3C **58**
Cyril's Nut Hut
Indoor Play Cen. 1G **73**

D

Dabell Av. NG6: Bulw......................5E **19**
Daffodil Gdns. NG12: Edwal 3C **68**
Dagmar Gro. NG3: Nott................. 6H **33**
Dagmar Gro. NG9: Bee 5G **55**
Dairy Sq. NG8: Bilb 2H **43**
Daisy Cl. NG12: Cotg 3E **71**
Daisy Farm Rd. NG16: Newth...... 4D **16**
Daisy Rd. NG3: Nott........................6C **34**
Dakeyne St. NG3: Nott....... 3H **5** (4A **46**)
Dakota Rd. NG13: Newt.................2B **50**
Dalbeattie Cl. NG5: Arn 5D **22**
Dalby Sq. NG8: Woll.......................6A **44**
Dale Av. NG10: Long E.....................4F **63**
Dale Av. NG3: Mapp..........................5C **34**
Dale Av. NG4: Car 2E **47**
Dalebrook Cres. NG15: Huck..........5C **6**
Dale Cl. DE72: Brea 5A **62**
Dale Cl. NG15: Huck 5C **6**
Dale Cl. NG2: West Br.................. 4D **58**
Dale Farm Av. NG3: Nott...............4C **46**
Dale Gro. NG2: Nott 5B **46**
Dalehead Rd. NG11: Clftn..............3B **66**
Dale La. DE7: D Ab 6D **38**
Dale La. NG9: Chil............................5E **55**
Dalemoor Gdns. NG8: Bilb........... 1H **43**
Dale Rd. DE7: Stly............................4A **38**
Dale Rd. NG12: Key 4G **79**
Dale Rd. NG16: Kimb 2H **29**
Dale Rd. NG4: Car.............................2E **47**
Dales, The DE7: West H.................2C **38**
Daleside NG12: Cotg.......................3E **71**
Daleside Rd. NG2: Nott...................6B **46**
Daleside Rd. E. NG2: Nott............ 5D **46**
Dale St. DE7: Ilk..............................2B **40**
Dale St. NG2: Nott...........................5A **46**
Dale Ter. NG2: Nott 5B **46**
Dale Vw. DE7: Ilk 3A **40**
Dale Vw. Rd. NG3: Nott.................. 2D **46**
Dalkeith Ter. NG7: Hys G 2D **44**
Dallaglio M. NG9: Chil 3B **64**
Dallas York Rd. NG9: Bee............ 5H **55**
Dalley Cl. NG9: Stfrd...................... 4G **53**
Dallimore Rd. DE7: Kirk H 5H **39**
Dallman Cl. NG15: Huck................. 6G **7**
Dalton Cl. NG9: Stfrd 6G **53**
Daltons Cl. NG16: Lang M 1E **15**
Damson Wlk. NG3: Nott................. 1D **46**
Danbury Mt. NG5: Sher 5H **33**
Dane Cl. NG3: Nott............ 1F **5** (3H **45**)
Dane Ct. NG3: Nott 1F **5** (3H **45**)
Danehurst Dr. NG4: Ged 6A **36**
Danes Cl. NG5: Arn 5H **21**
Danethorpe Va. NG5: Sher 3G **33**
Daniel M. NG10: Sand 6C **52**
Daniels Ct. NG16: Eastw................4B **16**
Daniels Way NG15: Huck...............1E **19**
Dann Pl. NG11: Wilf..........................3F **57**
Darfield Dr. DE75: Hea...................3E **15**
Darkey La. NG9: Stfrd..................... 6G **53**
.... (not continuous)
Dark La. NG13: Bing........................ 5G **51**
Dark La. NG14: Calv 5G **11**
Darley Av. NG4: Car......................... 6G **35**
Darley Av. NG7: Hys G 2C **44**
Darley Av. NG9: Toton...................... 2G **63**
Darley Dr. DE7: West H...................1C **38**
Darley Dr. NG10: Long E..................2C **72**
Darley Rd. NG7: Hys G.....................2C **44**
Darley Sq. DE7: Ilk...........................2A **28**
Darlison St. NG15: Huck................. 3G **7**
....*(off Ogle St.)*
Darlton Dr. NG5: Arn.......................6C **22**
Darnal Cl. NG5: Top V......................6C **20**
Darnhall Cres. NG8: Bilb 2D **42**
Daron Gdns. NG5: Bestw 6E **21**
Dart Ct. NG13: Bing 6D **50**
Dartmeet Ct. NG7: Radf...................2B **44**
Dartmoor Cl. NG11: Clftn................5B **66**
Darvel Cl. NG8: Bilb 3H **43**
Darwin Av. DE7: Ilk...........................2A **40**
Darwin Cl. NG5: Top V......................5C **20**
Darwin Rd. NG10: Long E.............. 2D **72**
David Gro. NG9: Bram 2D **54**
David La. NG6: Bas...........................4B **32**
David Lane Stop (NET)....................4B **32**
David Lloyd Leisure
Nottingham......................................2B **44**
David Lloyd Leisure
West Bridgford...............................5H **57**
Davidson Cl. NG5: Arn 6E **23**
Davidson Gdns. NG11: Rudd 6E **67**
Davidson St. NG2: Nott....................6B **46**
Davies Rd. NG2: West Br.................4B **58**
Davies Way NG5: Bestw 2E **33**
Davis Rd. NG9: Chil 2B **64**
Davy Cl. NG15: Lin............................ 1H **7**
Dawes Way NG7: Lent.....................4C **44**
Dawlish Cl. NG15: Huck 5D **6**
Dawlish Cl. NG3: Mapp 2E **35**
Dawlish Ct. NG16: Eastw............. 2H **15**
Dawlish Ct. NG3: Mapp 1F **35**
Dawlish Dr. NG5: Bestw 2F **33**
Dawn Cl. NG15: Huck........................2A **8**
Dawn Vw. NG9: Trow.........................1F **53**
Dawson Cl. NG16: Newth 4C **16**
Dawver Rd. NG16: Kimb................ 1H **29**
DAYBROOK 1A **34**
Daybrook Av. NG5: Sher............... 4G **33**
Daybrook Bus. Cen. NG5: Arn..... 1H **33**
DAYBROOK SQUARE.........................1A **34**
Daybrook St. NG5: Sher 4G **33**
Deabill Ct. NG4: Neth......................3A **48**
Deabill St. NG4: Neth......................3A **48**
Dead La. NG16: Coss.......................6F **29**
Deakins Pl. NG7: Radf 4C **44**
Deal Gdns. NG6: Bulw 6F **19**
Dean Av. NG3: Mapp...................... 4D **34**
Dean Cl. NG8: Woll 4D **42**
Deane Ct. NG11: Wilf 5E **57**
Deane Rd. NG11: Wilf 5E **57**
Dean Rd. NG5: Woodt 2A **34**
Deans Ct. NG12: Cotg..................... 2G **71**
Deans Cft. NG9: Bram 2B **54**
Dean St. NG1: Nott............5G **5** (5H **45**)
Dean St. NG16: Lang M 2G **15**
Debdale La. NG12: Key.....................4F **79**
De Buseli Cl. NG4: Ged....................6A **36**
Deddington La. NG9: Bram 1B **54**
Deeley Cl. NG16: Want......................5A **18**
Deepdale Av. NG9: Stfrd..................5F **53**
Deepdale Cl. NG2: Gam 4E **59**
Deepdale Ct. DE75: Hea 4C **14**
Deepdale Rd. NG10: Long E 1C **72**
Deepdale Rd. NG8: Woll 5D **42**
Deepdene Cl. NG8: Brox 5G **31**
Deepdene Way NG8: Brox 5G **31**
Deepdene Way NG8: Cin 5G **31**
Deep Furrow Av. NG4: Car 1F **47**
Deering Ct. NG2: Nott.......................1F **57**
Deerleap Dr. NG5: Arn 6G **21**
Deer Pk. NG8: Woll 5E **43**
Deer Pk. Dr. NG5: Arn 5F **21**
Defiant Cl. NG15: Huck.....................2E **19**
Delia Av. NG15: Huck.........................2A **8**
Dell Way NG11: Clftn 3D **66**
Dellwood Cl. NG4: Car.................... 5D **34**
Delta Ct. NG1: Nott 3G **45**
Delta St. NG7: Bas 6D **32**
Deltic Cl. NG16: Want 6A **18**
Delves Ct. DE75: Hea.......................5C **14**
Delves Rd. DE75: Hea.......................5B **14**
Delville Av. NG12: Key 3G **79**
Denacre Av. NG10: Long E............ 4H **63**
Denbury Ct. NG3: Mapp...................2F **35**
Denby Ct. NG4: Neth.........................2A **48**
Denby Hall Rd. DE7: Ilk 1A **28**
Denehurst Av. NG8: Aspl 6A **32**
Denewood Av. NG9: Bram 1C **54**
Denewood Cres. NG8: Bilb 1E **43**
Denholme Rd. NG8: Bilb............... 4D **42**
Denison Ct. NG7: Radf 3D **44**
Denison St. NG7: Radf 3D **44**
Denison St. NG9: Bee 4E **55**
Denman St. Central NG7: Radf.....4C **44**
Denman St. E. NG7: Radf................ 4D **44**
Denman St. W. NG7: Radf...............4C **44**
Denmark Gro. NG3: Nott................. 6H **33**
Dennett Cl. NG3: Nott 1H **5** (3A **46**)
Dennis Av. NG9: Bee..........................3E **55**
Dennis St. NG4: Neth.........................2A **48**
Denstone Rd. NG3: Nott 4A **46**
Dentdale Dr. NG8: Woll 5B **42**
Denton Av. NG10: Sand 5C **52**
Denton Dr. NG2: West Br 1H **67**
Denton Grn. NG8: Brox 5F **31**
Denver Ct. NG9: Stfrd 2G **53**
Denz Childrens Play Cen. 5H **55**
Depedale Av. DE7: Kirk H 4H **39**
Deptford Cres. NG6: Bulw 1A **32**
Derby Gro. NG7: Lent...................... 4D **44**
Derby Gro. NG7: Radf 4D **44**
Derby Rd. DE7: Ilk 2G **39**
Derby Rd. DE72: Ris 1A **62**
Derby Rd. DE75: Hea 4B **14**
....................................(not continuous)
Derby Rd. NG1: Nott.......... 3A **4** (4E **45**)
Derby Rd. NG10: Long E..................5C **62**
Derby Rd. NG10: Sand.....................6B **52**
Derby Rd. NG16: Eastw 3H **15**
Derby Rd. NG16: Lang M 2G **15**
Derby Rd. NG7: Lent..........................1B **56**
Derby Rd. NG7: Nott..........................1B **56**
Derby Rd. NG9: Bee...........................3A **54**
Derby Rd. NG9: Bram 3A **54**
Derby Rd. NG9: Lent...........................2F **55**
Derby Rd. NG9: Nott 2F **55**
Derby Rd. NG9: Nott 3A **54**
Derby Rd. NG9: Stfrd 6E **53**
Derby Rd. Ind. Est. DE75: Hea......4B **14**
Derby Rd. Ind. Est.
NG10: Sand..................................... 6D **52**
Derbyshire Av. DE7: West H 1C **38**
Derbyshire Av. NG9: Trow 5F **41**
Derbyshire Cl. DE7: West H...........1C **38**
Derbyshire Cres. NG8: Woll......... 4G **43**
Derbyshire Dr. DE7: Ilk 3A **40**
Derbyshire La. NG15: Huck 4G **7**
Derby St. DE7: Ilk 1B **40**
Derby St. NG1: Nott 3B **4** (4F **45**)
Derby St. NG5: Arn 6B **22**
Derby St. NG9: Bee...........................4F **55**
Derby Ter. NG7: Nott.......... 3A **4** (4E **45**)
Dereham Dr. NG5: Arn 1B **34**
Derry Dr. NG5: Arn............................3B **22**
Derry Hill Rd. NG5: Arn...................4A **22**
Derry La. NG13: Bing....................... 5H **51**
Derwent Av. DE7: Ilk........................ 5H **27**
Derwent Av. DE7: West H 1C **38**
Derwent Cl. NG2: Gam 4E **59**
Derwent Cl. NG9: Atten.....................2E **65**
Derwent Ct. NG7: Radf 3E **45**
Derwent Cres. NG5: Arn 1C **34**
Derwent Dr. NG15: Huck 1G **19**
Derwent St. NG10: Long E...............1E **73**
Derwent St. Ind. Est.
NG10: Long E.....................................1E **73**
Derwent Ter. NG5: Sher................. 5G **33**
Derwent Way NG7: Lent...................5B **44**
Desford Cl. NG5: Sher 3E **33**
De Vere Gdns. NG5: Woodt............2B **34**
Devitt Dr. NG15: Huck.........................2A **8**
Devon Cir. NG5: Redh 4H **21**
Devon Cl. NG10: Sand 6D **52**
Devon Cl. NG16: Newth 3D **16**
Devon Dr. NG11: Rudd 5H **67**
Devon Dr. NG5: Sher..........................5F **33**
Devonshire Av. NG10: Long E.......5A **64**
Devonshire Av. NG9: Bee 5F **55**
Devonshire Cl. DE7: Ilk.....................2A **28**
Devonshire Cres. NG5: Sher..........5F **33**
Devonshire Dr. NG16: Eastw 3B **16**
Devonshire Dr. NG9: Stfrd 1F **53**
Devonshire Prom. NG7: Lent........6C **44**
Devonshire Rd. NG2: West Br.......5A **58**
Devonshire Rd. NG5: Sher.............5F **33**
Devon St. DE7: Ilk..............................4C **40**
Devon St. NG3: Nott..........................4B **46**
Dewberry La. NG12: Rad T.......... 1H **61**
Dexters Gro. NG15: Huck.................4F **7**
DH Lawrence Birthplace Mus. 2B **16**
DH Lawrence Craft Cen..................2B **16**
.................................*(off Scargill Wlk.)*

A-Z Nottingham 97

DH Lawrence Pavilion 2B 56
DH Lawrence 'Sons & Lovers'
 Cottage...................................2C 16
Dial, The NG12: Cotg 4E 71
Diamond Cl. NG10: Long E 2C 72
Dickens Cl. NG16: Newth 2D 16
Dickinson St. NG3: Nott.............3A 46
Dicks La. NG16: Newth...............2E 17
Dickson Dr. NG11: Rudd..............1H 77
Didcot Dr. NG8: Bas.....................6B 32
Digby Av. NG3: Mapp..................4D 34
Digby Av. NG8: Woll....................5G 43
Digby Hall Dr. NG4: Ged 4E 35
Digby Ind. Est. NG16: Kimb 6F 17
Digby St. NG16: Kimb..................1F 29
Dirac Cl. NG11: Clftn...................5A 66
Discovery Dr. NG8: Aspl 2A 44
Diseworth Gro. NG2: Nott...........2H 57
Disraeli Cres. DE7: Ilk.................1B 40
Distillery St. NG11: Rudd.............1G 77
Dizzy Rascalz..............................5F 67
Djanogly Art Gallery 2B 56
Djanogly Community
 Leisure Cen...............................2E 45
DOBPARK 3F 7
Dob Pk. Cl. NG6: Bas..................3B 32
Dockholm Rd. NG10: Long E 3E 63
Dodford Ct. DE75: Hea 4E 15
Dogwood Av. NG6: Bulw..............6F 19
Dolphin Ct. NG5: Top V................5E 21
Donbas Cl. NG6: Bulw 3H 31
Doncaster Av. NG10: Sand 5D 52
Doncaster Gro. NG10: Long E.......4H 63
Doncaster Ter. NG2: Nott.............2G 57
Donington Rd. NG11: Clftn...........4C 66
Donkey La. NG11: Rudd...............4A 78
Donner Cres. DE7: Ilk..................2A 28
Dooland Dr. NG3: Nott.................6B 34
Dorchester Gdns.
 NG2: West Br...........................2A 68
Dorchester Rd. NG16: Kimb 6H 17
Doris Ct. NG9: Toton...................3A 64
Doris Rd. DE7: Ilk........................2C 40
Dorket Cl. NG5: Arn....................4C 22
Dorket Dr. NG8: Woll...................6B 44
DORKET HEAD 2C 22
Dorket Ho. NG4: Car...................1G 47
...................................(off Garden City)
Dorking Rd. NG7: Radf................3C 44
Dormy Cl. NG12: Rad T...............6H 49
Dormy Cl. NG9: Bram..................4C 54
Dormy Ct. NG6: Bulw..................6B 20
Dornoch Av. NG5: Sher................5H 33
Dorothy Av. NG10: Sand 6D 52
Dorothy Av. NG15: Huck..............2H 7
Dorothy Av. NG16: Newth............2C 16
Dorothy Boot Homes, The
 NG11: Wilf...............................3F 57
Dorothy Gro. NG8: Aspl 3A 44
Dorset Gdns. NG2: West Br 6G 57
Dorset St. NG8: Radf...................4B 44
Dorterry Cres. DE7: Ilk...............4C 40
Douglas Av. DE75: Hea...............3A 14
Douglas Av. DE75: Los................3A 14
Douglas Av. NG16: Aws..............2E 29
Douglas Av. NG4: Car.................3F 47
Douglas Cl. NG12: Rad T.............1F 61
Douglas Ct. NG9: Toton..............3A 64
Douglas Cres. NG4: Car..............3G 47
Douglas Rd. NG10: Long E 3D 62
Douglas Rd. NG13: Bing..............5H 51
Douglas Rd. NG7: Lent................4D 44
Douglas Rd. NG7: Radf................4D 44
Douro Dr. NG5: Arn....................4D 22
Dove Cl. NG3: Bing....................6F 51
Dovecote Dr. NG8: Woll...............5E 43
Dovecote La. NG9: Bee................5F 55
Dovecote Rd. NG16: Eastw..........3D 16

Dovecote Rd. NG16: Newth..........3D 16
Dovecotes, The NG9: Bee.............6F 55
Dovedale Av. NG10: Long E..........1D 72
Dovedale Circ. DE7: Ilk...............2A 28
Dovedale Ct. NG10: Long E 1D 72
Dovedale Rd. NG2: West Br..........6C 58
Dovedale Rd. NG3: Nott...............3E 47
Dove La. NG10: Long E................5E 63
Dovenby Rd. NG11: Clftn.............2D 66
Dover Beck Cl. NG14: Calv...........4A 12
Doverbeck Dr. NG14: Woodbo 1C 24
Doveridge Av. NG4: Car...............1A 48
Doveridge Rd. NG4: Car...............1H 47
Dove St. NG6: Bulw 6H 19
Doveys Orchard NG14: Calv..........4F 11
Downes Cl. NG6: Bulw.................6G 19
Downing Gdns. NG6: Bulw 5H 19
Downing St. NG6: Bulw................5H 19
Downs, The NG11: Wilf................1E 67
Dowson Cl. NG12: Rad T 5H 49
Dowson St. NG3: Nott.................3B 46
Doyne Ct. NG2: Nott...................2G 57
Drakemyre Cl. NG5: Arn..............4D 22
Drake Rd. NG4: Neth...................3B 48
Draycott Cl. DE75: Los................1A 14
Draycott Cl. DE7: Ilk...................4B 28
Draycott Rd. NG10: Long E...........2B 72
Draymans Cl. NG7: Bas...............6D 32
Drayton St. NG5: Sher.................5G 33
DREWRY ISLAND........................6F 31
Drift, The NG1: Clftn....................2C 66
Drift, The NG15: Huck..................2H 7
Drive, The NG9: Atten..................2E 65
Dronfield Pl. DE7: Ilk...................2A 28
Drummond Av. NG4: Neth 2B 48
Drummond Dr. NG16: Nuth...........3E 31
Drummond Dr. DE7: Ilk................6A 28
Drury Cl. NG15: Huck 6D 6
Drury Wlk. NG1: Nott.......... 5E 5 (5G 45)
Dryden Ct. NG9: Stfrd..................2G 53
Dryden St. NG1: Nott......... 1C 4 (3F 45)
Drysdale Rd. NG6: Bulw 2H 31
Duchess Gdns. NG6: Bulw 5H 19
Duchess St. NG6: Bulw................5H 19
Duckworth Cl. NG4: Ged 4G 35
Dudley Ct. NG9: Bram.................3A 54
Duffield Cl. NG10: Long E............2C 72
Duffield Cres. NG5: Top V.............5D 20
Duke Cl. NG6: Bulw 2F 31
Duke Cres. NG16: Gilt.................4E 17
Dukes Ct. NG15: Huck.................4H 7
Dukes Pl. DE7: Ilk......................3A 28
Dukes Rd. NG1: Nott.......... 4G 5 (5H 45)
Duke St. DE7: Ilk.......................4B 28
Duke St. NG5: Arn......................6H 21
Duke St. NG6: Bulw 6H 19
Duke St. NG7: Bas 1D 44
Duke St. E. NG15: Huck...............4H 7
Dukes Wharf NG7: Nott...... 6C 4 (6F 45)
Duke William Mt.
 NG7: Nott...................... 5A 4 (5E 45)
Dulverton Va. NG5: Arn...............4G 31
Dulwich Rd. NG7: Radf................4C 44
Dumbles, The NG4: Lamb............5B 24
Dumbles Cl. DE7: Kirk H..............3G 39
Dunbar Cl. NG10: Long E.............3G 73
Dunblane Rd. NG11: Rudd............1G 77
Duncombe Cl. NG3: Nott..............2A 46
Duncroft Av. NG4: Ged................6H 35
Dundas Cl. NG1: Nott.......... 1D 4 (3G 45)
Dunelm Dr. NG14: Calv...............4A 12
Dungannon Rd. NG11: Clftn..........5C 66
Dunholme Cl. NG6: Bulw 5H 19
Dunkery Rd. NG11: Clftn.............5D 66
DUNKIRK 1C 56
Dunkirk Rd. NG7: Lent.................2C 56
...................................(not continuous)

Dunlin Wharf NG7: Lent 1E 57
Dunlop Av. NG7: Lent 5C 44
Dunn Dr. NG10: Long E................6D 62
Dunoon Cl. NG5: Top V................3C 20
Dunsby Cl. NG11: Clftn................4C 66
Dunsford Dr. NG3: Mapp..............1F 35
Dunsil Dr. NG2: Nott...................3E 57
Dunsil Rd. NG16: Newth...............1D 16
Dunsmore Cl. NG9: Bee................1H 65
Dunstan St. NG4: Neth................2A 48
...................................(not continuous)
Dunster Rd. NG16: Newth 3D 16
Dunster Rd. NG2: West Br 5C 58
Dunston Cl. NG10: Long E............6H 63
Dunvegan Dr. NG5: Top V.............3D 20
Durham Av. NG2: Nott.................5B 46
Durham Chambers
 NG1: Nott.........................4E 5 (4G 45)
...................................(off Pelham St.)
Durham Cl. NG2: Nott..................5B 46
Durham Cres. NG6: Bulw 1A 32
Durham Ho. NG3: Mapp P 1G 45
Durham St. DE7: Ilk.....................6B 28
Durlston Cl. NG2: West Br 6F 57
Durnford St. NG7: Bas.................5D 32
Dursley Cl. NG6: Bulw 2H 31
Dusk till Dawn Casino..................3C 56
DW Fitness Nottingham.................3B 48
Dyce Cl. NG6: Bulw 6F 19
Dylan M. NG8: Bilb 1E 43
Dylan Thomas Rd. NG5: Bestw 5F 21

E

Eagle Cl. NG5: Arn......................6C 22
Eagle Cl. NG9: Bee.....................3D 54
Eagle Ct. NG6: Bulw....................6B 20
Eagle Rd. DE7: Ilk.......................5B 40
Ealing Av. NG6: Bas....................3B 32
Eames Cl. DE75: Hea...................4B 14
Eardley Rd. NG5: Bestw...............1C 32
Earl Cres. NG4: Ged....................4H 35
Earl Dr. NG16: Gilt......................4E 17
Earlham Cl. DE7: Kirk H...............3G 39
Earls Cl. NG8: Bilb 4C 42
Earlsfield Dr. NG5: Top V.............4B 20
Earlswood Dr. NG12: Edwal..........1D 68
Easedale Cl. NG2: Gam................4E 59
Easegill Ct. NG5: Top V................5D 20
...................................(off Aveline Cl.)
East Acres NG12: Cotg.................2F 71
East Bridgeford Rd.
 NG13: Newt..............................1B 50
East Circus St.
 NG1: Nott.........................4C 4 (5F 45)
Eastcliffe Av. NG4: Ged...............4F 35
Eastcote Av. NG12: Key...............5G 79
Eastcote Av. NG9: Bram...............1B 54
East Cres. NG9: Bee....................6H 55
Eastdale Rd. NG3: Nott................3E 47
East Dr. NG7: Nott......................2A 56
Easter Pk. NG7: Lent...................1D 56
Eastglade Rd. NG5: Bestw............1D 32
East Gro. NG13: Bing..................5F 51
East Gro. NG7: Bas.....................1E 45
Eastham Cl. NG3: Nott......... 2H 5 (3A 46)
Eastham Rd. NG5: Arn.................1D 34
Eastholme Cft. NG2: Colw............4F 47
Easthorpe Cotts. NG11: Rudd...... 6H 67
Easthorpe St. NG11: Rudd...........6G 67
East Midlands
 Conference Cen. 2H 55
East Moor NG12: Cotg.................4G 71
Eastmoor Dr. NG4: Car................1H 47
East Nelson St. DE75: Hea...........3C 14
East Rd. NG7: Nott......................1B 56
East St. DE7: Ilk........................1B 40
East St. DE75: Hea......................5E 15
East St. NG1: Nott............... 3F 5 (4H 45)

East St. NG10: Long E..................5H 63
East St. NG11: Goth.....................6H 75
East St. NG13: Bing....................5F 51
East Vw. NG2: West Br 5H 57
Eastview Ter. NG16: Lang M.........2F 15
Eastwell Cl. NG15: Huck..............3G 7
...................................(off Annesley Rd.)
Eastwell St. NG15: Huck..............3G 7
Eastwold NG12: Cotg...................3G 71
EASTWOOD...............................3B 16
Eastwood Cl. NG15: Huck.............1E 19
Eastwood Rd. NG12: Rad T 6G 49
Eastwood Rd. NG16: Kimb 6F 17
Eastwood St. NG6: Bulw...............2A 32
Eastwood Town FC......................3C 16
Eaton Av. DE7: Kirk H.................3H 39
Eaton Av. NG5: Arn....................6C 22
Eaton Gro. NG9: Bee...................5H 55
Eaton Grange Dr.
 NG10: Long E...........................5C 62
Eaton Pl. NG13: Bing..................5E 51
Eatons Rd. NG9: Stfrd.................5F 53
Eaton St. NG3: Mapp..................4B 34
Eaton Ter. NG3: Mapp.................4B 34
Ebenezer St. NG16: Lang M..........2F 15
Ebers Gro. NG3: Mapp P 1G 45
Ebers Rd. NG3: Mapp P 6G 33
Ebony Wlk. NG3: Nott.................1D 46
Ebury Rd. NG5: Sher...................6F 33
Eccles Way NG3: Nott.................2B 46
Eckington Cl. DE7: West H 1C 38
Eckington Ter. NG2: Nott.............2G 57
Ecton Cl. NG5: Top V..................4D 20
Ecton M. NG5: Top V...................5D 20
...................................(off Ecton Close)
Edale Cl. NG10: Long E................1D 72
Edale Cl. NG15: Huck...................5C 6
Edale Ri. NG9: Toton...................2G 63
Edale Rd. NG2: Nott....................4C 46
Edale Sq. DE7: Ilk.......................2A 28
Eddleston Dr. NG11: Clftn............4D 66
Edenbridge Ct. NG8: Woll............1D 54
Eden Cl. NG15: Huck....................5C 6
Eden Cl. NG5: Arn......................1C 34
Edenhall Gdns. NG11: Clftn..........3D 66
Eden Wlk. NG13: Bing.................6D 50
Edern Cl. NG5: Bestw..................6E 21
Edern Gdns. NG5: Bestw..............6E 21
Edgbaston Gdns. NG8: Aspl..........1B 44
Edgcote Way NG5: Bestw..............1E 33
Edge Hill Ct. NG10: Long E 3F 73
Edgeway NG8: Stre.....................6D 30
Edgewood Dr. NG15: Huck............6D 6
Edgewood Leisure Cen..................1D 18
Edgington Cl. NG12: Cotg.............3G 71
Edginton St. NG3: Nott................2B 46
Edginton Ter. NG3: Nott...............2B 46
Edgware Rd. NG6: Bulw...............1H 31
Edgwood Rd. NG16: Kimb............1H 29
Edinbane Cl. NG5: Top V..............3D 20
Edinboro Row NG16: Kimb...........6G 17
Edinburgh Dr. NG13: Bing............4D 50
Edinburgh Row NG8: Bram...........5B 42
Edingale Ct. NG9: Bram...............1B 54
Edingley Av. NG5: Sher................3G 33
Edingley Sq. NG5: Sher................3F 33
Edison Village NG7: Nott..............2C 56
Edison Way NG5: Arn..................6E 23
Edith Ter. NG7: Radf...................3C 44
...................................(off Hartley Rd.)
Edlington Dr. NG8: Woll...............6C 42
Edmond Gro. NG15: Huck.............3A 8
Edmonds Cl. NG5: Arn.................3E 21
Edmonstone Cres. NG5: Bestw 2D 32
Edmonton Ct. NG2: West Br 5H 57
Ednaston Rd. NG7: Nott...............2D 56
Edwald Rd. NG12: Edwal..............2D 68
EDWALTON 2D 68
Edwalton Av. NG2: West Br 4B 58

Edwalton Cl. NG12: Edwal........... 2D 68
Edwalton Ct. NG6: Bulw 1C 32
Edwalton Golf Course 2E 69
Edwalton Hall NG12: Edwal........2C 68
Edwalton Lodge Cl.
NG12: Edwal 2C 68
Edward Av. NG8: Aspl................1B 44
Edward Cl. NG15: Huck............ 1D 18
Edward Ct. NG2: West Br.........2B 58
Edward Rd. NG10: Long E 5F 63
Edward Rd. NG16: Eastw 3C 16
Edward Rd. NG5: Nuth 2C 30
Edward Rd. NG2: West Br...........2B 58
Edwards Ct. NG5: Sher................2F 33
Edwards La. NG5: Bestw 1F 33
Edwards La. NG5: Sher 1F 33
Edward St. NG16: Lang M 1F 15
Edward St. NG9: Stfrd 4F 53
Edwinstowe Av. NG2: West Br.....4B 58
Edwinstowe Dr. NG5: Sher 3G 33
Edwin St. NG5: Arn 1H 33
Eelwood Rd. NG15: Huck........... 1D 18
Egerton Dr. NG9: Stfrd 1F 53
Egerton Rd. NG5: Woodt............3H 33
Egerton St. NG3: Nott 2G 45
Egerton Wlk. NG3: Nott 2G 45
Egling Cft. NG4: Colw 5H 47
Egmont Ct. NG2: Nott 1G 57
Egreaves Av. DE75: Los.............1A 14
Egypt Rd. NG7: Bas 6D 32
.... (not continuous)
Eighth Av. NG7: Nott...................6A 56
Eileen Rd. NG9: Bee 2G 65
Eisele Cl. NG6: Bulw 1F 31
Ekowe St. NG7: Bas 5D 32
Eland St. NG7: Bas 6D 32
Elder Cl. NG5: Arn 4C 22
Elder Gdns. NG5: Top V 5E 21
Elder Gro. NG15: Huck...............1H 19
Elder Rd. NG14: Stoke B.............2C 48
Eldon Bus. Pk. NG9: Atten.........4C 64
Eldon Chambers
NG1: Nott 5D 4 (5G 45)
Eldon Rd. NG8: Aspl 4C 44
Eldon Rd. Ind. Est. NG9: Atten.....4C 64
Eldon Rd. Trad. Est. NG9: Chil.....4C 64
Eleanor Av. DE7: Ilk....................4C 40
Eleanor Cres. NG9: Stfrd 4H 53
Electric Av. NG2: Nott.................4E 57
Eley Cl. DE7: Ilk 5G 27
Elford Ri. NG3: Nott 5B 46
Elizabeth Cl. DE7: West H..........1B 38
Elizabeth Cl. DE7: Ilk..................6H 27
Elizabeth Gro. NG4: Ged 5G 35
Elizabeth Ho. NG5: Woodt..........2H 33
Elka Rd. DE7: Ilk.........................5B 40
Ella Bank Rd. DE75: Hea.............4E 15
Ella Rd. NG2: West Br 2B 58
Ellastone Av. NG5: Bestw 5G 21
Ellerby Av. NG11: Clftn 3C 66
Ellerslie Gro. NG10: Sand...........6C 52
Ellesmere Bus. Pk. NG5: Sher 5E 33
Ellesmere Cl. NG5: Arn 6D 22
Ellesmere Ct. DE7: Ilk................6H 27
Ellesmere Cres. NG5: Sher 5F 33
Ellesmere Dr. NG9: Trow 4E 41
Ellesmere Rd. NG2: West Br 1B 58
Ellington Rd. NG5: Arn................3B 22
Elliot St. NG7: Nott........3A 4 (4E 45)
Ellis Av. NG15: Huck...................5H 7
Ellis Cl. NG10: Long E 1E 73
Ellis Ct. NG3: Nott 3H 45
Ellis Gro. NG9: Bee 6F 55

Ellsworth Ri. NG5: Bestw 1D 32
Ellwood Cres. NG8: Woll..............4G 43
Elm Av. NG10: Long E 4E 63
Elm Av. NG10: Sand...................4D 52
Elm Av. NG12: Key 5H 79
Elm Av. NG13: Bing....................5G 51
Elm Av. NG15: Huck....................6E 7
Elm Av. NG16: Nuth 1B 30
Elm Av. NG3: Nott 2G 45
Elm Av. NG4: Car 2H 47
Elm Av. NG9: Atten....................3D 64
Elm Av. NG9: Bee 5E 55
Elm Bank NG3: Mapp P 1G 45
Elm Bank Dr. NG3: Mapp P..........1G 45
Elmbridge NG5: Bestw.................6F 21
Elm Cl. NG12: Key......................5H 79
Elm Cl. NG3: Mapp P..................2G 45
Elmdale Gdns. NG8: Bilb 1H 43
Elm Dr. NG4: Car 2H 47
Elm Gro. NG5: Arn 4C 22
Elmhurst Av. NG3: Mapp 5E 35
Elmore Ct. NG7: Radf..................3E 45
Elms, The NG16: Want................6H 17
Elms, The NG4: Colw 3H 47
Elms Cl. NG11: Rudd 1H 77
Elmsdale Gdns. NG14: Bur J 3F 37
Elmsfield Av. DE75: Hea..............3E 15
Elms Gdns. NG11: Rudd 1G 77
Elmsham Av. NG5: Top V............4C 20
Elms Pk. NG11: Rudd 1H 77
Elmsthorpe Av. NG7: Lent 5C 44
Elmswood Gdns. NG5: Sher 4H 33
Elm Tree Av. NG2: West Br 4H 57
Elmtree Rd. NG14: Calv...............4F 11
Elm Vw. NG7: Radf......................3D 44
Elnor St. NG16: Lang M 3G 15
Elson St. NG7: Bas......................1D 44
Elston Gdns. NG11: Clftn 1C 66
Elston M. NG3: Nott....................2D 46
Elstree Dr. NG8: Bilb 3G 43
Elswick Cl. NG5: Bestw 5F 21
Elswick Dr. NG9: Bee..................1H 65
Elterwater Dr. NG2: Gam.............4E 59
Eltham Cl. NG8: Cin....................4F 31
Eltham Dr. NG8: Cin...................4F 31
Eltham Rd. NG2: West Br............4B 58
Elton Cl. NG9: Stfrd....................3G 53
Elton M. NG5: Sher 6F 33
Elton Rd. Nth. NG5: Sher 6F 33
Elton Ter. NG7: Hys G................2D 44
Elvaston Ct. NG5: Bestw.............2D 32
Elvaston Dr. NG10: Long E...........3B 72
Elvaston Rd. NG8: Woll...............4G 43
Elveden Dr. DE7: Ilk 3G 27
Elwes Lodge NG4: Car................3H 47
Elwin Dr. NG9: Bram...................2C 54
Embley Rd. NG5: Sher 2E 33
Emerys Rd. NG4: Ged.................1B 48
Emery Rd. NG4: Neth..................1B 48
Emmanuel Av. NG3: Mapp...........6C 34
Emmanuel Av. NG5: Arn 4E 21
Emneth Cl. NG3: Nott.................1B 46
Emperor Cl. NG5: Sher 6F 33
Emperors Way NG15: Huck..........3A 8
Empingham Cl. NG9: Toton 3B 64
Empire Ct. DE75: Hea.................3C 14
.... (off Fletcher St.)
Emsworth Cl. DE7: Ilk.................4H 27
Ena Av. NG2: Nott 3B 46
Enderby Gdns. NG5: Redh...........4A 22
Enderby Sq. NG9: Lent A 3F 55
Endsleigh Gdns. NG12: Edwal......1C 68
Endsleigh Gdns. NG9: Bee 4F 55
Enfield Chambers
NG1: Nott 5E 5 (5G 45)
Enfield St. NG9: Bee...................5E 55
Engine La. NG16: Newth...............1D 16
England Cres. DE75: Hea.............3E 15
Ennerdale Cl. NG2: Gam..............4E 59

Ennerdale Ct. NG10: Long E.........3D 62
Ennerdale Rd. NG10: Long E........3D 62
Ennerdale Rd. NG5: Sher.............3H 33
Ennismore Gdns. NG8: Aspl.........3A 44
Ennismore M. NG2: West Br.........2G 67
Enterprise Ct. DE7: Ilk................6H 27
Enterprise Way NG16: Lang M 2G 15
Enterprise Way NG2: Nott 1E 57
Enthorpe St. NG8: Bilb................3H 43
EPPERSTONE.................................5G 13
Epperstone By-Pass
NG14: Woodbo 5E 13
Epperstone Ct. NG2: West Br.......3A 58
Epperstone Mnr. NG14: Epp 5F 13
Epperstone Rd. NG2: West Br......3A 58
Epperstone Rd. NG25: Oxton.......1B 12
Epsom Rd. NG9: Toton.............. 2G 63
Erdington Way NG9: Toton 2G 63
Erewash Ct. DE7: Ilk...................6H 27
Erewash Ct. NG10: Long E 4F 63
Erewash Dr. DE7: Ilk...................3C 40
Erewash Gdns. NG5: Top V..........5E 21
Erewash Gro. NG9: Toton 3H 63
.... (not continuous)
Erewash Indoor Bowling Club.......5A 64
Erewash Mus...............................1B 40
Erewash Sq. DE7: Ilk 3D 40
Erewash Valley Golf Course 2D 52
Eric Av. NG15: Huck.....................2F 7
Erith Cl. NG8: Stre 6D 30
Ernest Rd. NG4: Car 1D 46
Erskine Rd. NG5: Sher................6F 33
Escape Family
Entertainment Cen........................6E 17
Esher Gro. NG3: Mapp P 6G 33
Eskdale Cl. NG10: Long E............2D 72
Eskdale Ct. NG2: Gam.................4E 59
Eskdale Dr. NG8: Aspl.................1H 43
Eskdale Dr. NG9: Chil..................6A 54
Eskdale Drive Stop (NET) 6B 54
Esk Hause Cl. NG2: West Br 1E 69
Essex St. DE7: Ilk.......................6B 28
Essex St. NG16: Eastw................3B 16
Estwic Av. NG16: Eastw..............2B 16
Ethel Av. NG15: Huck................... 2H 7
Ethel Av. NG3: Mapp..................6C 34
Ethel Rd. NG2: West Br...............4B 58
Eton Cl. NG8: Aspl......................2B 44
Eton Ct. DE7: West H..................1B 38
Eton Gro. NG8: Woll 5H 43
Eton Pl. NG2: West Br.................6A 58
Eton Rd. NG2: West Br................5A 58
Eton Rd. NG5: Sher.....................6F 33
.... (off Claremont Rd.)
Eucalyptus Av. NG11: Clftn..........4A 66
Eugene Gdns. NG2: Nott.............1H 57
Eugene St. NG2: Nott..................6H 45
Europa Way NG2: West Br 2G 67
Evans Rd. NG6: Bas....................4B 32
Evedon Wlk. NG5: Top V.............4F 21
Evelyn St. NG2: Nott 5H 5 (5A 46)
Evelyn St. NG9: Bee....................4H 55
Eversley Wlk. NG5: Bestw...........5F 21
Evesham Ct. NG9: Toton..............4A 64
Ewart Rd. NG7: Hys G.................1D 44
Ewe Lamb Cl. NG9: Bram............2H 53
Ewe Lamb La. NG9: Bram............2H 53
Ewell Rd. NG8: Woll 4E 43
Exbourne Rd. NG8: Aspl..............6F 31
Exbury Gdns. NG2: West Br..........1F 67
Exchange Arc.
NG1: Nott 4E 5 (5G 45)
.... (off High St.)
Exchange Rd. NG2: West Br 4B 58
Exchange Wlk.
NG1: Nott 4E 5 (5G 45)
.... (off Pelham St.)

Exeter Cl. NG4: Ged....................5H 35
Exeter Rd. NG2: West Br..............5B 58
Exeter Rd. NG7: Hys G................1E 45
Experian Way NG2: Nott..............1E 57
Exton Rd. NG5: Sher....................4E 33
Eyam Cl. NG9: Bram....................1C 54
Eyre's Gdns. DE7: Ilk...................5B 28
Eyre St. NG2: Nott.............4H 5 (5A 46)

F

Fabis Dr. NG11: Clftn...................1C 66
Factory La. DE7: Ilk.....................5A 28
Factory La. NG9: Chil...................6E 55
Failsworth Cl. NG11: Clftn............2C 66
Fairbank Cres. NG5: Sher............5H 33
Fairburn Cl. NG8: Woll.................5C 42
Fairburn Cres. NG12: Edwal.........2C 68
Fairburn Way NG16: Want............6A 18
Faircroft Av. NG10: Sand.............6D 52
Fairdale Dr. NG16: Newth............3D 16
Fairfax Cl. NG5: Bas....................5D 32
Fairfield Cl. NG11: Wilf.................6F 57
Fairfield Cres. NG10: Long E.........3C 72
Fairfield St. NG13: Bing...............5E 51
Fairham Av. NG11: Goth..............6H 75
Fairham Brook Nature
Reserve 5D 66
Fairham Cl. NG11: Rudd..............5F 67
Fairham Cl. NG11: Wilf.................2E 67
Fairham Dr. NG8: Woll.................5B 44
Fairham Rd. NG12: Key...............4F 79
Fairholm Cl. NG3: Nott...... 1H 5 (3A 46)
Fairisle Cl. NG11: Clftn................4E 67
Fairland Cres. NG2: West Br........1H 67
Fairlawn Pl. NG5: Sher................5H 33
Fair Lea Cl. NG10: Long E............1F 73
Fairlight Way NG5: Bestw............6F 21
Fairmaid Gro. NG11: Clftn............3C 66
Fairmead Cl. NG3: Nott...............1C 46
Fairnley Rd. NG8: Bilb................1D 42
Fairview Ct. NG2: West Br...........3H 67
Fairview Rd. NG5: Woodt.............3A 34
Fairway NG12: Key......................4H 79
Fairway, The NG4: Ged................4G 35
Fairway Cres. NG13: Newt............1B 50
Fairway Dr. NG4: Car..................1E 47
Fairway Dr. NG6: Bulw................6B 20
Fairway Dr. NG9: Chil..................5D 54
Falcon Cl. NG7: Lent...................5C 44
Falcon Ct. DE7: Ilk......................6H 27
Falconers Wlk. NG5: Arn.............5G 21
Falcon Gro. NG7: Bas..................6E 33
Falcon St. NG7: Bas....................6E 33
Falcon Way NG15: Huck...............2B 8
Falconwood Gdns. NG11: Clftn 4A 66
Fallow Cl. NG11: Clftn..................3C 66
Fall Rd. DE75: Hea......................2C 14
Falstaff M. NG7: Bas...................6E 33
Falston Rd. NG8: Bilb..................3G 43
Faraday Bldg. NG7: Nott..............2B 56
Faraday Ct. NG9: Stfrd................2G 53
Faraday Rd. NG7: Lent................4C 44
Far Dales Rd. DE7: Ilk.................5A 28
Farfield Av. NG9: Bee..................3E 55
Farfield Gro. NG9: Bee................3E 55
Farfield Rd. DE7: Ilk....................6C 28
FARLEYS......................................2H 19
Farleys Gro. NG15: Huck...............6G 7
Farleys La. NG15: Huck.................5G 7
.... (not continuous)
Farley St. NG6: Bulw...................6H 19
Farm Av. NG15: Huck..................1D 18
Farm Cl. DE7: Ilk........................1C 40
Farm Cl. NG10: Long E................2G 73
Farm Cl. NG11: Clftn...................3C 66
Farmer St. NG11: Rudd................4A 78
Farm Rd. NG5: Arn 6D 22
Farm Rd. NG9: Chil.....................6C 54

Farnborough Rd. NG11: Clftn 1D **66**
Farndale Cl. NG10: Long E 2C **72**
Farndale Dr. NG8: Woll 5B **42**
Farndon Dr. NG9: Toton 2H **63**
Farndon Grn. NG8: Woll.............5A **44**
Farndon M. NG3: Nott................1C **46**
Far New Cl. NG10: Sand............. 6D **52**
Farnham Wlk. DE7: West H 1B **38**
Farnsfield Av. NG14: Bur J 2G **37**
Farnsworth Cl. NG16: Want.......4A **18**
Far Pastures Cl. NG12: Key 5G **79**
Farriers Cft. DE7: Ilk................. 4G **27**
Farriers Grn. NG11: Clftn 3A **66**
Farringdon Cl. NG16: Nuth 4D **30**
Farrington Way NG16: Eastw 3A **16**
Farr Row NG5: Bestw 2E **33**
Far Rye NG8: Woll......................3F **43**
Far St. NG11: Rudd 4A **78**
Farthing Ct. NG10: Long E 6D **62**
Farthings, The NG7: Lent...........5C **44**
Farwells Cl. NG6: Bas................4A **32**
Faulconbridge Cl. NG6: Bulw ... 1H **31**
Fearn Chase NG4: Car 2G **47**
Fearn Cl. DE72: Brea 6C **62**
Fearnleigh Dr. NG6: Bas 5B **32**
Featherstone Cl. NG4: Ged 4F **35**
Feignies Ct. NG12: Key 4G **79**
Felen Cl. NG5: Bestw 6E **21**
Fellbarrow Cl. NG2: West Br 6E **59**
Felley Cl. NG15: Huck................6E **7**
Fellows Rd. NG9: Bee................4E **55**
Fellows Yd. NG12: Plum 6G **69**
Fell Side NG5: Woodt.................2C **34**
Fellside Cl. NG2: Gam................5E **59**
Felstead Cl. NG9: Bram 2C **54**
Felstead Rd. NG8: Bilb...............3G **43**
Felton Cl. NG9: Chil...................6B **54**
Felton Rd. NG2: Nott..................2H **57**
Felton Way NG5: Arn 3B **22**
Fenchurch Cl. NG5: Arn.............4E **21**
Fenimore Ct. NG12: Rad T 5H **49**
Feniton Ct. NG3: Ged 2G **35**
Fenman Cl. DE7: Ilk...................2B **28**
Fenroth Cl. NG6: Bulw 5F **19**
Fenton Ct. NG5: Sher 3D **32**
Fenton Dr. NG6: Bulw 3A **20**
Fenton Rd. NG5: Sher................ 3D **32**
Fenwick Cl. NG5: Brox................5F **31**
Fenwick Ct. NG4: Neth 2A **48**
Fenwick Rd. NG8: Brox...............5F **31**
Fergus Cl. NG11: Clftn 5D **66**
Ferguson Cl. NG9: Chil 3C **64**
Fern Av. NG5: Sher 6F **33**
Fern Cl. NG9: Bram 4B **54**
Fern Cres. NG16: Eastw.............2A **16**
Ferndale Cl. NG9: Atten 3D **64**
Ferndale Gro. NG3: Nott 3D **46**
Ferndale Rd. NG3: Nott.............. 3D **46**
Ferndene Dr. NG10: Long E 6C **62**
Ferngill Cl. NG2: Nott.................2F **57**
Fernilee Cl. DE7: West H............1C **38**
Fern Lea Av. NG12: Cotg............3E **71**
Fernleigh Av. NG3: Mapp........... 5D **34**
Fernwood Commercial Workshops
  NG16: Want...............................5A **18**
Fernwood Cres. NG8: Woll 5C **42**
Fernwood Dr. NG12: Rad T 5F **49**
Fernwood Dr. NG16: Want...........5A **18**
Ferny Hollow Cl. NG5: Top V 5C **20**
Ferrers Wlk. NG3: Nott 2H **5** (4A **46**)
Ferriby Ter. NG2: Nott................ 2G **57**
Ferry Lodge NG4: Car 3G **47**
Ferryman Rd. NG11: Wilf.............5E **57**
Festival Cres. NG9: Trow............5E **41**
Festival Rd. DE7: Kirk H............. 4G **39**
Festus Cl. NG3: Nott 3H **45**
Festus St. NG4: Neth 2A **48**
Field, The DE75: Ship 6E **15**
Field Av. NG15: Huck.................. 1D **18**

Field Cl. DE72: Brea....................6B **62**
Field Cl. NG2: West Br 2E **59**
Field Cl. NG4: Ged 5H **35**
Field Cl. NG9: Chil......................1A **64**
Field Dr. DE7: Smal.....................5A **14**
Fieldfare Rd. NG9: Bram.............5C **54**
Fieldfare Rd. NG12: Cotg............6G **61**
Field Ho. Cl. NG8: Woll 4D **42**
Field La. NG14: Woodbo 1C **24**
Field La. NG9: Chil 1A **64**
Field Maple Dr. NG7: Hys G 1C **44**
Field Rd. DE7: Ilk.......................3B **40**
Fields Av. NG11: Rudd 2G **77**
Flds. Farm Rd. NG10: Long E 2E **73**
Field St. NG12: Cotg...................1E **71**
Field Vw. NG12: Rad T 5H **49**
Fieldway NG11: Wilf....................1F **67**
Fiennes Cres. NG7: Nott ... 6A **4** (6E **45**)
Fifth Av. NG7: Nott.....................5A **56**
Filey St. NG6: Bulw 5A **20**
Finch Cl. NG7: Lent.................... 3D **56**
Finchley Cl. NG11: Clftn.............4A **66**
Findern Grn. NG3: Nott...............3C **46**
Fingal Cl. NG11: Clftn 4D **66**
Finsbury Av. NG2: Nott...............5B **46**
Finsbury Pk. Cl. NG2: West Br 6G **57**
Finsbury Rd. NG5: Arn................3E **21**
Finsbury Rd. NG9: Bram.............6C **42**
Firbank Ct. NG9: Chil..................6B **54**
Firbeck Rd. NG5: Arn..................5C **22**
Firbeck Rd. NG8: Woll 5B **42**
Fir Cl. NG15: Huck......................1H **19**
Fir Cl. NG6: Bulw 6F **19**
Fircroft Av. NG8: Bilb.................1E **43**
Fircroft Dr. NG15: Huck..............6C **6**
Firdale NG12: Cotg 2G **71**
Firecrest Way NG6: Bas 3B **32**
Firefly Cl. NG13: Newt................2B **50**
Fire Ho., The NG5: Arn...............1A **34**
Firfield Av. DE72: Brea 5A **62**
Firs, The NG5: Sher.................... 4H **33**
Firs Av. NG9: Bee.......................4F **55**
Firsby Rd. NG8: Brox..................5F **31**
Firs Ho. NG5: Sher 4H **33**
Firs Rd. NG12: Edwal................. 6D **58**
Firs St. NG10: Long E 3C **72**
First Av. DE7: Ilk........................2B **40**
First Av. DE72: Ris 6B **52**
First Av. NG4: Car 2E **47**
First Av. NG4: Colw.....................4G **47**
First Av. NG4: Ged 6H **35**
First Av. NG6: Bulw.................... 6H **19**
First Av. NG7: Hys G 1F **45**
First Av. NG7: Nott.....................5A **56**
Firth Cl. NG5: Arn.......................4E **23**
Firth Dr. NG9: Chil......................3C **64**
Firth Way NG6: Bulw 5G **19**
Fir Wlk. NG3: Nott...................... 2D **46**
Fisher Av. NG5: Woodt................2B **34**
Fisher Cl. DE7: Ilk......................3B **28**
Fisher Ga. NG1: Nott.......5G **5** (5H **45**)
Fisher La. NG13: Bing.................5E **51**
Fisher St. NG7: Bas 1D **44**
  .... (not continuous)
Fishpond Dr. NG7: Nott... 6A **4** (6E **45**)
Fitzgerald Ct. NG15: Huck...........5G **7**
Five Acres NG11: Wilf.................1E **67**
Flagholme NG12: Cotg................3F **71**
Flake La. DE7: Stant D................2A **52**
Flamingo Ct. NG7: Lent..............1E **57**
Flamstead Av. DE75: Los............1A **14**
Flamstead Av. NG4: Lamb...........6B **24**
Flamstead Rd. DE7: Ilk...............6B **28**
Flamsteed Rd. NG8: Stre............6B **30**
Flatts, The NG9: Chil..................6B **54**
Flatts La. NG14: Calv.................1G **11**
Flawborough Ri. NG2: West Br.... 2G **67**
Flawforth Av. NG11: Rudd...........6H **67**
Flawforth La. NG11: Rudd...........6H **67**

Flaxendale NG12: Cotg............... 3G **71**
Flaxton Way NG5: Top V............. 6D **20**
Fleam Rd. NG11: Clftn 1C **66**
Fleeman Gro. NG2: West Br........2C **58**
Fleet Cl. NG7: Radf 3B **44**
Fleetway Cl. NG16: Newth.......... 4D **16**
Fleetwith Cl. NG2: West Br 6E **59**
Fleming Cl. NG16: Want..............5A **18**
Fleming Dr. NG4: Car..................2E **47**
Fleming Gdns. NG11: Clftn 4A **66**
Fleming Ho. NG3: Mapp..............5B **34**
Fletcher Ga. NG1: Nott.......4E **5** (5G **45**)
Fletcher Rd. NG9: Bee................ 4G **55**
Fletcher St. DE75: Hea...............3C **14**
Fletcher St. NG10: Long E 5F **63**
Fletcher Ter. NG3: Mapp.............5A **34**
Fletton Ct. NG3: Nott 2C **46**
Flewitt Gdns. NG3: Nott.....1H **5** (3A **46**)
Flinders Orchard NG12: Key....... 5G **79**
Flintham Dr. NG5: Sher...............3F **33**
Flixton Rd. NG16: Kimb 6H **17**
Florence Av. NG10: Long E 4H **63**
Florence Boot Cl. NG7: Nott 3H **55**
Florence Ct. DE7: Ilk..................6B **28**
Florence Cres. NG4: Ged 1B **48**
Florence Gro. NG3: Nott 2C **46**
Florence Rd. NG2: West Br.........3C **58**
Florence Rd. NG3: Nott...............6C **34**
Florence Rd. NG4: Ged 6B **36**
Florence St. NG15: Huck.............6G **7**
Florey Wlk. NG11: Clftn 5A **66**
Florimel Ct. NG5: Arn................. 6G **21**
Florin Gdns. NG10: Long E..........6C **62**
Flowers Cl. NG5: Arn.................. 1D **34**
Flying Horse Wlk.
  NG1: Nott...................4E **5** (5G **45**)
Foljambe Ter. NG3: Nott....2G **5** (4H **45**)
Folkton Gdns. NG3: Mapp...........6B **34**
Forbes Cl. NG10: Long E............. 2G **73**
Forbes Hole Local Nature
  Reserve 2G **73**
Ford Av. DE75: Los 1A **14**
Fordham Grn. NG11: Clftn 5C **66**
Ford St. NG7: Bas 6E **33**
Ford St. Nth. NG7: Bas 6E **33**
Foredrift Cl. NG11: Goth 6G **75**
Forest Cl. NG12: Cotg.................2E **71**
Forest Cotts. NG6: Bulw 4B **20**
Forest Ct. NG7: Radf...................3E **45**
Forester Cl. NG9: Chil.................1C **64**
Forester Gro. NG4: Car...............2F **47**
Forester Rd. NG3: Nott 1C **46**
Forester St. NG4: Neth 2A **48**
FOREST FIELDS 1E **45**
Forest Gro. NG1: Nott 2F **45**
Forest Gro. NG7: Radf.................3E **45**
Forest La. NG15: Pap..................1C **8**
Forest Park & Ride, The.............2E **45**
Forest Rd. NG13: Bing.................5C **50**
Forest Rd. NG14: Calv.................3F **11**
Forest Rd. E. NG1: Nott...............3E **45**
Forest Rd. W. NG7: Radf.............3E **45**
Forest Stop (NET), The................2E **45**
Forest Vw. Dr. NG15: Huck..........4E **7**
Forge, The NG9: Trow................. 4D **40**
Forge Av. NG14: Calv................. 3H **11**
Forge Hill NG9: Chil 1D **64**
Forge Mill Gro. NG15: Huck.........6B **8**
Forman Ho. NG5: Sher................ 6F **33**
Forman St. NG1: Nott........3D **4** (4G **45**)
Forster St. NG7: Radf..................3C **44**
  .... (not continuous)
Forsythia Gdns. NG7: Lent..........1C **56**
Forum Rd. NG5: Bestw 1C **32**
Fosbrooke Dr. NG10: Long E 2F **73**
Fosse, The NG12: Cotg 6H **71**
  .... (not continuous)
Fosse, The NG12: Crop Bi........... 6H **71**
  .... (not continuous)

Fosse, The NG12: Owt 6H **71**
  .... (not continuous)
Fosse Rd. NG13: Bing.................5B **50**
Fosse Rd. NG13: Car C 1E **51**
Fosse Rd. NG13: East B...............1E **51**
Fosse Rd. NG13: Knee.................1E **51**
Fosse Rd. NG13: Newt.................5B **50**
Fosse Rd. NG13: Saxon...............5B **50**
Fosse Rd. NG13: Scre..................1E **51**
Fosse Wlk. NG12: Cotg............... 3G **71**
Fosse Way NG13: Bing................6B **50**
Foster Av. NG9: Bee....................5F **55**
Foster Dr. NG5: Sher.................. 3H **33**
Fosters La. NG13: Bing................5F **51**
Fothergill Ct. NG3: Mapp............ 2G **45**
Fountain Dale Ct. NG3: Nott........2H **45**
Fountains Cl. NG2: West Br 5D **58**
Fountains Rd. NG9: Bee..............5G **55**
Fountayne Cl. NG15: Huck 1F **7**
Fourth Av. NG4: Car 1D **46**
Fourth Av. NG7: Hys G 1F **45**
Fourth Av. NG7: Nott...................5A **56**
Fowler M. NG16: Want.................6A **18**
Fowler Rd. NG12: Edwal.............2B **68**
Fowler St. NG3: Mapp P 1H **45**
Fox Cl. NG10: Long E 2F **73**
Fox Covert NG4: Colw..................5H **47**
Fox Covert La. NG11: Clftn 5H **65**
Fox Covert Local Nature
  Reserve 6F **63**
Foxearth Av. NG11: Clftn.............3E **67**
Fox End NG5: Sher..................... 5H **33**
Foxes Cl. NG7: Nott 6A **4** (6E **45**)
  .... (off Hermitage Wlk.)
Foxglove Cl. NG15: Huck.............1A **20**
Foxglove Rd. NG16: Newth..........5D **16**
Foxgloves, The NG13: Bing 6D **50**
Foxglove Way NG12: Cotg...........6G **61**
Fox Gro. NG5: Bas 4C **32**
Fox Gro. Ct. NG5: Bas.................4C **32**
Foxhall Rd. NG7: Hys G 1E **45**
Foxhill NG12: Cotg......................3E **71**
Foxhill Cl. NG4: Car.................... 1G **47**
Foxhill Rd. NG14: Bur J 2E **37**
Foxhill Rd. NG4: Car....................1E **47**
Foxhill Rd. Central NG4: Car....... 1D **46**
Foxhill Rd. E. NG4: Car................1F **47**
Foxhill Rd. W. NG4: Car...............1C **46**
Foxhollies Gro. NG5: Sher...........4F **33**
Foxley Rd. DE7: Ilk.....................2B **28**
Fox Mdw. NG15: Huck..................5F **7**
Fox Rd. NG2: West Br..................2B **58**
Foxton Cl. DE7: Ilk..................... 4G **27**
Foxton Cl. NG6: Bulw..................5F **19**
Foxton Gdns. NG8: Bilb 2G **43**
Foxwood Gro. NG14: Calv........... 4H **11**
Foxwood La. NG14: Woodbo 5H **11**
Fradley Cl. NG6: Bulw.................3A **20**
Frampton Rd. NG8: Bilb.............. 2G **43**
Frances Gro. NG15: Huck 2H **7**
Francis Gro. NG6: Bas 4C **32**
Francis Mill NG9: Bee..................4F **55**
Francis Rd. NG4: Car.................. 1H **47**
Francis St. NG7: Radf........ 1A **4** (3E **45**)
  .... (not continuous)
Franklin Cl. NG5: Arn................. 5G **21**
Franklin Dr. NG12: Toll................4F **69**
Franklin Ho. NG3: Mapp..............5B **34**
  .... (off Ockbrook Dr.)
Franklyn Gdns. NG12: Key 3G **79**
Franklyn Gdns. NG8: Aspl...........4A **44**
Fraser Cres. NG4: Car................. 6D **34**
Fraser Rd. NG2: Nott 3H **57**
Fraser Rd. NG4: Car.................... 5D **34**
Fraser Sq. NG4: Car.................... 6D **34**
Frearson Farm Ct.
  NG16: Eastw..............................4B **16**
Freckingham St.
  NG1: Nott..........................3H **5** (4H **45**)

Freda Av. – Glover Av.

Freda Av. NG4: Ged 5F **35**
Freda Cl. NG4: Ged 4F **35**
Frederic Av. DE75: Hea 6D **14**
Frederick Av. DE7: Ilk 4C **40**
Frederick Av. NG4: Car 2D **46**
Frederick Gro. NG7: Lent 6D **44**
Frederick Rd. NG9: Stfrd 4F **53**
Frederick St. NG10: Long E 6H **63**
Freeland Cl. NG9: Toton 2H **63**
Freemans Rd. NG4: Car 1A **48**
Freemans Ter. NG4: Car 1H **47**
Freemantle Wlk. NG5: Top V 5C **20**
Freeston Dr. NG6: Bulw 5F **19**
Freeth Ct. NG2: Nott 1B **58**
Freeth St. NG2: Nott 1A **58**
Freiston St. NG7: Hys G 2C **44**
Fremount Dr. NG8: Bilb 3F **43**
French St. DE7: Ilk 3C **40**
Fretwell St. NG7: Hys G 2C **44**
Friar La. NG1: Nott 5C **4** (5F **45**)
Friars Ct. DE7: Kirk H 3G **39**
Friars Ct. NG7: Nott 6A **4** (6E **45**)
Friar St. NG10: Long E 6F **63**
Friar St. NG7: Lent 1C **56**
Friar Wlk. NG13: Newt 1C **50**
Friary, The NG7: Lent 1C **56**
Friary Cl. NG7: Lent 1C **56**
Friday La. NG4: Ged 5H **35**
Friesland Dr. NG10: Sand 6B **52**
Frinton Rd. NG8: Brox 6E **31**
Frisby Av. NG10: Long E 1G **73**
Frobisher Gdns. NG5: Arn 1H **33**
Frogmore St.
NG1: Nott 1D **4** (3G **45**)
Frome Gdns. NG13: Bing 6D **50**
Front St. NG5: Arn 6B **22**
Frost Av. NG16: Lang M 1E **15**
Fryar Rd. NG16: Eastw 1B **16**
Fulforth St. NG1: Nott 1D **4** (3G **45**)
Fuller St. NG11: Rudd 1G **77**
Fullwood Av. DE7: Ilk 6A **28**
Fullwood St. DE7: Ilk 6A **28**
Fulwood Cl. NG9: Chil 1C **64**
Fulwood Cres. NG8: Aspl 6G **31**
Fulwood Dr. NG10: Long E 6C **62**
Funky Pots West Bridgford 5A **58**
Furleys Cotts. NG14: Lowd 2H **25**
Furlong Av. NG5: Arn 5A **22**
Furlong Cl. NG9: Stfrd 3F **53**
Furlong Ct. NG5: Arn 5A **22**
Furlong Pl. NG2: Nott 5C **46**
Furlong St. NG5: Arn 6A **22**
Furnace La. DE75: Los 1A **14**
Furnace Rd. DE7: Ilk 2D **40**
Furness Cl. NG2: West Br 4D **58**
Furness Rd. NG6: Bas 4A **32**
Furzebrook Rd. NG4: Colw 3G **47**
Furze Gdns. NG3: Nott 2H **45**
Fylde Cl. NG9: Toton 3G **63**
Fylingdale Way NG8: Woll 6B **42**

G

Gables, The NG3: Mapp 3C **34**
Gables, The NG7: Bas 6E **33**
Gabor Cl. NG11: Clftn 5A **66**
Gabor Ct. NG11: Clftn 4A **66**
Gabrielle Cl. NG6: Bulw 3B **32**
Gadd St. NG7: Radf 3D **44**
Gadsby Cl. DE7: Ilk 5C **40**
Gadwall Cres. NG7: Lent 1E **57**
Gainsborough Cl.
NG10: Long E 2G **73**
Gainsborough Cl. NG9: Stfrd 5G **53**
Gainsborough Ct. NG9: Bee 4G **55**
Gainsford Cl. NG5: Bestw 2D **32**
Gainsford Cres. NG5: Bestw 2D **32**
Gala Bingo Nottingham
Top Valley 1C **32**
Gala Way NG5: Bestw 1C **32**
Galeb, The NG7: Lent 1C **56**
(off Leen Ct.)
Gale Cl. NG9: Bee 5H **55**
Galena Dr. NG3: Nott 2C **46**
Gallery, The NG7: Nott 6C **4** (6F **45**)
GALLOWS INN 3C **40**
Gallows Inn Cl. DE7: Ilk 3C **40**
Gallows Inn Ind. Est. DE7: Ilk 3D **40**
Galway Rd. NG5: Arn 5H **21**
Galway Rd. NG7: Lent 6D **44**
Gamble St. NG7: Radf 3E **45**
GAMSTON 4E **59**
Gamston Cres. NG5: Sher 4G **33**
Gamston District Cen. 5E **59**
Gamston Lings Bar Rd.
NG12: Edwal 4C **68**
Gamston Lings Bar Rd.
NG12: Toll 4C **68**
Gamston Lings Bar Rd.
NG2: Gam 4F **59**
Gamston Lodge NG4: Car 3G **47**
Ganton Cl. NG3: Mapp 6B **34**
Garden Av. DE7: Ilk 4B **40**
Garden Av. NG4: Car 2F **47**
Garden City NG4: Car 1G **47**
Gardendale Av. NG11: Clftn 4B **66**
Gardeners Cl. NG13: Bing 4D **50**
Gardeners Cl. NG15: Huck 4F **7**
Gardeners Cl. NG4: Car 6F **35**
Gardeners Wlk. NG5: Sher 3D **32**
Gardenia Cl. NG9: Toton 3A **64**
Gardenia Cres. NG3: Mapp 5D **34**
Gardenia Gro. NG3: Mapp 5D **34**
Garden Rd. NG13: Bing 5D **50**
Garden Rd. NG15: Huck 4F **7**
Garden Rd. NG16: Eastw 2B **16**
Gardens, The DE75: Los 1A **14**
Gardens Ct. NG2: West Br 4C **58**
Garden St. NG7: Radf 4D **44**
Garfield Cl. NG9: Stfrd 2G **53**
Garfield Ct. NG7: Radf 4D **44**
Garfield Rd. NG7: Radf 3C **44**
(not continuous)
Garforth Cl. NG8: Bas 1C **44**
Garland, The NG7: Lent 1C **56**
(off Leen Ct.)
Garner Rd. NG16: Gilt 6D **16**
Garners Hill NG1: Nott 5E **5** (5H **45**)
Garnet Ct. NG3: Nott 2H **5** (4A **46**)
Garnet St. NG4: Neth 2H **47**
Garnett Av. DE75: Hea 3D **14**
Garrett Gro. NG11: Clftn 3A **66**
Garsdale Cl. NG2: Gam 5E **59**
Garsdale Dr. NG11: Wilf 2E **67**
Garton Cl. NG6: Bulw 2H **31**
Garton Cl. NG9: Chil 6B **54**
Gas St. NG10: Sand 5E **53**
Gatcombe Cl. NG12: Rad T 6G **49**
Gatcombe Gro. NG10: Sand 2C **62**
Gateford Cl. NG9: Bram 1C **54**
Gatehouse Ct. NG9: Chil 6D **54**
Gateside Rd. NG2: Nott 2E **57**
Gatling St. NG7: Radf 4C **44**
Gaul St. NG6: Bulw 6H **19**
Gauntley Ct. NG7: Bas 1D **44**
Gauntley St. NG7: Bas 1C **44**
Gautries Cl. NG5: Top V 5E **21**
Gavin M. NG7: Hys G 1D **44**
Gawthorne St. NG7: Bas 6D **32**
Gayhurst Grn. NG6: Bulw 2C **32**
Gayhurst Rd. NG6: Bulw 2C **32**
Gaynor Ct. NG8: Bilb 3H **43**
Gayrigg Ct. NG9: Chil 6B **54**
Gayton Cl. NG8: Bilb 1D **42**
Gayton Rd. DE7: Ilk 1H **39**
Gaywood Cl. NG11: Clftn 5D **66**
GEDLING 5H **35**
Gedling Country Pk. 2H **35**
Gedling Country Pk.
Visitor Cen. 2G **35**
Gedling Crematorium 4F **23**
Gedling Gro. NG5: Arn 6B **22**
Gedling Gro. NG7: Radf 1A **4** (3E **45**)
Gedling Rd. NG4: Car 1H **47**
Gedling Rd. NG5: Arn 6B **22**
Gedling St. NG1: Nott 4G **5** (5H **45**)
Gedney Av. NG3: Nott 1B **46**
Gell Rd. NG9: Chil 1A **64**
Genesis Pk. NG7: Radf 4B **44**
George Av. NG10: Long E 4H **63**
George Av. NG9: Bee 6F **55**
George Grn. Ct. NG2: Nott 5B **46**
(off Sneinton Blvd.)
George Grn. Way NG7: Nott 3B **56**
George Rd. NG2: West Br 4A **58**
George Rd. NG4: Car 2G **47**
George's La. NG14: Calv 5E **11**
George's La. NG5: Calv 6D **10**
George's La. NG5: Woodbo 6D **10**
George St. NG1: Nott 3F **5** (4H **45**)
George St. NG15: Huck 3G **7**
George St. NG16: Lang M 2F **15**
George St. NG5: Arn 1A **34**
George St. Trad. Ho.
NG1: Nott 4F **5** (5H **45**)
(off George St.)
Georgia Dr. NG5: Arn 3A **22**
Georgina Rd. NG9: Bee 6F **55**
Geraldine Cl. NG5: Bestw 5F **21**
Gerrard Cl. NG5: Arn 3E **21**
Gertrude Rd. NG2: West Br 3C **58**
Gervase Gdns. NG11: Clftn 3A **66**
Ghost Ho. La. NG9: Chil 6B **54**
(not continuous)
Gibbons Av. NG9: Stfrd 4F **53**
Gibbons St. NG7: Lent 3C **56**
Gibb St. NG10: Long E 6G **63**
Gibson Rd. NG7: Hys G 1E **45**
Gifford Gdns. NG2: Nott 1G **57**
Gilbert Av. NG11: Goth 6H **75**
Gilbert Blvd. NG5: Arn 6E **23**
Gilbert Cl. NG5: Bestw 2E **33**
Gilbert Gdns. NG3: Nott 3C **46**
Gilbert St. NG15: Huck 4G **7**
(not continuous)
Gilead St. NG6: Bulw 6H **19**
Giles Av. NG2: West Br 5H **57**
Giles Ct. NG2: West Br 4A **58**
Gillercomb Cl. NG2: West Br 6F **59**
Gilliver La. NG12: C'ton 3C **70**
Gillotts Cl. NG13: Bing 4E **51**
Gillott St. DE75: Hea 5E **15**
Gill St. NG1: Nott 1C **4** (3F **45**)
Gilpet Av. NG3: Nott 1B **46**
GILTBROOK 5E **17**
Giltbrook Cres. NG16: Gilt 5E **17**
Giltbrook Ind. Pk. NG16: Gilt 6E **17**
Giltbrook Retail Pk. 6E **17**
Gilt Hill NG16: Kimb 6F **17**
Giltway NG16: Gilt 6E **17**
Gimson Cl. DE7: Ilk 4G **27**
Gin Cl. Way NG16: Aws 1E **29**
Gin Cl. Way NG16: Gilt 1E **29**
Gipsy La. NG11: Clftn 3A **66**
Gipsy La. NG15: Huck 1D **6**
Girton Rd. NG5: Sher 4E **33**
Gisburn Cl. NG11: Wilf 1E **67**
Glade, The NG11: Clftn 6C **66**
Glade Av. NG8: Woll 4A **44**
Glade Bus. Cen., The
NG5: Bestw 1C **32**
Gladehill Rd. NG5: Arn 6G **21**
Gladehill Rd. NG5: Bestw 6G **21**
Glades, The NG5: Top V 5D **20**
Gladstone Av. DE75: Hea 3C **14**
Gladstone Av. NG11: Goth 6H **75**
Gladstone St. DE7: Ilk 2B **40**
Gladstone St. DE75: Hea 3C **14**
Gladstone St. NG10: Long E 1F **73**
Gladstone St. NG16: Lang M 2G **15**
Gladstone St. NG4: Car 2F **47**
Gladstone St. NG7: Bas 1D **44**
(not continuous)
Gladstone St. NG7: Hys G 1D **44**
(not continuous)
Gladstone St. NG9: Bee 6E **55**
Gladys St. NG7: Bas 6E **33**
Glaisdale Dr. E. NG8: Bilb 3D **42**
Glaisdale Dr. W. NG8: Bilb 4D **42**
Glaisdale Pk. Ind. Est.
NG8: Bilb 3D **42**
Glaisdale Parkway NG8: Bilb 4D **42**
Glamis Rd. NG5: Sher 5E **33**
Glanton Way NG5: Arn 3C **22**
Glapton La. NG11: Clftn 3B **66**
Glapton Rd. NG2: Nott 2G **57**
Glaramara Cl. NG2: Nott 2F **57**
Glasshouse, The
NG3: Nott 2F **5** (4G **45**)
Glasshouse St.
NG1: Nott 2E **5** (4G **45**)
Glastonbury Cl. NG12: Edwal 2C **68**
Glebe, The NG16: Coss 3D **28**
Glebe Cotts. NG11: Wilf 3F **57**
Glebe Cres. DE7: Ilk 2C **40**
Glebe Cres. DE7: Stly 3A **38**
Glebe Dr. NG14: Bur J 4D **36**
Glebe Farm Cl.
NG2: West Br 1G **67**
Glebe Farm Vw. NG4: Ged 4H **35**
Glebe La. NG12: Rad T 6F **49**
Glebe Rd. NG16: Nuth 1C **30**
Glebe Rd. NG2: West Br 4B **58**
Glebe Rd. NG4: Car 5E **35**
Glebe St. NG15: Huck 3G **7**
Glebe St. NG9: Bee 5E **55**
Glen, The NG11: Clftn 4C **66**
Glen Av. NG16: Eastw 4D **16**
Glenbrook NG12: Cotg 2G **71**
Glenbrook Cres. NG8: Bilb 2G **43**
Glencairn Dr. NG8: Bilb 1G **43**
Glencairn M. NG8: Bilb 1G **43**
Glencoe Rd. NG11: Clftn 4E **67**
Glencoyne Rd. NG11: Clftn 5C **66**
Glencross Cl. NG2: West Br 2E **59**
Glendale Cl. NG4: Car 5F **35**
Glendale Ct. NG9: Chil 2E **65**
Glendale Gdns. NG5: Arn 6B **22**
Glendoe Gro. NG13: Bing 5C **50**
Glendon Dr. NG15: Huck 6G **7**
Glendon Dr. NG5: Sher 4E **33**
Glendon Rd. DE7: Kirk H 5G **39**
Gleneagles Ct. NG12: Edwal 2D **68**
Gleneagles Dr. NG5: Arn 4D **22**
Glenfield Av. NG16: Kimb 6F **17**
Glenfield Rd. NG10: Long E 2F **73**
Glen Helen NG4: Colw 3H **47**
Glenlivet Gdns. NG11: Clftn 4D **66**
Glenloch Dr. NG11: Clftn 5D **66**
Glenmore Rd. NG2: West Br 5D **58**
Glenorchy Cres. NG5: Top V 5C **20**
Glen Parva Av. NG5: Redh 4A **22**
Glenridding Cl. NG2: West Br 6F **59**
Glen Rd. NG14: Bur J 2E **37**
Glensford Gdns. NG5: Top V 3C **20**
Glenside NG5: Woodt 2D **34**
Glenside Rd. NG9: Bram 2C **54**
Glenstone Ct. NG7: Hys G 1D **44**
Glentworth Rd. NG7: Radf 3C **44**
Glenwood Av. NG8: Woll 5D **42**
Glins Rd. NG5: Top V 5D **20**
Gloucester Av. NG10: Sand 1C **62**
Gloucester Av. NG16: Nuth 4F **31**
Gloucester Av. NG7: Lent 5C **44**
Gloucester Av. NG9: Bee 6F **55**
Glover Av. NG8: Woll 5D **42**

A-Z Nottingham 101

Glover Ho. NG5: Arn......................1C **34**
..............................*(off Derwent Cres.)*
Glue La. DE75: Los 3A **14**
Goatchurch Ct. NG5: Top V 5E **21**
Goathland Cl. NG5: Bestw 5F **21**
Godber Cl. NG16: Gilt..................5C **16**
Godber Rd. NG15: Huck................6E **7**
Goddard Ct. NG3: Arn..................1E **35**
Godfrey Dr. DE7: Kirk H 4G **39**
Godfrey La. NG7: Lent 5D **44**
Godfrey St. DE75: Hea................4C **14**
..............................*(not continuous)*
Godfrey St. NG4: Neth 3A **48**
Godkin Dr. NG16: Lang M............1E **15**
Goldcrest Cl. NG13: Bing.............6G **51**
Goldcrest Rd. NG6: Cin...............4H **31**
Goldenbrook Cl. DE72: Brea........6A **62**
Goldham Rd. NG8: Stre 1D **42**
Goldrill Cl. NG2: Gam.................4D **58**
Goldsmith Ct. NG1: Nott 2C **4** (4F **45**)
..............................*(off Chaucer St.)*
Goldsmith St. NG1: Nott 2C **4** (4F **45**)
Goldswong Ter. NG3: Nott 2G **45**
Golf Cl. NG6: Bulw 3A **20**
Golf Club Rd. DE7: Stant D 2C **52**
Golf Course Rd. NG12: Stant W ...5B **80**
Golf Rd. NG12: Rad T................6G **49**
Gonalston La. NG14: Epp 6H **13**
Gonalston La. NG14: Gon 6H **13**
Gonalston La. NG14: Hove..........6H **13**
Goodall Cres. NG15: Huck............5A **8**
Goodall St. NG7: Hys G 2D **44**
Goodhill Ct. DE7: Ilk 5D **40**
Goodliffe St. NG7: Hys G 1D **44**
Goodman Cl. NG16: Gilt..............5E **17**
Goodwin Cl. NG10: Sand 5C **52**
Goodwin Dr. NG16: Kimb 1G **29**
Goodwin St. NG7: Radf 1A **4** (3E **45**)
Goodwood Av. NG5: Arn 5A **22**
Goodwood Cres. DE7: Kirk H 5H **39**
Goodwood Dr. NG9: Toton 3H **63**
Goodwood Rd. NG8: Woll 5D **42**
Goole Av. DE7: Kirk H 4H **39**
Goosedale La. NG6: Bestw V 4C **8**
Goose Ga. NG1: Nott 4F **5** (5H **45**)
Goose Ga. NG12: Cotg 2E **71**
Gordon Cl. NG9: Atten................3D **64**
Gordon Gro. NG7: Bas 6D **32**
Gordon Ri. NG3: Mapp 5A **34**
Gordon Rd. NG14: Bur J 2G **37**
Gordon Rd. NG2: West Br...........4B **58**
Gordon Rd. NG3: Nott 3A **46**
Gordon Sq. NG2: West Br 4B **58**
Gordon St. DE7: Ilk 6B **28**
Gordon St. NG6: Bas..................3B **32**
Gorman Ct. NG5: Arn 6D **22**
Gorse Cl. NG10: Long E 3D **62**
Gorse Cl. NG14: Calv 4F **11**
Gorse Cl. NG15: Newth 4D **16**
Gorse Ct. NG6: Bulw 2C **32**
Gorse Rd. NG12: Key 4F **79**
Gorse Wlk. NG3: Nott 2D **46**
Gorsey Rd. NG3: Mapp P 2H **45**
Gosforth Av. DE7: Ilk 1A **28**
Gosforth Ct. NG2: Nott 2H **57**
Goshawk Rd. DE7: Ilk 6C **40**
GOTHAM 6H **75**
Gotheridge Dr. NG4: Ged 3F **35**
Gothic Cl. NG6: Bas 3C **32**
Gough Gro. NG10: Long E...........1E **73**
Govenors Fld. Recreation
Ground 1C **24**
Goverton Sq. NG6: Bulw.............2B **32**
Gowan Cl. NG9: Chil 3C **64**
Goyden Cl. NG5: Top V 5E **21**
Grace Av. NG9: Bee 5H **55**
Grace Cres. DE75: Hea 3D **14**
Grace Dr. NG8: Aspl 1B **44**
Grafton Av. NG5: Woodt.............2A **34**

Grafton Ct. NG7: Radf..... 3A **4** (4E **45**)
Graham St. DE7: Ilk 2B **40**
Graham St. NG7: Radf 4D **44**
Grainger Av. NG2: West Br 2A **68**
Graingers Ter. NG15: Huck..........5H **7**
Grainger St. NG2: Nott...............1A **58**
Grampian Dr. NG5: Arn...............3F **21**
Grampian Way NG10: Long E......5C **62**
Granby Ct. NG13: Bing................5D **50**
Granby St. DE7: Ilk 5A **28**
Granby Vs. NG2: Nott.................5B **46**
Grandfield Av. NG12: Rad T........5F **49**
Grandfield Cres. NG12: Rad T 5F **49**
Grandfield St. DE75: Los 1A **14**
Grange, The DE7: Smal...............5A **14**
Grange Av. DE72: Brea 5A **62**
Grange Av. NG11: Rudd 5F **67**
Grange Av. NG9: Bee 5F **55**
Grange Cl. NG11: Wilf 3F **57**
Grange Cl. NG4: Lamb 6C **24**
Grange Ct. NG11: Rudd 3G **67**
Grange Cres. NG4: Ged 4H **35**
Grange Dr. NG10: Long E 5H **63**
Grange Est. NG16: Coss..............6F **29**
Grange Farm NG2: Gam 4E **59**
Grange Farm Cl. NG9: Toton 4A **64**
Grange Farm Cotts.
NG14: Lowd 2F **25**
Grange Gdns. DE75: Los 2A **14**
Grange Gdns. NG15: Pap.............2B **8**
Grangelea Gdns. NG9: Bram 3B **54**
Grangemoor NG15: Pap...............2B **8**
Grange Pk. NG10: Long E 5H **63**
GRANGE PARK 5A **64**
Grange Pk. NG2: West Br 6D **58**
Grange Rd. NG10: Long E 5H **63**
Grange Rd. NG12: Edwal 1C **68**
Grange Rd. NG5: Woodt..............3A **34**
Grange Rd. NG6: Bas..................4B **32**
Grange Vw. NG16: Eastw.............2B **16**
Grangewood Av. DE7: Ilk.............2B **40**
Grangewood Rd. NG8: Woll.........6C **42**
Grannis Dr. NG8: Bilb.................1G **43**
Grantham Cl. NG16: Gilt..............6E **17**
Grantham Rd. NG12: Rad T 1D **60**
Grantham Rd. NG13: Aslo 5F **51**
Grantham Rd. NG13: Bing 5F **51**
Grantham Rd. NG13: What 5F **51**
Grantleigh Cl. NG8: Woll.............4F **43**
Granton Av. NG11: Clftn..............5B **66**
Grant St. NG7: Radf 4D **44**
Granville Av. NG10: Long E..........4F **63**
Granville Cl. NG3: Nott 4B **46**
Granville Cres. NG12: Rad T 1E **61**
Granville Gro. NG3: Nott 4B **46**
Grasby Wlk. NG11: Clftn..............3B **66**
Grasmere Av. NG8: Aspl 5A **32**
Grasmere Cl. NG15: Huck............3F **7**
Grasmere Ct. NG10: Long E.........3D **62**
Grasmere Gdns. NG11: Goth 5H **75**
Grasmere Rd. NG10: Long E 3D **62**
Grasmere Rd. NG9: Bram 3A **54**
Grasmere St. NG10: Sand 6D **52**
Grasmoor Cl. NG3: Nott..............1B **46**
Grassingdale Cl. NG4: Car...........5H **35**
Grassington Rd. NG8: Aspl..........3B **44**
Grassmere NG12: Cotg...............2G **71**
Grassy La. NG9: Bee..................6G **55**
Gravelly Hollow NG14: Calv..........1B **10**
Graveney Gdns. NG5: Arn...........1B **34**
Graylands Rd. NG8: Bilb 2D **42**
Grayson M. NG9: Chil 3B **64**
Graystones Cl. NG2: West Br.......6E **58**
Grazingfield NG11: Wilf 1E **67**
GREASLEY 2G **17**

Greasley Av. NG16: Newth...........3E **17**
Greasley Sports &
Community Cen. 3D **16**
Greasley St. NG6: Bulw 6H **19**
Great Central Railway
Ruddington Station 2G **77**
Great Central Railway
(Nottingham) Mus. 2G **77**
Gt. Freeman St.
NG3: Nott 1E **5** (3G **45**)
Gt. Hoggett Dr. NG9: Chil 5A **54**
Gt. Northern Cl. DE7: Ilk 5B **28**
Gt. Northern Cl., The
NG2: Nott 6G **5** (6H **45**)
Gt. Northern Cotts. NG15: Huck ... 2H **7**
Gt. Northern Rd. NG16: Eastw 3H **15**
Gt. Northern Way NG4: Neth........3B **48**
Greaves Cl. NG5: Arn..................2D **34**
Greaves Cl. NG8: Stre 6D **30**
Grebe Cl. NG14: Stoke B............2C **48**
Greek St. NG7: Radf...................4E **45**
Green, The DE72: Brea 5A **62**
Green, The NG11: Rudd 1G **77**
Green, The NG12: Rad T 6E **49**
Green, The NG14: Lowd...............3F **25**
Green, The NG4: Car...................1E **47**
Green, The NG9: Chil 1E **65**
Greenacre NG12: Edwal..............1D **68**
Greenacre NG14: Bur J...............2E **37**
Grn. Acre NG8: Woll....................4B **42**
Greenacre Av. DE75: Hea 2E **15**
Greenacres Cl. NG16: Newth........3E **17**
Greenacres Pk. NG2: West Br.....2F **59**
Green App. NG4: Car 1E **47**
Green Av. NG4: Neth 2A **48**
Greenbank NG4: Car 5F **47**
Greenbank Ct. NG5: Sher 5G **33**
Greenbanks NG5: Woodt.............3A **34**
Greenburn Cl. NG2: Gam 5F **59**
Green Cl. NG12: Key 3H **79**
Green Cl. NG7: Nott 1A **56**
Green Cl. NG13: Bing..................4E **51**
Greencroft NG11: Clftn 2D **66**
Greendale Gdns. NG8: Bilb 1H **43**
Greendale Rd. NG3: Nott 3E **47**
Greendale Rd. NG5: Arn 1B **34**
Greenfield Gro. NG4: Car............1D **46**
Greenfields NG16: Lang M 1E **15**
Greenfields Dr. NG12: Cotg 3F **71**
Greenfield St. NG7: Nott 2B **56**
Greenford Cl. NG16: Nuth............4E **31**
Greengage Rd. NG12: Cotg 6G **61**
Greengates Av. NG3: Mapp 4B **34**
Greenhalgh Cres. DE7: Ilk 5A **28**
Greenhill Cres. NG4: Car 3G **47**
Greenhill Ri. NG4: Car................2G **47**
Greenhill Rd. NG4: Car 3G **47**
Greenhills Av. NG16: Eastw 1H **15**
Greenhills Rd. NG16: Eastw 2B **16**
Greenland Cres. NG9: Chil..........1C **64**
Green La. DE7: Ilk.......................4C **40**
Green La. NG11: Clftn.................3B **66**
Green La. NG4: Lamb..................4B **24**
Grn. Leys NG2: West Br..............1G **67**
Green M., The NG5: Bestw 2E **33**
Grn. Platt NG12: Cotg.................2E **71**
Greens Ct. DE7: Ilk 5H **27**
Greens Farm La. NG4: Ged..........5A **36**
Greenside Cl. NG10: Long E 6G **63**
Greenside Wlk. NG3: Nott............3E **47**
Greens La. NG16: Kimb 1H **29**
Green St. NG11: Bart F 3E **75**
Green St. NG11: Thru..................3E **75**
Green St. NG2: Nott 2H **57**
Green's Windmill &
Science Cen. 5B **46**
Greenway, The NG10: Sand 5D **52**
Greenway Cl. NG12: Rad T..........6E **49**

Greenwich Av. NG6: Bas 3A **32**
Greenwich Pk. Cl.
NG2: West Br...........................6G **57**
Greenwood Av. DE7: Ilk...............2C **40**
Greenwood Av. NG15: Huck 3F **7**
Greenwood Av. NG3: Nott............4F **47**
Greenwood Bonsai Studio............4A **10**
Greenwood Cl. NG9: Chil.............6D **54**
Greenwood Cres. NG4: Car 3G **47**
Greenwood Gdns. NG11: Rudd....1H **77**
Greenwood Gdns. NG8: Bilb........2C **42**
Greenwood Rd. NG3: Nott 4C **46**
Greenwood Rd. NG4: Car 4F **47**
Greenwood Va. NG15: Huck.........3E **7**
Greet Cl. NG7: Radf 2B **44**
Greetwell Cl. NG8: Bilb...............3G **43**
Gregg Av. DE75: Hea 3D **14**
Gregory, The NG7: Lent 1C **56**
..............................*(off Leen Ct.)*
Gregory Av. NG16: Lang M 2E **15**
Gregory Av. NG3: Mapp 5C **34**
Gregory Av. NG7: Lent 6D **44**
Gregory Blvd. NG7: Hys G 2C **44**
Gregory Cl. NG9: Stfrd 3H **53**
Gregory Ct. NG7: Hys G 1D **44**
Gregory Ct. NG7: Lent 6C **44**
Gregory Ct. NG9: Chil 1B **64**
Gregory St. DE7: Ilk 1A **40**
Gregory St. NG7: Lent 6C **44**
Gregory Street Stop (NET) 1C **56**
Gregson Dr. NG5: Toton..............4B **64**
Gregson Rd. NG9: Chil 2A **64**
Grenay Ct. NG11: Rudd...............5F **67**
Grenfell Ter. NG6: Bas 3C **32**
Grenville Dr. DE7: Ilk..................4B **28**
Grenville Dr. NG2: West Br 4H **57**
Grenville Dr. NG9: Stfrd 3G **53**
Grenville Ri. NG5: Arn.................4B **22**
Grenville Rd. NG9: Bee 1H **65**
Gresham Cl. NG2: West Br..........4H **57**
Gresham Gdns. NG2: West Br 4H **57**
Gresham Gdns. NG5: Woodt........2C **34**
Gresham Pk. Rd. NG2: West Br ...4G **57**
Gresley Dr. NG2: Nott.................6B **46**
Gresley Rd. DE7: Ilk...................6B **28**
Gretton Rd. NG3: Mapp...............3C **34**
Greyfriar Ga. NG1: Nott...6D **4** (6G **45**)
Greyfriars Cl. DE75: Hea 4D **14**
Greyhound St. NG1: Nott ... 4E **5** (5G **45**)
Grey Meadow Rd. DE7: Ilk 5A **28**
Greymede Av. NG8: Stre 5C **30**
Greys Rd. NG5: Woodt................3B **34**
Greystoke Dr. NG8: Bilb..............2C **42**
Greythorn Dr. NG2: West Br........1H **67**
Grierson Av. NG5: Bestw.............5F **21**
Griffiths Way NG15: Huck............5H **7**
Griffon Ct. DE7: Ilk.....................5B **40**
Griffs Hollow NG4: Car 2G **47**
Grimesmoor Rd. NG14: Calv........3A **12**
Grimsby Ter. NG3: Nott ... 1E **5** (3G **45**)
Grimston Rd. NG7: Radf 3C **44**
Grindon Cres. NG6: Bulw.............3A **20**
Grindslow Av. DE7: West H 1C **38**
Grinsbrook NG7: Lent..................5C **44**
Gripps Comn. NG12: Cotg 3F **71**
Grisedale Ct. NG9: Chil 1A **64**
Gritley M. NG2: Nott....................1F **57**
Grizedale Gro. NG13: Bing...........5B **50**
Groome Av. DE75: Los.................1A **14**
Grosvenor Av. DE72: Brea 5B **62**
Grosvenor Av. NG10: Long E 3C **72**
Grosvenor Av. NG3: Mapp P 1G **45**
Grosvenor Ct. NG3: Mapp P.........1G **45**
Grosvenor Rd. NG16: Eastw.........2B **16**
Grove, The DE72: Brea 5B **62**
Grove, The NG14: Calv.................4A **12**

Grove, The NG5: Sher 5F **33**
Grove, The NG7: Radf 3D **44**
Grove Av. NG7: Radf 3E **45**
Grove Av. NG9: Chil 5E **55**
Grove Cl. NG14: Bur J..............2F **37**
Grove Ct. NG9: Chil.............. 5D **54**
Grove M. NG16: Eastw..............4A **16**
Grover Av. NG3: Mapp..............4C **34**
Grove Rd. NG13: Bing..............4F **51**
Grove Rd. NG7: Lent.............. 6D **44**
Groveside Cres. NG11: Clftn........2A **66**
Grove St. NG9: Bee.............. 6G **55**
Grundy St. NG7: Hys G 2C **44**
Guardian Ct. NG8: Aspl..............1A **44**
Guinea Cl. NG16: Eastw..............6C **62**
Gumtree Cl. NG12: Edwal..............4C **68**
Gunn Cl. NG6: Bulw 6G **19**
Gunnersbury Way NG16: Nuth 4D **30**
Gunthorpe Cl. NG5: Sher..............4F **33**
Gunthorpe Dr. NG5: Sher..............4F **33**
Gunthorpe Rd. NG4: Ged..............4E **35**
Gutersloh Ct. NG9: Stfrd.............. 3H **53**
Guy Cl. NG9: Stfrd.............. 5G **53**
Gwenbrook Av. NG9: Chil..............6E **55**
Gwenbrook Rd. NG9: Chil..............6E **55**
Gwndy Gdns. NG5: Bestw..............6E **21**
Gypsum Way NG11: Goth 6G **75**

H

H2 Fitness Nottingham....2E **5** (4G **45**)
Habitat, The NG1: Nott...... 4F **5** (5H **45**)
..............................(off Maiden La.)
Hackworth Cl. NG16: Newth.......... 2D **16**
Hadbury Rd. NG5: Sher 4D **32**
Hadden Cl. NG8: Bilb.............. 4D **42**
Haddon Cl. DE7: West H..............1C **38**
Haddon Cl. DE75: Hea..............3A **14**
Haddon Cl. NG15: Huck.............. 5G **7**
Haddon Cl. NG4: Car..............5F **35**
Haddon Cres. NG9: Chil..............2C **64**
Haddon Nurseries DE7: Ilk..............4A **28**
Haddon Rd. NG2: West Br..............5B **58**
Haddon St. DE7: Ilk 4A **28**
Haddon St. NG5: Sher..............5F **33**
Haddow Way NG10: Long E..............3B **72**
Haddow Way NG12: Rad T.......... 5G **49**
Hadleigh Cl. NG9: Toton 3G **63**
Hadley Cl. NG15: Huck 1A **8**
Hadley St. DE7: Ilk..............4C **40**
Hadrian Gdns. NG5: Top V..............3E **21**
Hadstock Cl. NG10: Sand 1D **62**
Hadston Dr. NG5: Arn..............3B **22**
Hagg La. DE7: D Ab..............4B **38**
Hagg La. DE7: West H..............4B **38**
Hagg La. NG14: Epp 6H **13**
Hagley Cl. NG3: Nott..............3C **46**
Haileybury Cres. NG4: West Br......6B **58**
Haileybury Rd. NG2: West Br..........6B **58**
Haise Ct. NG6: Bulw 2F **31**
Halberton Dr. NG2: West Br 1H **67**
Hales Cl. NG12: Cotg 2E **71**
Halfacre Gdns. DE7: Ilk..............5B **28**
Halfpenny Wlk. NG11: Wilf 5E **57**
Halifax St. NG8: Stre.............. 5D **30**
Halifax Pl. NG1: Nott.....5F **5** (5H **45**)
Halina Ct. NG9: Bee..............4F **55**
Hallam Ct. DE7: Ilk..............4B **28**
HALLAM FIELDS 5C **40**
Hallam Flds. Rd. DE7: Ilk..............5C **40**
Hallam Rd. NG3: Mapp..............5C **34**
Hallam Rd. NG9: Bee..............5F **55**
Hallam's La. NG5: Arn..............6B **22**
Hallams Cl. NG9: Chil..............1C **64**
Hallam Way DE7: West H..............1B **38**
Hallam Way NG16: Lang M..........2G **18**
Hall Cl. NG12: Rad T..............6E **49**
Hall Ct. DE7: West H 2C **38**

Hall Cft. NG9: Bee..............6F **55**
Hallcroft Rd. DE7: Ilk..............1B **40**
Hall Dr. NG10: Sand 5D **52**
Hall Dr. NG11: Goth..............6G **75**
Hall Dr. NG5: Arn..............5C **22**
Hall Dr. NG8: Woll..............6E **43**
Hall Dr. NG9: Chil..............6C **54**
Hall Farm Cl. NG12: Toll 4F **69**
Hall Farm Ct. DE7: Stant D 3B **52**
Hall Farm Ct. NG2: Gam 4E **59**
Hallfields NG12: Edwal 2D **68**
Hall Gdns. NG9: Bram..............4B **54**
Hallington Dr. DE75: Hea..............4B **14**
Hallowell Dr. NG8: Woll..............3F **43**
Hall Pk. Dr. NG16: Eastw..............2A **16**
Hall Rd. NG16: Lang M 1G **15**
Halls La. NG16: Newth..............5C **16**
Halls Rd. NG9: Stfrd..............5F **53**
Hall St. NG5: Sher..............4H **33**
Hall Vw. Dr. NG8: Bilb 3D **42**
Halstead Cl. NG8: Cin 4H **31**
Halstead Cl. NG9: Chil..............1C **64**
Haltham Wlk. NG11: Clftn..........5B **66**
Hambledon Dr. NG8: Woll..............4H **43**
Hambleton Cl. NG10: Long E..........4C **62**
Hambling Cl. NG6: Bulw..............6G **19**
Hamilton, The NG7: Lent..............1C **56**
..............................(off Leen Ct.)
Hamilton Cl. NG5: Arn 4E **23**
Hamilton Cl. NG9: Toton..............3H **63**
Hamilton Cl. NG11: Clftn..............2D **66**
Hamilton Ct. NG7: Nott...... 6B **4** (6F **45**)
Hamilton Dr. NG12: Rad T 5F **49**
Hamilton Ct. NG7: Nott...... 6B **4** (6F **45**)
Hamilton Gdns. NG5: Sher 6F **33**
..............................(off Alexandra St.)
Hamilton Pl. NG2: Nott..............5B **46**
Hamilton Rd. NG10: Long E..........4F **63**
Hamilton Rd. NG5: Sher 1F **45**
Hamlet, The DE75: Hea..............2C **14**
Hammersmith Cl. NG16: Nuth........3E **31**
Hampden Cl. NG16: Nuth 1C **4** (3F **45**)
Hampden Gro. NG9: Bee..............5E **55**
Hampden Rd. NG13: Newt..........2B **50**
Hampden St. NG1: Nott 1C **4** (3F **45**)
Hampden St. NG16: Gilt.............. 5D **16**
Hampden St. NG16: Lang M..........2F **15**
Hampshire Dr. NG10: Sand..........6D **52**
Hampstead Ct. NG5: Sher..............4G **33**
..............................(off St Albans St.)
Hampstead Rd. NG3: Nott..............6A **34**
Hampton Cl. DE7: West H..............1B **38**
Hampton Cl. NG9: Toton..............2G **63**
Hampton Ct. DE75: Hea..............3B **14**
Hampton Rd. NG2: West Br..........5A **58**
Handel St. NG3: Nott..........3H **5** (4A **46**)
Hand's Rd. DE75: Hea 4D **14**
Hankin St. NG15: Huck..............5A **8**
Hanley Av. NG9: Bram 3B **54**
Hanley St. NG1: Nott......3C **4** (4F **45**)
Hannah Cres. NG11: Wilf..............4F **57**
Hanover Ct. NG8: Bilb..............3D **42**
Hanselin Cl. NG4: Ged..............6A **36**
Hanslope Cres. NG8: Bilb 3D **42**
Hanson Cl. NG16: Kimb..............6H **17**
Hanson Cres. NG15: Huck..............4G **7**
Hanworth Gdns. NG5: Arn 5H **21**
Harberton Cl. NG5: Redh..........4A **22**
Harby Dr. NG8: Woll..............5A **44**
Harcourt Cl. DE7: Ilk..............6H **27**
Harcourt Cres. NG16: Nuth..........4F **31**
Harcourt Rd. NG7: Hys G..............1E **45**
Harcourt Rd. NG9: Bee..............5E **55**
Harcourt Ter. NG1: Nott....2G **5** (4H **45**)
Harden Ct. NG11: Clftn..............5A **66**
Hardstaff Almshouses
NG4: Ged..............5G **35**
Hardstaff Homes, The
NG16: Gilt..............5E **17**

Hardstaff Rd. NG2: Nott..............4C **46**
Hardwick Av. DE7: West H..............1C **38**
Hardwick Ct. NG10: Long E..........3B **72**
Hardwicke Rd. NG9: Chil..............2C **64**
Hardwick Gro. NG13: Bing 5D **50**
Hardwick Gro. NG2: West Br..........2B **58**
Hardwick Gro. NG7: Nott..............5E **45**
Hardwick Pl. DE7: Kirk H..............4G **39**
Hardwick Rd. NG5: Sher 4G **33**
Hardwick Rd. NG7: Nott..............6E **45**
Hardwood Cl. NG6: Bulw..............6G **19**
Hardy Barn DE75: Ship..............5E **15**
Hardy Cl. NG10: Long E 1F **73**
Hardy Cl. NG16: Kimb 6H **17**
Hardy's Dr. NG4: Ged..............6H **35**
Hardy St. NG16: Kimb..............6H **17**
Hardy St. NG7: Radf..............3E **45**
Harebell Gdns. NG13: Bing..........5C **50**
Harewood Av. NG6: Bulw 2B **32**
Harewood Cl. NG10: Sand..........1C **62**
Harewood Cl. NG12: Rad T..........6G **49**
Hargreaves Ct. DE7: Ilk 3C **40**
Harkstead Rd. NG5: Top V..............4F **21**
Harlaxton Dr. NG10: Long E..........4A **64**
Harlaxton Dr. NG7: Lent.............. 5D **44**
..............................(not continuous)
Harlaxton Wlk.
NG3: Nott..............1E **5** (3G **45**)
Harlech Cl. DE7: Ilk..............4G **27**
Harlech Ri. NG9: Chil..............1B **64**
HARLEQUIN..............6H **49**
Harlequin Cl. NG12: Rad T..........6H **49**
Harlequin Ct. NG16: Eastw..........2H **15**
Harlequin M. NG12: Rad T..........5H **49**
Harley St. NG7: Lent 6D **44**
Harlow Ct. DE7: West H..............2B **38**
Harlow Gro. NG4: Ged 5G **35**
Harmston Ri. NG5: Sher 3D **32**
..............................(not continuous)
Harnett Cl. NG1: Nott.... 5F **5** (5H **45**)
Harold Av. NG16: Lang M..............1F **15**
Harold Ct. NG2: Nott..............5A **46**
Harold St. NG2: Nott..........4H **5** (5A **46**)
Harpenden Sq. NG8: Cin..............4G **31**
Harpole Wlk. NG5: Arn..............3B **22**
Harrier Gro. NG15: Huck..............1E **19**
Harriett St. NG9: Stfrd 4F **53**
Harrimans Ct. NG7: Lent..............3C **56**
Harrimans Dr. DE72: Brea..........5B **62**
Harrimans La. NG7: Lent..............3C **56**
Harrington Cl. NG4: Ged..............6B **36**
Harrington Dr. NG7: Lent.............. 5D **44**
..............................(not continuous)
Harrington St. NG10: Long E 2D **72**
Harris Cl. NG8: Woll..............4F **43**
Harrison Ct. NG13: Bing..............5C **50**
Harrison Rd. NG9: Stfrd..............3F **53**
Harrison's Plantation
Nature Reserve..............4G **43**
Harris Rd. NG9: Chil..............5D **54**
Harrogate Rd. NG3: Nott..............4E **47**
Harrogate St. NG16: Newth..........2H **47**
Harrowby M. NG7: Lent.............. 5D **44**
Harrowby Rd. NG7: Lent.............. 5D **44**
Harrow Dr. DE7: Ilk..............5A **40**
Harrow Gdns. NG8: Woll..............5A **44**
Harrow Rd. NG15: Huck 6D **6**
Harrow Rd. NG2: West Br..........6A **58**
Harrow Rd. NG8: Woll..............5G **43**
Harry Peel Ct. NG9: Bee 5G **55**
Harry's Ct. NG16: Newth..............1D **16**
Harston Gdns. NG2: West Br 2F **67**
Hart Av. NG10: Sand..............5C **52**
Hartcroft Rd. NG5: Bestw..............1E **33**
Hartford Cl. NG2: Nott..............1H **57**
Hartill Cl. NG9: Chil..............5A **54**
Hartington Av. NG15: Huck..........5C **6**
Hartington Cl. DE7: West H 1C **38**

Hartington Pl. DE7: Ilk..............2A **28**
Hartington Rd. NG5: Sher..............4G **33**
Hartland Dr. NG3: Ged 2G **35**
Hart Lea NG10: Sand
Charles Av.............. 5D **52**
Hart Lea NG10: Sand
Hall Dr.............. 5D **52**
Hartley Ct. NG7: Radf 3D **44**
Hartley Dr. NG9: Bee..............5H **55**
Hartley Rd. NG7: Radf..............3C **44**
Hartness Rd. NG11: Clftn..............4A **66**
Hartshay Cl. DE7: Ilk..............2B **28**
Hartside Cl. NG2: Gam..............4E **59**
Hartside Gdns. NG10: Long E........5C **62**
Hartslade DE75: Hea..............4F **15**
Hart St. NG7: Lent.............. 6D **44**
Hartwell St. NG3: Nott 3H **45**
Hartwood Dr. NG9: Stfrd..............2F **53**
Harvest Cl. NG13: Bing.............. 5D **50**
Harvest Cl. NG5: Top V..............5D **20**
Harvest Cl. NG9: Bee.............. 4H **55**
Harvest Dr. NG12: Cotg..............6G **61**
Harvest Rd. NG16: Eastw..............4C **16**
Harvey Cl. NG11: Rudd..............2H **77**
Harvey Ct. NG7: Nott..............1C **56**
Harvey Cft. NG9: Trow..............5E **41**
Harvey Hadden Sports Village ...2F **43**
Harvey Hadden Stadium..............2F **43**
Harvey Rd. NG7: Nott..............1B **56**
Harvey Rd. NG8: Bilb..............2F **43**
Harviston Av. NG4: Ged..............3F **35**
Harwich Cl. NG6: Bulw..............5G **19**
Harwill Cres. NG8: Aspl..............5H **31**
Harwood Cl. NG5: Arn..............5D **22**
Haslam St. NG7: Nott...... 6C **4** (6F **45**)
Haslemere Rd. NG10: Long E...... 5D **62**
Haslemere Rd. NG8: Aspl..............1B **44**
Hassall Ct. NG13: Bing..............5F **51**
Hassock La. Nth. DE75: Ship........6F **15**
Hassock La. Sth. DE75: Ship........1G **27**
Hassocks Cl. NG9: Bee..............4H **55**
Hassocks La. NG9: Bee..............4H **55**
Hastings St. NG4: Car..............2E **47**
Haswell Rd. NG6: Bulw..............2H **31**
Hatfield Av. NG10: Sand..............1D **62**
Hatfield Dr. NG2: West Br 1G **67**
Hatfield Rd. NG3: Mapp P..........6G **33**
Hatherleigh Cl. NG3: Mapp..........1E **35**
Hathern Cl. NG10: Long E..............2F **73**
Hathern Grn. NG9: Lent A..........3G **55**
Hathersage Av. NG10: Long E........2B **72**
Hathersage Cl. NG5: Top V.......... 5D **20**
Hatley Cl. NG2: Nott..............2F **57**
Hatton Cl. NG5: Arn..............3E **21**
Hatton Crofts NG10: Long E........1E **73**
Hatton Gdns. NG16: Nuth..............4E **31**
Havelock Gdns.
NG3: Nott..............1G **5** (3H **45**)
Havelock St. DE7: Ilk..............2B **40**
Haven Cl. NG2: West Br..............6H **57**
Havenwood Ri. NG11: Clftn..........5B **66**
Haverhill Cres. NG5: Top V..........3B **20**
Haversham Cl. NG6: Bas..............5B **32**
Hawarden Ter. NG7: Hys G 2D **44**
Hawker Cl. NG9: Chil..............6B **54**
Hawkhurst Dr. NG8: Woll.............. 1D **54**
Hawkins Ct. DE7: Ilk..............3B **28**
Hawkridge Gdns.
NG3: Nott..............2G **5** (4A **46**)
..............................(not continuous)
Hawkshead Cl. NG2: West Br........6F **59**
Hawksley Gdns. NG11: Clftn........3A **66**
Hawksley Rd. NG7: Hys G..............2D **44**
Hawkswood Cl. NG9: Chil..............1B **64**
Hawksworth Av. NG5: Sher..............3H **33**
Hawksworth Rd. NG2: West Br......2B **58**
Hawksworth St.
NG3: Nott..............3H **5** (4A **46**)
Hawley Mt. NG5: Sher..............4B **34**

Haworth Ct. NG11: Clftn 4A 66
Hawthorn Av. DE72: Brea..........5B 62
Hawthorn Cl. NG12: Edwal 1D 68
Hawthorn Cl. NG12: Key............. 5G 79
Hawthorn Cl. NG14: Woodbo.........1C 24
Hawthorn Cl. NG2: Nott 2F 57
Hawthorn Cres. NG5: Arn..........4C 22
Hawthorne Av. NG10: Long E 1E 73
Hawthorne Av. NG12: Cotg..........3F 71
Hawthorne Av. NG15: Huck...........4F 7
Hawthorne Gro. NG9: Bee 5H 55
Hawthorne Lodge
    NG2: West Br..................... 2D 58
Hawthorne Ri. NG16: Aws........... 3D 28
Hawthorn Vw. NG2: Nott 1F 57
Hawthorn Wlk. NG3: Nott 2D 46
Hawton Cres. NG8: Woll 5A 44
Hawton Spinney NG8: Woll 5A 44
Hayden La. NG15: Lin.................. 1H 7
Haydn Av. NG5: Sher 5F 33
Haydn Rd. NG5: Sher 5E 33
Haydock Cl. NG16: Kimb 6G 17
Hayes Cl. DE7: West H............. 1C 38
Hayes Rd. NG12: Key.............. 4F 79
Hayles Cl. NG5: Bestw............. 1F 33
Hayley Cl. NG16: Kimb.............. 1F 29
Hayling Cl. DE7: Ilk.................. 4G 27
Hayling Dr. NG8: Bas...............6B 32
Haynes Av. NG9: Trow 4E 41
Haynes Cl. NG11: Clftn 2D 66
Hay's Cl. DE7: Ilk 5H 27
Haywood Ct. NG2: Nott..... 4H 5 (5A 46)
HAYWOOD HOUSE HOSPICE 3F 33
Haywood Rd. NG3: Mapp 5B 34
Haywood St. NG2: Nott...... 4H 5 (5A 46)
Hayworth Rd. NG10: Sand.......... 6D 52
Hazelbank Av. NG3: Nott 6B 34
Hazel Cl. DE75: Hea.................4B 14
Hazel Cl. NG13: Bing................ 5G 51
Hazel Ct. NG2: West Br 2E 59
Hazel Dr. NG16: Nuth.............. 1B 30
Hazel Gro. NG16: Huck 6G 7
Hazel Gro. NG3: Mapp 3C 34
HAZELGROVE 1H 19
Hazel Hill Cres. NG5: Bestw 5F 21
Hazel Hill Pl. NG5: Bestw........... 5F 21
Hazelhurst Gdns. NG6: Bulw 6H 19
Hazel Mdws. NG15: Huck 6G 7
Hazelmere Gro. NG7: Lent 5C 44
Hazel St. NG6: Bulw.................. 5H 19
.... (not continuous)
Hazel Way NG15: Lin 1H 7
Hazelwood NG12: Cotg.............. 2G 71
Hazelwood Cl. NG16: Newth 3D 16
Hazelwood Dr. NG15: Huck 5C 6
Hazelwood Rd. NG7: Hys G 2C 44
Headingley Gdns. NG8: Aspl 1B 44
Healey Cl. NG2: Nott 1G 57
HEANOR 4C 14
Heanor & District
    Heritage Cen. 5D 14
HEANOR GATE 5A 14
Heanor Ga. Ind. Est.
    DE75: Hea..........................4B 14
.... (not continuous)
Heanor Ga. Rd. DE75: Hea..........4A 14
HEANOR MEMORIAL
    HOSPITAL 4D 14
Heanor Retail Pk. 3C 14
Heanor Rd. DE7: Ilk 2H 27
Heanor Rd. DE75: Hea..............4A 14
Heanor Rd. DE75: Los 1A 14
Heanor Small Bus. Cen.
    DE75: Hea..........................5A 14
Heard Cres. NG9: Bee.............. 3F 55
Heath, The NG16: Gilt 5C 16
Heath Cl. NG7: Lent 5D 44

Heathcoat Bldg. NG7: Nott...........2B 56
Heathcoat Ho. NG1: Nott ... 5F 5 (5H 45)
Heathcoat St. NG1: Nott 4F 5 (5H 45)
Heather Cl. NG16: Newth...........4D 16
Heather Cl. NG3: Nott 2H 45
Heather Ct. DE75: Hea...............4F 15
Heather Cres. DE72: Brea..........5B 62
Heather Cft. NG2: West Br 1G 67
Heatherington Gdns.
    NG5: Top V.........................4E 21
Heatherley Dr. NG6: Bas...........3D 32
Heather Ri. NG9: Bram 2E 55
Heather Rd. NG4: Car 6F 35
Heathervale NG2: West Br 5F 57
Heathfield Av. DE7: Ilk..............1C 40
Heathfield Gro. NG9: Chil 2C 64
Heathfield Rd. NG5: Sher 3D 32
Heath Gdns. DE72: Brea............5C 62
Heaton Cl. NG3: Nott 6B 34
Heckington Dr. NG8: Woll..........4H 43
Hedderley Wlk.
    NG3: Nott 1F 5 (3H 45)
Heddington Gdns. NG5: Arn.........5H 21
Hedges Dr. DE7: Ilk..................5B 40
Hedingham Cl. DE7: Ilk 1H 39
Hedley St. NG7: Bas 1E 45
Hedley Vs. NG7: Bas 6E 33
Helen Cl. NG9: Chil 5D 54
Hellebore Cl. NG5: Top V...........6C 20
Helm Cl. NG6: Bulw 6F 19
Helmsdale Cl. NG5: Arn.............4D 22
Helmsdale Gdns. NG5: Top V 4D 20
Helmsley Dr. NG16: Eastw.........2H 15
Helston Dr. NG8: Stre................5D 30
Helvellyn Cl. NG2: Nott 1G 57
Helvellyn Way NG10: Long E......3D 62
Hemingway Cl. NG6: Newth 4E 17
Hemingway Cl. NG4: Car............2E 47
Hemlock Av. NG10: Long E..........4F 63
Hemlock Av. NG9: Stfrd.............3G 53
Hemlock Gdns. NG6: Bulw 1F 31
Hemlock La. DE7: Kirk H 4H 39
Hemlock Rd. NG12: Edwal..........4C 68
Hempshill Barns NG6: Bulw........2E 31
Hempshill La. NG6: Bulw
    Lillington Rd. 1H 31
Hempshill La. NG6: Bulw
    Rochester Ct. 1F 31
HEMPSHILL VALE 2F 31
Hemsby Cl. NG5: Arn................1B 34
Hemsby Gdns. NG6: Bulw 5H 19
.... (not continuous)
Hemscott Cl. NG6: Bulw 5F 19
Hemswell Cl. NG3: Nott 4C 46
Hendon Ct. NG3: Nott 1B 46
Hendon Ri. NG3: Nott...............1B 46
Hendre Gdns. NG5: Top V..........6E 21
Henley Cl. NG4: Neth 3A 48
Henley Gdns. NG9: Stfrd...........2G 53
Henley Ri. NG5: Sher 4E 33
Henley Way DE7: West H............1B 38
Hennessey Cl. NG9: Chil............3C 64
Henning Gdns. NG5: Top V 5E 21
Henrietta St. NG6: Bulw 1A 32
Henry Cl. NG2: Nott 1G 57
Henry Rd. NG2: West Br 3A 58
Henry Rd. NG7: Lent 6D 44
Henry Rd. NG9: Bee 5B 56
Henry St. NG15: Huck................5H 7
Henry St. NG2: Nott 4H 5 (5A 46)
Henry St. NG5: Redh................3A 22
Henshaw Av. DE7: Kirk H 4H 39
Henshaw Pl. DE7: Ilk 3A 28
Hensons Row NG6: Bas............5B 32
Hensons Sq. NG9: Bram 3B 54
.... (not continuous)
Hepple Dr. NG6: Bulw 5F 19
Hepworth Dr. NG16: Gilt 6D 16
Herald Cl. NG9: Bee 4H 55

Herbert Buzzard Ct. NG15: Huck....5A 8
.... (off Hankin St.)
Herbert Rd. NG5: Sher 6E 33
Hereford Rd. NG3: Nott............. 4D 46
Hereford Rd. NG4: Ged 4H 35
Hereford Rd. NG5: Woodt 2A 34
Hermitage Sq. NG2: Nott...........5B 46
Hermitage Wlk. DE7: Ilk 4B 40
Hermitage Wlk.
    NG7: Nott 6A 4 (6E 45)
Hermon St. NG7: Nott 3A 4 (4E 45)
Heron Ct. DE7: Ilk....................5B 40
Heron Cres. NG12: Cotg............6G 61
Heron Dr. NG7: Lent..................5C 44
Herons Cl. NG2: West Br 1E 69
Heron Wharf NG7: Lent 1D 56
Herrywell La. NG12: Owt............6H 71
Hertford M. NG4: Car................1E 47
Hervey Grn. NG11: Clftn 3C 66
Heskey Cl. NG3: Nott 1E 5 (3G 45)
Heskey Wlk. NG3: Nott 1E 5 (3G 45)
Heslington Av. NG8: Bas 1C 44
Hethbeth Ct. NG2: Nott 1G 57
Hethersett Gdns. NG6: Bulw......5H 19
Hetley Rd. NG9: Bee 3F 55
Hexham Av. DE7: Ilk 5C 40
Hexham Cl. NG2: West Br 5C 58
Hexham Gdns. NG5: Top V 3E 21
Heyford Ct. DE75: Hea...............4E 15
Hey St. NG10: Long E................3D 72
Hicking Bldg., The NG2: Nott 6H 45
Hickings La. NG9: Stfrd 3G 53
Hickling Cl. NG10: Long E 2E 73
Hickling Rd. NG3: Mapp 5C 34
Hickling Way NG12: Cotg 4G 71
Hickton Dr. NG9: Chil................4B 64
Highbank Dr. NG11: Clftn 5C 66
Highbury Av. NG6: Bulw 2A 32
Highbury Cl. NG16: Nuth 4D 30
HIGHBURY HOSPITAL 2A 32
Highbury Rd. NG12: Key.............3G 79
Highbury Rd. NG6: Bulw 6A 20
HIGHBURY VALE 2B 32
Highbury Vale Stop (NET)...........3B 32
Highbury Wlk. NG6: Bulw............1A 32
High Chu. St. NG7: Bas..............6D 32
.... (not continuous)
Highclere Dr. NG4: Car 1H 47
Highcliffe Rd. NG3: Nott 4C 46
High Court Dr. NG12: Key 5F 79
Highcroft NG3: Mapp..................3B 34
High Cft. Cl. NG10: Long E..........2G 73
Highcroft Dr. NG8: Woll..............4B 42
High Cross Leys
    NG3: Nott 1E 5 (3G 45)
High Cross St.
    NG1: Nott 3F 5 (4H 45)
Highfield Ct. NG9: Bee................5F 55
Highfield Dr. DE7: Kirk H 4F 39
Highfield Dr. NG16: Nuth 3F 31
Highfield Dr. NG4: Car 2D 46
Highfield Gro. NG2: West Br 4B 58
Highfield Rd. NG12: Key.............3G 79
Highfield Rd. NG16: Nuth 3E 31
Highfield Rd. NG2: West Br 4B 58
Highfield Rd. NG7: Nott 2B 56
Highfield Rd. NG9: Chil...............1A 64
Highfields Ct. NG15: Huck...........5G 7
Highfield St. NG10: Long E.........3E 63
Highgate Cl. NG4: Car 5E 35
Highgate Dr. DE7: Ilk.................4G 27
Highgrove Av. NG9: Chil.............5D 54
Highgrove Gdns. NG12: Edwal 1C 68
High Hazels Cl. NG16: Newth...... 1D 16
High Hazels Dr. NG4: Ged 4G 35
High Hazels Rd. NG12: Cotg........1G 71
High Holborn DE7: Ilk.................4A 28
High Hurst NG14: Calv................4G 11

Highland Ct. NG5: Bas................ 5D 32
High La. Central DE7: West H...... 6D 26
High La. E. DE7: West H..............6E 27
High La. W. DE7: West H.............1A 38
High Leys Rd. NG15: Huck...........5F 7
High Main Dr. NG6: Bestw V........1C 20
High Mdw. NG12: Toll.................4F 69
High Pavement
    NG1: Nott 5F 5 (5H 45)
High Rd. NG9: Bee 5F 55
High Rd. NG9: Chil....................2C 64
High Rd. NG9: Toton 3A 64
High Road / Central College
    Stop (NET) 6E 55
High School Stop (NET) 3E 45
High Spannia NG16: Kimb............6H 17
High St. DE7: Ilk........................1B 40
High St. DE75: Hea 3C 14
High St. NG1: Nott 4E 5 (5G 45)
High St. NG10: Long E................5G 63
High St. NG11: Rudd..................6G 67
High St. NG15: Huck...................4G 7
High St. NG16: Kimb 1H 29
High St. NG5: Arn......................6A 22
High St. NG9: Stfrd....................4G 53
High St. Av. NG5: Arn.................6A 22
High St. Pl. NG1: Nott 4E 5 (5G 45)
Highurst Ct. NG7: Radf 4E 45
Highurst St. NG7: Radf 4E 45
High Vw. Av. NG12: Key..............4H 79
High Vw. Ct. NG3: Mapp P 1H 45
Highwood Av. NG8: Bilb 1F 43
Highwray Gro. NG11: Clftn 4B 66
Hilary Cl. NG8: Woll 6D 42
Hilcot Dr. NG8: Aspl 6H 31
Hillary Pl. DE7: Kirk H................4F 39
Hillbeck Cres. NG8: Woll 5C 42
Hill Cl. NG16: Newth 4E 17
Hill Cl. NG2: West Br 5B 58
Hillcrest Cl. NG16: Want..............6A 18
Hillcrest Dr. NG15: Huck............. 5D 6
Hillcrest Gdns. NG14: Bur J 2E 37
Hillcrest Gro. NG5: Sher 4F 33
Hill Crest Pk. NG5: Calv...............2H 11
Hillcrest Rd. NG12: Key 3G 79
Hillcrest Vw. NG4: Car 6D 34
Hill Dr. NG13: Bing.....................4D 50
Hill Farm Ct. NG12: Edwal...........3C 68
Hillfield Gdns. NG5: Top V 3C 20
Hillfield Rd. NG9: Stfrd 3H 53
Hillgrove Gdns. NG5: Top V 5E 21
.... (off Whitchurch Cl.)
Hilliers Ct. NG5: Top V................ 5D 20
Hillingdon Av. NG16: Nuth 4D 30
Hillingdon Dr. DE7: Ilk 2C 40
Hillington Ri. NG5: Bestw............6G 21
Hill Ri. NG9: Trow 5E 41
Hill Rd. DE75: Hea 4B 14
Hill Rd. NG6: Bestw V 1C 20
Hill Rd. NG9: Chil......................2B 64
Hillsford Cl. NG8: Woll 4G 43
Hill Side NG7: Nott....................6B 44
Hillside NG16: Lang M................2E 15
Hillside Av. NG3: Mapp...............3C 34
Hillside Cres. NG9: Bram............3E 55
Hillside Dr. NG10: Long E 5D 62
Hillside Dr. NG14: Bur J..............2F 37
Hillside Gro. NG10: Sand............5C 52
Hillside Rd. NG12: Rad T.............6G 49
Hillside Rd. NG9: Bram...............2C 54
Hillside Rd. NG9: Chil.................2A 64
Hills Rd. NG5: Woodt 3A 34
Hill Syke NG14: Lowd.................3G 25
HILL TOP 3D 16
Hilltop Ri. NG16: Eastw 3D 16
Hillview Av. NG3: Mapp 5H 33
Hillview Rd. NG4: Car.................6C 34
Hillview Rd. NG9: Toton..............3A 64
Hilton Cl. NG10: Long E.............3B 72

Hilton Ct. NG2: West Br 6D 58
Hilton Cres. NG2: West Br 6D 58
Hilton Rd. NG3: Mapp 5B 34
Hinchin Brook NG7: Lent.............5C 44
Hine Hall NG3: Nott...................6B 34
Hinshelwood Ct. NG11: Ciftn......4A 66
Hinsley Cl. NG5: Arn 5D 22
Hinsley Ct. NG8: Bilb 4C 42
Hirst Cl. NG5: Arn 3H 31
Hirst Ct. NG7: Radf 2A 4 (4E 45)
Hirst Cres. NG8: Woll 5F 43
Hitchen Rd. NG10: Long E 6D 62
HMP Lowdham Grange...............3E 25
HMP Nottingham.......................4F 33
Hobart Cl. NG2: Nott 2G 57
Hobart Dr. NG9: Stfrd................2H 53
Hobben Cres. NG15: Huck............2B 8
Hobson Dr. DE7: Ilk...................3A 40
Hockerwood NG11: Ciftn.............1C 66
Hockley NG1: Nott 4G 5 (5H 45)
Hockley Ho. NG1: Nott........4G 5 (5H 45)
.............................(off Woolpack La.)
Hodgkin Cl. NG11: Ciftn..............4A 66
Hodgkinson St. NG4: Neth 3A 48
Hodson Ho. NG5: Sher 5G 33
Hoefield Cres. NG6: Bulw 1G 31
Hoe Hill Vw. NG12: Toll...............4F 69
Hoewood Rd. NG6: Bulw 6G 19
Hogan Gdns. NG5: Top V 4E 21
Hogarth Rd. NG9: Stfrd..............5G 53
Hogarth St. NG3: Nott................3B 46
Hoggbarn La. DE75: Los............1B 14
Hoggetts Cl. NG9: Chil...............5B 54
Hogg La. NG12: Rad T 6E 49
Hoggs Fld. NG16: Eastw............3B 16
Holbeck Rd. NG15: Huck 2H 7
Holbeck Rd. NG8: Aspl 3A 44
Holborn Av. NG2: Nott...............4B 46
Holborn Cl. NG16: Nuth 4D 30
Holborn Pl. NG6: Bulw 6A 20
Holbrook Ct. NG11: Ciftn 5C 66
Holbrook St. DE75: Hea............3E 15
Holby Cl. NG5: Top V 5D 20
Holcombe Cl. NG8: Aspl 5H 31
Holdale Rd. NG3: Nott................3D 46
Holgate NG11: Ciftn...................3A 66
Holden Ct. NG7: Radf 2A 4 (4E 45)
Holden Cres. NG16: Nuth...........1C 30
Holden Gdns. NG9: Stfrd 5G 53
Holden Rd. NG9: Bee 4E 55
Holden St. NG7: Radf 4E 45
Holgate NG11: Ciftn...................3A 66
Holgate Wlk. NG15: Huck 5E 7
Holkham Av. NG9: Chil...............6C 54
Holkham Cl. DE7: Ilk 4G 27
Holkham Cl. NG5: Arn................1C 34
Holland Cl. NG11: Goth 6H 75
Holland Mdw. NG10: Long E.......2F 73
Holland St. NG7: Hys G..............2D 44
Holles Cres. NG7: Nott.......6A 4 (6E 45)
Hollies, The NG10: Sand.............6C 52
Hollies, The NG16: Eastw 3B 16
Hollies Dr. NG12: Edwal.............1C 68
Hollington Rd. NG8: Bilb.............3G 43
Hollinwell Av. NG8: Woll.............4H 43
Hollins, The NG14: Calv 3A 12
Hollins Ct. NG7: Radf 4D 44
Hollinwell Av. NG8: Woll.............4H 43
Hollinwell Ct. NG12: Edwal.........2D 68
Hollinwood La. NG14: Calv..........4D 10
Hollis St. NG7: Bas 6E 33
Hollows, The NG10: Long E.........5A 64
Hollows, The NG11: Wilf 1E 67
Hollowstone NG1: Nott 5G 5 (5H 45)
Holly Av. DE72: Brea..................4B 62
Holly Av. NG11: Wilf..................3F 67
Holly Av. NG3: Nott...................2C 46
Holly Av. NG4: Car.....................2F 47
Hollybrook Gro. NG16: Want........6B 18

Holly Cl. NG13: Bing 5G 51
Holly Cl. NG15: Huck 6H 7
Holly Copse Nature Reserve......5H 29
Holly Ct. NG3: Nott....................2B 46
Holly Ct. NG9: Bram..................3C 54
Hollycroft NG2: West Br.............1C 68
Hollydale Rd. NG3: Nott.............3D 46
Hollydene Cl. NG15: Huck............6C 6
Hollydene Cres. NG6: Cin 3H 31
Holly Farm Cotts. NG12: Key......6G 79
Holly Farm Ct. NG16: Newth.......4E 17
Holly Gdns. NG3: Nott................2B 46
Hollygate Ind. Pk. NG12: Cotg....1G 71
Hollygate La. NG12: Cotg............2F 71
Hollyhock Cl. NG12: Edwal.........3B 68
Holly La. NG9: Chil.....................6E 55
Holly Leaf Rd. NG15: Huck.........1A 20
Holly Lodge NG2: West Br 2D 58
Holly Rd. NG16: Want.................6H 17
Hollythorpe Pl. NG15: Huck.........6C 6
Holme Cl. NG14: Woodbo.............1D 24
Holme Cft. DE7: West H..............2C 38
Holmefield Cres. DE7: Ilk...........1C 40
Holme Gro. NG2: West Br 1D 58
Holme La. NG12: Hol P 6B 48
Holme La. NG12: Rad T...............3H 59
Holme La. NG12: Rad T...............6B 48
Holme Lea NG10: Sand..............5D 52
Holme Lodge NG4: Car................3G 47
HOLME PIERREPONT 6A 48
Holme Pierrepont Country Pk. 6A 48
Holme Pierrepont Hall 6B 48
Holme Rd. NG13: Bing.................5F 51
Holme Rd. NG2: West Br.............2B 58
Holmes Cl. NG16: Lang M...........2E 15
Holmesfield Dr. DE75: Hea..........5D 14
Holme St. DE75: Hea..................3B 14
Holme St. NG2: Nott..................1A 58
Holmewood Av. DE7: Ilk.............2B 28
Holmewood Cres. NG5: Bestw.....1E 33
Holmewood Rd. NG16: Gilt..........5D 16
Holmfield Rd. NG9: Chil..............2C 64
Holmsfield NG12: Key.................5G 79
Holroyd Av. NG2: Nott................5B 46
Holt Gro. NG14: Calv..................3H 11
Holyoake Dr. NG10: Long E.........6H 63
Holyoake Rd. NG3: Mapp...........4E 35
Holyoake Vs. NG4: Colw.............3H 47
Holyrood Ct. NG9: Bram.............2C 54
Holy Trinity Stop (NET) 5C 66
Holywell Rd. DE7: Ilk.................4G 27
Home Cl. NG5: Arn.....................5H 21
Home Cft., The NG9: Bram..........4B 54
Home Farm Cl. NG11: Goth 6G 75
Homefield Av. NG5: Arn..............3C 22
Homefield Rd. NG8: Aspl............2B 44
Homestead NG16: Lang M...........1E 15
Homewell Wlk. NG11: Ciftn.........2D 66
Honeysuckle Cl. NG8: Brox.........6E 31
Honeysuckle Gro. NG13: Bing......6D 50
Honeysuckle Gro. NG6: Cin.........3H 31
Honeywood Ct. NG3: Nott...........2C 46
Honeywood Dr. NG3: Nott...........2C 46
Honingham Cl. NG5: Arn.............2B 34
Honingham Rd. DE7: Ilk.............4G 27
Honister Cl. NG11: Ciftn.............6B 66
Honister Cl. NG2: Gam................4E 59
Honiton Cl. NG9: Toton...............3A 64
Honiton Rd. NG8: Brox...............6E 31
Hood Cotts. NG5: Sher...............5H 33
Hood St. NG5: Sher...................5H 33
Hook Cl. NG9: Chil.....................3C 64
Hooley Cl. NG10: Long E.............1D 72
Hooley Pl. NG5: Sher.................4H 33
Hoopers Wlk. NG2: Nott..............1G 57
Hooton Rd. NG4: Car..................2E 47
Hooton St. NG3: Nott..................4B 46

Hope Cl. NG2: Nott.....................1F 57
Hopedale Cl. NG7: Radf 4C 44
Hope Dr. NG7: Nott...........6B 4 (6F 45)
Hope St. DE7: Ilk.......................2B 40
Hope St. NG9: Bee.....................4E 55
Hopewell Cl. NG12: Rad T 4G 49
HOPEWOOD.................................3H 33
Hopkin Ct. NG3: Mapp................1E 35
Hopkins Ct. NG16: Eastw............2B 16
Hopkinson Ct. NG6: Bestw V.......2C 20
Hopwood Dr. NG4: Ged................3F 35
Hopwood Rd. NG4: Ged...............4G 35
Horace Av. NG9: Stfrd................4E 53
Horizon Pl. NG8: Stre.................5C 30
Hornbeam Cl. DE7: Ilk................2D 40
Hornbeam Gdns. NG6: Bulw........6F 19
Hornbuckle Ct. NG7: Radf 4D 44
Hornchurch Rd. NG8: Bilb 1D 42
Hornsby Wlk. NG5: Top V............5C 20
Horridge St. DE7: Ilk..................3B 28
Horsecroft Cl. DE7: Ilk...............5G 27
Horsendale Av. NG16: Nuth.........3E 31
Horsham Dr. NG5: Top V.............5D 20
Horsley Cres. NG16: Lang M........2E 15
Horsley La. NG4: Ged.................4G 35
Horwood Dr. NG11: Wilf..............6C 67
Hoselett Fld. Rd. NG10: Long E....2G 73
Hoten Rd. NG2: Nott..................6B 46
Hotspur Cl. NG6: Bas.................2C 32
Hotspur Dr. NG4: Colw...............3G 47
Houghton Av. DE7: Ilk................4G 27
Houghton Cl. NG16: Nuth...........5D 30
Houghton Dr. NG8: Stre..............6C 30
Houldsworth Ri. NG5: Arn...........3A 22
Hound Rd. NG2: West Br.............3C 58
Hounds Ga. NG1: Nott........5C 4 (5G 45)
..................................(not continuous)
Houseman Gdns. NG2: Nott........1G 57
Houston Cl. NG5: Top V..............4C 20
Hovenden Gdns. NG7: Hys G.......2C 44
Hove Rd. NG5: Bestw.................2C 32
Howard Cl. NG10: Long E............4G 63
Howard St. NG1: Nott 2F 5 (4G 45)
Howarth Cl. NG10: Long E...........6C 62
Howbeck Rd. NG5: Arn................4D 22
Howden Rd. NG6: Bulw...............3A 20
Howell Jones Rd. NG9: Chil.........2B 64
Howells Cl. NG5: Arn..................5G 21
Howick Dr. NG6: Bulw.................6F 19
Howieson Cl. NG3: Mapp.............2D 34
Howitt St. NG10: Long E.............6G 63
Howitt St. DE75: Hea..................3D 14
Hoylake Cres. NG8: Bilb.............2D 42
Hoyland Av. NG7: Lent...............1C 56
Hoyle Rd. NG14: Calv.................2H 11
Hubert Ct. NG7: Hys G...............3D 44
Hubert St. NG7: Hys G...............3D 44
Huckerby Rd. DE7: Ilk................4D 26
Huckerbys Fld. NG4: Car.............6E 35
HUCKNALL...................................4G 7
Hucknall Aerodrome (disused)....3E 19
Hucknall By-Pass NG15: Huck......4E 7
Hucknall Cl. NG8: Stre................5D 30
Hucknall Cres. NG4: Ged............1A 48
Hucknall Ind. Pk. NG15: Huck......1F 19
Hucknall La. NG6: Bulw...............5A 20
Hucknall Leisure Cen..................3H 7
Hucknall Park & Ride 4A 8
Hucknall Rd. NG5: Bestw............1C 32
Hucknall Rd. NG5: Sher..............1C 32
Hucknall Rd. NG5: Top V.............1C 32
Hucknall Rd. NG6: Bulw..............4B 20
Hucknall Station (Rail & NET) 4A 8
Hudson St. NG3: Nott.................3B 46
Hudson Way NG12: Rad T............5H 49
Hufton's Ct. DE7: Hea.................6D 14
Hufton's Dr. DE7: Hea.................6D 14
Hugessen Av. NG15: Huck...........3A 8
Huggett Gdns. NG5: Top V..........5E 21

Hughes La. NG4: Ged..................3G 35
Humber Cl. NG2: Nott.................1G 57
Humber Lodge NG9: Bee..............4G 55
Humber Rd. NG10: Long E...........4E 63
Humber Rd. NG9: Bee.................4G 55
..................................(not continuous)
Humber Rd. Sth. NG9: Bee...........5H 55
Humberston Rd. NG8: Woll..........6C 42
HUNGERHILL GARDENS.................2H 45
Hungerhill La. NG14: Woodbo 3H 23
Hungerhill Rd. NG3: Nott............2H 45
Hungerton St. NG7: Lent............6D 44
Hunston Cl. NG8: Bilb.................2G 43
Hunt Av. DE75: Hea....................3C 14
Hunter Cl. NG12: Rad T..............6F 49
Hunter Rd. NG5: Arn..................1E 35
Hunters Cl. NG11: Wilf................5E 57
Hunter St. NG2: Nott..................2H 57
Huntingdon Dr.
  NG7: Nott 5B 4 (5F 45)
Huntingdon St. NG1: Nott...........3G 45
Huntingdon Wlk. NG10: Sand......6D 52
Huntingdon Way NG9: Toton 3H 63
Huntly Cl. NG11: Ciftn................4E 67
Hurcomb St. NG3: Nott...............2B 46
Hurley Cl. DE7: West H...............1C 38
Hurricane Rd. NG15: Huck...........2E 19
Hurst Dr. DE7: Stly.....................3A 38
Hurts Cft. NG9: Chil...................1D 64
Hurt's Yd. NG1: Nott........3D 4 (4G 45)
Hussar Ter. NG2: West Br............2H 67
Huss's La. NG10: Long E.............6H 63
Hutchinson Grn.
  NG3: Nott 1F 5 (3H 45)
Hutton Cl. NG9: Bram.................2D 54
Hutton St. NG2: Nott..................6B 46
Huxley Cl. NG8: Bilb...................2D 42
Hyde Cl. NG11: Ciftn..................1D 66
Hyde Pk. Cl. NG2: West Br...........6B 57
Hyson Cl. NG7: Hys G.................1D 44
HYSON GREEN..............................2D 44
Hyson Green Market
  Stop (NET)...............................2D 44
Hyson St. NG7: Hys G.................2D 44
Ian Gro. NG4: Car.......................1G 47
Ibbinson Ct. NG4: Ged................3F 35

I

Ice Ho., The NG1: Nott......4G 5 (5H 45)
..................................(off Belward St.)
Ikea Way NG16: Gilt....................6E 17
Ilam Sq. DE7: Ilk.......................2A 28
Ilford Cl. DE7: Ilk.......................4H 27
ILKESTON...................................6A 28
ILKESTON COMMUNITY
  HOSPITAL 3H 27
ILKESTON JUNCTION....................6C 28
Ilkeston Rd. DE7: Stant D
  Stanton Ga. 2E 53
Ilkeston Rd. DE7: Stant D
  Twelve Houses...........................6B 40
Ilkeston Rd. DE75: Hea...............4D 14
Ilkeston Rd. NG10: Sand.............3E 53
Ilkeston Rd. NG7: Lent...............4B 44
Ilkeston Rd. NG7: Nott................4B 44
Ilkeston Rd. NG7: Radf................4B 44
Ilkeston Rd. NG9: Bram...............1G 53
Ilkeston Rd. NG9: Stfrd...............1G 53
Ilkeston Rd. NG9: Trow...............4D 40
Ilkeston Station (Rail) 5C 28
Ilkeston Town FC........................4C 28
Imex Ent. Pk. NG15: Huck...........5B 8
Imperial Av. NG4: Car.................6G 35
Imperial Av. NG9: Bee.................5E 55
Imperial Rd. NG6: Bulw...............1B 32
Imperial Rd. NG9: Bee.................5E 55
Incher M. NG4: Car.....................6E 35
Inchwood Cl. NG9: Toton.............3H 63

Incinerator Rd. NG2: Nott............1A **58**
Independent St. NG7: Radf......... 3D **44**
Ingham Gro. NG7: Lent................6C **44**
Ingham Rd. NG10: Long E...........3E **63**
Ingleborough Gdns.
  NG10: Long E........................5C **62**
Ingleby Cl. NG12: Cotg...............3E **71**
Ingleby Cl. NG8: Woll..................5B **42**
Ingleby Rd. NG10: Long E...........3B **72**
Inglefield Rd. DE7: Ilk.................3B **40**
Inglewood Rd. NG11: Clftn..........4C **66**
Ingram Rd. NG6: Bulw.................1A **32**
Ingram Ter. NG6: Bulw.................1B **32**
Inham Cir. NG9: Chil...................5C **54**
Inham Cl. NG9: Chil....................6A **54**
Inham Rd. NG9: Chil...................6A **54**
Inham Road Stop (NET) 6A **54**
Inkerman Cl. DE7: Ilk.................2A **28**
Innes Cl. NG4: Car......................2E **47**
Innovation Pk. NG7: Lent.............5B **44**
Instow Cl. NG3: Ged....................2F **35**
Instow Ri. NG3: Nott..........1G **5** (3H **45**)
Intake Rd. NG12: Key..................4F **79**
Interchange 25 Bus. Pk.
  NG10: Sand.............................1C **62**
intu Broadmarsh Shop.
  Cen.........................5E **5** (5G **45**)
intu Victoria Cen. 2E **5** (4G **45**)
Invaders Cl. NG10: Long E.........5H **63**
Iona Dr. NG9: Trow......................6F **41**
Iona Gdns. NG5: Top V 4E **21**
Ipswich Cir. NG3: Nott................4C **46**
Ireland Av. NG9: Bee...................6G **55**
Ireland Cl. NG9: Bee...................6G **55**
Iremonger Rd. NG2: Nott..............1H **57**
Irene Ter. NG7: Bas....................5D **32**
Ireton Gro. NG9: Atten................3D **64**
Ireton St. NG7: Radf..........2A **4** (4E **45**)
Ireton St. NG9: Bee....................5E **55**
Ironwood Cl. NG12: Edwal...........3C **68**
Irwin Dr. NG6: Bulw.....................2F **31**
Isaac Newton Cen. NG7: Nott......2B **56**
Isaacs La. NG9: Stfrd.................4F **53**
Isabella St. NG1: Nott.........6D **4** (6G **45**)
Isandula Rd. NG7: Bas................5D **32**
Island, The NG16: Eastw..............4B **16**
Island La. NG12: Rad T...............5D **48**
Islay Cl. NG5: Arn......................4B **22**
Islay Cl. NG9: Trow.....................6F **41**
Ivatt Dr. NG2: Nott.....................6B **46**
Ives Cl. NG2: West Br.................1G **67**
Ivy Cl. NG16: Want.....................4H **17**
Ivy Gro. NG4: Car......................2F **47**
Ivy Gro. NG7: Bas......................1E **45**
Ivy La. NG16: Eastw...................3A **16**

J

Jacklin Gdns. NG5: Top V............4E **21**
Jackson Av. DE7: Ilk...................6A **28**
Jackson Av. NG10: Sand.............5C **52**
Jackson Dr. NG5: Bestw..............2E **33**
Jackson Rd. NG15: Huck..............1A **20**
Jacobite Cl. DE75: Hea................5A **14**
Jacoby Cl. NG5: Arn...................6G **21**
Jake Rd. NG9: Bee......................2G **65**
James Dr. NG4: Calv...................2G **11**
James St. NG16: Kimb.................1H **29**
James St. NG5: Arn......................5A **22**
Japonica Dr. NG6: Cin................3H **31**
Jardines, The NG9: Bram.............2C **54**
Jarrow Gdns. NG5: Top V.............3D **20**
Jarvis Av. NG3: Nott...................3D **46**
Jasmine Cl. NG11: Clftn..............4A **66**
Jasmine Cl. NG8: Brox.................6E **31**
Jasmine Cl. NG9: Bram................2D **54**
Jasmine Ct. DE75: Hea................4G **15**
Jasmine Gdns. NG12: Edwal 3B **68**
Jasmine Rd. NG5: Bas.................4C **32**

Jasper Cl. NG12: Rad T 1E **61**
Jayne Cl. NG4: Ged.....................5A **36**
Jayne Cl. NG8: Woll....................3E **43**
Jebb's La. NG13: Bing.................5F **51**
Jedburgh Cl. NG16: Kimb.............6G **17**
Jedburgh Cl. NG3: Nott......1G **5** (3H **45**)
Jedburgh Wlk.
  NG3: Nott.....................1G **5** (3H **45**)
Jeffries Cl. DE7: Ilk....................3H **27**
Jenned Rd. NG5: Arn...................3C **22**
Jenner Ho. NG3: Mapp.................5B **34**
Jenner St. NG5: Sher...................6F **33**
Jenness Av. NG5: Top V...............4C **20**
Jennison St. NG6: Bulw...............6A **20**
Jenny Burton Way NG15: Huck......6A **8**
Jensen Way NG5: Sher................6F **33**
Jermyn Dr. NG5: Arn...................4E **21**
Jersey Gdns. NG3: Nott...............3A **46**
Jervis Cl. DE7: Ilk......................4B **28**
Jesmond Rd. NG6: Bulw...............1B **32**
Jessamine Ct. NG9: Bee..............5G **55**
Jesse Boot Av. NG7: Nott.............2B **56**
Jessops La. NG4: Ged.................4H **35**
Jewitt Way NG11: Rudd................6F **67**
Jill-Iain Ct. NG9: Stfrd................5G **53**
Joan Av. DE75: Hea....................3C **14**
John & Eliza Jelley Homes
  NG7: Nott.................................6B **44**
John Carroll Ct. NG3: Nott...........3B **46**
John Carroll Leisure Cen. 4D **44**
John Quinn Ct. NG7: Bas.............6D **32**
Johnson Av. NG15: Huck..............6H **7**
Johnson Cl. NG16: Want...............6A **18**
Johnson Dr. DE75: Hea................3D **14**
Johnson Rd. NG7: Lent................5C **44**
Johnson Way NG9: Chil................3B **64**
John's Pl. DE75: Hea....................4B **14**
Johnson Rd. NG12: Rad T.............6A **49**
Johns Rd. NG9: Bee...................2G **65**
Johnstone Way NG6: Bestw V......5F **9**
John St. DE7: Ilk........................6B **28**
John St. DE75: Hea....................3B **14**
John St. NG7: Bas......................6D **32**
John Wright Cl. NG6: Bulw...........4B **20**
Joseph Ct. DE7: Ilk.....................4A **28**
Joshua Bus. Pk. NG16: Lang M...2G **15**
Joyce Av. NG5: Sher...................3H **33**
Joyce Av. NG9: Toton..................2H **63**
Joyce Cl. NG5: Sher...................3H **33**
Jubilee Cl. DE7: West H...............1A **38**
Jubilee Ct. NG15: Huck...............6E **7**
Jubilee Ct. NG8: Stre..................6D **30**
Jubilee Rd. NG5: Arn...................1A **34**
Jubilee St. NG16: Kimb................6G **17**
Jubilee St. NG2: Nott..................5B **46**
Judes Cl. NG3: Mapp...................5A **34**
Judson Av. NG9: Stfrd.................5H **53**
Julian Cl. DE7: Ilk......................3D **40**
Julian Rd. NG2: West Br..............3D **58**
Julie Av. DE75: Hea....................4E **15**
Julius Cl. NG16: Lang M..............1F **15**
Jumelles Dr. NG14: Calv..............4F **11**
Junction, The NG15: Huck............4H **7**
Junction Rd. NG10: Long E..........1A **74**
Jungletastic Play Cen. 3F **31**
Juniper Cl. NG11: Clftn...............4A **66**
Juniper Cl. NG16: Gilt..................5E **17**
Juniper Ct. NG7: Radf.................3E **45**
.........................(off Waterloo Prom.)
Juniper Gdns. NG13: Bing............5G **51**
Justice Cen. Nottingham 6E **5** (6G **45**)
Justnian Cl. NG15: Huck..............3A **8**

K

Kappler Cl. NG4: Neth.................2A **48**
Kapwood Cl. NG7: Radf...............4D **44**
Karen Gdns. NG9: Chil.................1D **64**
Karen Ri. NG5: Arn.....................4C **22**

Katherine Dr. NG9: Toton.............1H **63**
Kayes Ct. NG9: Stfrd..................4F **53**
Kayes Wlk. NG1: Nott....5F **5** (5H **45**)
Kay's Mdw. NG9: Bee..................4G **55**
Keats Cl. NG10: Long E...............2D **72**
Keats Cl. NG6: Nuth....................1B **30**
Keats Cl. NG5: Arn......................6H **21**
Keats Dr. NG15: Huck..................5D **6**
Keble Cl. DE75: Hea....................5C **14**
Kedleston Cl. NG10: Long E.........2C **72**
Kedleston Cl. NG9: Chil...............6C **54**
Kedleston Dr. DE7: Ilk.................4H **27**
Kedleston Dr. DE75: Hea.............3A **14**
Kedleston Dr. Sth. DE7: Ilk..........4A **28**
Keeling Cl. NG16: Newth..............4D **16**
Keepers Cl. NG6: Bestw V...........1C **20**
Keighton Dr. NG7: Nott................2A **56**
Kelfield Cl. NG6: Bulw.................2C **32**
Kelham Dr. NG5: Sher.................5E **33**
Kelham Grn. NG3: Nott................3B **46**
Kelham M. NG3: Nott...................1D **46**
Kelham Way NG16: Eastw.............2A **16**
Kelling Cl. NG5: Bestw................1E **33**
Kelly Wlk. NG11: Wilf...................4F **57**
Kelsey Cl. NG9: Atten.................2E **65**
Kelso Gdns. NG2: Nott................1F **57**
Kelstern Cl. NG8: Cin.................4H **31**
Kelvedon Gdns.
  NG3: Nott.....................1H **5** (3A **46**)
Kelvin Cl. NG9: Stfrd..................6E **53**
Kelvin Rd. NG3: Nott..................2C **46**
Kemmel Rd. NG6: Bulw................2B **32**
Kempsey Cl. NG5: Top V..............5C **20**
Kempson St. NG11: Rudd.............6G **67**
Kempton Cl. NG16: Kimb..............6G **17**
Kempton Dr. NG5: Arn.................4C **22**
Kenbrook Rd. NG15: Huck............2A **8**
Kenbrook Rd. NG15: Pap..............2A **8**
Kendal Cl. NG15: Huck.................3F **7**
Kendal Ct. NG2: West Br..............3D **58**
Kendal Dr. NG9: Bram.................3D **54**
Kendale Gro. NG3: Nott................6B **34**
Kendrew Ct. NG11: Clftn..............4A **66**
Kenia Cl. NG4: Car.....................1F **47**
Kenilworth Ct.
  NG7: Nott.......................6B **4** (6F **45**)
Kenilworth Cl. NG9: Bee...............3G **55**
Kenilworth Dr. DE7: Kirk H............4G **39**
Kenilworth Rd.
  NG7: Nott.......................6B **4** (6F **45**)
Kenilworth Rd. NG9: Bee..............4G **55**
Ken Martin Leisure Cen. 4A **20**
Kenmore Gdns.
  NG3: Nott.....................1G **5** (3H **45**)
Kennedy Av. NG10: Long E...........2E **73**
Kennedy Cl. NG5: Arn..................6H **21**
Kennedy Dr. NG9: Stfrd...............2G **53**
Kenneth Rd. NG5: Arn.................3B **22**
Kennington Rd. NG8: Radf............4B **44**
Kenny Av. NG11: Wilf...................6E **57**
Ken Reid Gdns. 5A **20**
.........................(off Ragdale Rd.)
Kenrick Rd. NG3: Mapp................6C **34**
Kenrick St. NG4: Neth..................2A **48**
Kensal Ct. NG2: West Br..............3A **58**
Kensington Av. DE75: Hea............4A **14**
Kensington Cl. NG9: Toton............4A **64**
Kensington Ct. NG5: Sher.............4G **33**
.........................(off St Albans St.)
Kensington Gdns. DE7: Ilk...........2C **40**
Kensington Gdns. NG4: Car..........2G **47**
Kensington Pk. Cl.
  NG2: West Br...........................6G **57**
Kensington Rd. NG10: Sand.........1C **62**
Kensington St. DE7: Ilk...............3B **40**
Kenslow Av. NG7: Hys G..............2C **44**
Kent Av. NG9: Bee......................1F **65**
Kentmere Cl. NG2: Gam...............4E **59**
Kenton Av. NG16: Nuth.................4D **30**

Kenton Ct. NG2: Nott..................2H **57**
Kent Rd. NG16: Gilt....................4E **17**
Kent Rd. NG3: Mapp...................5B **34**
Kent St. NG1: Nott........3F **5** (4H **45**)
Kentwood Rd. NG2: Nott..............5B **46**
Kenyon Rd. NG7: Lent.................6B **44**
Keppel Ct. DE7: Ilk....................4B **28**
Kersall Ct. NG6: Bulw..................2B **32**
Kersall Dr. NG6: Bulw..................2B **32**
Kersall Gdns. NG15: Huck............4H **7**
Kestrel Cl. DE7: Ilk.....................5B **40**
Kestrel Cl. NG4: Car...................6D **34**
Kestrel Dr. NG13: Bing................6F **51**
Kestrel Gro. NG15: Huck..............5F **7**
Keswick Cl. DE7: Kirk H...............4H **39**
Keswick Cl. NG2: Gam.................4E **59**
Keswick Cl. NG9: Bram................3D **54**
Keswick Cl. NG10: Long E............3D **52**
Keswick Cl. NG2: Nott.......4H **5** (5A **46**)
Keswick St. NG2: Nott.......4H **5** (5A **46**)
Ketton Cl. NG5: Bestw.................5F **21**
Kett St. NG6: Bulw.....................6H **19**
Keverne Cl. NG8: Aspl.................5A **32**
.........................(not continuous)
Kevin Rd. NG8: Woll...................1D **54**
Kew Cl. NG2: West Br.................2G **67**
Kew Cres. DE75: Hea..................4F **15**
Kew Gdns. NG16: Nuth.................4E **31**
Key VI Fitness 5G **79**
Keys Cl. NG6: Bulw....................6G **19**
Key St. NG3: Nott.......................4B **46**
KEYWORTH 5G **79**
Keyworth La. NG11: Bunny............6B **78**
Keyworth Leisure Cen. 4H **79**
Keyworth Rd. NG4: Ged...............4F **35**
Kibworth Cl. NG5: Sher...............3D **32**
Kiddier Av. NG5: Arn...................6D **22**
Kidley Cl. DE7: Hea....................5A **14**
Kidley Cl. DE7: Smal..................5A **14**
Kielder Dr. NG13: Bing................5C **50**
Kilbourne Rd. NG5: Arn................4D **22**
Kilburn St. NG3: Nott..................3G **45**
Kilburn Cl. NG9: Bram.................1B **54**
Kilburn Dr. DE7: Ilk....................4H **27**
Kilby Av. NG3: Nott....................3C **46**
Kilby Ho. NG10: Long E...............6F **63**
Kildare Rd. NG3: Nott..................1B **46**
Kildonan Cl. NG8: Stre................5D **30**
Killarney Pk. NG6: Bestw V..........5F **9**
Killerton Grn. NG11: Clftn............6D **66**
Killerton Pk. Dr.
  NG2: West Br...........................1F **67**
Killisick La. NG5: Arn..................3D **22**
Killisick Rd. NG5: Arn..................5D **22**
Kilnbrook Av. NG5: Arn................4D **22**
Kiln Cl. DE7: West H...................4D **22**
Kiln Pl. NG6: Bulw......................1G **31**
Kilnwood Cl. NG3: Nott................2C **46**
Kilsby Rd. NG11: Clftn.................3D **66**
Kilverston Rd. NG10: Sand...........5C **52**
Kilverton Cl. NG8: Woll................5A **44**
Kilvington Rd. NG5: Arn...............6D **22**
Kimber Cl. NG8: Bilb..................3D **42**
KIMBERLEY 1H **29**
Kimberley Cl. NG16: Kimb............2H **29**
Kimberley Eastwood By-Pass
  NG16: Eastw............................3H **15**
Kimberley Leisure Cen. 1A **30**
Kimberley Rd. NG16: Nuth............2B **30**
Kimberley St. NG2: Nott..............5C **46**
Kimbolton Av. NG7: Lent..............4D **44**
Kimbolton Av. NG7: Radf..............4D **44**
Kinchin Dr. NG9: Toton................3B **64**
King Charles St.
  NG1: Nott.......................5C **4** (5F **45**)
King Edward Ct.
  NG1: Nott.......................3F **5** (4H **45**)
King Edward Gdns.
  NG10: Sand.............................5D **52**

King Edward St.
NG1: Nott 3F **5** (4H **45**)
King Edward St. NG10: Sand 5D **52**
King Edward St. NG15: Huck 5G **7**
Kingfisher Cl. NG6: Bas 3B **32**
Kingfisher Cl. NG9: Bee...............6H **55**
Kingfisher Dr. NG12: Cotg 1G **71**
Kingfisher Rd. NG4: Neth 2C **48**
Kingfisher Rd. NG4: Stoke B 2C **48**
Kingfishers Ct. NG2: West Br 1E **69**
Kingfisher Wharf NG7: Lent 1E **57**
King George Av. DE7: Ilk 1A **40**
King John's Arc.
NG1: Nott 4E **5** (5G **45**)
.... (off Bridlesmith Ga.)
King John's Chambers
NG1: Nott 4E **5** (5G **45**)
.... (off Bridlesmith Ga.)
Kinglake Pl. NG2: Nott................. 1G **57**
Kingrove Av. NG9: Chil 5D **54**
Kings Av. NG4: Ged....................5G **35**
Kingsbridge Av. NG3: Mapp 1E **35**
Kingsbridge Way NG9: Bram....5C **54**
Kingsbury Dr. NG8: Bilb..............1G **43**
Kings Cl. DE75: Hea...................4A **14**
Kingsdale Cl. NG9: Chil 2C **72**
Kingsdown Mt. NG8: Woll 1E **55**
Kingsford Av. NG7: Radf............3C **44**
Kingsley Cres. NG10: Long E..... 3D **72**
Kingsley Dr. NG4: Neth...............3A **48**
Kingsley Rd. NG2: Nott...............5C **46**
Kingsmead Av. NG9: Trow.........1F **53**
Kingsmoor Cl. NG5: Top V 6C **20**
King's Pl. NG1: Nott............ 4F **5** (5H **45**)
Kings Rd. NG10: Sand 5D **52**
Kingsthorpe Cl. NG3: Nott 6B **34**
Kingston Av. DE7: Ilk 5C **40**
Kingston Ct. DE7: West H..........1B **38**
Kingston Ct. NG12: Rad T..........6F **49**
.... (off Bingham Rd.)
Kingston Ct. NG2: Nott 4H **5** (5A **46**)
Kingston Dr. NG12: Cotg...........4F **71**
Kingston Rd. NG2: West Br..........5A **58**
King St. DE7: Ilk.......................6B **28**
King St. NG1: Nott...............3D **4** (5G **45**)
King St. NG10: Long E 5F **63**
King St. NG10: Eastw................3B **16**
King St. NG9: Bee 5G **55**
Kings Wlk. NG1: Nott............3D **4** (4G **45**)
Kingsway DE7: Ilk.....................4B **40**
Kingsway DE75: Hea.................3B **14**
Kingsway NG12: Rad T..............1E **61**
Kingsway Gdns. NG15: Huck 1E **19**
Kingsway Rd. NG15: Huck 1E **19**
Kingswell Av. NG5: Arn 6B **22**
Kingswell Rd. NG5: Arn.............6B **22**
Kingswood Cl. NG2: West Br......6H **57**
Kingswood Rd. NG2: West Br 6H **57**
Kingswood Rd. NG8: Woll 4H **43**
Kinlet Rd. NG5: Bestw................1E **33**
KINOULTON WOLDS 6H **81**
Kinross Cres. NG8: Bilb 3G **43**
Kinsale Wlk. NG11: Clftn 3C **66**
Kipling Cl. NG11: Clftn...............5A **66**
Kipps St. NG1: Nott............. 3F **5** (4H **45**)
Kirby Cl. NG16: Newth................2C **16**
Kirby Rd. NG16: Newth................2C **16**
Kirkbride Ct. NG9: Chil................1B **64**
Kirkby Av. DE7: Ilk 3B **40**
Kirkby Gdns. NG2: Nott 1H **57**
Kirk Cl. NG9: Chil 1D **64**
Kirkdale Cl. NG8: Woll 5B **42**
Kirkdale Gdns. NG10: Long E...... 1D **72**
Kirkdale Rd. NG10: Long E........... 2D **72**
Kirkdale Rd. NG3: Nott 3D **46**
Kirkewhite Ct. NG2: Nott 1H **57**
Kirkewhite St. W. NG2: Nott 1G **57**
Kirkewhite Wlk. NG2: Nott 1G **57**
Kirkfell Cl. NG2: West Br 6E **59**

Kirkfield Dr. DE72: Brea 5A **62**
KIRK HALLAM.............................4H **39**
Kirkham Cl. DE75: Hea...............4B **14**
Kirkham Dr. NG9: Toton..............3H **63**
Kirkhill NG13: Bing 4E **51**
Kirkland Dr. NG9: Chil................3C **64**
Kirk La. NG11: Rudd...................6G **67**
Kirkley Dr. DE75: Hea 4A **14**
Kirkley Gdns. NG5: Arn...............5C **22**
Kirkman Rd. DE75: Los 1A **14**
Kirk Rd. NG3: Mapp....................5C **34**
Kirk's Bldgs. NG4: Car................2F **47**
Kirkstead Gdns. NG7: Hys G....... 2D **44**
Kirkstead St. NG7: Hys G 2D **44**
Kirkstone Av. DE75: Hea 4F **15**
Kirkstone Cl. NG10: Long E......... 3D **62**
Kirkstone Dr. NG2: Gam 4E **59**
Kirkwhite Av. NG10: Long E.........6F **63**
Kirkwhite Ho. NG10: Long E.........6F **63**
.... (off Kirkwhite Av.)
Kirtle Cl. NG8: Aspl 1H **43**
Kirtley Cl. NG16: Want.................5A **18**
Kirtley Dr. NG7: Lent...................1E **57**
Kirtling Cl. NG5: Bestw...............5G **21**
Kirton Av. NG10: Long E 6F **63**
Kittiwake Md. NG7: Lent 5C **44**
Kiwi Cl. NG15: Huck 6D **6**
KK Sports & Leisure Cen. 3C **46**
Knapp Av. NG16: Newth...............4B **16**
Kneesall Gro. NG15: Huck 4H **7**
Kneeton Cl. NG4: Ged 3F **35**
Kneeton Cl. NG5: Sher 3G **33**
Kneeton Va. NG5: Sher 3G **33**
Knighton Av. NG7: Radf...............3C **44**
Knighton Rd. NG5: Woodt............2H **33**
Knightsbridge Ct. NG5: Sher 4G **33**
.... (off St Albans St.)
Knightsbridge Dr.
NG2: West Br.............................. 1G **67**
Knightsbridge Gdns.
NG15: Huck 1F **7**
Knightsbridge Way NG15: Huck....2F **7**
Knight's Cl. NG2: West Br 2G **67**
Knights Cl. NG5: Top V 5D **20**
Knights Cl. NG9: Toton 3H **63**
Knights Ct. NG4: Neth 3H **47**
Knightsyard Ct. NG10: Long E.......2E **73**
Knightwood Dr. NG6: Bestw V......6F **9**
Kniveton Pk. DE7: Ilk 2H **27**
Knole Rd. NG8: Woll 4E **43**
Knoll Av. NG15: Huck 6D **6**
Knowle Hill NG16: Kimb 2A **30**
Knowle La. NG16: Kimb 3A **30**
Knowle Pk. NG16: Kimb 2A **30**
Knowles Wlk. NG5: Arn 5H **21**
Kozi Kots NG4: Neth 2H **47**
Krebs Cl. NG11: Clftn...................4A **66**
Kyle Vw. NG15: Top V 4E **21**
Kyme St. NG7: Radf 4D **44**
Kynance Gdns. NG11: Wilf 6F **57**
Kyte St. NG7: Lent 5D **44**

L

Labray Rd. NG14: Calv 3G **11**
Laburnum Av. NG12: Key 5A **80**
Laburnum Cl. NG10: Sand...........4D **52**
Laburnum Gdns. NG6: Bulw.........2C **32**
Laburnum Gro. NG15: Huck 6H **7**
Laburnum St. NG9: Bee 6H **55**
Laburnum St. NG3: Nott 2H **45**
Lace Cl. NG10: Long E 4E **63**
LACE MARKET.....................5F **5** (5H **45**)
Lace Mkt. Sq. NG1: Nott...... 4F **5** (5H **45**)
.... (off Warser Ga.)
Lace Market Stop (NET) 4E **5** (5G **45**)
Lace Market Theatre 5F **5** (5H **45**)
Lace Mill Ct. NG6: Bas 4B **32**

Lace Rd. NG9: Bee.....................4F **55**
Lace St. NG7: Lent......................2B **56**
Lace St. NG7: Nott......................2B **56**
Lace Way NG1: Nott............5H **5** (5A **46**)
Lacewood Cl. NG6: Bestw V 1B **20**
Lacey Av. NG15: Huck 6F **7**
Lacey Cl. DE7: Ilk.......................4G **27**
Laceyfields Rd. DE75: Hea...........4E **15**
Ladbrooke Cres. NG6: Bas...........4A **32**
Ladybank Ri. NG5: Arn................5E **23**
Lady Bay Av. NG2: West Br...........2B **58**
Lady Bay Bri. NG2: Nott 1A **58**
Lady Bay Bri. NG2: West Br...........1A **58**
Lady Bay Ct. NG2: West Br 2C **58**
Lady Bay Rd. NG2: West Br...........2C **58**
Ladybay Workshops
NG2: West Br..............................2B **58**
.... (off Lady Bay Av.)
Ladybridge Cl. NG9: Atten...........2E **65**
Ladycroft Av. NG15: Huck 4G **7**
Ladylea Rd. NG10: Long E............3C **72**
Ladysmith St. NG2: Nott..............5C **46**
Ladysmock Gdns. NG2: Nott 1H **57**
Ladywood Rd. DE7: D Ab 4F **39**
Ladywood Rd. DE7: Kirk H 4F **39**
Lake Av. DE75: Los.....................1A **14**
Lake Gdns. DE75: Los................1A **14**
Lakehead Ho. NG11: Clftn...........4C **66**
Lakeland Av. DE75: Los...............6A **8**
Lakeland Rd. NG14: Calv.............5C **12**
Lakeside Av. NG10: Long E 3E **73**
Lakeside Bus. Cen. DE75: Ship.....1E **27**
Lakeside Cres. NG10: Long E 2E **73**
Lake St. NG7: Radf 3D **44**
Lamartine St. NG3: Nott.....2G **5** (4H **45**)
Lamb Cl. DE7: Ilk.......................1A **28**
Lamb Cl. Dr. NG16: Eastw...........1C **16**
Lamb Cl. Dr. NG16: Newth...........1C **16**
Lambert Gdns. NG8: Aspl 1A **44**
Lambert Hill NG15: Huck 4F **7**
Lambert St. NG7: Hys G 2C **44**
Lambeth Ct. NG9: Bee.................4H **55**
Lambeth Rd. NG5: Arn.................3E **21**
Lambie Cl. NG8: Woll 4A **44**
LAMBLEY 6C **24**
Lambley Almshouses
NG3: Nott 1H **45**
Lambley Av. NG3: Mapp 4D **34**
Lambley Bridle Rd.
NG14: Bur J 1D **36**
Lambley Cl. NG3: Mapp................4B **34**
Lambley La. NG14: Bur J 2D **36**
Lambley La. NG4: Ged................. 2D **36**
Lambley Rd. NG14: Lowd.............5G **25**
Lambourne Cl. NG9: Bram............3C **54**
Lambourne Dr. NG8: Woll 4F **43**
Lambourne Gdns. NG5: Woodt......2C **34**
Lambton Cl. DE7: Ilk...................4A **28**
Lamcote Gdns. NG12: Rad T 2E **49**
Lamcote Gro. NG2: Nott 2H **57**
Lamcote M. NG12: Rad T 2E **49**
Lamcote St. NG2: Nott 2H **57**
Laming Gap La. NG12: Cotg..........3C **80**
Laming Gap La. NG12: Stant W......3C **80**
Lamins La. NG6: Bestw V..............6F **9**
Lammas St. NG2: Nott.................1H **57**
Lamorna Gro. NG11: Wilf.............5F **57**
Lamplands NG12: Cotg................2E **71**
Lamp Wood Cl. NG14: Calv 4G **11**
Lanark Cl. NG8: Woll 6A **44**
Lancaster Av. NG10: Sand...........1C **62**
Lancaster Av. NG9: Stfrd.............5G **53**
Lancaster Ct. NG3: Nott............... 2D **46**
Lancaster Rd. NG15: Huck 1D **18**
Lancaster Rd. NG6: Bestw V 1C **20**
Lancaster Way NG8: Stre 5D **30**
Lancelot Dr. NG16: Want..............4H **17**
Lancelyn Gdns. NG2: West Br 1A **68**
Landcroft Cres. NG5: Bestw..........1E **33**

Landmere Cl. DE7: Ilk.................. 4G **27**
Landmere Gdns. NG3: Nott 6B **34**
Landmere La. NG11: Rudd 3H **67**
Landmere La. NG12: Edwal...........4B **68**
Landmere La. NG2: West Br...........2F **67**
Landsdown Gro. NG10: Long E 4H **63**
Landseer Cl. NG7: Radf...............3C **44**
Lane, The NG16: Aws..................3E **29**
Laneham Av. NG5: Arn.................6C **22**
Laneside Av. NG9: Toton............. 3G **63**
Laneward Cl. DE7: Ilk.................. 3H **27**
Langar Cl. NG5: Sher 3G **33**
Langar Rd. NG13: Bing 6E **51**
Langbank Av. NG5: Top V.............4C **20**
Langdale Dr. NG10: Long E 1C **72**
Langdale Gro. NG13: Bing............5B **50**
Langdale Rd. NG3: Nott 4D **46**
Langdon Cl. NG10: Long E............6C **62**
Langdon Dr. NG5: Sher 5E **33**
Langdown Cl. NG6: Bulw.............5G **19**
Langen St. NG10: Long E 1G **73**
Langford Rd. NG5: Arn................ 6D **22**
Langham Av. NG3: Nott 3C **46**
Langham Dr. NG14: Bur J.............2F **37**
Langham Pk. DE7: Stant D 2D **52**
LANGLEY 4F **15**
Langley Av. DE7: Ilk....................2H **27**
Langley Av. NG5: Arn...................1B **34**
Langley Bri. Ind. Est.
NG16: Eastw 2H **15**
Langley Bus. Pk.
NG16: Lang M 3F **15**
Langley Cl. NG6: Bestw V.............1C **20**
Langley Farm Cl. DE75: Hea 4F **15**
LANGLEY MILL 2G **15**
Langley Mill By-Pass
NG16: Lang M 1E **15**
Langley Mill Station (Rail) 2F **15**
Langley Pk. NG16: Lang M............2F **15**
Langstrath Dr. NG2: West Br 1E **69**
Langstrath Rd. NG11: Clftn 4C **66**
Langton Rd. NG4: Colw................ 3G **47**
Langtry Gdns. NG13: Bing............4F **51**
Langtry Gro. NG7: Bas.................6E **33**
Langwith Cl. DE7: Ilk...................2B **28**
Lansdown Cl. NG9: Chil...............1B **64**
Lansdowne Dr. NG2: West Br 1H **67**
Lansdowne Rd. NG6: Bas.............3C **32**
Lansing Cl. NG11: Clftn 5D **66**
Lanthwaite Cl. NG11: Clftn............4C **66**
Lanthwaite Rd. NG11: Clftn 4D **66**
Lapford Cl. NG3: Mapp................1F **35**
Lapins Cl. NG8: Aspl 5G **31**
Larch Cl. NG13: Bing 5G **51**
Larch Cl. NG15: Huck 6H **7**
Larch Cl. NG2: West Br 2E **59**
Larch Cl. NG5: Arn......................5G **21**
Larch Cres. NG16: Eastw............3A **16**
Larch Cres. NG9: Bee 4E **55**
Larchdene Av. NG8: Woll 6D **42**
Larch Dr. NG10: Sand 4D **52**
Larch Gdns. NG6: Bulw 6G **19**
Larch Ho. NG5: Sher 4H **33**
Larch Way NG12: Key..................5A **80**
Largs Cl. NG5: Top V 3C **20**
Lark Cl. NG9: Chil 6F **55**
Larkdale St. NG7: Radf...... 1A **4** (3E **45**)
Larkfield Rd. NG16: Nuth 2B **30**
LARKFIELDS 2B **30**
Lark Hill Village NG11: Clftn..........5A **66**
LARKLANDS 2C **40**
Larkland's Av. DE7: Ilk.................2C **40**
Larkspur Av. NG5: Redh 3A **22**
Larkwood Cl. NG8: Bilb 1G **43**
Larkwood Gro. NG5: Sher 3G **33**
Lascelles Av. NG4: Ged................5F **35**
Latham St. NG6: Bulw 6H **19**
Lathkill Av. DE7: Ilk.....................2A **28**

Lathkill Cl. – Lit. Oakwood Dr.

Lathkill Cl. DE7: West H 1C 38
Lathkill Cl. NG6: Bulw 6H 19
Lathkilldale Cres.
NG10: Long E 2C 72
Latimer Cl. NG6: Bulw 1A 32
Latimer Dr. NG9: Bram 6B 42
Latin Gro. NG15: Huck 3A 8
Laughton Av. NG2: West Br 1G 67
Laughton Cres. NG15: Huck 1E 19
Launceston Cres. NG11: Wilf 1E 67
Launder St. NG2: Nott 1G 57
Laurel Av. NG12: Key 5H 79
Laurel Cres. NG10: Long E 1E 73
Laurel Cres. NG16: Nuth 6B 18
Laurel Rd. NG4: Car 1F 47
Lauren Gro. NG9: Toton 3H 63
Laurie Av. NG7: Hys G 1E 45
Laurie Cl. NG7: Hys G 1E 45
Lauriston Dr. NG6: Bulw 3B 32
Lavelle Ct. NG9: Chil 3C 64
Lavender Cl. NG8: Brox 6E 31
Lavender Cres. NG4: Car 6F 35
Lavender Gdns. DE75: Hea 4F 15
Lavender Gro. NG12: Cotg 6G 61
Lavender Gro. NG9: Bee 6H 55
Lavender Wlk. NG3: Nott 2H 45
Laver Cl. NG5: Arn 6D 22
Laverock Cl. NG16: Kimb 1H 29
Lavinia Cres. NG12: Edwal 3C 68
Lawdon Rd. NG5: Arn 4C 22
Lawley Av. NG9: Lent A 2G 55
Lawn Cl. DE75: Hea 3D 14
Lawn Gro. NG4: Car 6A 36
Lawn Gro. NG4: Ged 6A 36
Lawn Mill Rd. NG16: Kimb 6G 17
Lawn Mills NG16: Kimb 6F 17
Lawrence Av. DE72: Brea 5A 62
Lawrence Av. NG16: Aws 3E 29
Lawrence Av. NG16: Eastw 3B 16
Lawrence Av. NG4: Colw 4G 47
Lawrence Cl. NG12: Cotg 2F 71
Lawrence Dr. NG8: Stre 5C 30
Lawrence M. NG12: Cotg 2F 71
Lawrence St. NG10: Long E 5F 63
Lawrence St. NG10: Sand 4D 52
Lawrence St. NG9: Stfrd 5F 53
Lawrence Way NG7: Lent 1E 57
Lawson Av. NG10: Long E 6G 63
Lawson St. NG7: Radf 1A 4 (3E 45)
Lawton Dr. NG6: Bulw 4A 20
Laxton Av. NG6: Bulw 2B 32
Laxton Cl. NG8: Aspl 2H 43
Laxton Dr. NG15: Huck 5E 7
Leabrook Cl. NG11: Clftn 2A 66
Leabrook Gdns. NG15: Huck 3A 8
Lea Ct. NG13: Bing 6D 50
Leacroft Rd. NG8: Aspl 2B 44
Leadale Av. NG15: Huck 3A 8
Leaf Cl. NG15: Huck 2H 7
Leafe Cl. NG9: Chil 3C 64
Leafield Grn. NG11: Clftn 3C 66
Leafy La. DE75: Hea 4D 14
Leahurst Gdns. NG2: West Br 6D 58
Leahurst Rd. NG2: West Br 6C 58
Leahy Gdns. NG5: Bestw 1D 32
Leake Rd. NG11: Goth 6H 75
Leamington Dr. NG9: Chil 1C 64
Leander Cl. NG11: Wilf 5F 57
Leas, The NG14: Bulc 2H 37
Lechlade Cl. DE7: West H 1B 38
Lechlade Rd. NG5: Bestw 1E 33
Ledbury Va. NG8: Aspl 1H 43
Ledger Wlk. NG5: Sher 6F 33
.... (off Jensen Way)
Leech Ct. NG16: Gilt 6D 16
Lee Cres. DE7: Ilk 1D 40
Lee La. DE75: Hea 4F 15
Leen Cl. NG15: Huck 3A 8
Leen Cl. NG6: Bestw V 1D 20
Leen Ct. NG7: Lent 1C 56
Leen Dr. NG15: Huck 2H 7
Leen Dr. NG6: Bulw 4A 20
Leen Ga. NG7: Lent 1B 56
Leen Ga. NG7: Nott 1B 56
Leen Mills La. NG15: Huck 2H 7
Leen Pl. NG7: Radf 4C 44
Leen Valley Golf Course 4A 8
Leen Valley Way NG15: Huck 6A 8
Lee Rd. NG14: Bur J 2G 37
Lee Rd. NG14: Calv 3F 11
Lees Barn Rd. NG12: Rad T 1D 60
Lees Hill Footpath NG2: Nott 6A 46
Lees Hill St. NG2: Nott 5A 46
Leeson Cl. NG4: Colw 4G 47
Lees Rd. NG3: Mapp 6C 34
Lee Westwood Sports Cen. 2B 66
Leicester Ho. NG9: Bram 3H 53
Leicester St. NG10: Long E 1G 73
Leigh Cl. NG2: West Br 5G 57
Leigh Rd. NG9: Toton 2H 63
Leighton St. NG3: Nott 3B 46
Leiston Gdns. NG5: Top V 5E 21
Leivers Av. NG5: Arn 5B 22
Leivers Ho. NG5: Arn 1C 34
.... (off Derwent Cres.)
Lema Cl. NG6: Bulw 5B 20
Lendal Ct. NG7: Radf 2A 4 (4E 45)
Lendrum Ct. NG14: Bur J 3F 37
Leniscar Av. DE75: Los 1A 14
Len Maynard Ct. NG3: Nott 3C 46
Lennox St. NG1: Nott 3G 5 (4H 45)
LENTON ABBEY 2G 55
Lenton Av. NG12: Toll 4E 69
Lenton Av. NG7: Nott 5E 45
Lenton Blvd. NG7: Lent 4D 44
Lenton Bus. Pk. NG7: Lent 5C 44
Lenton Cen., The 6D 44
Lenton Cir. NG12: Toll 4E 69
Lenton Ct. NG7: Nott 6A 4 (6E 45)
Lenton Hall Dr. NG7: Nott 1A 56
Lenton Ind. Est. E. NG7: Lent 4D 56
Lenton Ind. Est. W. NG7: Lent 3D 56
Lenton La. NG7: Lent 1D 56
Lenton Mnr. NG7: Lent 6C 44
Lenton Rd. NG7: Nott 6A 4 (6E 45)
Lenton St. NG10: Sand 5E 53
Leonard Av. NG5: Sher 5F 33
Leonard Cheshire Cl.
DE75: Hea 4F 15
Leonard M. NG9: Chil 3B 64
Leonard St. NG6: Bulw 2H 31
Leopold St. NG10: Long E 5F 63
Le Page Ct. NG8: Bilb 1G 43
Leroy Wallace Av. NG7: Radf 3D 44
Lerwick Cl. NG11: Clftn 4E 67
Leslie Av. NG16: Kimb 2H 29
Leslie Av. NG7: Hys G 1E 45
Leslie Av. NG9: Bee 6F 55
Leslie Gro. NG14: Calv 4H 11
Leslie Rd. NG7: Hys G 1E 45
.... (not continuous)
Letchworth Cres. NG9: Chil 1C 64
Letcombe Rd. NG11: Clftn 2C 66
Levens Cl. NG2: West Br 6E 59
Leverton Ct. NG2: West Br 6B 58
Leverton Grn. NG11: Clftn 3C 66
Levertons Pl. NG15: Huck 1H 19
Leverton Wlk. NG5: Arn 5C 22
Levick Ct. NG2: Nott 1G 57
Lewcote La. DE7: West H 6E 27
Lewindon Ct. NG5: Woodt 3A 34
Lewis Cl. NG3: Nott 3H 45
Lewis Way NG6: Bestw V 6F 9
Lewsey Cl. NG9: Chil 3B 64
Lexington Gdns. NG5: Sher 3H 33
Lexington Pl. NG1: Nott 4G 5 (5H 45)
.... (off Plumptre St.)
Leybourne Dr. NG5: Bestw 1C 32
Leyland Cl. NG9: Toton 3H 63
Leys, The NG11: Clftn 4A 66
Leys, The NG12: Norm W 6H 69
Leys Ct. NG11: Rudd 1G 77
Leys Rd. NG11: Rudd 1G 77
Ley St. NG4: Neth 2A 48
Leyton Cres. NG9: Bee 6H 55
Library Rd. NG7: Nott 2A 56
Lichfield Cl. NG10: Long E 6H 63
Lichfield Cl. NG9: Toton 2G 63
Lichfield Rd. NG2: Nott 5C 46
Liddell Gro. NG8: Woll 4F 43
Liddington St. NG7: Bas 6D 32
Lido Cl. NG6: Bulw 4A 20
Lievesley Gro. NG4: Ged 4G 35
Lightning Gro. NG15: Huck 2D 18
Lilac Av. NG4: Car 1E 47
Lilac Cl. NG12: Key 5A 80
Lilac Cl. NG8: Brox 6E 31
Lilac Ct. NG11: Clftn 4A 66
Lilac Cres. NG9: Bee 6H 55
Lilac Gro. DE75: Hea 4C 14
Lilac Gro. NG9: Bee 6H 55
Lilac M. DE7: Ilk 4H 27
Lilac Rd. NG14: Calv 5C 12
Lilac Rd. NG15: Huck 6H 7
Lilacs, The NG9: Bee 5F 55
Lilian Hind Ct. NG6: Bulw 5F 19
Lilleker Ri. NG5: Arn 4A 22
Lillie Ter. NG2: Nott 5B 46
Lillington Rd. NG6: Bulw 6H 19
Lily Av. NG4: Neth 2A 48
Lily Gro. NG12: Edwal 3B 68
Lily Gro. NG9: Bee 6H 55
Lime Av. NG16: Lang M 3G 15
Lime Cl. NG12: Rad T 6F 49
Lime Cl. NG16: Nuth 1A 30
Limefield Ct. NG2: West Br 2C 58
Lime Gro. NG10: Long E 5F 63
Lime Gro. NG10: Sand 5D 52
Lime Gro. NG9: Stfrd 6F 53
Lime Gro. Av. NG9: Chil 6E 55
Limekiln Ct. NG6: Bulw 5G 19
Lime La. NG5: Arn 6A 10
Limes, The DE7: Mapp 4C 26
Limes, The NG11: Bart F 1E 75
Limes Cl. NG16: Lang M 1G 15
Lime St. DE7: Ilk 2B 40
Lime St. NG6: Bulw 6H 19
Lime Ter. NG10: Long E 5F 63
Lime Tree Av. NG8: Cin 4H 31
Lime Tree Av. NG8: Woll 6H 43
Limetree Cl. NG12: Key 5H 79
Lime Tree Ct. NG9: Nott 2G 55
Limetree Ct. DE7: Kirk H 3G 39
Lime Tree Ri. DE7: Kirk H 3G 39
Lime Tree Rd. NG15: Huck 1H 19
Limmen Gdns.
NG3: Nott 1H 5 (3A 46)
Limpenny St. NG7: Radf 3D 44
LINBY 1H 7
Linby Av. NG15: Huck 4H 7
Linby Cl. NG4: Ged 5G 35
Linby Cl. NG5: Sher 2H 33
Linby Dr. NG8: Stre 5D 30
Linby Gro. NG15: Huck 3H 7
Linby Ho. NG15: Lin 1H 7
Linby La. NG15: Lin 1H 7
Linby La. NG15: Pap 1H 7
Linby Rd. NG15: Huck 3H 7
Linby St. NG6: Bulw 5A 20
Linby Wlk. NG15: Huck 3G 7
Lincoln Av. NG10: Sand 1C 62
Lincoln Cir. NG7: Nott 5A 4 (5E 45)
Lincoln Cl. NG9: Stfrd 2G 53
Lincoln Ct. NG8: Bilb 2D 42
Lincoln Gro. NG12: Rad T 6F 49
Lincoln Ho. NG3: Mapp P 1H 45
Lincoln St. NG1: Nott 3E 5 (4G 45)
Lincoln St. NG6: Bas 4C 32
Lindale Cl. NG2: Gam 5E 59
Lindbridge Rd. NG8: Brox 5F 31
Linden Av. NG11: Clftn 4A 66
Linden Ct. NG9: Bee 6G 55
Linden Gro. NG10: Sand 4C 52
Linden Gro. NG4: Ged 6B 36
Linden Gro. NG9: Bee 6G 55
Linden Gro. NG9: Stfrd 5G 53
Linden Pl. NG3: Mapp 1E 35
Linden St. NG3: Nott 2H 45
Lindfield Cl. NG8: Brox 5G 31
Lindfield Rd. NG8: Brox 5F 31
Lindisfarne Gdns. NG5: Top V 4E 21
Lindley St. NG16: Newth 1D 16
Lindley Ter. NG7: Hys G 2C 44
Lindrick Cl. NG12: Edwal 1E 69
Lindsay St. NG7: Hys G 2D 44
Lindum Gro. NG2: Nott 6B 46
Lindum Rd. NG6: Bas 4B 32
Linen Ho. NG7: Radf 3C 44
.... (off Hartley Rd.)
Linette Cl. NG5: Sher 5E 33
Linford Ct. NG9: Bram 5B 42
Ling Cres. NG11: Rudd 5G 67
Lingfield Ct. NG8: Woll 6D 42
Lingford NG12: Cotg 2G 71
Lingford St. NG15: Huck 5H 7
Lingmell Cl. NG2: West Br 5E 59
LINGS BAR HOSPITAL 5F 59
Lings Bar Rd. NG2: Gam 5F 59
.... (off Ambleside)
Lings Cl. DE7: Ilk 2B 28
Lings La. NG12: Key 6G 79
Lingwood La. NG14: Woodbo 3B 24
Linkin Rd. NG9: Chil 5C 54
Linkmel Cl. NG2: Nott 2E 57
Linkmel Rd. NG16: Eastw 2G 15
Linksfield Ct. NG2: West Br 3G 67
Linley Ct. NG13: Bing 5E 51
.... (off Long Acre)
Linnell St. NG3: Nott 3B 46
Linnet Way NG15: Huck 4F 7
Linsdale Cl. NG8: Bilb 4B 42
Linsdale Gdns. NG4: Ged 3F 35
Linton Ri. NG3: Nott 3C 46
Linwood Cres. NG16: Eastw 4B 16
Lion Cl. NG8: Aspl 5A 32
Lismore Cl. NG7: Radf 4C 44
Lissett Av. DE7: Ilk 2A 40
Lister Ga. NG1: Nott 5E 5 (5G 45)
Listergate Sq.
NG1: Nott 5E 5 (5G 45)
Lister Ho. NG3: Mapp 5B 34
Lister Rd. NG7: Nott 1C 56
Listowel Cres. NG11: Clftn 5C 66
Litchen Cl. DE7: Ilk 5B 28
Litchfield Ri. NG5: Arn 3A 22
Litmus Bldg., The
NG1: Nott 2F 5 (4H 45)
.... (off Huntingdon St.)
Lit. Bounds NG2: West Br 4H 57
Little Drivers Soft Play Cen. 5F 53
Littlegreen Rd. NG5: Woodt 3A 34
LITTLE HALLAM 3B 40
Lit. Hallam Hill DE7: Ilk 4A 40
Lit. Hallam La. DE7: Ilk 3B 40
Lit. Hayes NG2: West Br 1G 67
Lit. Holland Gdns. NG16: Nuth 1B 30
Lit. John Wlk. NG3: Nott 2H 45
Little La. NG12: Toll 2G 69
Little La. NG14: Calv 4F 11
Little La. NG16: Kimb 2H 29
Lit. Lime La. NG5: Arn 6A 10
Lit. Lunnon NG11: Bart F 1E 75
Lit. Mdw. NG12: Cotg 3G 71
Little Mdw. Cl. DE7: Ilk 5A 28
Littlemoor La. NG11: Rudd 4A 78
Lit. Oakwood Dr. NG5: Top V 3B 20

Lit. Ox NG4: Colw......5H 47
Lit. Tennis St. NG2: Nott......6C 46
Lit. Tennis St. Sth. NG2: Nott...1C 58
Littlewell Ct. DE7: Stant D......1B 52
Lit. Wood Ct. NG15: Huck......6E 7
Littlewood Gdns. NG8: Bilb......4C 42
Litton Cl. DE7: Ilk......3A 28
Litton Cl. NG5: Woodt......3A 34
Liverpool St. NG3: Nott......3H 5 (4A 46)
Livingstone Rd. NG3: Nott......3A 46
LivingWell Health Club
Nottingham......3E 5 (4G 45)
Llanberis Gro. NG8: Aspl......5A 32
Lloyd St. NG5: Sher......5G 33
Loach Cl. NG8: Woll......4A 44
Lobelia Cl. NG3: Nott......2H 45
Lock Cl. DE7: Kirk H......3G 39
Lock Cl. NG8: Bee......2G 65
Lockerbie St. NG4: Colw......3H 47
Lock La. NG10: Long E......3D 72
Lock La. NG10: Sand......6D 52
Locksley Ho. NG3: Nott......3H 45
Locksley La. NG11: Clftn...1C 66
Lockton Av. DE75: Hea......5C 14
Lockwood Cl. NG5: Top V......4E 21
Lockwood Cl. NG9: Bee......1H 65
Lodge Cl. NG5: Redh......3A 22
Lodge Cl. NG8: Aspl......1B 44
Lodge Farm La. NG5: Arn......4A 22
Lodge Rd. DE7: Mapp......4D 26
Lodge Rd. NG10: Long E......2F 73
Lodge Rd. NG16: Newth......5C 16
Lodge Row DE7: Mapp......4C 26
Lodgewood Cl. NG6: Bulw......1G 31
Lodore Cl. NG2: West Br......5E 59
Logan Sq. NG6: Bas......2C 32
Logan St. NG6: Bulw......1A 32
Lois Av. NG7: Lent......6D 44
Lombard St. NG7: Lent......5D 44
Lombardy Lodge NG9: Toton......4A 64
London Rd. NG2: Nott......5G 5 (5H 45)
Long Acre NG13: Bing......5E 51
Long Acre NG15: Huck......4D 6
Longacre NG5: Woodt......3B 34
Long Acre E. NG13: Bing......5F 51
Longbeck Av. NG3: Nott......6C 34
Longbridge La. DE75: Los......2B 14
Longclose Ct. NG6: Bulw......1G 31
Longcroft DE7: Ilk......2A 28
Longdale Rd. NG5: Arn......1H 33
Longden Cl. NG9: Bram......1H 53
Longden Mill NG3: Nott...3H 5 (4A 46)
......(off Longden St.)
Longden St. NG3: Nott...3H 5 (4A 46)
LONG EATON......5G 63
Long Eaton Station (Rail)......2E 73
Longfellows Cl. NG5: Bestw......5F 21
Longfield Av. NG8: Bilb......2C 42
Longfield Cres. DE7: Ilk......4B 40
Longfield La. DE7: Ilk......4B 40
Longford Cres. NG6: Bulw......3A 20
Long Hill Ri. NG15: Huck......5F 7
Longhirst Dr. NG5: Arn......3B 22
Longlands Cl. NG9: Bee......1H 65
Longlands Dr. NG9: Bee......6F 59
Longlands Rd. NG9: Bee......1H 65
Long La. DE75: Ship......6H 15
Long La. NG16: Want......4A 18
Long La. NG9: Atten......3D 64
Longleat Cres. NG9: Chil......6C 54
Longmead Cl. NG5: Bestw......1G 33
Longmead Dr. NG5: Bestw......1G 33
Long Meadow Hill NG14: Lowd...3F 25
Longmoor Gdns. NG10: Long E......3C 62
Longmoor La. DE72: Brea......4A 62
Longmoor La. NG10: Sand......2D 62
Longmoor Rd. NG10: Long E......3C 62
Longmoor Rd. NG10: Sand......3C 62
Longore Sq. NG8: Woll......5B 44

Longridge Rd. NG5: Woodt......3B 34
Long Row NG1: Nott......4D 4 (5G 45)
......(not continuous)
Long Row W. NG1: Nott......4D 4 (5G 45)
Long Stairs NG1: Nott......5G 5 (5H 45)
......(off Pemberton St.)
Longthorpe Ct. NG5: Arn......6B 22
Longue Dr. NG14: Calv......4F 11
Longwall Av. NG2: Nott......2E 57
Long West Cft. NG14: Calv......4E 11
Longwood Ct. NG5: Top V......5D 20
Lonscale Cl. NG2: West Br......6E 59
Lonsdale Dr. NG9: Toton......3G 63
Lonsdale Rd. NG7: Radf......3C 44
Lord Haddon Rd. DE7: Ilk......6A 28
Lord Nelson St. NG2: Nott......5B 46
Lord St. NG2: Nott......5B 46
Lorimer Av. NG4: Ged......4H 35
Lorna Cl. NG3: Nott......6H 33
Lorne Gro. NG12: Rad T......6F 49
Lorne Wlk. NG3: Nott......2G 45
Lortas Rd. NG5: Sher......5D 32
LOSCOE......1A 14
Loscoe Gdns. NG5: Sher......6F 33
Loscoe Grange DE75: Los......2A 14
Loscoe Mt. Rd. NG5: Sher......5G 33
Loscoe Rd. DE75: Hea......2A 14
Loscoe Rd. NG5: Sher......6G 33
Lothian Rd. NG12: Toll......4E 69
Lothmore Ct. NG2: Nott......1F 57
Lotus Cl. NG3: Nott......2A 46
Loughborough Av. NG2: Nott......5B 46
Loughborough Rd.
NG11: Bunny......3H 67
Loughborough Rd.
NG11: Rudd......3H 67
Loughborough Rd.
NG2: West Br......5A 58
Loughrigg Cl. NG2: Nott......2F 57
Louisa Cl. NG5: Arn......5H 21
Louis Av. NG9: Bee......4E 55
Louise Av. NG4: Neth......1A 48
Lovelace Wlk. NG15: Huck......3H 7
Lovell Cl. NG6: Bulw......2F 31
Lovesey Av. NG15: Huck......3D 18
Lowater Pl. NG4: Car......2D 46
Lowater St. NG4: Car......2D 46
Lowcroft NG5: Woodt......3B 34
Lowdham La. NG14: Woodbo......1D 24
Lowdham Rd. NG14: Epp......1G 25
Lowdham Rd. NG4: Ged......4E 35
Lowdham St. NG3: Nott...3H 5 (4A 46)
Lowe Av. DE7: Smal......5A 14
LOWER BEAUVALE......2C 16
Lwr. Beauvale NG16: Newth......2C 16
Lwr. Bloomsgrove Rd. DE7: Ilk...5B 28
Lwr. Brook St. NG10: Long E......6G 63
Lwr. Canaan NG11: Rudd......5H 67
Lwr. Chapel St. DE7: Ilk......6B 28
Lwr. Claramount Rd.
DE75: Hea......4E 15
Lower Ct. NG9: Bee......4G 55
Lwr. Dunstead Rd.
NG16: Lang M......2E 15
Lwr. Eldon St.
NG2: Nott......5H 5 (5A 46)
Lwr. Gladstone St. DE75: Hea...3C 14
Lwr. Granby St. DE7: Ilk......5B 28
Lwr. Maples DE75: Ship......5E 15
Lwr. Middleton St. DE7: Ilk......6C 28
Lwr. Orchard St. NG9: Stfrd......4G 53
Lwr. Park St. NG9: Stfrd......5E 53
Lwr. Parliament St.
NG1: Nott......3E 5 (4G 45)
Lwr. Regent St. NG9: Bee......5G 55
Lower Rd. NG9: Bee......4H 55
Lwr. Stanton Rd. DE7: Ilk......3B 40
Lwr. Whitworth Dr. DE7: Ilk......3D 40
Loweswater Ct. NG2: Gam......4E 59

Lowlands Dr. NG12: Key......3H 79
Lowlands Lea DE75: Hea......3D 14
Low Pavement
NG1: Nott......5E 5 (5G 45)
Lows La. DE7: Stant D......1B 52
Low Wood Rd. NG6: Bulw......2E 31
Loxley Cl. NG15: Huck......6E 7
Loxley Mdw. NG14: Bur J......3E 37
Lucerne Cl. NG11: Wilf......5F 57
Lucillia Cl. NG15: Huck......3B 8
Lucknow Av. NG3: Mapp P......1H 45
Lucknow Ct. NG3: Mapp P......6H 33
Lucknow Dr. NG3: Mapp P......1H 45
Lucknow Rd. NG3: Mapp P......1H 45
Ludford Cl. NG10: Long E......3G 73
Ludford Rd. NG6: Bulw......5A 20
Ludgate Cl. NG5: Arn......3E 21
Ludham Av. NG6: Bulw......5H 19
Ludlam Av. NG16: Gilt......6C 16
Ludlow Av. NG2: West Br......4B 58
Ludlow Cl. NG9: Bram......2D 54
Ludlow Hill Rd. NG2: West Br...6B 58
Lulworth Cl. NG2: West Br......6G 57
Lulworth Ct. NG16: Kimb......6H 17
Lune Cl. NG9: Atten......2E 65
Lune Way NG13: Bing......6D 50
Lupin Cl. NG12: Edwal......3C 68
Lupin Cl. NG3: Nott......2H 45
Luther Cl. NG3: Nott......2A 46
Luton Cl. NG8: Aspl......6B 32
Lutterell Ct. NG2: West Br......6H 57
Lutterell Way NG2: West Br......6D 58
Lybster M. NG2: Nott......1F 57
Lychgate Ct. NG16: Want......5H 17
Lydia Gdns. NG16: Eastw......4A 16
Lydney Pk. NG2: West Br......5F 57
Lyle Cl. NG16: Kimb......6G 17
Lyme Pk. NG2: West Br......6F 57
Lymington Gdns. NG3: Nott......3C 46
Lymn Av. NG4: Ged......5H 35
Lynam Ct. NG6: Bulw......6H 19
Lyncombe Gdns. NG12: Key......3H 79
Lyndale Ct. DE7: Ilk......6H 27
Lyndale Rd. NG9: Bram......3A 54
Lynden Av. NG10: Long E......1F 73
Lyndhurst Gdns. NG2: West Br...1H 67
Lyndhurst Rd. NG2: Nott......5B 46
Lynemouth Ct. NG5: Arn......3C 22
Lyn Gilzean Ct.
NG3: Nott......1G 5 (3H 45)
Lynmoor Ct. NG15: Huck......2A 8
Lynmouth Cres. NG7: Radf......2C 44
Lynmouth Dr. DE7: Ilk......4H 27
Lynncroft NG16: Eastw......2C 16
Lynncroft St. NG8: Stre......5C 30
Lynstead Dr. NG15: Huck......6C 6
Lynton Cl. NG3: Bram......3B 46
Lynton Gdns. NG5: Arn......5C 22
Lynton Rd. NG9: Chil......5C 54
Lyons Cl. NG11: Rudd......5F 67
Lytham Dr. NG12: Edwal......2E 69
Lytham Gdns. NG5: Top V......4E 21
Lythe Cl. NG11: Wilf......6E 57
Lytton Cl. NG3: Nott......2H 5 (4A 46)

M

Mabel Gro. NG2: West Br......3C 58
Mabel St. NG2: Nott......1H 57
Macaulay Gro. NG16: Nuth......1B 30
McClelland Av. NG6: Bestw V......6F 9
McCracken Cl. NG5: Top V......4C 20
Macdonald Sq. DE7: Kirk H......4G 39
Machins La. NG12: Edwal......2C 68
McIntosh Rd. NG4: Ged......4F 35
Mackinley Av. NG9: Stfrd......2A 54
Maclaren Gdns. NG11: Rudd...1H 77
Maclean Rd. NG4: Car......2E 47
Macmillan Cl. NG3: Mapp......5B 34

Madden Cl. NG5: Bestw......2D 32
Madford Bus. Pk. NG5: Arn......1H 33
Madison Cl. NG7: Lent......5B 44
Madryn Wlk. NG5: Bestw......6E 21
Mafeking St. NG2: Nott......5C 46
Magdala Rd. NG3: Mapp P......1G 45
Magdalene Way NG15: Huck......3G 7
Magenta Way NG4: Neth......2C 48
Magenta Way NG4: Stoke B......2C 48
Magnolia Cl. NG12: Edwal......4C 68
Magnolia Cl. NG8: Brox......6E 31
Magnolia Ct. NG9: Bram......2D 54
Magnolia Gro. NG15: Huck......1D 54
Magnus Ct. NG9: Bee......5G 55
Magnus Rd. NG5: Sher......4G 33
Magson Cl. NG3: Nott......4A 46
Maiden La. NG1: Nott......4G 5 (5H 45)
Maidens Dale NG5: Arn......5H 21
Maid Marian Way
NG1: Nott......4C 4 (5F 45)
Maidstone Dr. NG8: Woll......1D 54
Main Rd. NG11: Wilf......5F 57
Main Rd. NG12: Cotg......4D 60
Main Rd. NG12: Plum......5G 69
Main Rd. NG12: Rad T......4D 60
Main Rd. NG12: Rad T......6E 49
Main Rd. NG12: S'frd......1H 49
Main Rd. NG14: Bur J......2G 37
Main Rd. NG14: Lowd......2G 37
Main Rd. NG14: Want......4H 17
Main Rd. NG4: Ged......6H 35
Main Rd. NG7: Nott......5A 56
Main St. DE7: Mapp......4C 26
Main St. DE7: Stant D......3B 52
Main St. DE72: Brea......5A 62
Main St. NG10: Long E......6G 63
Main St. NG11: Rudd......4A 78
Main St. NG12: Key......6G 79
Main St. NG13: Newt......1B 50
Main St. NG14: Bur J......3F 37
Main St. NG14: Calv......3D 10
Main St. NG14: Epp......5E 13
Main St. NG14: Woodbo......1B 24
Main St. NG15: Lin......1G 7
Main St. NG15: Pap......1B 8
Main St. NG16: Aws......2E 29
Main St. NG16: Eastw......4B 16
Main St. NG16: Kimb......1H 29
Main St. NG16: Newth......3E 17
Main St. NG2: Gam......4E 59
Main St. NG25: Oxton......1B 12
Main St. NG4: Lamb......6B 24
Main St. NG6: Bulw......1H 31
......(not continuous)
Main St. NG8: Stre......6B 30
Maitland Av. NG5: Woodt......3B 34
Maitland Rd. NG5: Woodt......3B 34
Major St. NG1: Nott......2D 4 (4G 45)
Malbon Cl. NG3: Nott......1B 46
Malcolm Cl. NG3: Mapp P......2G 45
Maldon Cl. NG10: Long E......2G 73
Malin Cl. NG5: Arn......5D 22
Malin Hill NG1: Nott......5F 5 (5H 45)
......(off Pemberton St.)
Malkin Av. NG12: Rad T......5G 49
Mallard Cl. NG13: Bing......6G 51
Mallard Ct. NG6: Bas......3D 32
Mallard Ct. NG9: Bee......6G 55
Mallard Rd. NG4: Neth......3B 48
Mallow Way NG13: Bing......5C 50
Malmesbury Rd. NG3: Mapp......3C 34
Maltby Cl. NG8: Aspl......5H 31
Maltby Rd. NG3: Mapp......3C 43
Malt Cotts. NG7: Bas......6D 32
Malthouse Cl. NG16: Eastw......4B 16
Malthouse Rd. DE7: Ilk......4B 40
Malting Cl. NG11: Rudd......1G 77

Maltings, The NG3: Nott 2B 46
Maltings, The NG6: Bas.............5C 32
Malton Rd. NG5: Sher................5D 32
Malt St. NG11: Goth....................6H 75
Malvern Cl. NG3: Nott.................6A 34
Malvern Ct. NG3: Mapp P 2G 45
Malvern Ct. NG9: Bee.................5H 55
Malvern Cres. NG2: West Br.......6B 58
Malvern Gdns. NG10: Long E 5C 62
Malvern Rd. NG2: West Br...........6A 58
Malvern Rd. NG3: Nott................6A 34
Manchester St. NG10: Long E......1F 73
Mandalay St. NG6: Bas 3B 32
Mandeville Cl. NG15: Huck.............4A 8
Manesty Cres. NG11: Cliftn.........6C 66
Manifold Gdns. NG2: Nott............1G 57
Manly Cl. NG5: Top V..................5C 20
Manners Av. NG3: Nott................6H 27
Manners Ind. Est. DE7: Ilk...........5H 27
Manners Rd. DE7: Ilk..................6A 28
Manners St. DE7: Ilk...................3C 40
Manning St. NG3: Nott.................2H 45
Manning Vw. DE7: Ilk..................5B 28
Mannion Cres. NG10: Long E 2D 72
Manns Leys NG12: Cotg...............3E 71
Mann St. NG7: Bas 1D 44
Manor Av. NG2: Nott...................5A 46
Manor Av. NG9: Atten..................2E 65
Manor Av. NG9: Bee....................5F 55
Manor Av. NG9: Stfrd..................3F 53
Manor Cl. NG12: Edwal................2D 68
Manor Ct. DE72: Brea.................5A 62
Manor Ct. NG4: Car....................2H 47
Manor Ct. NG9: Bram..................4C 54
Manor Cft. NG6: Bas...................4C 32
Mnr. Farm Cvn. & Camping Site
    NG11: Thru..........................4D 74
Mnr. Farm Cl. NG11: Rudd...........4A 78
Mnr. Farm La. NG11: Cliftn.........3C 66
Manor Flds. Dr. DE7: Ilk.............2H 27
Manor Grn. NG4: Car...................1H 47
Manor Grn. Wlk. NG4: Car............1H 47
Manor Health & Racquets
    Club, The 6A 28
Manor Ho. Cl. NG11: Wilf.............3F 57
Manor Ho. Rd. NG10: Long E........1H 73
Manorleigh DE72: Brea...............5A 62
Manor Pk. NG11: Rudd................6F 67
Manor Pk. La. NG14: Epp.............6G 13
Manor Rd. DE7: Ilk.....................6A 28
Manor Rd. NG11: Bart F..............1E 75
Manor Rd. NG12: Key..................4G 79
Manor Rd. NG13: Bing.................5F 51
Manor Rd. NG14: Calv.................4G 11
Manor Rd. NG16: Eastw...............4B 16
Manor Rd. NG4: Car....................1H 47
Manor St. NG2: Nott...................5A 46
Manor Wlk. NG14: Epp................6G 13
Manorwood Rd. NG12: Cotg.........3F 71
Mansell Cl. NG16: Eastw.............4D 16
Mansfield Cl. NG5: Sher..............1F 45
Mansfield Gro.
    NG1: Nott....................1C 4 (3F 45)
Mansfield La. NG14: Calv.............2H 11
Mansfield Rd. DE75: Hea..............3D 14
Mansfield Rd. NG1: Nott..............2F 45
Mansfield Rd. NG5: Arn...............2G 9
Mansfield Rd. NG5: Redh..............2G 9
Mansfield Rd. NG5: Sher..............1F 45
Mansfield Rd. NG5: Sher..............2G 9
Mansfield St. NG5: Sher..............5G 33
Manston M. NG7: Radf.................3D 44
Manthorpe Cres. NG5: Sher.........4B 34
Manton Cres. NG9: Lent A............3F 55
Manvers Bus. Pk. NG12: Cotg.......1G 71
Manvers Ct. NG2: Nott.......4H 5 (5A 46)
Manvers Gro. NG12: Rad T...........6F 49
Manvers Rd. NG2: West Br............5B 43

Manvers St. NG2: Nott.......4H 5 (5A 46)
Manvers St. NG4: Neth.................3A 48
Manville Cl. NG8: Aspl.................3A 44
Manville Cl. NG9: Bram................6B 42
Maori Av. NG15: Huck...................6D 6
Maple Av. NG10: Sand..................4D 52
Maple Av. NG9: Bee.....................6H 55
Maplebeck Rd. NG5: Arn..............6C 22
Maple Cl. NG12: Key....................5A 80
Maple Cl. NG12: Rad T..................1F 61
Maple Cl. NG13: Bing...................5G 51
Maple Cl. NG14: Calv...................4F 11
Maple Ct. NG16: Kimb..................1H 29
Maple Ct. NG7: Lent.....................6D 44
Mapledene Cres. NG8: Woll..........6C 42
Maple Dr. NG15: Huck..................6E 7
Maple Dr. NG16: Nuth...................1B 30
Maple Dr. NG9: Ged.....................5B 36
Maple Gdns. DE75: Hea................4B 14
Maple Gdns. NG16: Lang M...........2F 15
Maple Gro. DE72: Brea................5B 62
Maple Leaf Way NG15: Huck.........1A 20
Maples, The NG75: Ship...............5E 15
Maplestead Av. NG11: Wilf..........5F 57
Mapletree Cl. NG5: Bestw............6F 21
Maple Vw. NG11: Wilf..................1F 67
Maple Way NG2: West Br.............1H 67
MAPPERLEY.............................5C 26
MAPPERLEY.............................4B 34
Mapperley Brook DE7: Mapp.......5E 27
Mapperley Cres. NG3: Mapp........5A 34
Mapperley Golf Course...............3D 34
Mapperley Hall Dr.
    NG3: Mapp P 6G 33
Mapperley Hall Gdns.
    NG3: Mapp P 6H 33
Mapperley Hgts. NG5: Woodt......2D 34
Mapperley Orchard NG5: Arn......6D 22
MAPPERLEY PARK......................4B 26
MAPPERLEY PARK......................6G 33
Mapperley Pk. Dr.
    NG3: Mapp P 1G 45
Mapperley Plains NG3: Mapp.......2D 34
Mapperley Ri. NG3: Mapp............5A 34
Mapperley Rd. NG3: Mapp P 2G 45
Mapperley Sports Village
Mapperley St. NG5: Sher.............5G 33
Mapperley Wood Local
    Nature Reserve......................4D 26
March Cl. NG5: Top V..................6C 20
Marchesi Cl. NG15: Huck.............1E 19
Marchwood Cl. NG8: Radf............4B 44
Marciana Gro. NG15: Huck............3A 8
Marco Island NG1: Nott......3G 5 (4H 45)
    ....(off Huntington St.)
Mardale Cl. NG2: West Br............6E 59
Mardling Av. NG5: Bestw..............2E 33
Margaret Av. DE7: Ilk..................1B 40
Margaret Av. NG10: Long E..........4H 63
Margaret Av. NG10: Sand.............1D 62
Margaret Cres. NG4: Ged.............5G 35
Margaret Pl. NG13: Bing..............4D 50
Margarets Ct. NG9: Bram.............3A 54
Marham Cl. NG2: Nott.................6A 46
Marhill Rd. NG4: Car...................2H 47
Maria Ct. NG7: Nott.........6A 4 (6E 45)
Marie Gdns. NG15: Huck................6G 7
Marigold Cl. NG12: Edwal............3B 68
Marina Av. NG9: Bee....................6F 55
Marina Rd. DE7: Smal..................5A 14
Mariner Ct. NG6: Bulw.................1G 31
Marion Av. NG15: Huck.................2A 8
Maris Cl. NG11: Cliftn.................3A 66
Maris Dr. NG14: Bur J.................3E 37
Mkt. Pl. DE7: Ilk.........................1A 40
Mkt. Pl. DE75: Hea.....................4C 14
    ....(off Market St.)

Mkt. Pl. NG10: Long E.................5G 63
Mkt. Pl. NG13: Bing....................5E 51
Mkt. Pl. NG15: Huck.....................4G 7
Mkt. Pl. NG5: Arn.......................6B 22
Mkt. Pl. NG6: Bulw......................6H 19
Market Side NG6: Bulw.................6H 19
    ....(off Duke St.)
Mkt. St. DE7: Ilk.........................1B 40
Mkt. St. DE75: Hea.....................3C 14
Mkt. St. NG1: Nott...............3D 4 (4G 45)
Mkt. St. NG13: Bing....................5E 51
Markham Cres. NG5: Sher............3G 33
Markham Rd. NG9: Bram..............2D 54
Mark St. NG10: Sand...................6E 53
Marlborough, The NG3: Nott.........2G 45
Marlborough Ct. NG2: West Br......4B 58
Marlborough Ct. NG9: Bee...........3F 55
Marlborough Rd.
    NG10: Long E 4H 63
Marlborough Rd. NG5: Woodt......2H 33
Marlborough Rd. NG9: Bee...........3F 55
Marlborough St. NG7: Lent...........2C 56
Marl Cl. NG11: Rudd...................5F 67
Marldon Cl. NG8: Bilb.................4B 42
Marlow Av. NG6: Bas...................5C 32
Marlow Cres. DE7: West H...........1B 38
MARLPOOL................................6D 14
Marl Rd. NG12: Rad T.................6H 49
Marlwood NG12: Cotg.................4G 71
Marmion Ct. NG3: Nott................3B 46
Marmion Rd. NG3: Nott................2C 46
Marnham Dr. NG3: Nott...............6A 34
Marriott Av. NG9: Chil..................6A 54
Marriott Cl. NG9: Chil..................6A 54
Marsant Cl. NG8: Woll.................4A 44
Marsden Cl. NG6: Bulw................2C 32
Marshall Cl. NG14: Calv..............3F 11
Marshall Dr. NG11: Rudd.............6F 67
Marshall Dr. NG9: Bram..............3H 53
Marshall Hill Dr. NG3: Mapp.........6C 34
Marshall Rd. NG3: Mapp.............6C 34
Marshall St. DE75: Hea...............3D 14
Marshall St. NG5: Sher...............5G 33
Marshall Way DE7: Kirk H............3G 39
Marsham Dr. NG5: Arn................1B 34
Marsh Av. DE7: Ilk......................2A 28
Marston Rd. NG3: Nott................2D 46
Martell Ct. NG6: Bulw..................2C 64
Martin Cl. NG6: Bulw...................5F 19
Martin Ct. NG6: Bulw...................5G 19
Martin Cres. NG11: Rudd.............6F 67
Martindale Cl. NG2: Gam.............4E 59
Martinmass Cl. NG7: Lent............6C 44
Martin's Hill NG4: Car.................2G 47
Martin's Pond Nature Reserve 4E 43
Marton Rd. NG6: Bulw.................4A 20
Marton Rd. NG9: Chil..................2C 64
Marvyn Cl. NG6: Bulw.................1C 32
Marwood Cres. NG4: Car.............5E 35
Marwood Rd. NG4: Car................6E 35
Mary Ct. NG3: Nott.....................6A 34
Maryland Ct. NG9: Stfrd..............2G 53
MARY POTTER CEN., THE...........2D 44
Mary Rd. NG16: Eastw.................4D 16
Marziale Ct. NG4: Ged.................6A 36
Masonic Pl. NG1: Nott......3C 4 (4F 45)
Mason Rd. DE7: Ilk.....................5H 27
Massey Cl. NG14: Bur J..............4E 37
Massey Gdns. NG3: Nott.............3A 46
Masson Ct. NG5: Top V................4E 21
Matlock Ct. NG1: Nott.......2D 4 (4G 45)
Matlock Ct. NG10: Long E 2B 72
Matlock St. NG4: Neth.................1H 47
Matthews Ct. NG9: Stfrd.............1H 53
Matthew Thomas Ct. NG9: Bee....5G 55
Mattingly Rd. NG6: Bulw..............1G 31
Maud St. NG7: Bas.....................6E 33
Maun Av. NG7: Radf....................3B 44
Maun Gdns. NG7: Radf................3B 44

Maurice Dr. NG3: Mapp...............5A 34
Maws La. NG16: Kimb..................6G 17
Maxtoke Rd. NG7: Nott................6E 45
Maxwell Cl. NG7: Lent.................6D 44
Maxwell St. DE72: Brea...............5B 62
Maxwell St. NG10: Long E...........6G 63
May Av. NG8: Woll.......................5E 43
May Ct. NG5: Sher.....................6F 33
Maycroft Gdns. NG3: Nott............2C 46
Maydene Cl. NG11: Cliftn.............4B 66
Mayes Ri. NG6: Bestw V...............1C 20
Mayfair Gdns. NG5: Sher.............2D 32
Mayfield Av. NG14: Bur J.............2F 37
Mayfield Cl. NG2: Nott.................1G 57
Mayfield Dr. NG9: Stfrd...............1H 53
Mayfield Gro. NG10: Long E..........4G 63
Mayfield Rd. NG4: Car.................2D 46
Mayflower Cl. NG2: West Br.........4C 58
Mayflower Rd. NG16: Newth.........5D 16
Maygreen Av. NG12: Cotg............6G 61
Mayland Cl. NG8: Bilb.................3A 42
Maylands Av. DE72: Brea.............5A 62
Maynes Dr. NG14: Calv...............5C 12
Mayo Rd. NG5: Sher....................6F 33
Maypole NG11: Cliftn..................2C 66
Maypole Yd. NG1: Nott 3E 5 (4G 45)
May's Av. NG4: Car.....................3E 47
Mays Cl. NG4: Car......................3E 47
May St. DE7: Ilk..........................3A 28
Maythorn Cl. NG2: West Br..........2G 67
Maythorne Cl. NG5: Arn..............6D 22
Maythorne Wlk. NG5: Bestw.........5G 21
Maywood Golf Course.................5A 52
Meadowbank Ct.
    NG16: Eastw.........................2H 15
Meadowbank Way
    NG16: Eastw.........................2H 15
Meadow Brown Rd.
    NG7: Hys G...........................1C 44
Meadow Cl. DE72: Brea...............6A 62
Meadow Cl. NG15: Huck.................6D 6
Meadow Cl. NG16: Eastw.............1B 16
Meadow Cl. NG2: Nott.................1A 58
Meadow Cotts. NG4: Neth............2H 47
Meadow Ct.
    NG2: Nott Brand St................1B 58
Meadow Cres. NG12: Cotg...........6G 61
Meadow Cft. Gdns. NG15: Huck....6F 7
Meadow Dr. NG12: Key................4A 80
Mdw. End NG11: Goth..................6H 75
Mdw. End NG12: Rad T................6H 49
Meadow Gdns. DE75: Hea............4F 15
Meadow Gdns. NG9: Chil..............1E 65
Meadow Gro. NG2: Nott...............1A 58
Meadow La. NG10: Long E 6H 63
    ....(not continuous)
Meadow La. NG14: Bur J.............3F 37
Meadow La. NG2: Nott.................1A 58
    ....(not continuous)
Meadow La. NG9: Chil..................6E 55
Meadow Lane.............................1A 58
Meadow Ri. NG6: Bulw................1F 31
Meadow Ri. NG16: Aws................2E 29
Meadow Rd. NG4: Neth................3H 47
Meadow Rd. NG9: Bee..................6G 55
MEADOWS..................................1G 57
Meadows, The DE75: Hea.............4C 14
Meadows, The NG14: Woodbo......1B 24
Meadows, The NG16: Aws.............2E 29
Meadows Embankment
    Stop (NET)...........................2F 57
Meadow St. DE7: Ilk....................6B 28
Mdws. Way NG2: Nott..................2F 57
Meadows Way West
    Stop (NET)...........................1F 57
Meadowsweet Hill NG13: Bing.......5C 50
Meadow Trad. Est. NG2: Nott........6A 46
Meadowvale Cres. NG11: Cliftn 4C 66

Meadowvale Pl. NG11: Clftn........4C 66
Meadow Vw. NG9: Stfrd.........3F 53
Meadow Vw. Ct. DE72: Ris........1B 62
Mecca Bingo Beeston.............5H 55
Medawar Cl. NG11: Clftn........4A 66
Medbank Ct. NG11: Wilf.........6E 57
Meden Cl. NG11: Clftn........2C 66
Meden Gdns. NG7: Hys G........2B 44
Medina Dr. NG12: Toll.........4F 69
Medway Cl. NG9: Chil.........6C 54
Medway Dr. NG13: Bing.........6C 50
Medway St. NG8: Radf 4B 44
Meeks Rd. NG5: Arn 5D 22
Meerbrook Pl. DE7: Kirk H........4G 39
Meer Rd. NG9: Chil 6A 54
Melbourne Ct. NG10: Long E......3B 72
Melbourne Ct. NG8: Aspl 6A 32
Melbourne Rd. NG2: West Br......2B 58
Melbourne Rd. NG8: Aspl 1H 43
Melbourne Rd. NG9: Stfrd 1G 53
Melbury Rd. NG5: Woodt........3B 34
Melbury Rd. NG8: Bilb 1D 42
Meldreth Rd. NG8: Bilb.........3E 43
Melford Hall Dr. NG2: West Br 1G 67
Melford Rd. NG8: Bilb..........1D 42
Melksham Rd. NG5: Bestw......... 5G 21
Mellbreak Cl. NG2: West Br.......5E 59
Mellers Ct. NG3: Nott..........2C 46
Mellish Sports Cen...........2B 32
Mellors Rd. NG2: West Br........6B 58
Mellors Rd. NG5: Arn..........4B 22
Mellors Way NG8: Stre 5C 30
Melrose Av. NG5: Sher..........4G 33
Melrose Av. NG9: Bee...........6G 55
Melrose Gdns. NG2: West Br 1H 67
Melrose St. NG5: Sher 4G 33
Melton Ct. NG10: Sand 6C 52
Melton Gdns. NG12: Edwal.........1C 68
Melton Gro. NG2: West Br 4A 58
Melton Hall NG8: Woll 5A 44
Melton Rd. NG12: Edwal..........4C 68
Melton Rd. NG12: Key 4C 68
Melton Rd. NG12: Plum 4C 68
Melton Rd. NG12: Stant W........4C 68
Melton Rd. NG2: West Br 4A 58
Melville Ct. NG3: Mapp P........1G 45
Melville Gdns. NG3: Nott 1H 5 (3A 46)
Melville St. NG1: Nott 6E 5 (6G 45)
Melvyn Dr. NG13: Bing..........5E 51
Mendip Cl. NG10: Long E........4C 62
Mendip Ct. NG5: Top V.........5D 20
Mensing Av. NG12: Cotg........2E 71
Merchant St. NG6: Bulw.........5H 19
...............(not continuous)
Mercia Cl. NG16: Gilt..........5C 16
Mercian Cl. DE7: Ilk..........6A 28
Mercury Cl. NG6: Bas..........2C 32
Mere Av. NG14: Calv...........4H 11
Mere Cl. NG14: Calv...........4H 11
Meredith Cl. NG2: Nott.........2F 57
Meredith Ct. NG9: Stfrd 1G 53
Meregill Cl. NG5: Top V.........4D 20
Merevale Av. NG11: Clftn........1D 66
Mere Way NG11: Rudd 3H 77
Meriac Cl. NG5: Top V 5D 20
Meriden Av. NG9: Lent A 3G 55
Meridian Cl. DE7: Ilk..........3A 28
Meridian Ct. NG5: Sher.........5E 33
Merlin Cl. NG11: Clftn.........3C 66
Merlin Dr. NG15: Huck..........1E 19
Merlin Way DE7: Ilk..........5B 40
Merrivale Ct. NG3: Mapp P.......1G 45
Mersey St. NG6: Bulw..........6H 19
Merton Cl. DE75: Hea..........4D 14
Merton Ct. NG5: Arn..........4D 22
Metcalf Rd. NG16: Newth........2D 16
Meteor Cl. NG15: Newt..........2B 50
Meteor Rd. NG15: Huck..........3D 18

Mettham St. NG7: Lent..........6D 44
Mevell Ct. NG7: Nott........5A 4 (5E 45)
Mews, The NG7: Bas...........1E 45
Mews La. NG14: Calv..........4G 11
Meynell Gro. NG7: Bas.........6E 33
Meynell Rd. NG10: Long E........2F 73
MFA Bowl Ilkeston.............2A 40
Miall Ct. NG7: Lent...........4C 44
Miall St. NG7: Lent...........4C 44
Michael Gdns. NG5: Sher........6F 33
Michael Rayner Ct. NG6: Bas.....4B 32
Mickleborough Av. NG3: Nott.....1B 46
Mickleborough Way
    NG2: West Br...........2G 67
Mickledon Cl. NG10: Long E......5D 62
Mickledon Cl. NG2: Nott........1G 57
Micklemoor La. NG13: Car C......1H 51
Mickleover Rd. NG16: Kimb.......6G 17
Middlebeck Av. NG5: Arn........5E 23
Middlebeck Dr. NG5: Arn........5D 22
Middlefell Cl. NG11: Clftn.......4B 66
Middlefell Way NG11: Clftn......4B 66
Middle Furlong Gdns.
    NG2: Nott...........1F 57
Middle Furlong M. NG2: Nott.....1F 57
Middle Hill NG1: Nott......5E 5 (5G 45)
Middle La. NG9: Chil..........6E 55
Middle Nook NG8: Woll........4E 43
...............(off Cottage Wlk.)
Middle Orchard St. NG9: Stfrd 4F 53
Middle Pavement
    NG1: Nott...........5E 5 (5G 45)
Middle St. NG9: Bee..........5F 55
Middle Street Stop (NET)........4G 55
Middleton Blvd. NG8: Woll.......5A 44
Middleton Cl. NG16: Nuth.......1C 30
Middleton Ct. NG8: Bilb.........4D 42
Middleton Cres. NG9: Bee.......2E 55
Middleton Rd. DE7: Ilk.........4C 40
Middleton St. DE7: Ilk.........6C 28
Middleton St. NG16: Aws........3E 29
Middleton St. NG7: Lent........4C 44
Middleton St. NG9: Bee........4C 54
Midhurst Cl. NG9: Chil.........1C 64
Midhurst Way NG11: Clftn.......3C 66
Midlame Gdns. NG6: Bulw........6F 19
Midland Av. NG4: Neth.........2A 48
Midland Av. NG7: Lent.........6C 44
Midland Av. NG9: Stfrd.........6E 53
Midland Cotts. NG2: West Br.....4B 58
Midland Ct. NG7: Radf.........3B 44
Midland Cres. NG4: Car........2H 47
Midland Gro. NG4: Neth........1A 48
Midland Rd. DE75: Hea.........3C 14
Midland Rd. NG16: Eastw.......3B 16
Midland Rd. NG4: Car..........2H 47
Midland St. NG10: Long E.......5G 63
Midland Way NG7: Radf.........3B 44
Midway, The NG7: Lent.........3C 56
Mikado Rd. NG10: Long E........2E 73
Mikado Rd. NG13: Bing........5C 50
Mildenhall Cres. NG5: Bestw.....5G 21
Mile End Rd. NG4: Colw........4G 47
Milford Av. NG10: Long E........2D 62
Milford Cl. NG6: Bulw.........5G 19
Milford Ct. NG5: Arn..........1H 33
Milford Dr. DE7: Ilk..........4H 27
Milford St. NG3: Nott.........2E 47
Mill Acre Cl. DE7: Ilk.........5H 27
Millbank DE75: Hea...........4E 15
Millbank Cl. DE7: Ilk.........4H 27
Millbank Pl. NG6: Bestw V......2B 20
Millbeck Av. NG8: Woll.........5C 42
Millbeck Cl. NG2: Gam.........5E 59
Millbeck Cl. NG5: Arn.........4C 22
Mill Cl., The NG6: Bas........4C 32
Mill Ct. NG10: Long E..........6G 63

Mill Cres. NG5: Arn..........5A 22
Milldale Cl. NG11: Clftn.......3A 66
Milldale Rd. NG10: Long E.......1D 72
Millennium Cl. DE7: Ilk........4A 28
Millennium Ct. NG6: Bulw.......2B 32
Millennium Way NG8: Cin.......3G 31
Millennium Way E. NG8: Cin 3G 31
Millennium Way W. NG8: Cin 3G 31
Miller Hives Cl. NG12: Cotg......2E 71
Millers Bri. NG12: Cotg........3E 71
Millers Ct. NG7: Radf.........3C 44
Millersdale Av. DE7: Ilk........2A 28
Millers Grn. NG2: Nott........5C 46
Millership Way DE7: Ilk........5B 28
Mill Fld. Cl. NG14: Bur J.......4E 37
Millfield Cl. DE7: Ilk.........3G 27
Millfield Rd. DE7: Ilk.........2C 40
Millfield Rd. NG16: Kimb.......6G 17
Mill Hill La. DE72: Brea.......4A 62
Mill Hill Rd. NG13: Bing........6D 50
MILL HILL RDBT..............5A 66
Millicent Gro. NG2: West Br.....3B 58
Millicent Rd. NG2: West Br......3A 58
Millidge Cl. NG5: Bestw........2D 32
Mill La. NG10: Sand...........5E 53
Mill La. NG11: Rudd..........3B 78
Mill La. NG12: C'ton..........4D 70
Mill La. NG12: Cotg...........1E 71
...............(not continuous)
Mill La. NG12: Cotg..........4D 70
...............(not continuous)
Mill La. NG16: Coss...........1D 40
Mill La. NG4: Lamb..........6B 24
Mill La. NG5: Arn...........5A 22
Mill La. NG6: Bestw V.........2B 20
Mill Rd. DE75: Hea...........5E 15
Mill Rd. NG16: Newth.........2C 16
Mill Rd. NG9: Stfrd..........3F 53
Mills Bldgs. NG1: Nott......5G 5 (5H 45)
...............(off Stoney St.)
Mill St. DE7: Ilk...........6B 28
Mill St. NG6: Bas...........4B 32
Millview Ct. NG2: Nott.....5H 5 (5A 46)
Mill Yd. NG15: Huck..........4G 7
Milner Rd. NG10: Long E........5F 63
Milner Rd. NG5: Sher.........5G 33
Milnhay Rd. DE75: Hea........4G 15
Milnhay Rd. NG16: Lang M.......3G 15
Milton Av. DE7: Ilk..........3A 28
Milton Cres. NG5: Arn.........6D 22
Milton Ct. NG5: Sher..........4F 33
Milton Cres. NG9: Atten.......3D 64
Milton Ho. NG1: Nott......3E 5 (4G 45)
Milton Ri. NG15: Huck.........6D 6
Milton Rd. DE7: Ilk..........3A 28
Milton St. DE7: Ilk..........3B 28
Milton St. NG1: Nott......2E 5 (4G 45)
Milton St. NG10: Long E.......6F 63
Milton Ter. NG10: Long E.......6F 63
Milverton Rd. NG5: Bestw.......5G 21
Milward Rd. DE75: Los.........3B 14
Mimosa Cl. NG11: Clftn........4A 66
Minerva Gro. NG15: Huck.......3A 8
Minerva St. NG6: Bulw.........5H 19
...............(not continuous)
Minkley Dr. NG16: Lang M.......1G 15
MINOR INJURIES UNIT (ILKESTON
HOSPITAL)................3H 27
Minster Cl. NG15: Huck.........3H 7
Minster Ct. NG5: Sher.........2F 45
Minster Gdns. NG16: Newth.....4D 16
Minstrel Av. NG5: Sher........5E 33
Minstrel Cl. NG15: Huck........6G 7
Mint Gro. NG10: Long E.........6C 62
Minton Cl. NG9: Chil.........4B 64
Minver Cres. NG8: Aspl........6G 31
Minver Crescent Sports Cen.....6H 31
Mirberry M. NG7: Lent.........6C 44

Miriam Ct. NG2: West Br........4A 58
Misk Hollows NG15: Huck........3F 7
Misk Vw. NG16: Eastw.........3D 16
Mission St. NG3: Mapp.........5A 34
Mitchell Av. NG16: Lang M.......1E 15
Mitchell Cl. NG6: Bulw.........1G 31
Mitchell St. NG10: Long E.......6G 63
Mitchell Ter. DE7: Ilk.........4C 40
Mitford Dr. NG5: Arn..........3B 22
Moffat Cl. NG3: Nott..........2B 46
Mohan Bus. Cen.
    ....6F 63
Mollington Sq. NG6: Cin.......3H 31
Monarch Way DE75: Hea........3B 14
Mona Rd. NG2: West Br........2C 58
Mona St. NG9: Bee...........5G 55
Monks Cl. DE7: Ilk...........1C 40
Monk's La. NG11: Goth........6H 75
Monksway NG11: Wilf..........1E 67
Monkton Cl. DE7: Ilk..........4H 27
Monkton Dr. NG8: Bilb.........2E 43
Monmouth Cl. NG8: Woll........5B 42
Monroe Wlk. NG5: Bestw........6E 21
Monsaldale Cl. NG10: Long E.....1D 72
Monsall Av. DE7: Ilk..........2A 28
Monsall St. NG7: Bas.........6D 32
Monsell Dr. NG5: Redh.........4A 22
Montague Rd. NG15: Huck........3G 7
Montague St. NG6: Bulw........6A 20
Montague St. NG9: Bee.........4E 55
Montfort Cres. NG5: Sher.......3H 33
Montfort St. NG7: Radf........4E 45
Montgomery Cl. NG9: Chil......3C 64
Montgomery St.
    NG7: Radf............1A 4 (3E 45)
Montpelier Rd. NG7: Lent.......2C 56
Monyash Cl. DE7: Ilk.........4A 28
Moody Cl. NG9: Chil..........3B 64
Moon Cres. NG16: Eastw........4A 16
Moor, The DE7: D Ab..........6E 39
Moor, The NG9: Trow..........3A 42
Moorbridge Cvn. Pk.
    NG6: Bulw............3B 20
Moorbridge Cotts. NG6: Bulw 3B 20
Moorbridge Ct. NG13: Bing......4E 51
Moorbridge La. NG9: Stfrd......2F 53
Moor Bridge Park & Ride........3B 20
Moorbridge Rd. NG13: Bing......4E 51
Moorbridge Rd. E. NG13: Bing ...4E 51
Moor Bridge Stop (NET)........3B 20
Moore Cl. NG2: West Br........2D 58
Moore Ga. NG9: Bee..........5F 55
Moore Rd. NG3: Mapp.........5C 34
Moores Av. NG10: Sand........4E 53
Moores Pl. NG5: Sher.........5E 33
Moore St. NG6: Bulw..........2A 32
Moor Farm Holiday & Home Pk.
    ....5C 12
Moor Farm Inn La. NG9: Bram ...1A 54
Moorfield Ct. NG9: Stfrd.......2G 53
Moorfield Cres. NG10: Sand.....6D 52
Moorfields Av. NG16: Eastw.....2B 16
Moorgate St. NG7: Radf........4E 45
MOORGREEN.................2F 17
Moorgreen Dr. NG8: Stre.......5D 30
Moorgreen Ind. Pk.
    NG16: Newth...........1D 16
Moorhouse Rd. NG8: Bilb.......3E 43
Moorings, The NG7: Lent.......1D 56
Moorland Av. NG9: Stfrd.......5F 53
Moorlands Cl. NG10: Long E.....3D 62
Moor La. NG11: Rudd
    Leys Ct.............1G 77
Moor La. NG11: Rudd
    Littlemoor La.........5H 77
Moor La. DE7: D Ab..........6D 38
Moor La. NG11: Bunny.........6G 77
Moor La. NG11: Goth..........6H 75

Moor La. – New St.

Moor La. NG11: Rudd ... 6H **75**
Moor La. NG13: Bing ... 4E **51**
Moor La. NG14: Calv ... 5C **12**
Moor La. NG14: Epp ... 5C **12**
Moor La. NG9: Bram ... 1B **54**
Moor Rd. NG14: Calv ... 4A **12**
Moor Rd. NG15: Pap ... 1B **8**
Moor Rd. NG6: Bestw V ... 2B **20**
Moor Rd. NG8: Stre ... 6D **30**
Moorsholm Dr. NG8: Woll ... 5C **42**
Moor St. NG4: Neth ... 2H **47**
Moray Ct. NG16: Kimb ... 6H **17**
Morden Cl. NG8: Bilb ... 1D **42**
Morden Rd. NG16: Gilt ... 5E **17**
Moreland Ct. NG2: Nott ... 6B **46**
Moreland Ct. NG4: Car ... 2E **47**
Moreland Pl. NG2: Nott ... 6B **46**
Moreland St. NG2: Nott ... 6B **46**
Morel Cl. NG16: Eastw ... 4B **16**
Morel Ho. NG7: Lent ... 4C **44**
... *(off Faraday Rd.)*
Morello Av. NG4: Car ... 2H **47**
Morello Dr. NG8: Aspl ... 2A **44**
Moreton Rd. NG11: Clftn ... 6C **66**
Morgan M. NG11: Clftn ... 3B **66**
Morkinshire Cres. NG12: Cotg ... 1F **71**
Morkinshire La. NG12: Cotg ... 1E **71**
Morley Av. NG3: Mapp ... 5A **34**
Morley Ct. NG2: Nott ... 3H **5** (5A **46**)
Morley Dr. DE7: Ilk ... 4H **27**
Morley Gdns. NG12: Rad T ... 5G **49**
Morley Gdns. NG5: Sher ... 6F **33**
Morley Pl. NG3: Nott ... 1B **46**
Morley Rd. NG3: Nott ... 6C **34**
Morley St. NG5: Arn ... 1H **33**
Mornington Cl. NG10: Sand ... 5E **53**
Mornington Cres. NG16: Nuth ... 4D **30**
Morrell Bank NG5: Bestw ... 1D **32**
Morris Av. NG9: Chil ... 4B **64**
Morris Ct. NG4: Colw ... 4A **48**
Morris Rd. NG8: Stre ... 6D **30**
Morris St. NG4: Neth ... 2A **48**
Morton Av. DE7: Ilk ... 2B **28**
Morton Gdns. NG12: Rad T ... 6H **49**
Morval Rd. NG8: Bilb ... 2E **43**
Morven Av. NG15: Huck ... 5H **7**
Mosley St. NG15: Huck ... 5G **7**
Mosley St. NG7: Bas ... 1D **44**
Mosquito Gro. NG15: Huck ... 3E **19**
Moss Cl. NG5: Arn ... 5G **21**
Mosscroft Av. NG11: Clftn ... 4B **66**
Mossdale Rd. NG5: Sher ... 2G **33**
Moss Dr. NG9: Bram ... 4B **54**
Moss Ri. NG3: Mapp ... 5D **34**
Moss Rd. DE7: Ilk ... 2A **40**
Moss Rd. NG15: Huck ... 4F **7**
Moss Side NG11: Wilf ... 2E **67**
Mosswood Cres. NG5: Bestw ... 6F **21**
Mottram Rd. NG9: Chil ... 5C **54**
Mount, The NG3: Mapp ... 5E **35**
Mount, The NG5: Redh ... 4H **21**
Mount, The NG6: Bestw V ... 1C **20**
Mount, The NG8: Stre ... 6E **31**
Mount, The NG9: Stfrd ... 5F **53**
Mountain Ash Cres.
NG12: Edwal ... 3C **68**
Mountbatten Ct. DE7: Ilk ... 4B **28**
Mountbatten Gro. NG4: Ged ... 5G **35**
Mountbatten Way NG9: Chil ... 3B **64**
Mountfield Av. NG10: Sand ... 1C **62**
Mountfield Dr. NG5: Bestw ... 6E **21**
Mount Hgts. NG7: Bas ... 6E **33**
Mt. Hooton NG1: Nott ... 3E **45**
Mt. Hooton Rd. NG7: Radf ... 2E **45**
Mt. Pleasant DE7: Ilk ... 3A **28**
Mt. Pleasant NG12: Key ... 4H **79**
Mt. Pleasant NG12: Rad T ... 6E **49**
Mt. Pleasant NG4: Car ... 2G **47**
Mt. Pleasant NG6: Bas ... 5B **32**
Mountsorrel Dr. NG2: West Br ... 5D **58**
Mount St. DE72: Brea ... 6B **62**
Mount St. DE75: Hea ... 4C **14**
Mount St. NG1: Nott ... 4C **4** (5F **45**)
... (not continuous)
Mount St. NG7: Bas ... 6D **32**
Mount St. NG9: Stfrd ... 4G **53**
Mount St. Arc.
NG1: Nott ... 4C **4** (5F **45**)
... *(off Mount St.)*
Mowbray Ct. NG3: Nott ... 2G **5** (4H **45**)
Mowbray Gdns. NG2: West Br ... 6B **58**
Mowbray Ri. NG5: Arn ... 4B **22**
Moyra Dr. NG5: Arn ... 6G **21**
Moyra Ho. NG5: Arn ... 6A **22**
Mozart Cl. NG7: Radf ... 4C **44**
Mudpie La. NG2: West Br ... 2D **58**
Muir Av. NG12: Toll ... 5F **69**
Muirfield Rd. NG5: Arn ... 4D **20**
Muirfield Rd. NG5: Top V ... 4D **20**
Mulberry Cl. NG2: West Br ... 6F **57**
Mulberry Gdns. NG6: Bulw ... 5G **19**
Mulberry Gro. NG15: Huck ... 1H **19**
Mundella Rd. NG2: Nott ... 2H **57**
Mundy's Dr. DE75: Hea ... 5D **14**
Mundy St. DE7: Ilk ... 5B **28**
Mundy St. DE75: Hea ... 4C **14**
Munford Cir. NG8: Cin ... 4G **31**
Munks Av. NG15: Huck ... 4F **7**
Murby Cres. NG6: Bulw ... 5H **19**
Murden Way NG9: Bee ... 5H **55**
Muriel Gdns. NG6: Bulw ... 6H **19**
Muriel Rd. NG9: Bee ... 4F **55**
Muriel St. NG6: Bulw ... 6H **19**
Murray Cl. NG5: Bestw ... 2D **32**
Museum of Nottingham
Life ... 6C **4** (6F **45**)
Mushroom Farm Ct.
NG16: Eastw ... 2H **15**
Muskham Av. DE7: Ilk ... 4B **28**
Muskham St. NG2: Nott ... 2H **57**
Mustang Cl. NG15: Huck ... 3E **19**
Musters Ct. NG15: Huck ... 5A **8**
Musters Ct. NG2: West Br ... 3A **58**
Musters Cres. NG2: West Br ... 6B **58**
Musters Cft. NG4: Colw ... 6H **47**
Musters Rd. NG11: Rudd ... 1F **77**
Musters Rd. NG13: Bing ... 5D **50**
Musters Rd. NG2: West Br ... 3A **58**
Musters Wlk. NG6: Bulw ... 6G **19**
Muston Cl. NG3: Mapp ... 6B **34**
Myrtle Av. NG10: Long E ... 1E **73**
Myrtle Av. NG7: Hys G ... 1F **45**
Myrtle Av. NG9: Stfrd ... 5G **53**
Myrtle Gro. NG9: Bee ... 4G **55**
Myrtle Rd. NG4: Car ... 1E **47**
Myrtus Cl. NG11: Clftn ... 3A **66**
Mytholme Cl. NG10: Long E ... 3E **63**

N

Nabarro Ct. NG14: Calv ... 4G **11**
Nabbs La. NG15: Huck ... 5D **6**
Naburn Ct. NG8: Bas ... 6B **32**
Nairn Cl. NG5: Arn ... 4D **22**
Nairn M. NG4: Car ... 2G **47**
Nansen Gdns. NG5: Bestw ... 1D **32**
Nansen St. NG6: Bulw ... 1A **32**
Naomi Ct. NG6: Bulw ... 4A **20**
Naomi Cres. NG6: Bulw ... 4A **20**
Naranjan M. NG7: Radf ... 1A **4** (3E **45**)
Narrow La. NG16: Want ... 4H **17**
Naseby Cl. NG5: Sher ... 3D **32**
Naseby Dr. NG10: Long E ... 2G **73**
Nathaniel Rd. NG10: Long E ... 6H **63**
Nathans La. NG12: Rad T ... 4A **60**
Nat. Ice Cen., The ... 4G **5** (5H **45**)
National Justice Mus. ... 5F **5** (5H **45**)
National Water Sports Cen. ... 1G **59**
National Water Sports Cen.
Holme Pierrepont Cvn. &
Camping Pk.
NG2: West Br ... 2F **59**
Natural History Mus.
Nottingham ... 6G **43**
Navdeep Ct. NG2: West Br ... 4A **58**
Navenby Wlk. NG11: Clftn ... 3C **66**
Navigation St. NG2: Nott ... 1B **58**
Naworth Cl. NG6: Bulw ... 2C **32**
Naylor Av. NG11: Goth ... 6H **75**
Naylor Ho. NG5: Arn ... 1C **34**
... *(off Derwent Cres.)*
Nazareth Ct. NG7: Lent ... 1C **56**
Nazareth Rd. NG7: Lent ... 1C **56**
Neal Ct. NG16: Lang M ... 2E **15**
Neale St. NG10: Long E ... 6G **63**
Near Mdw. NG10: Long E ... 2G **73**
Nearsby Dr. NG2: West Br ... 5D **58**
Needham Rd. NG5: Arn ... 5C **22**
Needham St. NG13: Bing ... 5E **51**
Needwood Av. NG9: Trow ... 1F **53**
Neeps Cft. NG14: Epp ... 5G **13**
Negus Ct. NG4: Lamb ... 6B **24**
Neighwood Cl. NG9: Toton ... 3G **63**
Nell Gwyn Cres. NG5: Arn ... 4G **21**
Nelper Cres. DE7: Ilk ... 4C **40**
Nelson Rd. NG5: Arn ... 6A **22**
Nelson Rd. NG6: Bulw ... 6A **20**
Nelson Rd. NG9: Bee ... 1G **65**
Nelson St. DE7: Ilk ... 3B **28**
Nelson St. DE75: Hea ... 3B **14**
Nelson St. NG1: Nott ... 4G **5** (5H **45**)
Nelson St. NG10: Long E ... 1F **73**
Nene Cl. NG15: Huck ... 2E **19**
Nene Way NG13: Bing ... 6D **50**
Nesfield Ct. DE7: Ilk ... 6A **28**
Nesfield Rd. DE7: Ilk ... 6A **28**
Neston Dr. NG6: Cin ... 3H **31**
Nether Cl. NG16: Eastw ... 1B **16**
Nether Cl. NG3: Nott ... 3C **46**
NETHERFIELD ... 3H **47**
Netherfield Rd. NG10: Long E ... 3D **72**
Netherfield Rd. NG10: Sand ... 6D **52**
Netherfields La. DE72: Shar ... 6B **72**
Netherfield Station (Rail) ... 3H **47**
Nethergate NG11: Clftn ... 3A **66**
NETHER GREEN ... 1B **16**
Nether Grn. NG16: Eastw ... 2B **16**
Nethermere La. NG8: Stre ... 5C **30**
Nether Pasture NG4: Neth ... 3A **48**
Nether Slade Rd. DE7: Ilk ... 5A **28**
Nether St. NG9: Bee ... 5G **55**
Nettlecliff Wlk. NG5: Top V ... 5C **20**
Neville Rd. NG14: Calv ... 5H **11**
Neville Sadler Ct. NG9: Bee ... 4G **55**
New Alexandra Ct., The
NG3: Nott ... 1H **45**
Newall Dr. NG9: Chil ... 3C **64**
Newark Av. NG2: Nott ... 5H **5** (5A **46**)
Newark Ct. NG5: Bestw ... 2D **32**
Newark Cres. NG2: Nott ... 5H **5** (5A **46**)
Newark Hall NG8: Woll ... 5B **44**
Newark St. NG2: Nott ... 5H **5** (5A **46**)
New Art Exchange ... 2D **44**
NEW BASFORD ... 6D **32**
New Basford Bus. Area
NG7: Bas ... 6D **32**
... *(off Palm St.)*
Newbery Av. NG10: Long E ... 1H **73**
Newbridge Cl. DE7: West H ... 1B **38**
New Brook Ho. NG7: Radf ... 3D **44**
Newbury Cl. NG3: Mapp ... 3C **34**
Newbury Ct. NG5: Sher ... 1F **45**
Newbury Dr. NG16: Nuth ... 4D **30**
Newcastle Av. NG4: Ged ... 6G **35**
Newcastle Av. NG9: Bee ... 5F **55**
Newcastle Chambers
NG1: Nott ... 4D **4** (5G **45**)
Newcastle Cir.
NG7: Nott ... 5A **4** (5E **45**)
Newcastle Ct. NG7: Nott ... 5A **4** (5E **45**)
Newcastle Dr. NG7: Nott ... 4A **4** (5E **45**)
Newcastle Farm Dr.
NG8: Aspl ... 6A **32**
Newcastle St. NG6: Bulw ... 5A **20**
Newcastle Ter.
NG7: Nott ... 3A **4** (4E **45**)
Newcastle Ter. NG8: Aspl ... 6B **32**
Newcombe Dr. NG5: Arn ... 6E **23**
New Ct. NG1: Nott ... 4F **5** (5H **45**)
... *(off Ristes Pl.)*
New Derby Rd. NG16: Eastw ... 2H **15**
Newdigate Rd. NG16: Want ... 6A **18**
Newdigate St. DE7: Ilk ... 3C **40**
Newdigate St. DE7: West H ... 1A **38**
Newdigate St. NG16: Kimb ... 1H **29**
Newdigate St.
NG7: Radf ... 2A **4** (4E **45**)
Newdigate Vs.
NG7: Radf ... 2A **4** (4E **45**)
NEW EASTWOOD ... 4B **16**
New Eaton Rd. NG9: Stfrd ... 5F **53**
New Farm La. NG16: Nuth ... 1C **30**
Newfield Rd. NG5: Sher ... 4D **32**
Newgate Cl. NG4: Car ... 2G **47**
Newgate St. NG13: Bing ... 4E **51**
Newgate St. NG7: Lent ... 5D **44**
Newhall Gro. NG2: West Br ... 2B **58**
Newham Cl. DE75: Hea ... 4E **15**
Newholm Dr. NG11: Wilf ... 6E **57**
Newland Cl. NG8: Aspl ... 4A **44**
Newland Cl. NG9: Toton ... 3A **64**
NEWLANDS ... 3E **15**
Newlands Cl. NG12: Edwal ... 1E **69**
Newlands Dr. DE75: Hea ... 2C **14**
Newlands Dr. NG4: Ged ... 6H **35**
New Lawn Rd. DE7: Ilk ... 1A **40**
NEW LENTON ... 6D **44**
Newlyn Dr. NG8: Aspl ... 1B **44**
Newlyn Gdns. NG8: Aspl ... 1B **44**
Newmanleys Rd. NG16: Eastw ... 5A **16**
Newmanleys Rd. Sth.
NG16: Eastw ... 4A **16**
New Manor Ground ... 4C **28**
Newman Rd. NG14: Calv ... 3G **11**
Newmarket Rd. NG6: Bulw ... 1H **31**
Newmarket Way NG9: Toton ... 4H **63**
NEW NUTHALL ... 1C **30**
Newport Dr. NG8: Bas ... 6B **32**
Newquay Av. NG7: Radf ... 2C **44**
New Ri. NG11: Clftn ... 5A **66**
New Rd. NG11: Bart F ... 1E **75**
New Rd. NG12: Rad T ... 6F **49**
New Rd. NG16: Newth ... 1F **17**
New Rd. NG16: Want ... 1F **17**
New Rd. NG7: Radf ... 3B **44**
New Rd. NG9: Stfrd ... 2F **53**
New Row NG14: Woodbo ... 1C **24**
New Row NG4: Car ... 2F **47**
NEW SAWLEY ... 2D **72**
NEW STANTON ... 6A **40**
NEW STAPLEFORD ... 2G **53**
Newstead Av. NG12: Rad T ... 5G **49**
Newstead Av. NG3: Mapp ... 5D **34**
Newstead Ct. NG5: Woodt ... 2C **34**
Newstead Dr. NG2: West Br ... 4D **58**
Newstead Gro.
NG1: Nott ... 1C **4** (3F **45**)
Newstead Gro. NG13: Bing ... 5C **50**
Newstead Ind. Est. NG5: Arn ... 6C **22**
Newstead Rd. NG10: Long E ... 2E **63**
Newstead Rd. Nth. DE7: Ilk ... 4H **27**
Newstead Rd. Sth. DE7: Ilk ... 4H **27**
Newstead St. NG5: Sher ... 4G **33**
Newstead Ter. NG15: Huck ... 3G **7**
Newstead Way NG8: Stre ... 5D **30**
New St. DE7: Stly ... 3A **38**

112 A-Z Nottingham

New St. – Oakland Ct.

New St. NG10: Long E 5G 63
New St. NG5: Redh 4A 22
New St. NG5: Sher 6F 33
New Ter. NG10: Sand 5D 52
NEWTHORPE 4E 17
NEWTHORPE COMMON 5D 16
Newthorpe Comn. NG16: Newth 4C 16
Newthorpe St. NG2: Nott 1H 57
NEWTON 1B 50
Newton Airfield (disused) 1A 50
Newton Av. NG12: Rad T 5G 49
Newton Av. NG13: Bing 5D 50
(not continuous)
Newton Cl. NG5: Arn 1D 34
Newtondale Cl. NG8: Aspl 6B 32
Newton Dr. DE75: Hea 4E 15
Newton Dr. NG2: West Br 1G 67
Newton Dr. NG9: Stfrd 5G 53
Newton Gdns. NG13: Newt 3C 50
Newton Rd. NG4: Ged 4F 35
Newton's La. NG16: Coss 4C 28
(not continuous)
Newton St. NG7: Lent 3C 56
Newton St. NG9: Bee 5E 55
New Tythe St. NG10: Long E 6H 63
New Vale Rd. NG4: Colw 4F 47
New Windmill Ct. NG2: Nott 5B 46
New Works Cotts. NG14: Stoke B 1C 48
ng2 Bus. Pk. NG2: Nott 1E 57
ng2 Stop (NET) 1E 57
Nicholas Cl. DE7: Ilk 3B 40
Nicholas Rd. NG9: Bram 2D 54
Nicker Hill NG12: Key 3H 79
Nicklaus Ct. NG5: Top V 5E 21
(off Crossfield Dr.)
Nidderdale NG8: Woll 5C 42
Nidderdale Cl. NG8: Woll 6C 42
Nightingale Cl. NG16: Nuth 1D 30
Nightingale Cl. NG7: Nott 2G 55
Nightingale Ho. NG3: Mapp 5B 34
Nightingale Way NG13: Bing 6G 51
Nile St. NG1: Nott 3G 5 (4H 45)
Nilsson Rd. NG9: Chil 2B 64
Nimbus Way NG16: Want 6H 17
Nine Acre Gdns. NG6: Bulw 6F 19
Nine Corners NG16: Kimb 1H 29
Nixon Ri. NG15: Huck 6D 6
Nobel Rd. NG11: Clftn 5A 66
Noel St. NG16: Kimb 1A 30
Noel St. NG7: Bas 1D 44
(not continuous)
Noel St. NG7: Hys G 1D 44
(not continuous)
Noel Street Stop (NET) 2D 44
No Man's La. DE72: Ris 4A 52
No Man's La. NG10: Sand 4A 52
Nook, The DE75: Los 1A 14
Nook, The NG14: Calv 4H 11
Nook, The NG16: Kimb 2A 30
Nook, The NG8: Woll 5E 43
Nook, The NG9: Bee 4G 55
Nook, The NG9: Chil 1E 65
Nook End Rd. DE75: Hea 4B 14
Norbett Cl. NG9: Chil 2C 64
Norbett Ct. NG5: Arn 4C 22
Norbett Rd. NG5: Arn 5C 22
Norbreck Cl. NG8: Cin 4H 31
Norburn Cres. NG6: Bas 4D 32
Norbury Way NG10: Sand 5C 52
Nordean Rd. NG5: Woodt 2C 34
Norfolk Av. NG9: Toton 4A 64
Norfolk Cl. NG15: Huck 6D 6
Norfolk Pk. NG5: Arn 2D 34
Norfolk Pl. NG1: Nott 3D 4 (4G 45)
Norfolk Rd. NG10: Long E 4H 63
Norfolk Wlk. NG10: Sand 6D 52
Norland Cl. NG3: Nott 2A 46
(not continuous)
Normanby Rd. NG8: Woll 6C 42
Norman Cl. NG3: Nott 1E 5 (3G 45)
Norman Cl. NG9: Chil 6C 54
Norman Cres. DE7: Ilk 4A 28
Norman Dr. NG15: Huck 1E 19
Norman Dr. NG16: Eastw 3D 16
Norman Rd. NG3: Nott 1C 46
Norman St. DE7: Ilk 3A 28
Norman St. NG16: Kimb 6H 17
Norman St. NG4: Neth 3A 48
Normanton La. NG12: Key 4H 79
NORMANTON-ON-THE-WOLDS 1A 80
Norris Homes NG7: Hys G 1F 45
Northall Av. NG6: Bulw 1H 31
Northampton St. NG3: Nott 3A 46
North Av. NG10: Sand 5C 52
Nth. Church St. NG1: Nott 2D 4 (4G 45)
Nth. Circus St. NG1: Nott 3B 4 (5F 45)
Northcliffe Av. NG3: Mapp 5C 34
Northcote St. NG10: Long E 6G 63
Northcote Way NG6: Bulw 2A 32
Northdale Rd. NG3: Nott 2D 46
Northdown Dr. NG9: Chil 1C 64
Northdown Rd. NG8: Aspl 3B 44
North Dr. NG9: Chil 5E 55
Northern Ct. NG6: Bas 3B 32
Northern Dr. NG6: Bestw V 1D 20
Northern Dr. NG9: Trow 6F 41
Northern Rd. DE75: Hea 3B 14
Northfield Av. DE7: Ilk 5A 28
Northfield Av. NG10: Long E 3D 72
Northfield Av. NG12: Rad T 5H 49
Northfield Cres. NG9: Chil 1H 63
Northfield Rd. NG9: Chil 1A 64
Northfields NG10: Long E 3D 72
North Ga. NG7: Bas 6D 32
North Ga. Pl. NG7: Bas 6D 32
(off High Chu. St.)
Northgate St. DE7: Ilk 6A 28
North Grn. NG14: Calv 2E 11
North Hill Av. NG15: Huck 4F 7
North Hill Cres. NG15: Huck 4F 7
Northolme Av. NG6: Bulw 6A 20
Northolt Dr. NG16: Nuth 4D 30
North Rd. NG7: Nott West Rd 1B 56
North Rd. NG7: Nott Western Ter 5E 45
North Rd. NG10: Long E 1E 73
North Rd. NG11: Rudd 5F 67
North Rd. NG2: West Br 5A 58
North Rd. NG5: Sher 3E 33
(not continuous)
Nth. Sherwood St. NG1: Nott 2F 45
Northside Wlk. NG5: Arn 3B 22
North St. DE7: Ilk 6B 28
North St. NG16: Kimb 2A 30
North St. NG16: Lang M 2F 15
North St. NG16: Newth 3E 17
North St. NG2: Nott 4H 5 (5A 46)
North St. NG9: Bee 5E 55
Northumberland Cl. NG3: Nott 1F 5 (3H 45)
Northville Ct. NG3: Nott 2H 45
Northwold Av. NG2: West Br 5H 57
Northwood Cres. NG5: Bestw 1G 33
Northwood Rd. NG5: Bestw 1G 33
Northwood St. NG9: Stfrd 3F 53
Norton Ct. NG7: Radf 3C 44
Norton St. NG7: Radf 3C 44
(not continuous)
Norwich Gdns. NG6: Bulw 4H 19
Norwood Cl. DE7: Ilk 2B 28
Norwood Rd. NG7: Radf 4C 44
Noskwith St. DE7: Ilk 4C 40
Notintone Pl. NG2: Nott 5A 46
Notintone St. NG2: Nott 5A 46
NOTTINGHAM 4E 5 (5G 45)
Nottingham Airport 6H 59
Nottingham Arts Theatre 4F 5 (5H 45)
Nottingham Bus. Pk. NG2: Nott 6H 5 (6A 46)
Nottingham Bus. Pk. NG8: Stre 5C 30
Nottingham Castle 6C 4 (5F 45)
Nottingham Castle Caves 6C 4 (6F 45)
(within Nottingham Castle)
Nottingham City Golf Course 3G 19
Nottingham Climbing Cen. 1D 44
Nottingham Contemporary 5E 5 (5H 45)
Nottingham Forest FC 2A 58
Nottingham Forest Football Academy 4H 57
Nottingham Greyhound Stadium 5D 46
Nottingham Indoor Bowls Cen. 2G 43
Nottingham Industrial Mus. 6G 43
Nottingham Lakeside Arts 2B 56
NOTTINGHAM NEURODISABILITY SERVICE HUCKNALL 6A 8
NOTTINGHAM NHS TREATMENT CEN. 1C 56
Nottingham One NG1: Nott 6F 5 (6H 45)
Nottingham Playhouse 4C 4 (5F 45)
Nottingham Racecourse 6E 47
Nottingham RFC 2B 58
Nottingham Rd. DE7: Ilk 2B 40
Nottingham Rd. NG10: Long E 5G 63
Nottingham Rd. NG11: Goth 6H 75
Nottingham Rd. NG12: Key 5G 79
Nottingham Rd. NG12: Rad T 1D 60
Nottingham Rd. NG13: Bing 5B 50
Nottingham Rd. NG14: Bur J 4D 36
Nottingham Rd. NG14: Woodbo 3F 23
Nottingham Rd. NG15: Huck 6A 8
Nottingham Rd. NG16: Cin 2D 30
Nottingham Rd. NG16: Eastw 3B 16
Nottingham Rd. NG16: Gilt 4D 16
Nottingham Rd. NG16: Kimb 1A 30
Nottingham Rd. NG16: Newth 4D 16
Nottingham Rd. NG16: Nuth 2D 30
Nottingham Rd. NG25: Oxton 1B 12
Nottingham Rd. NG5: Arn 1A 34
Nottingham Rd. NG6: Bas 4C 32
(not continuous)
Nottingham Rd. NG7: Bas 5D 32
Nottingham Rd. NG8: Cin 3G 31
Nottingham Rd. NG9: Chil 4A 64
Nottingham Rd. NG9: Stfrd 4F 53
Nottingham Rd. NG9: Toton 4A 64
Nottingham Rd. NG9: Trow 5E 41
Nottingham Rd. E. NG16: Eastw 4D 16
Nottingham Rd. E. NG16: Gilt 4D 16
Nottingham Rd. E. NG16: Newth 4D 16
Nottingham Sailing Club 1F 59
Nottingham St Barnabas' RC Cathedral 3B 4 (5F 45)
Nottingham Science & Technology Pk. NG7: Nott 2B 56
Nottinghamshire County Cricket Ground 2A 58
Nottinghamshire Golf Course, The 4C 60
NOTTINGHAMSHIRE HOSPICE 1H 45
Nottingham South & Wilford Ind. Est. NG11: Wilf 1F 67
Nottingham Station (Rail & NET) 6F 5 (6H 45)
Nottingham Tennis Cen. 3B 56
Nottingham Tourism Cen. 4E 5 (5G 45)
Nottingham Trent University City Campus 2C 4 (4F 45)
Nottingham Trent University Clifton Campus 2B 66
Nottingham Trent University Union Rd. 4G 45
Nottingham Trent University Waverley St. 1B 4 (3F 45)
Nottingham Trent University Stop (NET) 2C 4 (4F 45)
Nottingham University Academy of Science & Technology 2C 56
Nottingham Wholesale & Trade Pk. NG2: Nott 1A 58
Nottingham Wildcats Arena 4D 46
Notts County FC 1A 58
Notts Gymnastics Academy 1B 68
Nuart Rd. NG9: Bee 5F 55
Nuffield Health Nottingham 3D 34
Nugent Gdns. NG3: Nott 1H 5 (3A 46)
Nunn Cl. NG15: Huck 1A 8
Nurseries, The NG16: Eastw 3C 16
Nursery Av. DE7: West H 2C 38
Nursery Av. NG10: Sand 6B 52
Nursery Av. NG9: Chil 6C 54
Nursery Cl. NG12: Rad T 6H 49
Nursery Cl. NG15: Huck 1G 19
Nursery Dr. NG4: Car 1F 47
Nursery Hollow DE7: Ilk 3A 40
Nursery La. NG6: Bas 3C 32
Nursery Rd. NG12: Rad T 6H 49
Nursery Rd. NG13: Bing 5H 51
Nursery Rd. NG5: Arn 6B 22
Nutbrook Cres. DE7: Kirk H 5H 39
NUTHALL 2D 30
Nuthall Circ. DE7: Kirk H 5G 39
Nuthall Gdns. NG8: Aspl 1B 44
Nuthall Rd. NG8: Aspl 4H 31
Nuthall Rd. NG8: Cin 4H 31

O

Oak Acres NG9: Chil 6A 54
Oak Apple Cres. DE7: Ilk 3A 40
Oakash Ct. NG16: Nuth 1B 30
Oak Av. NG10: Sand 4C 52
Oak Av. NG12: Rad T 5E 49
Oak Av. NG13: Bing 5G 51
Oak Av. NG16: Lang M 1F 15
Oakdale Dr. NG9: Chil 1C 64
Oakdale Rd. NG3: Nott 3D 46
Oakdale Rd. NG4: Car 3F 47
Oakdale Rd. NG5: Arn 5D 22
Oak Dr. NG16: Eastw 3A 16
Oak Dr. NG16: Nuth 1B 30
Oakenhall Av. NG15: Huck 4A 8
Oakfield NG12: Rad T 5G 49
Oakfield Cl. NG8: Woll 6C 42
Oakfield Ct. NG12: Rad T 6H 49
Oakfield Dr. NG10: Sand 2D 62
Oakfield Rd. NG15: Huck 5H 7
Oakfield Rd. NG8: Woll 6C 42
Oakfield Rd. NG9: Stfrd 4F 53
Oakfields Rd. NG2: West Br 2C 58
Oak Flatt NG9: Chil 5A 54
Oakford Cl. NG8: Brox 5G 31
Oak Gro. NG15: Huck 1H 19
Oakham Cl. NG5: Top V 6D 20
Oakham Ct. NG4: Ged 4F 35
Oakham Rd. NG11: Rudd 3H 67
Oakham Way DE7: Ilk 4H 27
Oakington Cl. NG5: Bestw 2F 33
Oakland Av. NG10: Long E 2E 73
Oakland Ct. NG9: Bram 2A 54

A-Z Nottingham 113

Oakland Gro. NG14: Calv............4H 11
Oaklands Av. DE75: Hea.........3E 15
Oakland St. NG7: Hys G........2C 44
Oakland Ter. NG10: Long E.........2E 73
Oakland Way NG8: Bilb.............1D 42
Oakleaf Cl. NG6: Bestw V 1C 20
Oakleigh Av. NG3: Mapp...........5E 35
Oakleigh St. NG6: Bulw.............3B 32
Oakley M. NG6: Bulw..............1F 31
Oakley's Rd. NG10: Long E........6G 63
Oakley's Rd. W.
  NG10: Long E.......................1F 73
Oak Lodge NG13: Bing 5G 51
Oak Lodge Dr. NG16: Kimb.........6H 17
Oakmead Av. NG8: Bilb 1F 43
Oakmere Cl. NG12: Edwal 1E 69
Oaks, The NG3: Nott.......2H 5 (4H 45)
Oak St. NG5: Sher....................6F 33
Oak Tree Av. NG12: Rad T..........5F 49
Oak Tree Cl. NG15: Huck 1D 18
Oak Tree Cl. NG2: West Br.........3C 58
Oak Tree Cl. NG12: Toll...........4E 69
Oak Tree Dr. NG4: Ged.............5A 36
Oak Vw. NG7: Radf 3D 44
Oakwell Cres. DE7: Ilk..............1A 40
Oakwell Dr. DE7: Ilk................1A 40
Oakwood Dr. NG8: Aspl...........2A 44
Oakwood Gdns. NG16: Nuth.......4D 30
Oban Rd. NG9: Chil.................5C 54
Occupation Rd. NG15: Huck.......6G 7
Occupation Rd. NG6: Bulw........2H 31
Oceans of Fun 4G 7
Ockbrook Ct. DE7: Ilk...............4B 28
Ockbrook Dr. NG3: Mapp...........5B 34
Ockerby St. NG6: Bulw.............1A 32
Odesa Dr. NG6: Bulw 3H 31
Odin Ct. NG4: Car 1H 47
Ogdon Ct. NG3: Nott...............3B 46
Ogle Dr. NG7: Nott...........6B 4 (6F 45)
Ogle St. NG15: Huck 4G 7
Okehampton Cres. NG3: Mapp.....1E 35
Oldacres NG14: Woodbo...........1D 24
Old Bank Ct. NG6: Bas..............5B 32
Old Bar Cl. NG6: Bas...............5A 32
OLD BASFORD 3C 32
Old Brickyard NG3: Nott...........2C 46
Oldbury Cl. NG11: Clftn............6B 66
Old Church St. NG7: Lent...........1C 56
Old Coach Rd. NG8: Bilb...........3E 43
Old Coach Rd. NG8: Woll..........3E 43
Old Coppice Side DE75: Hea
  Roper Av. 5C 14
Old Coppice Side DE75: Hea
  Sunningdale Av. 5D 14
Old Derby Rd. NG16: Eastw........2H 15
Old Dr. NG8: Bee 3D 54
Old Epperstone Rd.
  NG14: Lowd 1G 25
Old Farm Cl. NG11: Bart F..........1E 75
Old Farm Rd. NG5: Top V..........5D 20
Old Hall Cl. NG14: Calv.............4G 11
Old Hall Dr. NG3: Mapp P.........6H 33
Oldham Cl. NG9: Chil................1C 64
Old Kiln La. NG16: Eastw...........4C 16
Oldknow St. NG7: Hys G............3D 44
OLD LENTON 6C 44
Old Lenton St.
  NG1: Nott 3F 5 (4H 45)
Old Lodge Dr. NG5: Sher...........3H 33
Old Main Rd. NG14: Bulc...........2G 37
Old Mnr. Cl. NG16: Woodbo 1D 24
Old Market Square
  Stop (NET) 4D 4 (5G 45)
Old Melton Rd. NG12: Plum........6G 69
  .... (not continuous)
Old Mill Cl. NG6: Bestw V 2B 20
Old Mill Cl. NG7: Radf...............4D 44
Old Mill Cl. NG9: Toton............3A 64
Old Mill Cl. NG13: Bing............4E 51

Old Mission Forge Wlk.
  NG16: Newth.........................3E 17
Oldmoor Wood Nature
  Reserve 1H 41
Old Oak Rd. NG11: Clftn 3E 67
Old Pk., The NG12: Cotg............1F 71
Old Pk. Cl. NG8: Bilb 2E 43
Old Pond, The DE75: Hea...........5E 15
OLD RADFORD 3B 44
Old Rd. NG11: Rudd.................4H 67
Old Rd. NG2: West Br...............2A 68
Old School Cl. NG11: Clftn..........5C 66
Old School La. NG16: Aws..........2E 29
Old Station Dr. NG11: Rudd.........6F 67
Old St. NG1: Nott..........2E 5 (4G 45)
Old Tollerton Rd. NG2: Gam........4E 59
Olga Ct. NG3: Nott 3B 46
Olga Rd. NG3: Nott 3B 46
Olive Av. NG10: Long E 4F 63
Olive Gro. NG14: Bur J..............2F 37
Oliver Cl. DE72: Brea................5A 62
Oliver Cl. DE75: Hea.................3F 15
Oliver Rd. DE7: Kirk H...............4G 39
Oliver St. NG7: Radf.........1A 4 (3E 45)
Ollerton Rd. NG14: Calv.............1B 10
Ollerton Rd. NG5: Arn................1A 22
  .... (not continuous)
Olton Av. NG9: Lent A 2F 55
Olympus Ct. NG15: Huck...........2D 18
Omer St. NG16: Want................6A 18
Onchan Av. NG4: Car 3G 47
Onchan Dr. NG4: Car 3G 47
Open University
  Nottingham, The 1F 45
Orange Gdns. NG2: Nott 1H 57
Orby Cl. NG3: Nott 3B 46
Orby Wlk. NG3: Nott.................4B 46
Orchard, The DE7: Stant D 3B 52
Orchard Av. NG13: Bing............5D 50
Orchard Av. NG4: Car 2G 47
Orchard Bus. Pk. DE7: Ilk...........6H 27
Orchard Cl. DE7: West H............2C 38
Orchard Cl. DE72: Brea.............5H 62
Orchard Cl. NG11: Clftn............3A 66
Orchard Cl. NG12: Rad T...........6E 49
Orchard Cl. NG12: Toll..............5F 69
Orchard Cl. NG14: Bur J............2F 37
Orchard Cl. NG15: Huck............. 5G 7
Orchard Ct. NG6: Bas...............1C 44
Orchard Ct. NG4: Car...............2G 47
Orchard Ct. NG4: Ged..............5F 35
Orchard Cres. NG9: Chil............6C 54
Orchard Dr. NG12: Cotg............6G 61
Orchard Dr. NG14: Calv............4A 12
Orchard Gro. NG5: Arn.............1G 33
Orchard Pk. NG3: Mapp...........1E 35
Orchard Pk. Ind. Est.
  NG10: Sand..........................5E 53
Orchard Pl. NG8: Stre...............5C 30
Orchard Ri. DE75: Hea..............3D 14
Orchard Ri. NG4: Lamb.............6C 24
Orchards, The NG4: Ged............6A 36
Orchard St. DE7: Ilk.................2B 40
Orchard St. NG10: Long E..........6G 63
Orchard St. NG11: Goth.............6H 75
Orchard St. NG15: Huck............. 5G 7
Orchard St. NG16: Kimb............1H 29
Orchard St. NG16: Lang M.........2F 15
Orchard St. NG16: Newth...........4C 16
Orchard Way NG10: Sand..........2C 62
Orchid Cl. NG2: West Br............1G 67
Orchid Cft. NG15: Huck.............1A 20
Orchil St. NG16: Gilt.................5D 16
Ordnance Ct. NG9: Chil.............2C 64
Orford Av. NG11: Clftn 1D 66
Orford Av. NG12: Rad T.............1E 61
Orient M. NG16: Want...............6A 18

Orion Cl. NG8: Bilb..................2E 43
Orion Dr. NG8: Bilb..................2E 43
Orlando Dr. NG4: Car 1H 47
Orlock Wlk. NG5: Bestw 2F 33
Ormiston Cl. NG11: Clftn 4D 66
Ormonde St. NG16: Lang M........1F 15
Ormonde Ter. NG16: Lang M 1F 15
Ormonde Ter. NG5: Sher............5G 33
Ornsay Cl. NG5: Top V.............4C 20
Orpean Way NG9: Toton 3G 63
Orston Cl. NG5: Arn.................6C 22
Orston Dr. NG8: Woll................5A 44
Orston Grn. NG8: Woll..............6B 44
Orston Rd. E. NG2: West Br 2B 58
Orston Rd. W. NG2: West Br 2A 58
Orton Av. NG9: Bram................5C 54
Orton Flds. NG9: Bram..............5B 54
Ortzen Cl. NG7: Radf 3D 44
Ortzen St. NG7: Radf 3D 44
Orville Rd. NG5: Bestw.............2C 32
Osborne Av. NG5: Sher.............4G 33
Osborne Cl. NG10: Sand...........1D 62
Osborne Gro. NG5: Sher............4G 33
Osborne St. NG7: Radf..............3C 44
Osbourne Cl. NG15: Huck..........1A 20
Osbourne Cl. NG16: Want..........6B 18
Osgood Rd. NG5: Arn...............2E 35
Osier Rd. NG2: Nott 2G 57
Osman Cl. NG2: Nott................2F 57
Osmaston Cl. NG10: Long E........2B 62
Osmaston St. NG10: Sand..........6E 53
Osmaston St. NG7: Lent............6D 44
Osprey Cl. NG11: Clftn..............4A 66
Osprey Cl. NG13: Bing..............6F 51
Osprey Gro. NG15: Huck............2B 8
Ossington Cl.
  NG1: Nott 1D 4 (3G 45)
Ossington St. NG7: Radf............3D 44
Ostara Rd. NG9: Nott...............4H 55
Osterley Gro. NG16: Nuth 4D 30
Oughton Cl. NG12: Edwal..........2B 68
Oulton Cl. NG5: Arn 1B 34
Oulton Lodge NG5: Top V..........4B 20
Oundle Dr. DE7: Ilk 2D 40
Oundle Dr. NG8: Woll...............6A 44
Ousebridge Cres. NG4: Car 1A 48
Ousebridge Dr. NG4: Car 1A 48
Out Track, The DE7: Mapp.........5C 26
  .... (off Church La.)
Oval Gdns. NG8: Aspl...............1B 44
Overdale Cl. NG10: Long E..........1B 72
Overdale Rd. NG6: Bas.............5A 32
Overstrand Cl. NG5: Arn............1B 34
Owen Av. NG10: Long E.............1A 74
Owers Av. DE75: Hea................6D 14
Owlston Cl. NG16: Eastw...........2B 16
Owsthorpe Cl. NG5: Top V..........5E 21
Owthorpe Gro. NG5: Sher...........5F 33
Owthorpe Rd. NG12: Cotg..........3F 71
Oxborough Rd. NG5: Arn............6G 21
Oxbow Cl. NG2: Nott................2G 57
Oxbury Rd. NG16: Want.............5H 17
Oxclose La. NG5: Arn................1F 33
Oxendale Cl. NG2: West Br.........5E 59
Oxengate NG5: Arn 1G 33
Oxford Rd. NG2: West Br............4C 58
Oxford St. DE7: Ilk..................2B 40
Oxford St. NG1: Nott........4B 4 (5F 45)
Oxford St. NG10: Long E............6D 63
Oxford St. NG16: Eastw.............3B 16
Oxford St. NG4: Car.................6G 35
Oxgang Cl. NG14: Calv..............3E 11
Oxton Av. NG5: Sher................3G 33
Oxton Rd. NG14: Calv...............2F 11
Oxton Rd. NG14: Epp................3C 12
Oxton Rd. NG25: Oxton.............1B 12
Oxton Rd. NG5: Arn.................4B 10
Ozier Holt NG10: Long E............1E 73
Ozier Holt NG4: Colw...............5G 47

P

Packham Ct. NG6: Bas 3C 32
Packman Dr. NG11: Rudd...........5H 67
Paddington M. NG3: Nott...........2C 46
Paddock, The NG13: Bing...........5E 51
Paddock, The NG9: Atten...........3D 64
Paddock Cl. NG12: Rad T...........1E 61
Paddock Cl. NG14: Calv.............4H 11
Paddock Cl. NG6: Bulw..............2H 31
Paddock Dr. DE7: Smal 5A 14
Paddock Farm Cotts.
  NG14: Epp...........................6G 13
Paddocks, The NG10: Sand.........6C 52
Paddocks, The NG12: Edwal 2D 68
Paddocks, The NG14: Bur J 3E 37
Paddocks, The NG16: Nuth 2B 30
Paddocks Vw. NG10: Long E........5C 62
Padge Rd. NG9: Bee 5H 55
Padgham Cl. NG5: Top V...........5E 21
Padley Cl. NG6: Bulw................1A 32
Padley Ct. NG6: Bulw................1G 31
Padleys La. NG14: Bur J.............2E 37
Padstow Rd. NG5: Bestw............1D 32
Paetina Gro. NG15: Huck............3B 8
Page Av. NG5: Bestw.................2E 33
Paget Cres. NG11: Rudd.............5G 67
Pagett Cl. NG15: Huck...............5A 8
Paige Gdns. NG10: Sand............6C 52
Paignton Cl. NG8: Aspl..............5H 31
Paisley Gro. NG9: Chil...............4C 64
Palatine St. NG7: Nott........6B 4 (6F 45)
Palin Cl. NG7: Hys G.................2D 44
Palin Gdns. NG12: Rad T............6G 49
Palin St. NG7: Hys G.................3D 44
Palm Cotts. NG5: Sher...............4H 33
Palm Ct. NG7: Bas 6D 32
Palmer Av. NG15: Huck 3G 7
Palmer Bus. Ct. NG10: Long E......1H 73
Palmer Cres. NG4: Car 2F 47
Palmer Dr. NG9: Stfrd...............6F 53
Palmerston Gdns.
  NG3: Nott 1E 5 (3G 45)
  .... (not continuous)
Palmerston Rd. DE7: Ilk.............1B 40
Palm St. NG7: Bas 6D 32
Palmwood Ct. NG6: Bulw 2A 32
Papplewick Farm Cl. NG15: Pap....2B 8
Papplewick Grange NG15: Pap......2B 8
Papplewick La. NG15: Huck.........4H 7
Parchment M. NG5: Sher............6F 33
Park, The NG12: Cotg................1F 71
PARK, THE 4B 4 (5F 45)
Park & Ride Clifton South 6A 66
Park & Ride Cotgrave 2F 71
Park & Ride Hucknall 4A 8
Park & Ride Moor Bridge............3B 20
Park & Ride Phoenix Park...........3G 31
Park & Ride Queen's Drive..........4E 57
Park & Ride Racecourse.............4B 58
Park & Ride Stragglethorpe.........4D 60
Park & Ride The Forest 2E 45
Park & Ride Toton Lane..............1H 63
Park & Ride Wilkinson Street........1C 44
Park Av. NG12: Key Croft Rd........4F 79
Park Av. NG12: Key Park Rd.........3H 79
Park Av. DE7: Ilk......................1B 40
Park Av. DE7: Stly....................3A 38
Park Av. NG14: Bur J.................3F 37
Park Av. NG14: Woodbo.............1B 24
Park Av. NG15: Huck 4F 7
Park Av. NG16: Aws..................2D 28
Park Av. NG16: Eastw................2A 16
Park Av. NG16: Kimb.................3A 30
Park Av. NG2: West Br...............3B 58
Park Av. NG3: Mapp P...............1G 45
Park Av. NG4: Car....................1H 47
Park Av. NG5: Woodt.................2A 34
Park Av. E. NG12: Key...............4F 79

Park Av. W. NG12: Key	4F **79**	Parkway Ct. NG8: Bilb	4D **42**
Pk. Chase NG6: Bulw	2H **31**	Park W. NG7: Nott	3A 4 (4E **45**)
Park Cl. DE7: Stant D	3B **52**		(off Derby Rd.)
Park Cl. NG3: Mapp	5A **34**	Pk. Wharf NG7: Nott	6C 4 (6F **45**)
Park Ct. DE75: Hea	4D **14**	Parkwood Ct. NG6: Bulw	2C **32**
Park Ct. NG7: Lent	2C **56**	Parkwood Cres. NG5: Sher	4A **34**
Park Cres. DE7: Ilk	1C **40**	Park Yacht Club	1C **58**
Park Cres. NG16: Eastw	1B **16**	Parkyn Rd. NG5: Arn	1H **33**
Park Cres. NG8: Woll	5C **42**	Parkyns St. NG11: Rudd	6G **67**
Parkcroft Rd. NG2: West Br	5B **58**	Parliament Ter.	
Parkdale Rd. NG3: Nott	3D **46**	NG1: Nott	3C 4 (4F **45**)
Parkdale Rd. NG4: Car	3E **47**	Parr Ct. NG12: Rad T	6F **49**
Park Dr. DE7: Ilk	2B **40**	Parr Ga. NG9: Chil	6A **54**
Park Dr. NG10: Sand	2C **62**	Parrs, The NG9: Bee	5H **55**
Park Dr. NG15: Huck	6G **7**	Parry Ct. NG3: Mapp	3C **34**
Park Dr. NG7: Nott	5A 4 (5E **45**)	Parry Rd. NG3: Nott	3C **46**
Parker Cl. NG5: Arn	5E **23**	Parry Way NG5: Arn	5D **22**
Parker Gdns. NG9: Stfrd	3H **53**	Parsons Mdw. NG4: Colw	5G **47**
Parker St. NG15: Huck	4H **7**	Partridge Cl. NG13: Bing	6F **51**
Parkes Bldg. NG9: Bee	4F **55**	Pasteur Ho. NG3: Mapp	5B **34**
Parkgate NG15: Huck	2H **7**	Pasture Ct. NG2: Colw	5G **47**
Pk. Hall DE7: Mapp	4B **26**	Pasture La. NG10: Long E	1A **74**
Park Hall La. DE7: Mapp	5B **26**	Pasture La. NG11: Rudd	1D **76**
Park Hall La. DE7: West H	5B **26**	Pasture Rd. NG9: Stfrd	2F **53**
Parkham Rd. NG16: Kimb	6H **17**	Pastures, The NG14: Calv	4F **11**
Park Hgts. NG7: Nott	6A 4 (6E **45**)	Pastures, The NG16: Gilt	5D **16**
Pk. Hill NG16: Aws	2D **28**	Pastures, The NG8: Bilb	2H **43**
Pk. Hill NG7: Nott	3A 4 (4E **45**)	Pastures Av. NG11: Clftn	5B **66**
Parkham Rd. NG16: Kimb		Pastures Dr. DE7: Smal	5A **14**
Parkland Cl. NG11: Clftn	2A **66**	Pateley Rd. NG3: Mapp	3C **34**
Parkland M. NG10: Long E	5F **63**	Pates Cl. NG15: Huck	1B **8**
	(off Derby Rd.)	Patient Cl. NG9: Chil	6B **54**
Parklands Cl. NG5: Top V	4F **21**	Paton Cl. NG14: Calv	2G **11**
Park La. NG14: Epp	6G **13**	Paton Rd. NG5: Bestw	2C **32**
Park La. NG4: Lamb	6C **24**	Patricia Dr. NG5: Arn	4C **22**
Park La. NG6: Bas	3C **32**	Patrick Rd. NG2: West Br	3A **58**
Park La. NG6: Bulw	3C **32**	Patriot Cl. NG16: Want	6A **18**
Park La. Bus. Cen. NG6: Bulw	2C **32**	Patterdale Cl. NG2: Gam	4E **59**
Park Lodge Rd. NG16: Gilt	6C **16**	Patterdale Ct. NG9: Chil	6A **54**
Park M. NG3: Mapp P	1G **45**	Patterdale Rd. NG5: Woodt	2B **34**
Pk. Ravine NG7: Nott	6A 4 (6E **45**)	Patterson Rd. NG7: Hys G	2D **44**
Park Rd. DE7: Ilk	2B **40**	Paulina Av. NG15: Huck	3A **8**
Park Rd. NG12: Key	3H **79**	Pavilion, The NG7: Hys G	2E **45**
Park Rd. NG12: Rad T	5F **49**	Pavilion Ct. NG16: Nott	2H **57**
Park Rd. NG14: Calv	3F **11**	Pavilion Ct. DE7: West H	2B **38**
Park Rd. NG15: Huck	4F **7**	Pavilion Rd. NG2: West Br	2A **58**
Park Rd. NG4: Car	2H **47**	Pavilion Rd. NG5: Arn	4F **21**
Park Rd. NG5: Woodt	2A **34**	Pavior Rd. NG5: Bestw	2D **32**
Park Rd. NG6: Bestw V	1C **20**	Paxton Gdns. NG3: Nott	2H 5 (4A **46**)
Park Rd. NG7: Lent	6D **44**		(not continuous)
Park Rd. NG9: Bram	3H **53**	Payne Rd. NG9: Chil	2A **64**
Park Rd. NG9: Chil	5E **55**	Peace Gro. NG12: Edwal	3C **68**
Park Rd. E. NG14: Calv	3H **11**	Peache Way NG9: Bram	4A **54**
Park Rd. Nth. NG9: Chil	5E **55**	Peachey St. NG1: Nott	2D 4 (4G **45**)
Pk. Rock NG7: Lent	6A 4 (6E **45**)	Peach St. DE75: Hea	4B **14**
Pk. Row NG1: Nott	5C 4 (5F **45**)	Peacock Cl. NG11: Rudd	1F **77**
Parkside NG12: Key	3H **79**	Peacock Cres. NG11: Clftn	3C **66**
Parkside NG8: Woll	6E **43**	Peacock Dr. NG16: Eastw	4A **16**
Parkside Av. NG10: Long E	5D **62**	Peacock Gdns. NG8: Stre	5C **30**
Parkside Dr. NG10: Long E	5D **62**	Peacock Pl. DE7: Ilk	3H **27**
Parkside Gdns. NG8: Woll	6E **43**	Peakdale Cl. NG10: Long E	1C **72**
Parkside Ri. NG8: Woll	1E **55**	Pearce Dr. NG8: Bilb	2H **43**
Parkstone Cl. NG2: West Br	6G **57**	Pearmain Dr. NG3: Nott	2B **46**
Park St. DE72: Brea	5B **62**	Pearson Av. NG9: Chil	6B **54**
Park St. DE75: Hea	3B **14**	Pearson Cl. NG9: Chil	6B **54**
Park St. NG10: Long E	4E **63**	Pearson Ct. NG5: Arn	6A **22**
Park St. NG7: Lent	5D **44**	Pearson St. NG4: Neth	3A **48**
Park St. NG9: Bee	5E **55**	Pearson St. NG7: Bas	5D **32**
Park St. NG9: Stfrd	5E **53**	Pear Tree Ct. NG6: Bas	3C **32**
Park Ter. NG1: Nott	4B 4 (5F **45**)	Peartree Orchard NG11: Rudd	6G **67**
Park Ter. NG12: Key	2H **79**	Pear Tree Yd. NG10: Sand	5D **52**
Pk. Valley NG7: Nott	5B 4 (5F **45**)	Peashill La. NG12: Cotg	6C **60**
Park Vw. DE75: Hea	4B **14**	Peas Hill Rd. NG3: Nott	3H **45**
Park Vw. NG15: Huck	5H **7**	Peatfield Ct. NG9: Stfrd	2F **53**
Park Vw. NG16: Eastw	4B **16**	Peatfield Rd. NG9: Stfrd	2F **53**
Park Vw. NG3: Mapp	5A **34**		
Park Vw. Ct. NG1: Nott	3G 5 (4H **45**)		
Park Vw. Ct. NG5: Bestw	5D **54**		
Parkview Dr. NG5: Bestw	6E **21**		

Peck La. NG1: Nott	4E 5 (5G **45**)	Perlethorpe Dr. NG4: Ged	5F **35**
Pedley St. DE7: Ilk	2B **40**	Perry Gro. NG13: Bing	5F **51**
Pedmore Cl. NG5: Bestw	6F **21**	Perry Rd. NG5: Sher	5D **32**
Pedmore Valley NG5: Bestw	6E **21**	Perry Rd. NG9: Stfrd	2G **53**
Peel St. NG1: Nott	1C 4 (3F **45**)	Perth St. NG1: Nott	2E 5 (4G **45**)
Peel St. NG10: Long E	5G **63**	Perth St. NG16: Newth	3E **17**
Peel St. NG6: Lang M	2F **15**	Peters Cl. NG5: Arn	1E **35**
Peel Vs. NG3: Mapp	5A **34**	Petersfield Cl. NG5: Top V	6D **20**
Pegswood Dr. NG5: Arn	3C **22**	Petersgate NG10: Long E	4C **62**
Pelham Av. DE7: Ilk	6A **28**	Petersgate Cl. NG10: Long E	3C **62**
Pelham Av. NG5: Sher	1F **45**	Petersham Ct. NG10: Long E	3D **62**
Pelham Cotts. NG7: Nott	5D **44**	Petersham M. NG7: Lent	6D **44**
	(off Pelham Cres.)	Petersham Rd. NG10: Long E	3C **62**
Pelham Ct. NG5: Sher	1F **45**	Petworth Av. NG9: Toton	2H **63**
Pelham Cres. NG7: Nott	5D **44**	Petworth Dr. NG5: Sher	3D **32**
Pelham Cres. NG9: Bee	4H **55**	Peveril Hall NG11: Clftn	2B **66**
Pelham Rd. NG5: Sher	1F **45**	Peverel Rd. NG15: Huck	1F **7**
Pelham St. DE7: Ilk	6A **28**	Peveril Ct. NG2: West Br	4A **58**
Pelham St. NG1: Nott	4E 5 (5G **45**)	Peveril Cres. NG10: Long E	2B **72**
Pemberton St.		Peveril Dr. DE7: Ilk	5H **27**
NG1: Nott	5G 5 (5H **45**)	Peveril Dr. NG2: West Br	2A **68**
Pembrey Cl. NG9: Trow	1F **53**	Peveril Dr. NG7: Nott	6B 4 (6F **45**)
Pembridge Cl. NG6: Bas	5B **32**	Peveril M. NG7: Nott	5E **44**
Pembroke Dr. NG3: Mapp P	6G **33**		(off Alexander Rd.)
Pembury Rd. NG8: Woll	4E **43**	Peveril Rd. NG9: Bee	3F **55**
Penarth Gdns. NG5: Sher	4A **34**	Peveril St. NG15: Huck	3G **7**
Penarth Ri. NG5: Sher	4A **34**	Peveril St. NG7: Radf	3D **44**
Pendennis Cl. NG4: Ged	6B **36**	Pewit Golf Course	1H **39**
Pendine Cl. NG5: Redh	4H **21**	Philip Av. NG16: Eastw	4C **16**
Pendle Cres. NG3: Nott	6B **34**	Philip Av. NG16: Nuth	1C **30**
Pendock Ct. NG12: Toll	4F **69**	Philip Gro. NG4: Ged	5G **35**
Pendock La. NG11: Rudd	5B **78**	Phoenix Av. NG4: Ged	5G **35**
Penhale Dr. NG15: Huck	6C **6**	Phoenix Cen. NG8: Cin	3G **31**
Penhurst Cl. NG11: Wilf	1E **67**	Phoenix Cl. NG2: Nott	1F **57**
Penllech Cl. NG5: Bestw	6E **21**	Phoenix Ct. NG16: Eastw	3C **16**
Penllech Wlk. NG5: Bestw	6E **21**	Phoenix Ct. NG7: Lent	3D **56**
Pen Moor Cl. NG10: Long E	1C **72**	Phoenix Park Park & Ride	3G **31**
Pennant Rd. NG6: Bas	5B **32**	Phoenix Park Stop (NET)	3G **31**
Pennard Wlk. NG11: Clftn	5B **66**	Phoenix Pl. NG8: Cin	3H **31**
Penn Av. NG7: Lent	6C **44**	Phoenix Rd. NG16: Newth	1D **16**
Pennhome Almshouses NG5: Sher	5G **33**	Phyllis Cl. NG15: Huck	2F **7**
	(off Haydn Rd.)	Phyllis Gro. NG10: Long E	6H **63**
Pennhome Av. NG5: Sher	5G **33**	Piccadilly NG6: Bulw	1B **32**
Pennie Cl. NG10: Long E	3F **73**	Pickering Av. NG16: Eastw	3B **16**
Pennine Cl. NG10: Long E	4C **62**	Pieris Dr. NG11: Clftn	4A **66**
Pennine Cl. NG5: Arn	4F **21**	Pierrepont Av. NG4: Ged	6G **35**
Pennyfields Blvd.		Pierrepont Cl. NG2: West Br	2D **58**
NG10: Long E	6C **62**	Pierrepont Rd. NG2: West Br	3C **58**
Pennyfoot St. NG1: Nott	5H 5 (5A **46**)	Piggott Av. NG4: Ged	4G **35**
Penrhyn Cl. NG3: Nott	1F 5 (3H **45**)	Pilcher Ga. NG1: Nott	4E 5 (5H **45**)
Penrhyn Cres. NG9: Chil	1B **64**	Pilkington Rd. NG3: Mapp	6C **34**
Penrith Av. NG12: Rad T	5G **49**	Pilkington St. NG6: Bulw	6H **19**
Penrith Cres. NG8: Aspl	5A **32**	Pilot Dr. NG15: Huck	1E **19**
Penshore Cl. NG11: Clftn	4B **66**	Pimlico DE7: Ilk	1A **40**
Pentland Dr. NG5: Arn	3F **21**	Pimlico Av. NG9: Bram	6B **42**
Pentland Gdns. NG10: Long E	4C **62**	Pine Av. NG16: Lang M	2E **15**
Pentrich Rd. NG16: Gilt	6E **17**	Pine Gro. NG15: Huck	1H **19**
Pentridge Dr. DE7: Ilk	4G **27**	Pine Hill Cl. NG5: Top V	4D **20**
Pentwood Av. NG5: Arn	3B **22**	Pinehurst Av. NG15: Huck	6C **6**
Peoples Hall Cotts.		Pines, The NG9: Bram	3C **54**
NG1: Nott	4F 5 (4H **45**)	Pines Ct. NG5: Sher	3H **33**
	(off Heathcoat St.)	Pine Tree Wlk. NG16: Eastw	3A **16**
Peppercorn Gdns. NG8: Woll	3A **44**	Pine Vw. NG7: Radf	3D **44**
Pepper La. DE7: Stant D	3A **52**	Pinewood Av. NG5: Arn	4D **22**
Pepper Rd. NG14: Calv	3G **11**	Pinewood Gdns. NG11: Clftn	5B **66**
Pepper St. NG1: Nott	5E 5 (5G **45**)	Pinfold NG13: Bing	5F **51**
Percival Rd. NG5: Sher	5F **33**	Pinfold Cl. NG12: Cotg	1F **71**
Percy St. DE7: Ilk	2B **40**	Pinfold Cl. NG14: Woodbo	1C **24**
Percy St. NG16: Eastw	3C **16**	Pinfold Cres. NG14: Woodbo	1C **24**
Percy St. NG6: Bas	4B **32**	Pinfold La. NG11: Wilf	5F **57**
Peregrine Cl. NG7: Lent	5C **44**	Pinfold La. NG12: Plum	6H **69**
Peregrine Rd. NG15: Huck	2B **8**	Pinfold La. NG9: Stfrd	4F **53**
Perivale Cl. NG16: Nuth	4D **30**	Pinfold La. NG9: Stfrd	4F **53**
Perkins Way NG9: Chil	2D **64**	Pinfold Rd. NG16: Gilt	4E **17**
Perlethorpe Av. NG15: Huck	5B **46**	Pingle, The NG10: Long E	4F **63**
Perlethorpe Av. NG4: Ged	5F **35**	Pingle Cres. NG5: Top V	5D **20**
Perlethorpe Cres. NG4: Ged	5G **35**	Pintail Cl. NG4: Neth	3B **48**
Perlethorpe Dr. NG15: Huck	4H **7**	Pioneer Meadows Local Nature Reserve	5G **39**

Piper Cl. NG15: Huck 2H 7
Pippin Cl. NG3: Nott.....................2B 46
Pitcairn Cl. NG2: Nott 2G 57
Pitch Cl. NG6: Gilt......................5E 17
Pitch Cl. NG4: Car......................1E 47
Pit La. DE7: Ilk.........................1F 27
Pit La. DE75: Ship......................1F 27
Plackett Cl. NG9: Stfrd 3H 53
Plains Farm Cl. NG3: Mapp 2E 35
Plains Gro. NG3: Mapp 3C 34
Plains Rd. NG3: Mapp..................4B 34
Plane Cl. NG6: Bulw.....................6F 19
Plane Rd. NG12: Edwal.................3C 68
Plane Tree Ct. NG15: Huck 6H 7
Plantagenet Ct.
   NG3: Nott 1G 5 (4H 45)
Plantagenet St.
   NG3: Nott 2G 5 (4H 45)
Plantation Cl. NG5: Arn 4F 21
Plantation Cotts. NG14: Epp.........5F 13
Plantation Rd. NG12: Key.............4F 79
Plantation Rd. NG8: Woll..............5C 42
Plantations, The NG10: Long E....5C 62
Plantation Side NG7: Hys G........2C 44
Plantin Rd. NG5: Sher..................6F 33
Plant La. NG10: Long E...............3C 72
Platt La. NG12: Key 3H 79
Platt La. NG12: Norm W..............3H 79
Platts Av. DE75: Hea....................4A 14
Player Ct. NG7: Radf....................3C 44
Player St. NG7: Radf....................3C 44
Plaza Gdns. NG6: Bas..................3C 32
Pleasant Ct. NG7: Hys G..............2D 44
Pleasant Row NG7: Hys G...........2D 44
Plimsoll St. NG7: Hys G...............1C 44
Plough La. NG1: Nott........5H 5 (5A 46)
Ploughman Av. NG14: Woodbo... 1D 24
Plover Wharf NG7: Lent...............1E 57
Plowman Ct. NG9: Stfrd 5F 53
Plowright Ct. NG3: Nott 2H 45
Plowright St. NG3: Nott 2H 45
Plumb Rd. NG15: Huck.................4F 7
Plumptre Cl. NG16: Eastw...........4B 16
Plumptre Gdns. NG16: Eastw 3B 16
Plumptre Pl. NG1: Nott...... 5F 5 (5H 45)
Plumptre Rd. NG16: Lang M.........1F 15
Plumptre Sq. NG1: Nott......5G 5 (5H 45)
Plumptre St. NG1: Nott...... 5F 5 (5H 45)
Plumptre Way NG16: Eastw 4B 16
PLUMTREE 6G 69
Plumtree Ct. NG12: Plum.............6G 69
Plumtree Gdns. NG14: Calv..........4H 11
PLUMTREE PARK 3H 79
Plumtree Rd. NG12: Cotg 3D 70
Plungar Cl. NG8: Bilb..................3H 43
Podder La. NG3: Mapp.................1E 35
Poets Cl. NG15: Huck..................1E 19
Point, The NG1: Nott........5G 5 (5H 45)
   ....(off Plumptre St.)
Point, The NG2: West Br..............4A 58
   ....(off Loughborough Rd.)
Point, The NG3: Mapp P............. 1H 45
Pointers Cl. NG3: Nott.................2C 46
Pollard Ct. NG9: Bee...................4F 55
Polperro Way NG15: Huck............6C 6
Pompeia Cl. NG15: Huck...............3B 8
Pond Hills La. NG5: Arn...............5B 22
Poole Av. NG4: Ged.....................3G 35
Pool Mdw. NG4: Colw..................5H 47
Popham Ct. NG1: Nott 5F 5 (5H 45)
Poplar Av. NG10: Sand................4C 52
Poplar Av. NG5: Sher 5E 33
Poplar Cl. NG12: Cotg.................6G 61
Poplar Cl. NG13: Bing.................5G 51
Poplar Cl. NG4: Car.....................3F 47
Poplar Cres. NG16: Nuth..............1A 30
Poplar Rd. DE72: Brea.................4B 62
Poplars, The NG2: Plum...............1G 79
Poplars, The NG2: West Br...........4B 58

Poplars, The NG7: Hys G 1C 44
Poplars, The NG9: Bee.................4F 55
Poplars Av. NG14: Bur J 2G 37
Poplars Cl. NG12: Key 3H 79
Poplars Ct. NG7: Lent..................1D 56
Poplars Rd. NG7: Lent 1D 56
Poplar St. NG1: Nott 5G 5 (5H 45)
   ....(not continuous)
Poplar Way DE7: Kirk H...............4H 39
Poppy Cl. NG12: Cotg 1G 71
Poppy Cl. NG2: West Br 4H 57
Poppy M. NG15: Huck..................1B 20
PORCHESTER 5D 34
Porchester Cl. NG15: Huck...........4A 8
Porchester Ct. NG3: Nott............1C 46
Porchester Rd. NG13: Bing..........5D 50
Porchester Rd. NG3: Mapp...........5B 34
Porchester Rd. NG3: Nott.............5B 34
Porlock Cl. NG10: Long E............5C 62
Portage Cl. NG12: Rad T..............1E 61
Port Arthur Rd. NG2: Nott............5B 46
Porter Cl. NG11: Clftn.................5A 66
Porters Wlk. NG3: Nott................2C 46
Portinscale Cl. NG2: West Br.......6E 59
Portland Cl. NG5: Bestw..............2F 33
Portland Cres. NG9: Stfrd 5G 53
Portland Gdns. NG15: Huck..........4F 7
Portland Grange NG15: Huck 4E 7
Portland Hill NG7: Nott 2A 56
Portland Leisure Cen. 2H 57
Portland Pk. Cl. NG15: Huck.........4F 7
Portland Rd. DE7: Ilk..................4B 28
Portland Rd. NG10: Long E..........3C 72
Portland Rd. NG15: Huck..............4H 7
Portland Rd. NG16: Gilt 5D 16
Portland Rd. NG2: West Br...........5B 58
Portland Rd. NG4: Car.................5E 35
Portland Rd. NG7: Radf ... 2A 4 (4E 45)
Portland Rd. NG9: Toton...............4H 63
Portland Sq. NG7: Radf.... 2A 4 (4E 45)
Portland St. NG5: Arn 1H 33
Portland St. NG9: Bee..................4G 55
Portree Dr. NG5: Top V................4D 20
Port Said Vs. NG7: Bas................6D 32
Portside St. NG2: Nott.................1B 58
Postern St. NG1: Nott....... 4C 4 (5F 45)
Pot 'n' Kettle (Ceramic Cafe)........4G 55
   ....(off High Rd.)
Potomac M. NG7: Nott........ 5A 4 (5E 45)
Potters Cl. NG5: Top V.................6E 21
Potters Ct. NG9: Bram.................2D 54
Potters Hill Vw. DE75: Hea...........4E 15
Potters Hollow NG6: Bulw 2A 32
Potters Way DE7: Ilk...................1C 40
Pottery Ct. NG6: Bulw.................6G 19
Pottery Way NG6: Bulw...............6G 19
Poulter Cl. NG7: Radf..................2B 44
Poulton Dr. NG2: Nott..................6B 46
Poultry NG1: Nott........................2H 57
Poultry Arc. NG1: Nott.... 4E 5 (5G 45)
   ....(off St Peter's Ga.)
Powerleague Nottingham 5C 56
Powis St. NG6: Bulw 6H 19
Powtrell Pl. DE7: Ilk....................3D 40
Poynter Cl. DE75: Hea 4A 14
Poynton St. NG1: Nott... 3C 4 (4F 45)
Poyser Cl. NG7: Bas...................6E 33
Premier Rd. NG7: Hys G..............1E 45
Prendwick Gdns. NG5: Bestw.......5F 21
Prestwick Cl. NG8: Stre...............5D 30
Prestwood Dr. NG8: Aspl..............2H 43
Pretoria Vs. NG5: Aspl.................5A 32
Previn Gdns. NG3: Nott................3B 46
Primrose Bank NG13: Bing 5D 50
Primrose Cl. NG4: Car.................2H 45
Primrose Cotts. DE72: Ris............2A 62
Primrose Cres. NG4: Car.............2H 47
Primrose Gdns. NG15: Huck..........1B 20
Primrose Hill DE7: Ilk..................4A 28

Primrose Ri. NG16: Newth...........5C 16
Primrose St. DE7: Ilk...................4A 28
Primrose St. NG4: Car 2H 47
Primula Cl. NG11: Clftn...............3A 66
Prince Edward Cres.
   NG12: Rad T........................1D 60
Princess Av. NG9: Bee.................5G 55
Princess Blvd. NG8: Stre.............5C 30
Princess Cl. DE75: Hea................3B 14
Princess Cl. NG4: Ged.................5G 35
Princess Dr. NG10: Sand.............1D 62
Princess St. NG10: Long E 5F 63
Princes St. NG16: Eastw..............2B 16
Prince St. DE7: Ilk......................3A 28
Prince St. NG10: Long E 5F 63
Prioridge NG12: Cotg..................3G 71
Prior Rd. NG5: Arn 1H 33
Priors Cl. NG13: Bing..................4G 51
Priory Av. NG5: Toll....................4E 69
Priory Cir. NG12: Toll..................4E 69
Priory Cl. DE7: Kirk H.................3G 39
Priory Ct. NG3: Mapp..................6A 34
Priory Ct. NG4: Ged....................6H 35
Priory Ct. NG7: Lent....................6C 44
Priory Cres. NG4: Ged.................6H 35
PRIORY HOSPITAL
   NOTTINGHAM 1A 46
Priory M. NG7: Lent....................1C 56
Priory Rd. NG15: Huck.................4E 7
Priory Rd. NG16: Eastw..............4B 16
Priory Rd. NG2: West Br..............3B 58
Priory Rd. NG4: Ged....................6H 35
Priory St. NG7: Lent....................6C 44
Pritchard Dr. NG9: Stfrd..............5G 53
Private Rd. NG12: Key.................4A 80
Private Rd. NG16: Woodbo...........6B 12
Private Rd. NG15: Huck................4E 7
Private Rd. NG3: Mapp................5H 33
Private Rd. NG5: Sher.................5G 33
Private Rd. No. 1 NG4: Colw 3H 47
Private Rd. No. 2 NG4: Colw 4H 47
Private Rd. No. 3 NG4: Colw 4A 48
Private Rd. No. 4 NG4: Colw 4B 48
Private Rd. No. 5 NG4: Colw 4B 48
Private Rd. No. 7 NG4: Colw 3H 47
Private Rd. No. 8 NG4: Colw 4H 47
Prize Cl. NG11: Clftn...................4A 66
Promenade NG3: Nott.......2G 5 (4H 45)
Prospect Ct. NG4: Ger.................6C 34
Prospect Pl. NG7: Lent................6D 44
Prospect Rd. DE75: Hea...............5E 15
Prospect Rd. NG4: Car 6C 34
Prospect Rd. NG7: Radf...............3C 44
Prospect Ter. NG7: Radf..............3C 44
Providence Pl. DE7: Ilk................6A 28
Provident Works
   NG7: Radf....................2A 4 (4E 45)
   ....(off Newdigate St.)
Prudhoe Cl. NG2: Nott.................2H 57
Pulborough Cl. NG5: Sher............3D 32
Pullman Rd. NG2: Nott.................5B 46
Pump Works Cl. NG5: Sher 4G 33
Purbeck Cl. NG10: Long E............5C 62
Purbeck Dr. NG2: West Br 6G 57
Purchase Av. DE75: Los...............3A 14
Purdy Mdw. NG10: Long E...........2B 72
Pyatt St. NG2: Nott.....................2H 57
Pygall Av. NG11: Goth.................6G 75
Pym Leys NG10: Long E...............2B 72
Pym St. NG3: Nott.......................3B 46
Pym Wlk. NG3: Nott........1H 5 (3A 46)

Quantock Cl. NG5: Arn 3F 21
Quantock Gro. NG13: Bing 5C 50
Quantock Rd. NG10: Long E........4C 62
Quarry Av. NG6: Bulw 1H 31
Quarrydale NG15: Huck...............2F 7

Quarry Hill DE7: Stant D..............3B 52
Quarry Hill Ind. Est. DE7: Ilk........5B 40
Quarry Hill Rd. DE7: Ilk...............4B 40
Quasar Elite
   Nottingham 3G 5 (4H 45)
Quays, The NG7: Lent.................6E 45
Quayside Cl. NG2: Nott...............2A 58
Queen Elizabeth Rd. NG9: Chil....1A 64
Queen Elizabeth Way
   DE7: Kirk H..........................4G 39
Queens Av. DE7: Ilk....................4C 40
Queens Av. DE7: Stly..................3A 38
Queens Av. DE75: Hea.................3B 14
Queens Av. NG4: Ged..................5G 35
Queensberry St. NG6: Bas............3C 32
Queen's Bower Rd.
   NG5: Bestw 5F 21
Queens Bri. Rd. NG2: Nott...........6G 45
Queensbury Av. NG2: West Br.... 2G 67
Queens Ct. NG13: Bing 4D 50
Queens Ct. NG2: Nott..................4E 57
Queens Dr. DE7: Ilk....................1A 40
Queen's Dr. NG2: Nott.................4E 57
Queen's Dr. NG9: Bee.................5G 55
Queens Dr. NG10: Sand...............1D 62
Queens Dr. NG16: Nuth................1C 30
Queens Dr. Ind. Est. NG2: Nott 2E 57
Queens Gro. NG2: Nott................6G 45
Queen's Medical Centre
   Stop (NET)...........................1B 56
QUEEN'S MEDICAL CENTRE
   UNIVERSITY HOSPITAL..........1B 56
Queen's Rd. NG12: Rad T............5F 49
Queens Rd. NG9: Bee..................6G 55
Queens Rd. NG2: Nott.................6G 45
Queen's Rd. E. NG9: Bee.............4H 55
Queens Rd. Nth. NG16: Eastw......3B 16
Queens Rd. Sth. NG16: Eastw......4B 16
Queen's Rd. W. NG9: Bee.............1D 64
Queen's Rd. W. NG9: Chil............1D 64
Queens Sq. NG16: Eastw.............3B 16
Queen St. DE7: Ilk......................1A 40
Queen St. NG1: Nott........3D 4 (4G 45)
Queen St. NG10: Long E..............6G 63
Queen St. NG15: Huck.................3F 7
Queen St. NG16: Lang M..............2G 15
Queen St. NG5: Arn....................4B 22
Queen's Wlk. NG2: Nott...............2F 57
Queen's Walk Stop (NET)............1G 57
Queen Ter. DE7: Ilk....................1A 40
Querneby Av. NG3: Mapp 5A 34
Querneby Rd. NG3: Mapp.............5A 34
Quinton Cl. NG11: Wilf................6E 57
Quorn Cl. NG9: Atten..................2E 65
Quorndon Cres. NG10: Long E......2F 73
Quorn Gro. NG5: Sher.................4E 33
Quorn Rd. NG5: Sher..................4E 33

Racecourse Park & Ride...............6D 46
Racecourse Rd. NG2: Colw 5D 46
Racecourse Rd. NG2: Nott............5D 46
Radbourne Rd. NG2: Nott.............6B 46
Radburn Ct. NG9: Stfrd................2G 53
Radcliffe Gdns. NG4: Car.............1F 47
Radcliffe Lodge NG12: Rad T........6E 49
Radcliffe Mt. NG2: West Br...........2B 58
RADCLIFFE ON TRENT 6F 49
Radcliffe on Trent Golf Course.....1H 61
Radcliffe Rd. NG12: Hol P............3G 59
Radcliffe Rd. NG2: Gam...............2A 58
Radcliffe Rd. NG2: West Br..........2A 58
Radcliffe Station (Rail)................6F 49
Radcliffe St. NG2: Nott................2H 57
RADFORD 4D 44
Radford Blvd. NG7: Radf 3C 44
Radford Bri. Rd. NG8: Aspl...........3A 44

Radford Bri. Rd. – Robin Hood St.

Radford Bri. Rd. NG8: Woll 3A **44**
Radford Ct. NG7: Bas 5D **32**
(off Radford Rd.)
Radford Ct. NG7: Radf 4D **44**
Radford Cres. NG4: Ged 5G **35**
Radford Gro. La. NG7: Radf 3C **44**
Radford Rd. NG7: Bas 5D **32**
Radford Rd. NG7: Hys G 5D **32**
Radford Road Stop (NET) 1D 44
Radham Ct. NG5: Sher 5G **33**
Radley Sq. NG6: Bulw 2B **32**
Radmarsh Rd. NG7: Lent 6C **44**
Rad Mdws. NG10: Long E 1E **73**
Radnor Gro. NG13: Bing 5C **50**
Radstock Rd. NG3: Nott 2C **46**
Radway Dr. NG11: Wilf 6E **57**
Raeburn Dr. NG9: Toton 3G **63**
Rafters, The NG7: Bas 5D **32**
Ragdale Pl. NG6: Bulw 5A **20**
Ragdale Rd. NG6: Bulw 5H **19**
(not continuous)
Raglan Cl. NG3: Nott 2H **45**
Raglan Ct. NG9: Lent A 2G **55**
Raglan Dr. NG4: Ged 6B **36**
Raglan St. NG16: Eastw 4C **16**
Raibank Gdns. NG5: Woodt 2A **34**
Railway Cotts. NG16: Kimb 1H **29**
Rainbow Rd. NG14: Calv 5C **12**
Rainham Gdns. NG11: Rudd 1G **77**
Raithby Cl. NG5: Bestw 1E **33**
Raleigh Cl. DE7: Ilk 4B **28**
Raleigh Cl. NG11: Clftn 4A **66**
Raleigh Ct. NG7: Radf 1A **4** (3E **45**)
Raleigh Pk. NG7: Lent 4B **44**
Raleigh Sq. NG7: Radf 2A **4** (4E **45**)
Raleigh St. NG7: Radf 2A **4** (4E **45**)
Ralf Cl. NG2: West Br 1A **68**
Ralph Way NG5: Sher 2G **33**
Ramblers Cl. NG4: Colw 4G **47**
Ramsdale Av. NG14: Calv 3F **11**
Ramsdale Cres. NG5: Sher 4H **33**
Ramsdale Pk. NG5: Arn 5D **10**
Ramsdale Pk. Golf Cen. 4D 10
Ramsdale Rd. NG4: Car 6G **35**
Ramsey Cl. NG9: Stfrd 1G **53**
Ramsey Ct. NG5: Sher 6F **33**
Ramsey Dr. NG5: Arn 1D **34**
Ranby Wlk. NG3: Nott 3B **46**
Rancliffe Av. NG12: Key 3F **79**
Randal Gdns. NG7: Hys G 2D **44**
Randal St. NG7: Hys G 2C **44**
(not continuous)
Ranelagh Gro. NG8: Woll 4G **43**
Rani Dr. NG5: Bas 3D **32**
Ranmere Rd. NG8: Bilb 2G **43**
Ranmoor Rd. NG4: Ged 6H **35**
Ranmore Cl. NG9: Bram 1B **54**
Rannerdale Cl. NG2: West Br 5D **58**
Rannoch Ri. NG5: Arn 4B **22**
Rannock Gdns. NG12: Key 4H **79**
Ranskill Gdns. NG5: Top V 5E **21**
Ransom Dr. NG3: Mapp 6A **34**
Ransom Dr. NG3: Nott 6A **34**
Ransom Rd. NG3: Nott 6A **34**
Ranson Rd. NG9: Chil 4B **64**
Ratcliffe St. NG16: Eastw 3B **16**
Rathgar Cl. NG8: Woll 5D **42**
Rathmines Cl. NG7: Lent 6C **44**
Rathvale Ct. NG9: Chil 1A **64**
Raven Av. NG5: Sher 3F **33**
Raven Ct. DE75: Hea 3C **14**
Ravenhill Cl. NG9: Chil 1B **64**
Ravens Ct. NG5: Bestw 2F **33**
Ravensdale Av. NG10: Long E 3D **62**
Ravensdale Dr. NG8: Woll 6C **42**
Ravensdene Ct. NG3: Mapp P 1G **45**
Ravensmore Rd. NG5: Sher 5F **33**
Ravenstone Ct. NG15: Huck 2E **19**
Ravenswood Rd. NG5: Arn 6B **22**
Ravensworth Rd. NG6: Bulw 5H **19**
Rawson St. NG7: Bas 6D **32**
Raymede Cl. NG5: Bestw 1D **32**
Raymede Dr. NG5: Bestw 1C **32**
Raymond Dr. NG13: Bing 5G **51**
Rayneham Rd. DE7: Ilk 3G **27**
Rayner Ct. NG7: Lent 4D **44**
Raynford Av. NG9: Chil 1D **64**
Raynham Lodge NG5: Top V 4B **20**
Rays Av. DE75: Hea 4C **14**
Ray St. DE75: Hea 4B **14**
Read Av. NG9: Bee 5G **55**
Read Lodge NG9: Bee 5G **55**
Readman Rd. NG9: Chil 2A **64**
Rearsby Cl. NG8: Bilb 4D **42**
Recreation Rd. NG10: Sand 5D **52**
Recreation St. NG10: Long E 5H **63**
Recreation Ter. NG9: Stfrd 5F **53**
Rectory Av. NG8: Woll 5E **43**
Rectory Ct. NG2: West Br 4B **58**
Rectory Dr. NG11: Wilf 3F **57**
Rectory Dr. NG4: Ged 5H **35**
Rectory Gdns. NG8: Woll 5F **43**
Rectory Pl. NG11: Bart F 1E **75**
Rectory Rd. DE72: Brea 5A **62**
Rectory Rd. NG12: Cotg 2E **71**
Rectory Rd. NG2: West Br 4A **58**
Rectory Rd. NG4: Colw 4G **47**
Redbourne Dr. NG8: Aspl 3A **44**
Redbridge Cl. DE7: Ilk 2C **40**
Redbridge Dr. NG16: Nuth 4D **30**
Redcar Cl. NG4: Ged 5G **35**
Redcliffe Gdns. NG3: Mapp P 1G **45**
Redcliffe Rd. NG3: Mapp P 1F **45**
Redens, The NG10: Long E 3D **72**
Redfield Rd. NG7: Lent 3C **56**
Redfield Way NG7: Lent 2C **56**
Redgates Ct. NG14: Calv 4F **11**
REDHILL 4A 22
Redhill Leisure Cen. 4A 22
Redhill Lodge Dr. NG5: Redh 4H **21**
Redhill Marina 6G 73
Redhill Rd. NG5: Arn 4A **22**
Red Kite Cl. NG15: Huck 3B **8**
Redland Av. NG4: Car 1H **47**
Redland Cl. DE7: Ilk 4B **28**
Redland Cl. NG9: Chil 1C **64**
Redland Dr. NG9: Chil 2C **64**
Redland Gro. NG4: Car 1G **47**
Red Lion Sq. DE75: Hea 3C **14**
Red Lion Yd. NG15: Huck 4G **7**
(off High St.)
Redmays Dr. NG14: Bulc 1H **37**
Redmile Cl. NG15: Huck 3F **7**
Redmile Rd. NG8: Aspl 5A **32**
Redoubt St. NG7: Radf 4C **44**
Redruth Cl. NG8: Bilb 3C **42**
Redwood NG2: West Br 5F **57**
Redwood Av. NG8: Woll 6D **42**
Redwood Cl. NG8: Bilb 2D **42**
Redwood Ct. NG15: Huck 3F **7**
Redwood Ct. NG7: Lent 5C **44**
(off Faraday Rd.)
Redwood Cres. NG9: Bee 6G **55**
Reeders Cft. NG9: Chil 2D **64**
Reedham Wlk. NG5: Bestw 5F **21**
Reedman Rd. NG10: Long E 3D **72**
Reel Cinema Ilkeston 1A 40
Rees Gdns. NG5: Top V 4E **21**
Regan Way NG9: Chil 3B **64**
Regatta Way NG2: West Br 3E **59**
Regency Ct. NG9: Bee 4G **55**
Regency Point NG2: West Br 3B **58**
Regent M. NG1: Nott 3B **4** (4F **45**)
Regents Pk. Cl. NG2: West Br 6G **57**
Regents Pl. NG11: Wilf 5F **57**
Regent St. DE7: Ilk 2B **40**
Regent St. NG1: Nott 4B **4** (5F **45**)
Regent St. NG10: Long E 5F **63**
Regent St. NG10: Sand 6E **53**
Regent St. NG16: Kimb 1H **29**
Regent St. NG16: Lang M 2F **15**
Regent St. NG7: Bas 6E **33**
Regent St. NG9: Bee 4G **55**
Regina Cl. NG12: Rad T 1E **61**
Reid Gdns. NG16: Want 1B **30**
Reigate Cl. NG9: Atten 3E **65**
Reigate Dr. NG9: Atten 3E **65**
Reigate Rd. NG7: Bas 5D **32**
Remembrance Way
NG11: Clftn 4A **66**
Rempstone Dr. NG6: Bulw 2B **32**
Renals Way NG14: Calv 5H **11**
Renfrew Dr. NG8: Woll 5E **43**
Rennie Hogg Rd. NG2: Nott 2D **56**
Renshaw Dr. NG4: Ged 4G **35**
Repton Dr. DE7: Ilk 2D **40**
Repton Rd. NG10: Long E 3B **72**
Repton Rd. NG2: West Br 6A **58**
Repton Rd. NG6: Bulw 1B **32**
Retford Rd. NG5: Sher 4E **33**
Retlaw Ct. NG9: Chil 6D **54**
Revelstoke Av. NG5: Top V 4B **20**
Revelstoke Way NG5: Top V 4B **20**
Revena Cl. NG4: Colw 3H **47**
Revesby Gdns. NG8: Aspl 2A **44**
Revesby Rd. NG5: Woodt 2B **34**
Revill Cl. DE7: Ilk 5G **27**
Revill Cres. NG9: Stfrd 3H **53**
Reydon Dr. NG8: Bas 6B **32**
Reynolds Dr. NG8: Woll 4F **43**
Rhodes Way NG6: Bestw V 5F **9**
Rhyl Cres. NG4: Ged 5H **35**
Ribblesdale DE7: Kirk H 4G **39**
Ribblesdale Ct. NG9: Chil 1A **64**
Ribblesdale Rd.
NG10: Long E 2C **72**
Ribblesdale Rd. NG5: Sher 2G **33**
Riber Cl. DE7: West H 1C **38**
Riber Cl. NG10: Long E 2F **73**
Riber Cres. NG5: Bestw 2D **32**
Richard Herrod Cen. 1E 47
Richardson Cl. NG11: Clftn 4A **66**
Richborough Pl. NG8: Woll 1D **54**
Richey Cl. NG5: Arn 6D **22**
Richmond Av. DE7: Ilk 3B **28**
Richmond Av. DE72: Brea 5C **62**
Richmond Av. NG10: Sand 1C **62**
Richmond Av. NG14: Calv 3A **12**
Richmond Av. NG16: Newth 3D **16**
Richmond Av. NG3: Nott 2B **46**
Richmond Cl. DE7: West H 1B **38**
Richmond Ct. NG9: Chil 6E **55**
Richmond Dr. NG12: Rad T 5F **49**
Richmond Dr. NG3: Mapp P 5H **33**
Richmond Dr. NG9: Chil 6E **55**
Richmond Gdns. NG5: Redh 4A **22**
Richmond Rd. NG2: West Br 2B **58**
Richmond Ter. NG12: Rad T 6F **49**
Ricklow Ct. NG5: Top V 5E **21**
(off Gautries Cl.)
Rick St. NG1: Nott 3F **5** (4H **45**)
Riddings, The NG4: Neth 2A **48**
(off Morris St.)
Ridding Ter. NG3: Nott 1E **5** (3G **45**)
Riddles Ct. NG16: Want 5A **18**
Ridge La. NG12: Rad T 4G **49**
Ridgeway DE75: Hea 5D **14**
Ridgeway NG5: Top V 6C **20**
Ridgeway Dr. DE7: Kirk H 4F **39**
Ridgeway Wlk. NG5: Top V 5E **21**
Ridgewood Dr. NG9: Chil 1C **64**
Ridgmont Wlk. NG11: Clftn 5B **66**
Ridgway Cl. NG2: West Br 6E **59**
Ridgway St. NG3: Nott 3A **46**
Ridings, The NG12: Key 4A **80**
Ridings, The NG14: Bulc 2G **37**
Ridsdale Rd. NG5: Sher 2G **33**
Rifle St. NG7: Radf 4C **44**
Rigley Av. DE7: Ilk 6B **28**
Rigley Dr. NG5: Top V 6C **20**
Ring Leas NG12: Cotg 3F **71**
Ringstead Cl. NG2: West Br 6G **57**
Ringstead Wlk. NG5: Bestw 5F **21**
Ringwood Cres. NG8: Woll 4A **44**
Ringwood Rd. NG13: Bing 5C **50**
Ripon Rd. NG3: Nott 4D **46**
Rise, The NG5: Sher 4H **33**
Riseborough Wlk. NG6: Bulw 4H **19**
(not continuous)
Rise Ct. NG5: Sher 1F **45**
Risegate NG12: Cotg 2F **71**
Risegate Gdns. NG12: Cotg 2F **71**
Riseholme Av. NG8: Woll 6C **42**
RISE PARK 4C 20
Rise Pk. Rd. NG5: Top V 4B **20**
Rise Pk. Shop. Cen. 4D 20
RISLEY 1A 62
Risley Ct. DE7: Ilk 4B **28**
Risley Dr. NG2: Nott 1F **57**
Risley La. DE72: Brea 2A **62**
Risley La. DE72: Ris 2A **62**
Riste's Pl. NG1: Nott 4F **5** (5H **45**)
Ritchie Cl. NG12: Cotg 3G **71**
Ritson Cl. NG3: Nott 1G **5** (3H **45**)
River Cres. NG2: Nott 1C **58**
Riverdale Rd. NG9: Chil 3D **64**
Rivergreen NG11: Clftn 2C **66**
Rivergreen Cl. NG9: Bram 1C **54**
Rivergreen Cres. NG9: Bram 1C **54**
Rivergreen Stop (NET) 3D 66
Rivermead NG12: Cotg 2F **71**
Rivermead NG2: West Br 4H **57**
River Rd. NG4: Colw 5G **47**
Riverside NG14: Stoke B 1F **49**
Riverside Cl. NG9: Bee 2H **65**
Riverside Family Golf Cen. 5D 56
Riverside Golf Course 5D 56
Riverside Point NG7: Lent 6C **44**
Riverside Retail Pk.
Nottingham 3E 57
Riverside Rd. NG9: Bee 2G **65**
Riverside Way NG2: Nott 2F **57**
River Vw. NG10: Long E 4C **72**
River Vw. NG2: Nott 2H **57**
Riverway Gdns. NG2: Nott 1H **57**
Rivington Rd. NG9: Toton 3G **63**
Robbie Burns Rd. NG5: Bestw 5G **21**
Robbinetts La. NG16: Babb 6F **29**
(not continuous)
Robbinetts La. NG16: Coss 6F **29**
(not continuous)
Robbinetts La. NG8: Stre 6A **30**
Roberts La. NG15: Huck 4F **7**
Roberts St. DE7: Ilk 3C **40**
Roberts St. NG2: Nott 5A **46**
Roberts Yd. NG9: Bee 4G **55**
Robert Wilkinson Smith Homes
NG3: Mapp P 2G **45**
Robey Cl. NG15: Lin 2H **7**
Robey Dr. NG16: Eastw 2B **16**
Robey Ter. NG7: Hys G 2D **44**
Robina Dr. NG16: Gilt 5E **17**
Robin Bailey Way NG15: Huck 5A **8**
Robinet Rd. NG9: Bee 6F **55**
Robin Gdns. NG12: Edwal 3C **68**
Robin Hood Chase NG3: Nott 2H **45**
Robin Hood Cl. NG16: Eastw 4B **16**
Robin Hood Dr. NG15: Huck 1E **19**
Robin Hood Experience,
The 5C 4 (5F 45)
(off Friar La.)
Robin Hood Ind. Est.
NG3: Nott 2H **5** (4A **46**)
Robin Hood Rd. NG5: Arn 4G **21**
Robin Hood St.
NG3: Nott 3H **5** (4A **46**)

A-Z Nottingham 117

Robin Hood Ter. – St Albans Rd.

Robin Hood Ter.
NG3: Nott ... 2G 5 (4H 45)
Robin Hood Way NG2: Nott ... 2F 57
Robinia Ct. NG2: West Br ... 6C 58
Robinson Ct. NG9: Chil ... 3B 64
Robinson Gdns. NG11: Clftn ... 4A 66
Robinson Rd. NG3: Mapp ... 4B 34
Robinsons Hill NG6: Bulw ... 6H 19
Robin's Row NG15: Huck ... 6E 7
... (off Knoll Av.)
Robins Wood House ... 2H 43
Robins Wood Rd. NG8: Aspl ... 3H 43
Rob Roy Av. NG7: Lent ... 6D 44
Roche Cl. NG5: Arn ... 6E 23
Rochester Av. NG4: Neth ... 2A 48
Rochester Cl. NG10: Long E ... 6C 62
Rochester Ct. NG6: Bulw ... 1F 31
Rochester Wlk. NG11: Clftn ... 4D 66
Rochford Ct. NG12: Edwal ... 2E 69
Rock City ... 3C 4 (4F 45)
... (off Talbot St.)
Rock Ct. NG6: Bas ... 4B 32
Rock Dr. NG7: Nott ... 6A 4 (6E 45)
Rocket Cl. NG16: Want ... 6A 18
Rockford Ct. NG9: Stfrd ... 2G 53
Rockford Rd. NG5: Sher ... 4D 32
Rockingham Gro. NG13: Bing ... 5C 50
Rockley Av. NG12: Rad T ... 5F 49
Rockley Av. NG16: Newth ... 4C 16
Rockley Cl. NG15: Huck ... 5C 6
Rockleys Vw. NG14: Lowd ... 3G 25
Rock Side NG16: Kimb ... 1H 29
... (off Edgwood Rd.)
Rockside Gdns. NG15: Huck ... 4E 7
Rock St. NG6: Bulw ... 5G 19
Rockwell Ct. NG9: Stfrd ... 4G 53
Rockwood Cres. NG15: Huck ... 5D 6
Rockwood Wlk. NG15: Huck ... 5E 7
Rodel Ct. NG3: Nott ... 1F 5 (3H 45)
Roden St. NG3: Nott ... 3H 5 (4A 46)
Roderick St. NG6: Bas ... 3B 32
Rodice Ct. NG7: Lent ... 4C 44
Rodney Rd. NG2: West Br ... 5C 58
Rodney Way DE7: Ilk ... 4B 28
Rodwell Cl. NG8: Aspl ... 3A 44
Roebuck Cl. NG5: Arn ... 5F 21
Roecliffe NG2: West Br ... 1A 68
Roe Gdns. NG11: Rudd ... 6F 67
Roehampton Dr. NG9: Trow ... 1F 53
Roe Hill NG14: Woodbo ... 5C 12
Roe La. NG14: Woodbo ... 1C 24
Roes La. NG14: Calv ... 4A 12
Roker Cl. NG8: Aspl ... 6G 31
Roland Av. NG11: Wilf ... 4F 57
Roland Av. NG16: Nuth ... 3E 31
Rolleston Cl. NG15: Huck ... 6D 6
Rolleston Cres. NG16: Want ... 4H 17
Rolleston Dr. NG16: Newth ... 5C 16
Rolleston Dr. NG5: Arn ... 6C 22
Rolleston Dr. NG7: Lent ... 5D 44
Rolls Royce Leisure ... 2E 19
Roman Cres. NG15: Huck ... 3B 8
Roman Dr. NG6: Bas ... 3C 32
Romans Ct. NG6: Bas ... 5C 32
Romilay Cl. NG9: Lent A ... 2G 55
Romney Av. NG8: Woll ... 1D 54
Romorantin Pl. NG10: Long E ... 6G 63
Rona Ct. NG6: Bulw ... 2C 32
Ronald St. NG7: Radf ... 4D 44
Rookery Gdns. NG5: Arn ... 5B 22
Rookwood Cl. NG9: Bee ... 5E 55
Roosa Cl. NG6: Bulw ... 2F 31
Roosevelt Av. NG10: Long E ... 2E 73
Roper Av. DE75: Hea ... 5C 14
Ropewalk, The DE7: Ilk ... 6C 28
Ropewalk, The DE7: Stan C ... 6A 26
Ropewalk, The DE75: Hea ... 5D 14
Ropewalk, The
NG1: Nott ... 3A 4 (4E 45)
Ropewalk Ct. NG1: Nott ... 3B 4 (4F 45)
ROPEWALK HOUSE ... 4B 4 (5F 45)
Ropewalk Ind. Est. DE7: Ilk ... 6C 28
Ropsley Cres. NG2: West Br ... 2C 58
Rosa Ct. NG4: Ged ... 6A 36
Roscoe Av. NG5: Redh ... 3A 22
Roseacre NG9: Bee ... 6G 55
Rose Ash La. NG5: Bestw ... 5F 21
Rose Av. DE7: Ilk ... 5A 28
Rosebank Dr. NG5: Arn ... 4D 22
Rosebay Av. NG7: Hys G ... 1C 44
Roseberry Gdns. NG15: Huck ... 5A 8
Rosebery Av. NG2: West Br ... 2A 58
Rosebery St. NG6: Bas ... 3C 32
Rose Cl. NG3: Nott ... 2H 45
Rose Cotts. NG14: Bur J ... 2E 37
Rose Ct. NG10: Long E ... 4D 62
Rosecroft Dr. NG5: Bestw ... 1G 33
Rosedale Cl. NG10: Long E ... 1D 72
Rosedale Dr. NG8: Woll ... 5B 42
Rosedale Gdns. NG15: Huck ... 4E 7
Rosedale Rd. NG3: Nott ... 3E 47
Rose Flower Gro. NG15: Huck ... 1A 20
Rosegarth Wlk. NG6: Bas ... 3B 32
Rose Gro. NG12: Key ... 3H 79
Rose Gro. NG9: Bee ... 6H 55
Rosegrove Av. NG5: Arn ... 4B 22
Rose Hill NG12: Key ... 4G 79
Roseland Cl. NG12: Key ... 5G 79
Roseleigh Av. NG3: Mapp ... 5D 34
Rosemary Cl. NG8: Brox ... 6E 31
Rose M. NG3: Nott ... 2H 45
Roseneath Av. NG5: Top V ... 4C 20
Rosetta Rd. NG7: Bas ... 6D 32
... (not continuous)
Rosewall Ct. NG5: Arn ... 6D 22
Rose Way NG12: Edwal ... 3C 68
Rosewood Cres. DE75: Hea ... 3F 15
Rosewood Gdns. NG2: West Br ... 2G 67
Rosewood Gdns. NG6: Bulw ... 6F 19
Roslyn Av. NG4: Ged ... 5G 35
Roslyn Ct. NG14: Bur J ... 2F 37
Rossell Dr. NG9: Stfrd ... 6G 53
Rossendale DE7: Ilk ... 3A 28
Rossett Cl. NG2: Gam ... 5F 59
Rossington Rd. NG2: Nott ... 4B 46
Ross La. NG4: Lamb ... 6C 24
Rosslyn Dr. NG15: Huck ... 3A 8
Rosslyn Dr. NG8: Aspl ... 5G 31
Rosthwaite Cl. NG2: West Br ... 6E 59
Rothbury Av. NG9: Trow ... 1F 53
Rothbury Cl. NG5: Arn ... 3B 22
Rothbury Gro. NG13: Bing ... 4C 50
Rothesay Av. NG7: Lent ... 4D 44
Rothley Av. NG3: Nott ... 4B 46
Rothwell Cl. NG11: Wilf ... 1E 67
Roughs Wood La. NG15: Huck ... 1D 18
Round Ho. Cl. DE75: Hea ... 5A 14
Roundwood Rd. NG5: Arn ... 6G 21
Rowan Av. NG9: Stfrd ... 1G 53
Rowan Cl. DE7: Ilk ... 4B 40
Rowan Cl. NG12: Cotg ... 6G 61
Rowan Cl. NG13: Bing ... 5G 51
Rowan Cl. NG14: Calv ... 4F 11
Rowan Ct. NG15: Huck ... 3A 8
Rowan Ct. NG16: Nuth ... 1B 30
Rowan Dr. NG11: Wilf ... 1E 67
Rowan Dr. NG12: Key ... 5A 80
Rowan Gdns. NG6: Bulw ... 6F 19
Rowans Cres. NG6: Cin ... 3H 31
Rowan Wlk. NG3: Nott ... 1C 46
Rowe Ct. NG10: Long E ... 6G 63
Rowe Gdns. NG6: Bulw ... 1B 32
Rowland Av. NG3: Mapp ... 5C 34
Rowland M. NG3: Nott ... 2A 46
Rowley Ct. NG5: Sher ... 5E 33
Rowley Dr. NG5: Sher ... 5E 33
Rowsley Av. NG10: Long E ... 2C 72
Roxburgh Cl. NG5: Arn ... 5E 23
Roxby Ho. NG5: Arn ... 1C 34
Roxley Ct. NG9: Bee ... 4E 55
Roxton Ct. NG16: Kimb ... 6H 17
Royal Albert Ct. NG7: Radf ... 3E 45
... (off Russell St.)
Royal Av. NG10: Long E ... 4F 63
Royal Cen. NG1: Nott ... 3D 4 (4G 45)
... (off Sth. Sherwood St.)
Royal Centre Stop (NET) ... 3D 4 (4F 45)
Royal Concert Hall ... 3D 4 (4G 45)
Royal Ct. NG5: Sher ... 5G 33
... (off Haydn Rd.)
Royal M. NG9: Chil ... 2C 64
Royal Standard Ho.
NG1: Nott ... 5C 4 (5F 45)
Royal Standard Pl.
NG1: Nott ... 5C 4 (5F 45)
... (off St James's Ter.)
Royal Victoria Ct.
NG7: Radf ... 1A 4 (3E 45)
Roy Av. NG9: Bee ... 1H 65
Royce Av. NG15: Huck ... 1E 19
Royston Cl. NG2: Nott ... 2F 57
Royston Ct. NG4: Car ... 1E 47
Ruby Paddocks NG16: Kimb ... 2H 29
RUDDINGTON ... 6G 67
Ruddington Flds. Bus. Pk.
NG11: Rudd ... 2H 77
Ruddington Framework
Knitters Mus. ... 1G 77
Ruddington Gdns. NG11: Wilf ... 2F 67
Ruddington Grange
Golf Course ... 3G 67
Ruddington La. NG11: Wilf ... 5F 57
Ruddington Station Great
Central Railway ... 2G 77
Ruddington Village Mus. ... 6G 67
Rudge Cl. NG8: Woll ... 4F 43
Ruffles Av. NG5: Arn ... 2D 34
Rufford Av. NG4: Ged ... 5F 35
Rufford Av. NG9: Bram ... 3A 54
Rufford Cl. NG15: Huck ... 5A 8
Rufford Gro. NG13: Bing ... 5D 50
Rufford Hall NG2: Nott ... 1C 58
Rufford Rd. NG10: Long E ... 3D 72
Rufford Rd. NG11: Rudd ... 6H 67
Rufford Rd. NG5: Sher ... 4G 33
Rufford Wlk. NG11: Rudd ... 6H 67
Rufford Wlk. NG6: Bulw ... 6H 19
Rufford Way NG2: West Br ... 5D 58
RUFFS ... 6E 7
Ruffs Dr. NG15: Huck ... 6E 7
Rugby Cl. NG5: Top V ... 6C 20
Rugby Ct. NG2: West Br ... 6A 58
Rugby Rd. NG2: West Br ... 6G 57
Rugby Ter. NG7: Hys G ... 2D 44
Rugeley Av. NG10: Long E ... 6H 63
Ruislip Cl. NG16: Kimb ... 6G 17
Runcie Cl. NG12: Cotg ... 3F 71
Runnymede Ct.
NG7: Radf ... 2A 4 (4E 45)
Runnymede Ct. NG9: Bee ... 6G 55
... (off Grove St.)
Runswick Dr. NG5: Arn ... 5B 22
Runswick Dr. NG8: Woll ... 4G 43
Runton Dr. NG6: Bas ... 3D 32
Rupert Rd. NG13: Bing ... 5D 50
Rupert St. DE7: Ilk ... 6C 28
Ruscombe Pl. NG3: Nott ... 3H 45
Rushcliffe Arena ... 5H 57
Rushcliffe Av. NG12: Rad T ... 6F 49
Rushcliffe Av. NG4: Car ... 1F 47
Rushcliffe Country Pk. ... 2G 77
Rushcliffe Ct. NG6: Bulw ... 1B 32
Rushcliffe Ri. NG5: Sher ... 2H 33
Rushcliffe Rd. NG15: Huck ... 6E 7
Rushes, The NG11: Goth ... 6H 75
Rushes Cl. NG9: Bee ... 5G 55
Rushford Dr. NG8: Woll ... 5C 42
Rush Leys NG10: Long E ... 2F 73
Rushmere Wlk. NG5: Woodt ... 2B 34
Rushton Gdns. NG3: Nott ... 2A 46
Rushworth Av. NG2: West Br ... 3A 58
Rushworth Cl. NG3: Nott ... 2A 46
Rushworth Ct. NG2: West Br ... 3A 58
Rushy Cl. NG8: Bilb ... 4D 42
Rushy La. DE72: Ris ... 6A 52
Rushy La. NG10: Sand ... 5A 52
Ruskin Av. NG10: Long E ... 2D 72
Ruskin Av. NG9: Chil ... 1D 64
Ruskin Cl. NG5: Arn ... 6H 21
Ruskin St. NG7: Radf ... 4C 44
Russell Av. NG8: Woll ... 4F 43
Russell Ct. NG10: Long E ... 4F 63
Russell Cres. NG8: Woll ... 4F 43
Russell Dr. NG8: Woll ... 4E 43
Russell Farm Cl. NG12: Toll ... 4F 69
Russell Gdns. NG9: Chil ... 3C 64
Russell Pl. NG1: Nott ... 3C 4 (4F 45)
Russell Rd. NG7: Hys G ... 1D 44
Russell St. NG10: Long E ... 4F 63
Russell St. NG7: Radf ... 3E 45
... (not continuous)
Russet Av. NG4: Car ... 2G 47
Russett Way NG8: Aspl ... 2H 43
Russley Rd. NG9: Bram ... 3A 54
Ruth Dr. NG5: Arn ... 4C 22
Rutherford Ho. NG7: Nott ... 2B 56
Ruthwell Gdns. NG5: Top V ... 3E 21
Rutland Av. NG9: Toton ... 3A 64
Rutland Cl. NG2: Nott ... 1F 57
Rutland Ct. DE7: Ilk ... 6H 27
Rutland Gro. NG10: Sand ... 6E 53
Rutland Rd. NG13: Bing ... 5F 51
Rutland Rd. NG2: West Br ... 2B 58
Rutland Rd. NG4: Ged ... 4F 35
Rutland St. DE7: Ilk ... 5B 28
Rutland St. NG1: Nott ... 5C 4 (5F 45)
Rutland Ter. DE7: Ilk ... 5B 28
Rutland Vs. NG2: Nott ... 5B 46
Ryan Way NG9: Bee ... 2G 65
Rydal Av. NG10: Long E ... 3D 62
Rydal Dr. NG15: Huck ... 3F 7
Rydal Dr. NG9: Bram ... 3D 54
Rydale Rd. NG5: Sher ... 2G 33
Rydal Gdns. NG2: West Br ... 6C 58
Rydal Gro. NG6: Bas ... 4C 32
Ryder St. NG6: Bas ... 3B 32
Ryecroft St. NG9: Stfrd ... 2G 53
Ryefield Av. DE7: Ilk ... 2B 28
Ryehill Cl. NG2: Nott ... 1H 57
Ryehill St. NG2: Nott ... 1H 57
Ryeland Gdns. NG2: Nott ... 1G 57
Ryemere Cl. NG16: Eastw ... 3A 16
Ryemere Ct. NG16: Eastw ... 3A 16
... (off Bailey Gro. Rd.)
Rye St. NG7: Bas ... 6D 32
Ryknield Rd. NG15: Huck ... 3A 8
RYLANDS ... 6H 55
Rylands Cl. NG9: Bee ... 1H 65
Rylands Ct. NG9: Bee ... 6G 55
Ryton Ct. NG2: Nott ... 2H 57
Ryton Sq. NG8: Aspl ... 6H 31

S

Sabina Rd. NG15: Huck ... 3A 8
Saco Ho. NG1: Nott ... 4B 4 (5F 45)
Saddlers Ga. NG12: Rad T ... 6F 49
Saddlers Yd. NG12: Plum ... 6G 69
Saddleworth Ct. NG3: Nott ... 2G 45
Saffron Gdns. NG2: Nott ... 1F 57
St Agnes Cl. NG8: Bilb ... 1D 42
St Aidans Ct. NG6: Bas ... 3C 32
St Albans Cl. NG10: Long E ... 2G 73
St Albans M. NG6: Bulw ... 1B 32
St Albans Rd. NG5: Arn ... 6H 21
St Albans Rd. NG6: Bestw V ... 1C 20

St Albans Rd. – Serina Ct.

St Albans Rd. NG6: Bulw.............5A **20**
St Albans St. NG5: Sher.............4G **33**
St Andrew Cl. NG11: Goth..........6H **75**
St Andrews Cl. NG15: Huck..........3F **7**
St Andrews Cl. NG6: Bulw...........6A **20**
St Andrew's Ct. DE7: Ilk..............6H **27**
St Andrews Ct. NG6: Bulw..........6B **20**
St Andrew's Dr. DE7: Ilk...............1A **40**
St Andrews Ho. NG3: Mapp..........4E **35**
St Andrew's M. DE7: Stly............4A **38**
St Andrew's Rd. NG3: Mapp P.....2F **45**
ST ANN'S..............................3H 45
St Ann's Gdns. NG3: Nott.............2A **46**
St Ann's Hill NG3: Nott...............2G **45**
St Ann's Hill Rd. NG3: Nott..........2G **45**
St Ann's St. NG1: Nott.......2E **5** (4G **45**)
St Ann's Valley NG3: Nott............3A **46**
St Ann's Way NG3: Nott...............3G **45**
St Ann's Well Rd.
NG3: Nott.......................2F **5** (4H **45**)
St Anthony Ct. NG7: Lent............1C **56**
St Augustines Cl. NG7: Bas..........6E **33**
St Austell Dr. NG11: Wilf..............6F **57**
St Austins Ct. NG4: Car...............1H **47**
St Austins Dr. NG4: Car...............1H **47**
St Bartholomews Ct.
NG3: Nott....................................2B **46**
St Bartholomew's Rd.
NG3: Nott....................................2B **46**
St Catherines St. NG12: Rad T.....1E **61**
St Cecilia Gdns. NG3: Nott..........3H **45**
St Chads NG4: Car.......................2H **47**
St Chad's Rd. NG3: Nott..............4A **46**
St Christopher St. NG2: Nott........5B **46**
St Cuthbert's Rd. NG3: Nott.........4A **46**
St Emmanuel Vw. NG5: Arn..........4F **21**
St Ervan Rd. NG11: Wilf................5F **57**
St Francis Dr. NG11: Rudd............5G **67**
St George's Dr. NG2: Nott.............1G **57**
St Georges Dr. NG9: Toton...........3H **63**
St Helen's Cres. NG14: Bur J........3F **37**
St Helens Cres. NG9: Trow...........5E **41**
St Helen's Gro. NG14: Bur J.........4E **37**
St Helens Rd. NG2: West Br..........5B **58**
St Helen's St. NG7: Nott.... 3A **4** (4E **45**)
St Helier NG7: Nott........... 5A **4** (5E **45**)
St James Av. DE7: Ilk...................2C **40**
St James Ct. NG10: Sand...........2D **62**
St James Ct. NG3: Mapp..............5D **34**
St James's St.
NG1: Nott........................ 5C **4** (5F **45**)
St James's Ter.
NG1: Nott........................ 5C **4** (5F **45**)
St James St. NG9: Stfrd...............5E **53**
St James Ter. NG9: Stfrd..............5E **53**
St John's Ct. NG4: Car..................2F **47**
St John's Cres. NG15: Huck...........6A **8**
St John's Rd. DE7: Ilk...................2C **40**
St John's Rd. NG11: Rudd............6G **67**
St Johns St. NG10: Long E............6F **63**
St Jude's Av. NG3: Mapp..............5H **33**
St Laurence Ct. NG10: Long E.......1G **73**
St Lawrence Blvd.
NG12: Rad T.................................1D **60**
St Lawrence Cl. DE75: Hea..........3D **14**
St Lawrence Cl. NG11: Goth.........6H **75**
St Leonard's Dr. NG8: Woll...........5F **43**
St Leven Cl. NG8: Bilb..................1D **42**
St Lukes Cl. NG2: West Br...........6D **58**
St Luke's St. NG3: Nott......3H **5** (4A **46**)
St Lukes Way NG14: Stoke B.......1F **49**
St Margaret's Av. NG8: Aspl.........1A **44**
St Mark's St. NG3: Nott..... 2F **5** (4H **45**)
St Martins Cl. NG8: Stre...............1E **43**
St Martin's Gdns. NG8: Stre.........1D **42**
St Martin's Rd. NG8: Stre.............1E **43**
St Mary Ct. DE7: Ilk......................1A **40**
....................................*(off St Mary St.)*
St Mary's Av. NG4: Ged...............5G **35**
St Mary's Church
Nottingham....................5F **5** (5H **45**)
St Mary's Cl. NG5: Arn.................4B **22**
St Mary's Cl. NG9: Atten..............4D **64**
St Mary's Cres. NG11: Rudd........6G **67**
St Mary's Ga. NG1: Nott.... 4F **5** (5H **45**)
St Mary's Pl. NG1: Nott..... 4F **5** (5H **45**)
St Marys Rd. NG13: Bing..............4F **51**
St Mary St. DE7: Ilk......................1A **40**
St Marys Vw. NG15: Huck.............4G **7**
....*(off Ogle St.)*
St Marys Way NG15: Huck............3F **7**
St Matthias Rd. NG3: Nott............3A **46**
St Mawes Av. NG11: Wilf..............5F **57**
St Michael's Av. NG4: Ged...........5G **35**
St Michael's Av. NG8: Bilb............1D **42**
St Michaels Sq. NG9: Bram..........3B **54**
St Michaels Vw. NG15: Huck.........2H **7**
St Nicholas Cl. NG5: Arn..............6A **22**
St Nicholas St.
NG1: Nott........................5D **4** (5G **45**)
St Norbert Dr. DE7: Kirk H...........4G **39**
St Patrick's Rd. NG15: Huck..........4F **7**
St Patrick's Rd. NG16: Nuth.........1B **30**
St Paul's Av. NG7: Hys G..............2D **44**
St Pauls Ct. NG16: Kimb..............1H **29**
St Paul's St. NG8: Radf.................4B **44**
St Paul's Ter. NG7: Hys G.............2D **44**
St Peters Chambers
NG1: Nott........................ 4E **5** (5G **45**)
....*(off Bank Pl.)*
St Peter's Chu. Wlk.
NG1: Nott........................ 4E **5** (5G **45**)
St Peters Ct. NG7: Radf...............4B **44**
St Peters Cres. NG11: Rudd.........6G **67**
St Peter's Ga. NG1: Nott.... 4E **5** (5G **45**)
St Peter's Sq. NG1: Nott....4D **4** (5G **45**)
...............................*(off St Peter's Ga.)*
St Peter's St. NG7: Radf...............4C **44**
St Saviours Gdns. NG2: Nott.......1H **57**
St Stephen's Av. NG2: Nott...........5B **46**
St Stephen's Rd. NG2: Nott..........5A **46**
St Thomas More Cl. NG8: Woll.....5D **42**
St Vincent Cl. NG10: Long E........1G **73**
St Wilfrids Chu. Dr. NG11: Wilf.....3F **57**
St Wilfrid's Rd. DE7: West H........2C **38**
St Wilfrid's Sq. NG14: Calv..........4H **11**
Salamander Cl. NG4: Car.............5F **35**
Salcey Dr. NG9: Trow...................1F **53**
Salcombe Cir. NG5: Redh.............4H **21**
Salcombe Cl. NG16: Newth..........4E **17**
Salcombe Cres. NG11: Rudd.........5H **67**
Salcombe Dr. NG5: Redh..............4H **21**
Salcombe Rd. NG5: Sher...............4D **32**
Salford Gdns. NG3: Nott....2G **5** (4H **45**)
...................................(not continuous)
Salisbury Ct. NG3: Mapp...............5A **34**
Salisbury Sq. NG7: Lent................5C **44**
Salisbury St. NG10: Long E..........6G **63**
Salisbury St. NG7: Lent................4C **44**
Salisbury St. NG9: Bee.................4G **55**
Salmon Cl. NG6: Bulw...................6F **19**
Salop St. NG5: Arn.......................6H **21**
Saltburn Rd. NG8: Bilb..................3G **43**
Saltby Grn. NG2: West Br..............2F **67**
Salterford Av. NG14: Calv..............3H **11**
Salterford Rd. NG15: Huck............6E **7**
Saltford Cl. NG4: Ged...................5H **35**
Salthouse Cl. NG9: Bee.................3G **55**
Salthouse Ct. NG9: Bee.................3G **55**
Salthouse La. NG9: Bee.................3G **55**
Saltney Way NG11: Wilf.................2E **67**
Samson Ct. NG11: Rudd.................5F **67**
Sandale Cl. NG2: Gam....................5E **59**
Sandays Cl. NG2: Nott....................2G **57**
Sandby NG1: Nott.............. 2C **4** (4F **45**)
..................................*(off Hampden St.)*
Sandby Ct. NG9: Chil.....................6C **54**
Sanders Cl. DE7: Ilk.......................5G **27**
Sanderson Dr. NG3: Mapp.............1F **35**
Sandfield Ct. NG6: Bulw.................1G **31**
Sandfield Rd. NG5: Arn..................1B **34**
Sandfield Rd. NG7: Lent.................5D **44**
Sandfield Rd. NG9: Toton...............3G **63**
Sandford Av. NG10: Long E............6G **63**
Sandford Rd. NG3: Mapp................5B **34**
Sandgate NG9: Bram......................2D **54**
Sandham Wlk. NG11: Clftn.............2C **66**
Sandhurst Dr. NG11: Rudd.............1F **77**
Sandhurst Dr. NG9: Chil.................3C **64**
Sandhurst Rd. NG6: Bulw...............4H **19**
SANDIACRE.....................................6D 52
Sandiacre Friesland
Sports Cen.....................................6B 52
Sandiacre Rd. NG9: Stfrd...............5E **53**
Sandon St. NG7: Bas......................6E **33**
Sandown Rd. NG9: Toton...............2H **63**
Sandpiper Cl. NG13: Bing..............6F **51**
Sandpiper Way NG7: Lent..............5C **44**
Sandringham Av.
NG2: West Br.................................3A **58**
Sandringham Cres. NG8: Woll......4C **42**
Sandringham Dr. DE75: Hea.........3A **14**
Sandringham Dr. NG9: Bram.........2C **54**
Sandringham Pl. DE7: Kirk H.........4H **39**
Sandringham Pl. NG15: Huck.........3H **7**
Sandringham Rd. NG10: Sand.......2D **62**
Sandringham Rd. NG2: Nott..........5B **46**
Sands Cl. NG4: Colw......................4G **47**
Sandside NG12: Cotg.....................3F **71**
Sandstone Ct. NG6: Bulw..............5G **19**
Sandwell Cl. NG10: Long E............1C **72**
Sandyford Cl. NG6: Bas..................4A **32**
Sandy La. NG12: Hol P..................1B **60**
Sandy La. NG15: Huck....................4G **7**
Sandy La. NG9: Bram......................1D **54**
Sanger Cl. NG11: Clftn...................5A **66**
Sanger Gdns. NG11: Clftn..............5A **66**
Sankey Dr. NG6: Bulw...................6G **19**
Sapele Cl. NG4: Ged.....................5A **36**
Sarah Av. NG5: Sher......................5E **33**
Sargent Gdns. NG3: Nott................3B **46**
Saskatoon Cl. NG12: Rad T............1E **61**
Saunby Cl. NG5: Arn......................6D **22**
Saunton Cl. NG12: Edwal................1E **69**
Savages Rd. NG11: Rudd...............5G **67**
Savages Row NG11: Rudd...............5G **67**
Saville Cl. NG9: Stfrd....................3G **53**
Saville Rd. NG5: Woodt..................2B **34**
Savoy Cinema Nottingham...............5D 44
SAWLEY...3C 72
Sawley Rd. DE72: Brea....................6A **62**
Sawley Rd. DE72: Dray....................6A **62**
Sawmand Cl. NG10: Long E.............1E **73**
Sawmills Ind. Pk. DE75: Los............2B **14**
Saxby Ct. NG11: Rudd....................6H **67**
Saxelby Gdns. NG6: Bulw................5H **19**
SAXONDALE......................................5A 50
Saxondale Ct. NG6: Bulw.................4A **20**
Saxondale Dr. NG6: Bulw.................2B **32**
Saxon Grn. NG7: Lent......................6C **44**
Saxon Way NG12: Cotg....................4F **71**
Saxton Av. DE75: Hea......................3D **14**
Saxton Av. NG8: Stre.......................6C **30**
Saxton Cl. NG9: Bee.........................4H **55**
Saxton Ct. NG5: Arn.........................6E **23**
Scafell Cl. NG2: West Br..................6E **59**
Scafell Way NG11: Clftn...................6B **66**
Scalby Cl. NG16: Eastw.....................3H **15**
Scalford Dr. NG8: Woll.....................5A **44**
Scarborough Av. DE7: Ilk.................1H **39**
Scarborough St.
NG3: Nott.........................2G **5** (4H **45**)
Scarf Wlk. NG11: Wilf.......................4F **57**
Scargill Av. NG16: Newth..................4D **16**
Scargill Cl. NG16: Newth...................4D **16**
Scargill Rd. DE7: West H....................1C **38**
Scargill Wlk. NG16: Eastw..................2B **16**
Scarrington Rd. NG2: West Br.....2B **58**
Sceptre St. NG5: Sher.................5G **33**
Scholar Cl. DE7: Ilk.......................3B **40**
School Av. NG15: Huck...............1D **18**
School Cl. NG2: Nott....................2H **57**
School Gdns. NG25: Oxton...........1B **12**
School La. DE7: Stant D...............4B **52**
School La. NG13: Bing..................4E **51**
School La. NG9: Chil......................1C **64**
School Sq. DE7: West H.................2C **38**
School Wlk. NG6: Bestw V.............1C **20**
School Way NG2: Nott...................2H **57**
School Woods Cl. DE75: Ship.......1E **27**
Science Rd. NG7: Nott...................2B **56**
Scollins Ct. DE7: Ilk......................5A **28**
Scotholme Av. NG7: Hys G............1D **44**
Scotland Bank NG12: Cotg.............2F **71**
Scotland Rd. NG5: Bas...................4D **32**
Scott Av. NG9: Bee.........................5F **55**
Scott Cl. NG6: Bulw........................2F **31**
Scrimshire La. NG12: Cotg.............2E **71**
Script Dr. NG6: Bas........................3C **32**
Scrivelsby Gdns. NG9: Chil............1D **64**
Scrooby Row NG5: Top V...............5E **21**
Seaburn Rd. NG9: Toton.................2G **63**
Seaford Av. NG8: Woll....................4H **43**
Seagrave Ct. NG5: Arn....................6A **22**
Seagrave Ct. NG8: Stre...................6D **30**
Seagrave Rd. NG8: Stre..................6D **30**
Seamer Rd. NG16: Kimb..................6H **17**
Sean Upton Cl. NG9: Chil...............2D **64**
Seatallan Cl. NG2: West Br.............5E **59**
Seathwaite Cl. NG2: West Br..........1E **69**
Seatoller Cl. NG2: West Br..............6E **59**
Seaton Cres. NG8: Aspl...................6G **31**
Seaton Way NG3: Ged......................2G **35**
Second Av. DE7: Ilk..........................2B **40**
Second Av. DE72: Ris........................1B **62**
Second Av. NG4: Car.........................2E **47**
Second Av. NG4: Ged........................6H **35**
Second Av. NG6: Bulw.......................6H **19**
Second Av. NG7: Hys G.....................1F **45**
Second Av. NG7: Nott........................5A **56**
Sedgebrook Cl. NG6: Bas..................4A **32**
Sedgemoor Rd. NG10: Long E..........2G **73**
Sedgewood Gro. NG11: Clftn............2C **66**
Sedgley Av. NG2: Nott........................4B **46**
Sedgley Rd. NG12: Toll.......................5F **69**
Sedgwick St. NG16: Lang M...............2F **15**
Sedley Av. NG16: Nuth........................1C **30**
Seeley Ho. NG1: Nott...........5G **5** (5H **45**)
....*(off Malin Hill)*
Seely Av. NG14: Calv............................3F **11**
Seely Rd. NG7: Lent..............................4D **44**
Seely Rd. NG7: Radf..............................4D **44**
Sefton Av. NG9: Stfrd............................3G **53**
Sefton Dr. NG3: Mapp P.........................6H **33**
Selbourne Gdns.
NG3: Nott...............................1H **5** (3A **46**)
Selby Cl. NG9: Toton...............................2G **63**
Selby La. NG12: Key.................................5G **79**
Selby Rd. NG2: West Br............................5B **58**
Selhurst Ct. NG7: Hys G............................2D **44**
Selhurst St. NG7: Hys G.............................2D **44**
Selkirk Way NG5: Sher...............................6F **33**
Sellars Av. NG11: Rudd...............................1G **77**
Sellers Wood Dr. NG6: Bulw........................5F **19**
Sellers Wood Dr. W.
NG6: Bulw...6E **19**
Seller's Wood Nature Reserve.....6E 19
Selsby Cl. NG8: Stre......................................5C **30**
Selside Ct. NG9: Chil.....................................1A **64**
Selston Dr. NG8: Woll....................................6A **44**
Selwyn Cl. NG6: Bulw.....................................2C **32**
Senator Cl. NG15: Huck..................................3A **8**
Senso Ct. NG4: Ged..6B **36**
Serif Cl. NG5: Sher...6F **33**
Serina Ct. NG2: West Br...................................4A **58**
Serina Ct. NG9: Bee..4H **55**

A-Z Nottingham 119

Serlby Ri. NG3: Nott....3B 46
Serlby Rd. NG16: Newth....2C 16
Seven Oaks Cres. NG9: Bram....2B 54
Seven Oaks Rd. DE7: Stant D....2C 52
Seventh Av. NG7: Nott....6A 56
Severals NG9: Stfrd....4H 53
Severn Ind. Est. NG6: Bulw....6H 19
Severn St. NG6: Bulw....6H 19
Seymour Cl. DE7: Ilk....2B 28
Seymour Ct. NG7: Radf....1A 4 (3E 45)
Seymour Pl. NG2: West Br....2D 58
Seymour Rd. NG15: Huck....6E 7
Seymour Rd. NG16: Eastw....4B 16
Seymour Rd. NG2: West Br....3D 58
Seymour St. NG3: Nott....4A 46
Shackleton Cl. NG8: Stre....5D 30
Shacklock Cl. NG5: Arn....3E 21
Shadwell Gro. NG12: Rad T....6E 49
Shady La. NG9: Atten....3D 64
Shaftesbury Av. NG10: Long E....3D 72
Shaftesbury Av. NG10: Sand....6C 52
Shaftesbury Av. NG14: Bur J....2G 37
Shaftesbury St. NG7: Bas....6E 33
Shakespeare Cl. NG4: Colw....4G 47
Shakespeare Ho.
  NG1: Nott....2E 5 (4G 45)
Shakespeare Rd. NG16: Aws....2E 29
Shakespeare St.
  NG1: Nott....2C 4 (4F 45)
Shakespeare Vs.
  NG1: Nott....2D 4 (4G 45)
Shakir Ct. NG7: Bas....6E 33
Shaldon Cl. NG3: Ged....2F 35
Shaldon Cl. NG5: Top V....4D 20
Shandwick Cl. NG5: Arn....4D 22
Shanklin Dr. NG9: Stfrd....4F 53
Shanwell Cl. NG8: Stre....5D 30
Shardale Gdns. NG6: Bas....3B 32
Sharnford Way NG9: Bram....5B 42
Sharp Cl. DE7: Kirk H....3G 39
Sharp Cl. NG10: Long E....1E 73
Sharpes Way NG6: Bestw V....6F 9
Sharphill Rd. NG12: Edwal....1D 68
Shaw Cres. NG15: Huck....1E 19
Shaw Gdns. NG11: Clftn....5A 66
Shaw Gdns. NG4: Ged....1B 48
Shaw Rd. NG9: Chil....3B 64
Shaw St. NG11: Rudd....6G 67
Shaw St. E. DE7: Ilk....3C 40
Shaw St. W. DE7: Ilk....3C 40
Shearing Cl. NG4: Ged....6A 36
Shearing Hill NG4: Ged....6A 36
Sheepfold La. NG11: Rudd....1G 77
Sheerness Cl. NG16: Gilt....6D 16
Sheets Stores Ind. Est.
  NG10: Long E....2F 73
Shelby Cl. NG7: Lent....5C 44
Sheldon Cl. NG10: Long E....2D 62
Sheldon Rd. DE75: Los....1A 14
SHELFORD....6H 37
Shelford Cl. NG12: Rad T....5G 49
Shelford Cl. NG9: Chil....1D 64
Shelford Cres. NG14: Bur J....2G 37
Shelford Dr. NG13: Bing....5D 50
Shelford Ri. NG3: Nott....3C 46
Shelford Rd. NG12: Rad T....6F 49
Shelford Rd. NG12: S'frd....6F 49
Shelford Rd. NG4: Ged....4E 35
Shellburne Cl. NG5: Top V....5C 20
Shelley Av. NG11: Clftn....2C 66
Shelley Cl. NG15: Huck....5D 6
Shelley Cl. NG16: Nuth....1B 30
Shelley Rd. NG5: Arn....6H 21
Shelt Hill NG14: Woodbo....1D 24
Shelton Av. NG15: Huck....1A 20
Shelton Gdns. NG11: Rudd....6E 67
Shelton St. NG3: Nott....1E 5 (3G 45)
Shenfield Gdns. NG5: Top V....4B 20

Shepard Cl. NG6: Bulw....1F 31
Shepherd Ct. NG15: Huck....1D 18
Shepherd Ho. NG5: Bestw....2E 33
Shepherds Cl. NG8: Bilb....2G 43
Shepherds Wood Dr. NG8: Aspl....2A 44
Shepton Cl. DE7: Ilk....4H 27
Shepton Cres. NG8: Aspl....5H 31
Sheraton Dr. NG8: Woll....6E 43
Sherborne Rd. NG2: West Br....6B 58
Sherborne Rd. NG8: Aspl....6G 31
Sherbrook Av. NG5: Arn....1H 33
Sherbrook Bus. Cen. NG5: Arn....1H 33
Sherbrooke Cl. NG14: Calv....3G 11
Sherbrooke Rd. NG5: Sher....6F 33
Sherbrooke Ter. NG5: Sher....6F 33
Sherbrook Rd. NG5: Arn....1G 33
Sherbrook Ter. NG5: Arn....1H 33
Sheridan Ct. NG1: Nott....1D 4 (3G 45)
  ....(off Mansfield Rd.)
Sheridan Ct. NG9: Stfrd....2H 53
Sheridan Way NG15: Huck....6G 7
Sheridan Way NG5: Sher....4E 33
Sheriffs Lea NG9: Toton....3G 63
Sheriffs Way NG2: Nott....6G 45
Sheringham Cl. NG5: Arn....1B 34
Sherman Dr. NG9: Chil....3C 64
Sherrington Cl. NG11: Clftn....4A 66
Sherwin Gro. NG7: Lent....6C 44
Sherwin Rd. NG7: Lent....6C 44
Sherwin Rd. NG9: Stfrd....2H 53
Sherwin Wlk. NG3: Nott....3G 45
SHERWOOD....4E 33
Sherwood Av. NG14: Calv....3F 11
Sherwood Av. NG5: Sher....4H 33
Sherwood Ct. NG14: Calv....3H 11
Sherwood Ct. NG9: Chil....2C 64
Sherwood Gro. NG13: Bing....5D 50
Sherwood Gro. NG14: Calv....3H 11
Sherwood Lodge Dr. NG5: Arn....1G 9
Sherwood Ri. NG16: Eastw....4B 16
Sherwood Ri. NG7: Sher....6E 33
SHERWOOD RISE....1F 45
Sherwood St. NG15: Huck....5A 8
Sherwood Va. NG5: Sher....4A 34
Sherwood Wlk. NG15: Lin....1G 7
Shilling Way NG10: Long E....6C 62
Shilo Way NG16: Aws....3D 28
SHIPLEY....1F 27
SHIPLEY COMMON....4G 27
Shipley Comn. La. DE7: Ilk....3G 27
Shipley Country Pk....3D 26
Shipley Country Pk. Vis. Cen....6C 14
Shipley Ct. DE7: Ilk....6H 27
Shipley Ct. DE75: Hea....5B 14
Shipley Ga. NG16: Eastw....6A 16
Shipley La. DE75: Hea....2D 26
Shipley La. DE75: Ship....2D 26
Shipley Pk. Gdns. DE75: Hea....6C 14
Shipley Ri. NG4: Car....2G 47
Shipley Rd. NG8: Brox....5F 31
Shipstones Bus. Cen.
Shipstone St. NG7: Bas....1D 44
Shipstone Street Stop (NET)....1D 44
Shipstones Yd. NG6: Bulw....5A 20
Shirebrook Cl. DE7: Ilk....1B 28
Shirebrooke Cl. NG6: Bas....4A 32
Shires Dr. NG3: Mapp....5A 34
Shirland Cl. DE7: Ilk....2B 28
Shirley Ct. NG9: Toton....3A 64
Shirley Cres. DE72: Brea....5A 62
Shirley Dr. NG5: Arn....6D 22
Shirley Rd. NG3: Mapp P....1G 45
Shirley St. NG10: Long E....3C 72
Shoreswood Cl. NG5: Bestw....5F 21
Short Hill NG1: Nott....5G 5 (5H 45)
Short Stairs NG1: Nott....5G 5 (5H 45)
  ....(off Short Hill)

Shortwood Av. NG15: Huck....6F 7
Shortwood Cl.
  NG1: Nott....5F 5 (5H 45)
Shorwell Rd. NG3: Nott....2E 47
Shotton Dr. NG5: Arn....3C 22
Showcase Cinema
  Nottingham....3C 56
Shrewsbury Rd. NG2: Nott....5C 46
Shrimpton Cl. NG11: Rudd....1H 77
Shrubberies, The NG5: Sher....4F 33
Sibson Wlk. NG5: Arn....3B 22
Sidbury Cl. NG3: Ged....1G 35
Sidings, The NG16: Kimb....1H 29
Sidings La. NG9: Bram....6A 42
Sidlaw Ri. NG5: Arn....3F 21
Sidmouth Cl. NG12: Key....3G 79
Sidney Rd. NG9: Bee....4E 55
Sidney St. NG10: Long E....1F 73
Sidney St. NG16: Kimb....1H 29
Silbury Cl. NG11: Clftn....6B 66
Sillitoe Cl. NG7: Lent....4A 44
Sillitoe Way NG7: Lent....5B 44
Silver Birch Cl. NG6: Cin....3H 31
SILVERDALE....1E 67
Silverdale NG9: Stfrd....6G 53
Silverdale Rd. NG7: Bas....5D 32
Silverdale Wlk. NG11: Clftn....2E 67
Silverdale Wlk. NG11: Wilf....2E 67
Silverhill Cl. NG8: Stre....5D 30
Silverhow Cl. NG2: West Br....6E 59
Silverwood Rd. NG9: Bee....6E 55
Simkin Av. NG3: Mapp....6C 34
Simkin Wlk. NG10: Long E....6D 62
Simone Gdns. NG11: Clftn....3C 66
Simons Ct. NG9: Bram....2D 54
Sinclair Cl. DE75: Hea....5B 14
Sir John Robinson Way
  NG5: Arn....6H 21
Siskin Cl. NG9: Bram....5C 54
Sisley Av. NG9: Stfrd....5G 53
Sixth Av. NG7: Nott....6A 56
Skeavingtons La. DE7: Ilk....2A 28
Skelwith Cl. NG2: West Br....6E 59
Sketchley Cl. NG6: Bulw....6G 19
Sketchley St. NG3: Nott....3B 46
Skiddaw Cl. NG2: West Br....6E 59
Skipton Cir. NG3: Nott....3C 46
Skipton Cl. DE7: Ilk....4H 27
Skylark Cl. NG13: Bing....6F 51
Skylark Dr. NG6: Bas....3B 32
Slack La. DE75: Hea....5C 14
Slack Rd. DE7: Mapp....4D 26
Slade Cl. DE7: Ilk....4C 40
Slade Rd. NG9: Chil....6B 54
Slaidburn Av. NG11: Wilf....6E 57
Slalom Run NG4: Car....6E 35
Slaters Way NG5: Bestw....2D 32
Sloan Dr. NG9: Bram....6B 42
Sloane Ct. NG2: West Br....6E 59
Sloethorne Gdns. NG5: Arn....5H 21
Smalley Farm Cl. DE75: Hea....5A 14
Smalley Mnr. Dr. DE7: Smal....5A 14
Small's Cft. NG14: Woodbo....1C 24
Smedley Av. DE7: Ilk....2C 40
Smedley Cl. NG8: Aspl....5H 31
Smedley's Av. NG10: Sand....6D 52
Smeeton St. DE75: Hea....4F 15
Smite Ct. NG7: Radf....2B 44
Smith Dr. NG16: Lang M....2E 15
Smithfield Av. NG9: Trow....5F 41
Smithurst Rd. NG16: Gilt....5C 16
Smithy Cl. NG11: Clftn....3B 66
Smithy Cl. NG14: Woodbo....2C 24
Smithy Cres. NG5: Arn....5H 21
Smithy Row NG1: Nott....4E 5 (5G 45)
Smithy Vw. NG14: Calv....4G 11
Smithy Vw. NG6: Bestw V....6F 9
Smythson Dr. NG8: Woll....5E 43
Snape Nook Ct. NG6: Bulw....6F 19

Snape Wood Rd. NG6: Bulw....6F 19
Snead Ct. NG5: Top V....4E 21
SNEINTON....5B 46
Sneinton Blvd. NG2: Nott....5B 46
Sneinton Dale NG2: Nott....5B 46
Sneinton Dale NG3: Nott....4C 46
Sneinton Hermitage
  NG2: Nott....6H 5 (6A 46)
Sneinton Hollows NG2: Nott....5B 46
Sneinton Mkt. Sq.
  NG1: Nott....3H 5 (4A 46)
  ....(off Bath St.)
Sneinton Rd. NG2: Nott....4H 5 (5A 46)
Snowdon Cl. NG5: Top V....4F 21
Snowdrop Cl. NG15: Huck....1A 20
Soarbank Cl. NG16: Kimb....6G 17
Sobers Gdns. NG5: Arn....1D 34
Softwood Cl. NG6: Bulw....6F 19
Soloman Pk. DE7: Ilk....5D 28
Soloman Rd. DE7: Ilk....5D 28
Solway Cl. NG9: Chil....6E 55
Somerby Ct. NG9: Bram....5B 42
Somerleyton Dr. DE7: Ilk....5C 40
Somersby Rd. NG3: Mapp....2C 34
Somersby Rd. NG5: Woodt....2B 34
Somerset Cl. NG10: Long E....5A 64
Somerton Av. NG11: Wilf....1E 67
Songthrush Av. NG6: Bas....3B 32
Sophie Rd. NG7: Hys G....3D 44
Sorrel Dr. NG13: Bing....5C 50
Soudan Dr. NG2: Nott....2F 57
Sough Wood Cl. DE75: Los....3A 14
Southampton St. NG3: Nott....3A 46
South Av. NG12: Rad T....5H 49
Southchurch Ct. NG11: Clftn....2D 66
Southchurch Dr. NG11: Clftn....5C 66
Southchurch Drive North
  Stop (NET)....2D 66
Southcliffe Rd. NG4: Car....2F 47
South Ct. NG9: Bee....1H 65
Southdale Dr. NG4: Car....2F 47
Southdale Rd. NG4: Car....2F 47
Sth. Devon Av. NG3: Mapp....5D 34
Southey St. NG7: Radf....3D 44
Southfield Gro. NG13: Bing....6E 51
Southfield Rd. NG8: Aspl....3B 44
Southfields NG10: Long E....6G 63
Southfields NG9: Chil....5B 54
Southglade Food Pk.
  NG5: Bestw....1C 32
Southglade Leisure Cen....6D 20
Southglade Rd. NG5: Bestw....1C 32
Southlea Rd. NG4: Car....2F 47
South Pde. NG1: Nott....4D 4 (5G 45)
Southport Ter. NG7: Hys G....2C 44
South Rd. NG7: Nott
  Newcastle Cir....5A 4 (6E 45)
South Rd. NG7: Nott
  West Rd....1B 56
South Rd. NG2: West Br....5A 58
South Rd. NG5: Sher....3F 33
South Rd. NG9: Bee....1G 65
Sth. Sherwood St.
  NG1: Nott....2D 4 (4G 45)
Southside NG5: Arn....5E 23
Sth. Snape Cl. NG6: Bulw....6F 19
South St. DE7: Ilk....1A 40
South St. NG10: Long E....6G 63
South St. NG15: Huck....4G 7
South St. NG16: Eastw....3A 16
South St. NG16: Gilt....5E 17
South Vw. Rd. NG4: Car....5F 35
Southwark St. NG6: Bas....4C 32
Southwell Hall NG8: Woll....5B 44
Southwell Rd. NG16: Gilt....6D 16
Southwell Rd.
  NG1: Nott....4H 5 (5H 45)
Southwell Rd. NG25: Oxton....1C 12
  ....(not continuous)

Southwell Rd. NG25: S'well 1C 12
.... (not continuous)
Southwold Dr. NG8: Aspl 4A 44
Sovereign Ct. NG9: Bee 6G 55
Sovereign Gro. NG10: Long E 6D 62
Sovereign Way DE75: Hea 4B 14
Sowbrook La. DE7: D Ab 5H 39
Sowbrook La. DE7: Stant D 5H 39
Spalding Rd. NG3: Nott 4A 46
Spaniel Row NG1: Nott 5D 4 (5G 45)
Sparrow Cl. DE7: Ilk 4C 40
Spean Ct. NG8: Woll 4G 43
Spean Dr. NG8: Aspl 2H 43
Speedway Cl. NG10: Long E....... 5H 63
Speedwell Cl. NG13: Bing 5C 50
Speedwell La. NG16: Kimb 1G 29
Spencer Av. NG10: Sand 4D 52
Spencer Av. NG3: Mapp.............2E 35
Spencer Cl. NG11: Rudd 6F 67
Spencer Ct. NG7: Hys G 1F 45
Spencer Cres. NG9: Stfrd 3H 53
Spencer Rd. NG16: Nuth 1C 30
Spey Cl. NG15: Huck...................2D 18
Spicer Cl. NG9: Chil 3C 64
Spindle Gdns. NG6: Bulw 6G 19
Spindle La. NG14: Calv................6E 11
Spindle La. NG14: Woodbo 6E 11
Spindle Vw. NG14: Calv............. 5H 11
Spinney, The NG16: Nuth
   Harcourt Cres. 4F 31
Spinney, The NG16: Nuth
   Keats Cl. 1B 30
Spinney, The DE7: Ilk.................3A 40
Spinney, The DE7: Stant D 3B 52
Spinney, The NG14: Bulc 2H 37
Spinney, The NG5: Woodt 3A 34
Spinney, The NG6: Bestw V 6C 8
Spinney Cl. NG12: Cotg 3F 71
Spinney Cl. NG2: West Br 1D 68
Spinney Cres. NG9: Toton 2H 63
Spinney Dr. NG10: Long E 3E 63
Spinney Hill NG2: West Br 3A 68
Spinney Ri. NG9: Toton...............2G 63
Spinney Rd. DE7: Ilk....................3A 40
Spinney Rd. NG10: Long E 3E 63
Spinney Rd. NG12: Key 4F 79
Spinney Rd. NG13: Bing 5D 50
Spinney Way NG11: Wilf 1E 67
Spinningdale NG5: Arn 4D 22
Spinning Dr. NG5: Sher................2G 33
SPIRE NOTTINGHAM
HOSPITAL 6H 59
Spire Vw. NG10: Long E.............. 3D 72
Spitfire Way NG15: Huck 2D 18
Spondon St. NG5: Sher...............5G 33
Spray Cl. NG4: Colw 4G 47
Spridgeon Cl. NG10: Long E 3D 62
Spring, The NG10: Long E 2F 73
Spring Cl. NG16: Want.................6A 18
Spring Cl. NG2: West Br 3D 58
Spring Ct. NG9: Stfrd 4G 53
Springdale Gdns. NG9: Trow.......1F 53
Springfield Av. NG10: Long E....... 5H 63
Springfield Av. NG10: Sand 2C 62
Springfield Av. NG16: Eastw 3C 16
Springfield Cl. NG9: Stfrd............2H 53
Springfield Dr. NG6: Bulw 1F 31
Springfield Gdns. DE7: Ilk............5B 28
Springfield Mill NG10: Sand......... 5D 52
SPRINGFIELD PARK 2D 62
Springfield Pastures
   NG3: Nott 1H 45
Springfield Retail Pk.
   Nottingham 5A 20
Springfield Rd. NG15: Huck 5D 6
Springfield Rd. NG5: Redh 4A 22
Springfields NG2: West Br 5H 57
Springfield St. NG7: Bas 6D 32
Spring Gdns. NG8: Bilb...............2C 42

Spring Garden Ter. DE7: Ilk 5B 28
Spring Grn. NG11: Clftn..............6C 66
Springhead Ct. NG6: Bulw........... 1G 31
Spring Hill NG16: Kimb................2H 29
Springhill Cl. NG6: Bulw 4H 19
   NG16: Nuth 1D 30
.... (off Watnall Rd.)
Spring La. DE75: Hea 4C 14
Spring La. NG3: Mapp 1E 35
Spring La. NG4: Lamb 2A 36
Spring Mdw. NG12: Cotg 2G 71
Spring Moor NG2: Colw...............4F 47
Spring Rd. NG6: Bulw..................6A 20
Spring St. NG15: Huck................... 3G 7
Spring Ter. NG16: Nuth 2D 30
Spring Ter. Gdns. NG16: Nuth......1D 30
Springwater Golf Course 5C 12
Springwood Cl. NG14: Calv..........4A 12
Springwood Gdns. NG5: Woodt....4B 34
Spruce Gdns. NG6: Bulw 6G 19
Spruce Gro. NG15: Huck.............. 6H 7
Sprydon Wlk. NG11: Clftn........... 6D 66
Square, The NG11: Goth 6H 75
Square, The NG12: Key................5G 79
Square, The NG6: Bestw V 1C 20
Square, The NG8: Woll 5E 43
Square, The NG9: Bee 5F 55
Squires Av. NG6: Bulw 4H 19
Squires Ct. NG6: Bestw V 5F 9
Squires Way NG2: West Br 5H 57
Stacey Av. NG5: Top V 6D 20
Stadford Av. NG6: Bulw 1H 31
Stafford Ct. NG6: Bulw 2F 31
Staffords Ct. NG4: Neth...............2A 48
Stafford St. NG10: Long E 5H 63
Stagsden Cres. NG8: Bilb 4C 42
Staindale Ct. NG8: Aspl 6A 32
Staindale Dr. NG8: Aspl 6A 32
Stainmore Gro. NG13: Bing 5C 50
Stainsborough Rd. NG15: Huck....5C 6
Stainsby Av. DE75: Hea...............4C 14
Stakeford Cl. NG5: Arn................3B 22
Stamford Cl. NG10: Long E 3G 73
Stamford Ct. DE75: Hea................3C 14
.... (off Nelson St.)
Stamford Ct. NG5: Bestw 5F 21
Stamford Rd. NG2: West Br.........6B 58
Stamford St. DE7: Ilk..................6A 28
Stamford St. DE75: Hea 3C 14
Stamford St. NG16: Aws..............3E 29
Stamford St. NG16: Newth 4E 17
Stancliffe Av. NG6: Bulw 6A 20
Standard Ct. NG1: Nott 5C 4 (5F 45)
Standard Hill NG1: Nott....5C 4 (5F 45)
STANDARD HILL 5C 4 (5F 45)
Standhill Av. NG4: Car.................1D 46
Standhill Rd. NG4: Car 6C 34
Stanesby Ri. NG11: Clftn............ 4C 66
Stanford Gdns. NG12: Rad T 1H 67
Stanford St. NG1: Nott.....5D 4 (5G 45)
Stanhome Ct. NG2: West Br 1H 67
Stanhome Dr. NG2: West Br 1H 67
Stanhome Sq. NG2: West Br 1H 67
Stanhope Av. NG5: Sher 6F 33
Stanhope Cl. NG16: Newth 3D 16
Stanhope Cres. NG14: Stoke B 2F 49
Stanhope Cres. NG5: Arn 5A 22
Stanhope Rd. NG4: Ged 2F 35
Stanhope Rd. NG5: Arn 5A 22
Stanhope St. DE7: Ilk..................3C 40
Stanhope St. DE7: Stant D 3B 52
Stanhope St. NG1: Nott 4G 5 (5H 45)
Stanhope St. NG10: Long E 5F 63
Stanhope Way NG13: Bing 5E 51
Stanier Dr. NG12: Edwal 2C 68
Staniland Cl. NG9: Chil 3C 64
STANLEY 3A 38
Stanley Av. NG7: Hys G...............1E 45

Stanley Cl. DE7: Ilk......................2A 40
STANLEY COMMON 6A 26
Stanley Ct. NG16: Eastw..............4B 16
Stanley Dr. NG9: Bram................3A 54
Stanley M. NG16: Kimb................6F 17
Stanley Pl. NG1: Nott 3C 4 (4F 45)
Stanley Rd. NG2: West Br............5B 58
Stanley Rd. NG3: Mapp 5C 34
Stanley Rd. NG7: Hys G 1E 45
.... (not continuous)
Stanley St. DE7: Ilk.....................2B 40
Stanley St. NG10: Long E 6G 63
Stanmore Cl. NG16: Nuth 4E 31
Stanmore Gdns. NG5: Arn 1A 34
.... (not continuous)
Stannier Way NG16: Want............6A 18
Stansfield St. NG7: Lent 4C 44
Stanstead Av. NG12: Toll.............5F 69
Stanstead Av. NG5: Top V 5B 20
Stanthorne Cl. NG11: Wilf 1E 67
STANTON-BY-DALE 3B 52
Stanton Ga. DE7: Stant D 2E 53
STANTON GATE 2E 53
Stanton La. NG12: Stant W..........5B 80
Stanton M. NG12: Stant W...........5C 80
STANTON-ON-THE-WOLDS..........6B 80
Stanton-on-the-Wolds
   Golf Course 5B 80
Stanton Rd. DE7: Ilk....................3B 40
Stanton Rd. NG10: Sand 4B 52
Stanway Cl. NG3: Nott.................3E 47
Stanwick Cl. NG8: Bilb 1E 43
STAPLEFORD 4F 53
Stapleford By-Pass
   NG10: Sand 1C 62
Stapleford La. NG9: Toton 1H 63
Stapleford Rd. NG9: Trow 5E 41
Staplehurst Dr. NG5: Sher 3E 33
Staples St. NG3: Mapp 5A 34
Stapleton Rd. DE7: Ilk 3A 28
Starch La. NG10: Sand 4D 52
Starnhill Way NG13: Bing.............6E 51
Starthe Bank DE75: Hea 3D 14
Starthe Vw. DE75: Hea 4E 15
Starth Wood Rd. NG15: Huck 1D 18
Stathern Wlk. NG5: Bestw............6F 21
Station Av. NG4: Ged 6A 36
Station Cl. DE7: Ilk......................6A 28
.... (off Bath Rd.)
Station Rd. DE7: Ilk.....................6B 28
Station Rd. DE7: Stly...................1A 38
Station Rd. DE7: West H...............1A 38
Station Rd. NG10: Long E 5H 63
Station Rd. NG10: Sand 6E 53
Station Rd. NG12: Key..................1G 79
Station Rd. NG12: Plum 1G 79
Station Rd. NG14: Bur J 4F 37
Station Rd. NG15: Huck................. 4H 7
Station Rd. NG16: Aws.................2E 29
Station Rd. NG16: Kimb 1H 29
Station Rd. NG16: Lang M 3E 15
Station Rd. NG4: Car 2G 47
Station Rd. NG6: Bulw 1A 32
Station Rd. NG9: Bee 5F 55
.... (not continuous)
Station St. DE7: Ilk 5C 28
Station St. NG10: Long E 6G 63
Station St. NG13: Bing 4F 51
Station St. NG2: Nott 6E 5 (6G 45)
Station Ter. NG12: Rad T 6F 49
Station Ter. NG15: Huck 4H 7
Station Vs. NG9: Bee 6G 55
Staunton Dr. NG5: Sher 3G 33
Stavely Way NG2: Gam.................6H 57
Staverton Rd. NG8: Bilb...............3D 42
Steadfold Cl. NG6: Bulw 1H 31
Steads Cl. NG4: Car....................2H 47
Steedman Av. NG3: Mapp.............3C 34
Steeles Way NG4: Lamb 6B 24

Steinbeck Rd. NG4: Car...............2E 47
Stella Av. NG12: Toll....................5F 69
Stella Gro. NG12: Toll..................5F 69
Stepney Ct. NG8: Brox.................6E 31
Sterndale Rd. NG10: Long E......... 1D 72
Steven Cl. NG9: Toton..................1H 63
Stevens Rd. NG5: Bestw ...1E 33
Steven's La. DE72: Brea 5A 62
Stevenson Gdns. NG11: Rudd 1H 77
Stevens Rd. NG10: Sand 6C 52
Stewarton Cl. NG5: Arn 4D 22
Stiles Rd. NG5: Arn 1E 35
Stinsford Cl. NG5: Bestw 5G 21
Stirling Av. NG9: Chil..................3B 64
Stirling Gro. NG11: Clftn..............5D 66
Stirling Gro. NG15: Kimb 6G 17
Stockdale Cl. NG5: Arn 3E 21
Stockgill Cl. NG2: West Br............5E 59
Stockhill Cir. NG6: Bas 4A 32
Stockhill La. NG6: Bas 4A 32
Stocks Rd. NG16: Kimb 6A 18
Stockton St. NG6: Bulw................6H 19
Stock Well NG6: Bulw 1H 31
Stoddard Dr. DE75: Hea................3D 14
STOKE BARDOLPH 1F 49
Stoke Ferry La. NG12: S'frd 6F 37
Stoke La. NG14: Stoke B 1D 48
.... (not continuous)
Stoke La. NG4: Ged 6B 36
Stokesay Wlk. NG2: West Br 6B 58
Stolle Cl. NG5: Arn 6E 23
Stoneacre NG5: Bestw..................5F 21
Stone Av. DE75: Hea....................4E 15
Stonebridge City Farm......2H 5 (4A 46)
Stonebridge Ct.
   NG3: Nott 2H 5 (4A 46)
Stonebridge Rd.
   NG3: Nott 2H 5 (4A 46)
Stonebridge Way NG14: Calv.......3E 11
Stonehaven Cl. NG5: Arn 4D 22
Stoneleigh Cl. NG9: Chil 6C 54
Stoneleigh St. NG7: Radf...2A 4 (4E 45)
Stone Mdws. NG10: Long E 2G 73
Stonepit Cl. NG3: Nott 6B 34
Stonesby Va. NG2: West Br 2F 67
Stones Cl. NG16: Eastw 3C 16
Stonesdale Cl. NG5: Sher 2G 33
Stoneycroft Rd. NG6: Bulw...........2C 32
Stoney Houghton Gdns.
   NG6: Bulw 5F 19
Stoney La. NG9: Trow...................3D 40
Stoney St. NG1: Nott 4F 5 (5H 45)
Stoney St. NG9: Bee 4F 55
Stony Clouds Local Nature
   Reserve 3D 52
Stoppard Cl. DE7: Ilk...................5H 27
Storey Av. NG4: Ged 5G 35
Stornoway Cl. NG9: Bee...............6G 55
Storth Av. NG15: Huck.................. 5G 7
Story Gdns. NG15: Huck...............6A 8
Stotfield Rd. NG8: Bilb 4B 42
Stourdale Cl. NG10: Long E..........1C 72
Stowe Av. NG2: West Br 6H 57
STRAGGLETHORPE 4G 61
Stragglethorpe La.
   NG12: Rad T 2C 60
Stragglethorpe Park & Ride 4D 60
Strand, The NG9: Atten 4D 64
Stratford Cl. NG4: Colw 4G 47
Stratford Rd. NG2: West Br 4B 58
Stratford St. DE7: Ilk...................3B 28
Strathglen Cl. NG16: Kimb 6G 17
Strathmore Cl. NG15: Huck..........6E 7
Strathmore Rd. NG5: Arn 4D 22
STRELLEY 1D 42
Strelley Cl. NG15: Huck................1F 7
Strelley La. NG8: Stre 1B 42
Strelley Rd. NG8: Bilb 1C 42
Strelley Rd. NG8: Stre..................1C 42

Strelley St. – Three Tuns Rd.

Strelley St. NG6: Bulw 6H **19**
Stretton, The NG7: Lent 1C **56**
(off Leen Ct.)
Stretton St. NG3: Nott 1F **5** (3H **45**)
Striding Edge Cl. NG10: Long E 3D **62**
Stripes Vw. NG14: Calv 5H **11**
Strome Cl. NG2: Nott 1G **57**
Strome Ct. NG2: Nott 1G **57**
Stuart Cl. NG5: Arn 5D **22**
Studio Theatre, The 5D 58
Studland Way NG2: West Br 6G **57**
Sturgeon Av. NG11: Clftn 1D **66**
Sturmer Way NG8: Aspl 2H **43**
Sturton St. NG7: Hys G 1E **45**
Styring St. NG9: Bee 5F **55**
Sudbury Av. DE7: Ilk 2C **40**
Sudbury Av. NG10: Sand 4C **52**
Sudbury Ct. NG10: Long E 3B **72**
Sudbury M. NG16: Eastw 4A **16**
Suez St. NG7: Bas 6D **32**
Suffolk Av. NG15: Huck 6C **6**
Suffolk Av. NG9: Bee 1A **66**
Sullivan Cl. NG3: Nott 2B **46**
Sullivan St. NG7: Radf 4C **44**
Sumburgh Rd. NG11: Clftn 4E **67**
Summer Cres. NG9: Bee 4H **55**
Summer Dr. NG2: West Br 6H **57**
Summerfields Way DE7: Ilk 3G **27**
Summerfields Way Sth. DE7: Ilk 5H **27**
Summer Leys Rd. NG2: Nott 6H **45**
Summer Way NG12: Rad T 5E **49**
Summerwood La. NG11: Clftn 5B **66**
Summerwood Lane Stop (NET) 5B 66
Sunbourne Ct. NG7: Radf 3E **45**
Sunbury Gdns. NG5: Arn 4C **22**
Sunderland Gro. NG8: Stre 5D **30**
Sundown Dr. NG12: Cotg 6G **61**
Sundridge Pk. Cl. NG2: West Br 6G **57**
Sunflower Dr. NG12: Edwal 3C **68**
Sunlea Cres. NG9: Stfrd 6H **53**
Sunnindale Dr. NG12: Toll 4F **69**
Sunningdale Av. DE75: Hea 5D **14**
Sunningdale Dr. DE7: Kirk H 4F **39**
Sunningdale Dr. NG14: Woodbo 6C **12**
Sunningdale Rd. NG6: Bulw 1B **32**
Sunninghill Cl. DE7: West H 1B **38**
Sunninghill Dr. NG11: Clftn 2C **66**
Sunninghill Ri. NG5: Arn 4C **22**
Sunnydale Rd. NG3: Nott 3D **46**
Sunny Row NG8: Woll 4E **43**
Sunnyside Rd. NG9: Chil 5C **54**
Sunridge Ct. NG3: Mapp P 1G **45**
Sunrise Av. NG5: Bestw 2D **32**
Sunrise Av. NG6: Bestw V 6G **9**
Surbiton Ct. DE7: West H 1B **38**
Surbiton Ct. NG3: Mapp 6A **34**
Surbiton Sq. NG8: Cin 4H **31**
Surfleet Cl. NG8: Woll 6C **42**
Surgey's La. NG5: Arn 4B **22**
Surrey Ct. NG3: Mapp 6A **34**
Susan Cl. NG15: Huck 2H **7**
Susan Dr. NG6: Bulw 3B **32**
Sussex Cl. NG16: Gilt 5C **16**
Sussex St. NG1: Nott 5E **5** (5G **45**)
Sussex Way NG10: Sand 6D **52**
Sutherland Dr. NG2: West Br 1C **68**
Sutherland Rd. NG3: Nott 2D **46**
Sutton Ct. NG16: Eastw 3B **16**
Sutton Gdns. NG11: Rudd 1G **77**
Sutton Gro. NG9: Chil 5D **54**
Sutton Passeys Cres. NG8: Woll 5H **43**
Sutton Rd. NG5: Arn 3B **22**
Swain's Av. NG3: Nott 3C **46**
Swale Cl. NG6: Bulw 6B **20**
Swaledale Cl. NG8: Aspl 6B **32**
Swale Gro. NG13: Bing 6D **50**
Swallow Cl. NG6: Bas 3B **32**
Swallow Dr. NG13: Bing 6F **51**
Swallow Gdns. NG4: Car 6D **34**
Swan Mdw. NG4: Colw 5G **47**
Swansdowne Dr. NG11: Clftn 3D **66**
Swanwick Rd. DE7: Ilk 2B **28**
Sweeney Ct. NG5: Top V 5E **21**
Sweet Leys Rd. NG2: Nott 2G **57**
Swenson Av. NG7: Lent 6C **44**
Swift Ct. NG16: Eastw 3B **16**
Swigert Cl. NG6: Bulw 2F **31**
Swildon Wlk. NG5: Top V 5D **20**
Swinburne St. NG3: Nott 3B **46**
Swinburne Way NG5: Arn 6G **21**
Swindale Cl. NG2: Gam 4D **58**
Swindell Cl. NG3: Mapp 2D **34**
Swindon Cl. NG16: Gilt 6E **17**
Swiney Way NG9: Chil 3H **63**
Swiney Way NG9: Toton 3H **63**
Swingate NG16: Kimb 2A **30**
SWINGATE 2A 30
Swinley Ct. NG13: Bing 5C **50**
Swinscoe Gdns. NG5: Top V 5D **20**
Swinstead Cl. NG8: Bilb 3F **43**
Swithland Dr. NG2: West Br 1A **68**
Sycamore Cl. DE7: Mapp 4D **26**
Sycamore Cl. NG11: Rudd 6H **67**
Sycamore Cl. NG12: Rad T 1F **61**
Sycamore Cl. NG13: Bing 5G **51**
Sycamore Cl. NG15: Huck 6E **7**
Sycamore Ct. NG9: Bee 4G **55**
Sycamore Cres. NG10: Sand 4C **52**
Sycamore Dr. DE7: Ilk 2D **40**
Sycamore Gdns. DE75: Hea 4B **14**
Sycamore Pl. NG3: Mapp P 1G **45**
Sycamore Ri. NG6: Cin 3H **31**
Sycamore Rd. NG10: Long E 2E **73**
Sycamore Rd. NG16: Aws 2D **28**
Sycamores, The NG16: Eastw 4A **16**
Syderstone Wlk. NG5: Arn 2B **34**
Sydney Gro. NG12: Rad T 6E **49**
Sydney Rd. NG8: Woll 4H **43**
Syke Rd. NG5: Top V 5D **20**
Synge Cl. NG11: Clftn 5A **66**
Syon Pk. Cl. NG2: West Br 6G **57**

T

Taft Av. NG10: Sand 5D **52**
Talbot Ct. NG12: Rad T 6E **49**
Talbot Dr. NG9: Stfrd 1F **53**
Talbot St. NG1: Nott 3B **4** (4F **45**)
Tamarix Cl. NG4: Ged 5A **36**
Tambling Cl. NG5: Arn 1D **34**
Tame Cl. NG11: Clftn 1C **66**
Tamworth Gro. NG11: Clftn 3D **66**
Tamworth Rd. NG10: Long E 3D **72**
(not continuous)
Tangmere Cres. NG8: Stre 6E **31**
Tanners Wlk. NG1: Nott 5E **5** (5G **45**)
Tannery Rd. NG16: Gilt 6E **17**
Tannin Cres. NG6: Bulw 2A **32**
Tansy Way NG13: Bing 6C **50**
Tantum Av. DE75: Los 1A **14**
Tanwood Rd. NG9: Toton 4B **64**
Tarbert Cl. NG2: Nott 1F **57**
Target St. NG7: Radf 4C **44**
Tarn Cl. NG16: Lang M 1F **15**
Tarrat St. DE7: Ilk 5A **28**
Tasmania Cl. NG2: Nott 2G **57**
Tatham's La. DE7: Ilk 5A **28**
Tattershall Dr. NG7: Nott 4A **4** (5E **45**)
Tattershall Dr. NG9: Bee 4H **55**
Taunton Rd. NG2: West Br 5B **58**
Taupo Dr. NG15: Huck 6C **6**
Tavern Av. NG8: Aspl 5A **32**
Tavistock Av. NG3: Mapp P 6G **33**
Tavistock Cl. NG15: Huck 6D **6**
Tavistock Ct. NG5: Sher 6G **33**
Tavistock Dr. NG3: Mapp P 6G **33**
Tavistock Rd. NG2: West Br 5B **58**
Taylor Cl. NG2: Nott 5C **46**
Taylor Cres. NG9: Stfrd 3H **53**
Taylor La. DE75: Los 2B **14**
Taylor La. Ind. Est. DE75: Los 2B **14**
Taylor Pl. NG3: Nott 1B **46**
Taylors Cft. NG14: Woodbo 1B **24**
Taylor St. DE7: Ilk 6B **28**
Teak Cl. NG3: Nott 2H **45**
Tealby Cl. NG6: Bulw 6F **19**
Teal Cl. NG4: Neth 2B **48**
Teal Wharf NG7: Lent 1E **57**
Teasels, The NG13: Bing 6D **50**
Technology Dr. NG9: Bee 6G **55**
Teesbrook Dr. NG8: Woll 5B **42**
Tees Ct. NG13: Bing 6D **50**
Teesdale Ct. NG9: Chil 1A **64**
Teesdale Rd. NG10: Long E 1C **72**
Teesdale Rd. NG5: Sher 5E **33**
Telford Dr. NG16: Newth 2D **16**
Teme Ct. NG2: West Br 6B **58**
Templar Lodge NG9: Bee 5H **55**
Templar Rd. NG9: Bee 5H **55**
Templars Ct. NG7: Radf 3B **44**
(off New Rd.)
Temple Cres. NG16: Nuth 3D **30**
Temple Dr. NG16: Nuth 3E **31**
Templeman Cl. NG11: Rudd 5F **67**
Templeoak Dr. NG8: Woll 6C **42**
Tenants Hall Cl. NG9: Lent A 2G **55**
Tenbury Cres. NG8: Aspl 6H **31**
Tene Cl. NG5: Arn 3B **22**
Tennis Ct. Ind. Est. NG2: Nott 6C **46**
Tennis Dr. NG7: Nott 4A **4** (5E **45**)
Tennis M. NG7: Nott 4A **4** (5E **45**)
Tennis Vw. NG7: Nott 4A **4** (5E **45**)
Tennyson Av. NG4: Ged 6H **35**
Tennyson Ct. NG15: Huck 5D **6**
Tennyson Ct. NG5: Sher 4F **33**
Tennyson Dr. NG9: Atten 3D **64**
Tennyson Grange NG4: Ged 6A **36**
Tennyson Rd. NG5: Woodt 3A **34**
Tennyson Sq. NG16: Aws 3E **29**
Tennyson St. DE7: Ilk 4A **28**
Tennyson St. NG7: Radf 1A **4** (3E **45**)
(not continuous)
Tenpin Nottingham 2C 56
Tenter Cl. NG10: Long E 2F **73**
Tenter Cl. NG5: Top V 5D **20**
Terrace St. NG7: Hys G 2D **44**
Terrian Cres. NG2: West Br 4B **58**
Terton Rd. NG5: Top V 5D **20**
Tetney Wlk. NG8: Bilb 2G **43**
Tettenbury Rd. NG5: Sher 4D **32**
Teversal Av. NG7: Lent 5D **44**
Tevery Cl. NG9: Stfrd 3G **53**
Teviot Rd. NG5: Bestw 2D **32**
Tewkesbury Cl. NG2: West Br 5C **58**
Tewkesbury Dr. NG16: Kimb 6G **17**
Tewkesbury Dr. NG6: Bas 3C **32**
Tewkesbury Rd. NG10: Long E 3G **73**
Thackeray's La. NG5: Woodt 2H **33**
Thackeray St. NG7: Radf 4D **44**
Thales Dr. NG5: Arn 6E **23**
Thames St. NG6: Bulw 6H **19**
Thane Rd. NG7: Lent 5B **56**
Thane Rd. NG7: Nott 5B **56**
Thatcham Cl. NG8: Aspl 2B **44**
Thatchmarsh Cl. DE7: Ilk 1B **28**
Thaxted Cl. NG8: Bilb 3D **42**
Theatre Royal Nottingham 3D 4 (4G 45)
Theatre Sq. NG1: Nott 3D **4** (4G **45**)
(off Wollaton St.)
Thelda Av. NG12: Key 4G **79**
Thetford Cl. NG5: Arn 1C **34**
Third Av. DE7: Ilk 2B **40**
Third Av. NG4: Car 1D **46**
(not continuous)
Third Av. NG4: Ged 6H **35**
Third Av. NG6: Bulw 6H **19**
Third Av. NG7: Hys G 1F **45**
Third Av. NG7: Nott 5A **56**
Thirlmere NG2: West Br 6E **59**
Thirlmere Cl. NG10: Long E 3D **62**
Thirlmere Cl. NG3: Nott 2B **46**
Thirlmere Rd. NG10: Long E 3D **62**
Thirston Cl. NG6: Bulw 6F **19**
Thistle Cl. NG16: Newth 5D **16**
Thistledown Rd. NG11: Clftn 6C **66**
Thistlegreen Cl. DE75: Hea 4F **15**
Thistle Rd. DE7: Ilk 5C **40**
Thomas Av. NG12: Rad T 5H **49**
Thomas Cl. NG3: Nott 1G **5** (3H **45**)
Thomas Forman Ct. NG5: Sher 6F **33**
Thompson Cl. NG9: Chil 2C **64**
Thompson Ct. NG9: Chil 4B **64**
Thompson Gdns. NG5: Top V 4E **21**
Thompson St. NG16: Lang M 2F **15**
Thoresby Av. NG2: Nott 6B **46**
Thoresby Av. NG4: Ged 5F **35**
Thoresby Ct. NG12: Rad T 5G **49**
Thoresby Ct. NG3: Mapp P 1H **45**
Thoresby Dale NG15: Huck 4H **7**
Thoresby Rd. NG10: Long E 1D **72**
Thoresby Rd. NG13: Bing 5C **50**
Thoresby Rd. NG9: Bram 2C **54**
Thoresby St. NG1: Nott 5H **5** (5A **46**)
Thor Gdns. NG5: Top V 4D **20**
Thornbury Way NG5: Top V 6D **20**
Thorncliffe Ho. NG5: Top V 5C **20**
Thorncliffe Ri. NG3: Mapp P 1G **45**
Thorncliffe Rd. NG3: Mapp P 1G **45**
Thorndale Rd. NG14: Calv 4H **11**
Thorndale Rd. NG6: Bas 5A **32**
Thorn Dr. NG16: Newth 5D **16**
Thorndyke Cl. NG9: Bee 1H **65**
Thorner Cl. NG6: Bulw 2C **32**
Thorney Hill NG3: Nott 2B **46**
THORNEYWOOD 1C 46
Thorneywood Mt. NG3: Nott 2B **46**
Thorneywood Ri. NG3: Nott 2B **46**
Thorneywood Rd. NG10: Long E 5H **63**
Thornfield Ind. Est. NG3: Nott 4B **46**
Thornfield Sq. NG10: Long E 5H **63**
Thorn Gro. NG15: Huck 1H **19**
Thornhill Cl. NG9: Bram 1B **54**
Thornley St. NG7: Hys G 2C **44**
Thornthwaite Cl. NG2: West Br 5E **59**
Thornton Av. NG5: Redh 4H **21**
Thornton Cl. NG8: Woll 5E **43**
Thorntons Cl. NG12: Cotg 2G **71**
Thornton's Holt Camping Pk. NG12: Rad T 3D **60**
Thorntree Cl. DE72: Brea 4B **62**
Thorn Tree Gdns. NG16: Eastw 1B **16**
Thorold Cl. NG11: Clftn 3C **66**
Thoroton Rd. NG2: West Br 2B **58**
Thoroton St. NG7: Radf 4E **45**
Thorpe Cl. NG5: Top V 5D **20**
Thorpe Cl. NG9: Stfrd 4E **53**
Thorpe Cres. NG3: Mapp 5D **34**
Thorpe Hill Dr. DE75: Hea 6C **14**
Thorpe Leys NG10: Long E 2F **73**
Thorpe Rd. NG16: Eastw 1B **16**
Thorpe's Rd. DE75: Hea 4B **14**
Thorpes Rd. Ind. Est. DE75: Hea 5B **14**
Thorpe St. DE7: Ilk 4A **28**
Thrapston Av. NG5: Arn 3B **22**
Thraves Yd. NG12: Rad T 6E **49**
Threeleys Cl. DE7: Ilk 4B **40**
Three Tuns Rd. NG16: Eastw 3C **16**

122 A-Z Nottingham

Threlkeld Cl. NG2: West Br 5E 59
THRUMPTON 4B 74
Thrumpton Av. NG10: Long E 6H 63
Thrumpton Dr. NG2: Nott...........2F 57
Thrumpton La. NG11: Bart F 3F 75
Thurgarton Av. NG2: Nott 5B 46
Thurgarton St. NG2: Nott...........5B 46
Thurland St. NG1: Nott 4E 5 (5G 45)
Thurlbeck NG12: Cotg 4G 71
Thurlby La. NG12: Stant W 6B 80
Thurlestone Dr. NG3: Mapp.......1E 35
Thurloe Ct. NG2: West Br 2G 67
Thurman Dr. NG12: Cotg 2F 71
Thurman St. DE7: Ilk 3C 40
Thurman St. NG7: Hys G 3D 44
Thursby Rd. NG11: Clftn...........2C 66
Thymus Wlk. NG11: Clftn 4A 66
Thyra Ct. NG3: Nott....................6A 34
Thyra Gro. NG3: Nott 6H 33
Thyra Gro. NG9: Bee 5G 55
Tiberius Gdns. NG15: Huck 3A 8
Tidworth Cl. NG8: Bilb 3G 43
Tilberthwaite Cl. NG2: Gam........5E 59
Tilbury Ri. NG8: Cin 4G 31
Tilford Gdns. NG9: Stfrd 5G 53
Tilstock Ct. NG16: Want 5A 18
Tilton Gro. DE7: Kirk H............. 4G 39
Tim La. NG14: Bur J 3F 37
Tindall Cl. NG9: Chil................3B 64
Tinker Cft. DE7: Ilk 2A 40
Tinkers Way NG7: Lent...............6F 45
Tinsley Rd. NG16: Eastw 4A 16
Tintagel Arch. NG11: Clftn.........4C 66
Tintern Dr. NG8: Bas 5B 32
Tippett Ct. NG3: Nott 3B 46
Tip Tree Cl. NG16: Kimb 6H 17
Tiree Cl. NG9: Trow....................1F 53
Tishbite St. NG6: Bulw.............. 6H 19
Tissington Cl. NG7: Hys G 1E 45
Tissington Cl. NG3: Chil............4C 64
Tissington Rd. NG7: Hys G 1E 45
Titchfield Cl. NG15: Huck 5G 7
Titchfield St. NG15: Huck 4G 7
Titchfield Ter. NG15: Huck 4H 7
Tithby Dr. NG5: Sher 3H 33
Tithby Rd. NG13: Bing 6E 51
.... (not continuous)
Tithby Rd. NG13: Lang...............6E 51
.... (not continuous)
Tithby Rd. NG13: Tith 6E 51
.... (not continuous)
Tithe Gdns. NG5: Top V 4E 21
Tithe La. NG14: Calv 4H 11
Tiverton Cl. NG15: Huck 6D 6
Tiverton Cl. NG8: Aspl 5H 31
Toad Hole Cl. DE7: Kirk H 3G 39
Toad La. NG14: Epp 6G 13
Tobias Cl. NG5: Top V 5D 20
Todd Cl. NG11: Clftn..................5A 66
Todd Ct. NG11: Clftn..................5A 66
Toft Cl. NG12: Cotg 3E 71
Toft Rd. NG9: Chil 4E 64
Token Ho. Yd. NG1: Nott 4E 5 (5G 45)
.... (off Fletcher Ga.)
TOLLERTON 4F 69
Tollerton Grn. NG6: Bulw...........2B 32
Tollerton La. NG12: Toll 5F 59
Tollerton Pk. Cvn. Pk.
   NG12: Toll 5G 59
Tollhouse Hill NG1: Nott 3C 4 (4F 45)
Tom Blower Cl. NG8: Woll 4G 43
Tomlinson Av. NG11: Goth.........6G 75
Tonbridge Mt. NG8: Woll 1D 54
Tongue Way NG11: Rudd............6E 67
Tonnelier Rd. NG7: Lent.............2C 56
Toothill Cl. NG14: Calv...............3E 11
Topliff Rd. NG9: Chil 3C 64
Top Rd. NG11: Rudd..................1G 77
Top Row NG14: Stoke B 2D 48

TOP VALLEY...............................5C 20
Top Valley Dr. NG5: Top V 5C 20
Top Valley Way NG5: Top V 6C 20
Torbay Cres. NG5: Bestw............1F 33
Torkard Ct. NG15: Huck............. 6G 7
Torkard Dr. NG5: Top V 5D 20
Torkard Way NG15: Huck 4H 7
Torrington Ct. NG5: Sher 5H 33
Torvill Dr. NG8: Woll..................4E 43
Torvill Hgts. NG8: Woll...............4E 43
Toston Dr. NG8: Woll..................5A 44
Totland Dr. NG8: Bas 5B 32
Totland Rd. NG8: Bram..............1C 54
Totley Cl. NG6: Bulw 3A 20
Totnes Cl. NG15: Huck............... 5D 6
Totnes Rd. NG3: Nott 4D 46
TOTON 3A 64
Toton Cl. NG6: Bulw..................2B 32
Toton La. NG9: Stfrd 4F 53
Toton Lane Park & Ride...............1H 63
Toton Lane Stop (NET)................1H 63
Toton Sidings NG9: Toton..........2F 63
Tottle Gdns. NG7: Radf 3B 44
Tottle Rd. NG2: Nott 3E 57
Tower Cres. NG16: Kimb 3A 30
Towe's Mt. NG4: Car.................. 2G 47
Towle St. NG10: Long E 3C 72
Towlson Ct. NG9: Chil................2D 64
Towlsons Cft. NG6: Bas 4B 32
Town End Cotts. NG12: Plum 6A 68
Townsend Cl. NG5: Top V 4E 21
Townside Cl. NG10: Long E 3D 72
Town St. NG10: Sand..................6D 52
Town St. NG9: Bram 3B 54
Town Vw. NG16: Kimb 6H 17
Townson Av. NG16: Lang M........ 3G 15
Towyn Ct. NG5: Bestw................6E 21
Tracy Cl. NG9: Bram 2E 55
Trafalgar Cl. NG7: Radf..............3D 44
Trafalgar Rd. NG10: Long E........1F 73
Trafalgar Rd. NG9: Bee...............1G 65
Trafalgar Sq. NG10: Long E 6H 63
Trafalgar Ter. NG10: Long E........6G 63
Traffic St. NG2: Nott 6G 45
Trafford Gdns. NG8: Aspl...........2A 44
Tranby Gdns. NG8: Woll.............5F 43
Travers Rd. NG10: Sand 5C 52
Treegarth Sq. NG5: Top V 4F 21
TREETOPS HOSPICE 1A 62
Tree Vw. Cl. NG5: Arn 4G 21
Trefan Gdns. NG5: Bestw...........6E 21
Trefoil Cl. NG13: Bing 6D 50
Trelawn Cl. NG5: Sher 5H 33
Tremadoc Ct. NG5: Sher 1F 45
Tremayne Rd. NG8: Bilb 3C 42
Trenchard Cl. NG13: Newt..........2B 50
Trent Av. NG11: Rudd.................. 5G 67
Trent Blvd. NG2: West Br 2B 58
Trent Bri. NG2: Nott 2A 58
Trent Bri. NG2: West Br 2A 58
Trent Bridge 2A 58
Trent Bri. Bldgs.
   NG2: West Br 2A 58
Trent Bus. Cen. NG10: Long E 3E 63
Trent Cotts. NG10: Long E 1H 73
Trent Ct. NG2: West Br 2C 58
Trent Cres. NG9: Atten 2E 65
Trentdale Rd. NG4: Car...............3F 47
Trent Dr. NG15: Huck 2D 18
Trent Gdns. NG14: Bur J 3G 37
Trentham Gdns. NG14: Bur J 4D 36
Trentham Gdns. NG8: Aspl.........2A 44
Trent Ho. NG10: Long E 3C 72
Trent La. NG10: Long E 3G 73
Trent La. NG14: Bur J 3G 37
Trent La. NG2: Nott 6B 46
.... (not continuous)
TRENTLOCK................................4G 73

Trent Lock Golf Course 3F 73
Trenton Cl. NG9: Bram...............2A 54
Trenton Dr. NG10: Long E 5A 64
Trent Rd. DE7: Kirk H................. 5H 39
Trent Rd. NG2: Nott 5B 46
Trent Rd. NG9: Bee 1G 65
Trent Side NG11: Bart F..............6C 64
Trentside NG2: West Br 3A 58
Trentside NG9: Bee.....................2G 65
.... (off Riverside Rd.)
Trent Side Nth. NG2: West Br 2A 58
Trent Sth. Ind. Pk. NG2: Nott 6C 46
Trent St. NG10: Long E 5G 63
Trent St. NG2: Nott...........6F 5 (6H 45)
Trent Vale Rd. NG9: Bee.............1G 65
Trent Valley Rd. NG14: Bur J.......1C 48
Trent Valley Rd. NG4: Ged..........2B 48
Trent Valley Rd. NG4: Neth.........2B 48
Trent Valley Sailing Club............4G 73
Trent Valley Vw. NG3: Mapp........6C 34
.... (off Hickling Rd.)
Trentview Ct. NG2: Nott..............1B 58
Trent Vw. Gdns. NG12: Rad T 4G 49
Tressall Cl. DE7: Ilk 1C 40
Trevelyan Rd. NG2: West Br 3B 58
Trevino Gdns. NG5: Top V 4E 21
Trevone Av. NG9: Stfrd 5G 53
Trevor Rd. NG2: West Br 5C 58
Trevor Rd. NG9: Bee 6F 55
Trevose Gdns. NG5: Sher 4H 33
Treyford Cl. NG11: Wilf...............1E 67
Triangle, The DE7: Ilk 3C 40
Triangle, The NG2: Nott 1E 57
Tricornia Dr. NG6: Cin 3H 31
Tring Va. NG5: Sher 3E 33
Trinity Av. NG7: Lent..................6C 44
Trinity Cl. DE7: Ilk 4A 28
Trinity Cres. NG4: Lamb 6C 24
Trinity Row NG1: Nott...........3D 4 (4G 45)
Trinity Sq. NG1: Nott...........3D 4 (4G 45)
Trinity Vw. NG10: Long E 5G 63
Trinity Wlk. NG1: Nott.......3E 5 (4G 45)
Trinity Way DE75: Hea................5C 14
Trinstead Way NG5: Bestw..........6G 21
Triumph Cl. NG7: Lent................5B 44
Triumph Rd. NG7: Lent...............5B 44
Trivett Sq. NG1: Nott.........5G 5 (5H 45)
.... (off Short Hill)
Troon Cl. NG16: Kimb 6G 17
Trough La. NG16: Want...............5H 17
Trough Rd. NG16: Want..............5H 17
Troutbeck NG12: Cotg 2G 71
Troutbeck Cres. NG9: Bram........3C 54
TROWELL...................................5E 41
Trowell Av. DE7: Ilk 4C 40
Trowell Av. NG8: Woll 4B 42
Trowell Gdns. NG8: Bilb.............4C 42
Trowell Gro. NG10: Long E 3D 62
Trowell Gro. NG9: Trow 6F 41
Trowell Gro. NG9: Stfrd 1G 53
TROWELL MOOR 4B 42
Trowell Pk. Dr. NG9: Trow 1F 53
Trowell Rd. NG8: Woll................5B 42
Trowell Rd. NG9: Stfrd 1G 53
TROWELL SERVICE AREA...........3G 41
Trueman Gdns. NG5: Arn............1D 34
Trueman St. DE7: Ilk 3B 28
Truman Cl. NG3: Nott........1F 5 (3H 45)
Truman Dr. NG15: Huck..............5G 7
Trumans Rd. NG2: Nott 2H 57
Truman St. NG16: Kimb 6F 17
Truro Cres. NG7: Radf.................2C 44
Tudor Cl. NG10: Long E 4G 63
Tudor Cl. NG4: Colw...................4G 47
Tudor Ct. NG15: Huck.................6C 6
Tudor Ct. NG9: Stfrd...................6F 53
Tudor Falls DE75: Hea................2C 14
Tudor Gro. NG1: Nott 2F 45
Tudor Pl. DE7: Kirk H 4G 39
Tudor Rd. NG2: West Br 4B 58

Tudor Sq. NG2: West Br 4B 58
Tudwal Cl. NG5: Bestw...............6E 21
Tudwal Wlk. NG5: Bestw............6E 21
Tulip Av. NG3: Nott..................... 2H 45
Tulip Cl. NG12: Cotg.................. 6G 61
Tulip Rd. NG16: Aws................... 2D 28
Tumble Town Play Cen. 5A 22
Tunnel Rd. NG7: Nott 5A 4 (5E 45)
Tunnicliffe Cl. DE7: Ilk 5A 28
Tunnicliffe Cl. DE7: Ilk 5A 28
Tunstall Cres. NG8: Aspl............ 6G 31
Tunstall Dr. NG5: Sher 3D 32
Tunstall Rd. NG5: Woodt............3B 34
Turnberry Cl. DE7: Ilk 5G 27
Turnberry Cl. NG8: Bram 5C 54
Turnberry Ct. NG12: Edwal.........2E 69
Turnberry Rd. NG6: Bulw............1B 32
Turner Av. NG16: Lang M............2E 15
Turner Cl. NG5: Sher 2F 33
Turner Cl. NG9: Stfrd 5G 53
Turner Dr. NG16: Gilt..................6D 16
Turner Rd. NG10: Long E 3E 73
Turner St. NG15: Huck................ 4G 7
Turneys Ct. NG2: Nott 2A 58
Turney St. NG2: Nott.................. 2H 57
Turnook Av. DE7: Ilk 2B 28
Turnpike La. NG9: Bee................3G 55
Turnpike Village NG9: Bee 3G 55
Turnpike Village Halls of Residence
   NG9: Bee 4G 55
Turnstone Wharf NG7: Lent........1D 56
Turpin Av. NG4: Ged 4F 35
Turton Cl. NG16: Lang M 2E 15
Turton Dr. NG5: Arn 6A 22
Tuxford Wlk. NG3: Nott..............3B 46
Twells Cl. NG3: Nott...................2B 46
Twelve Ho.'s. DE7: Stant D 6A 40
Twitchell, The NG9: Chil 1E 65
Twycross Rd. NG5: Bestw...........6F 21
Twyford Cl. DE7: West H.............1B 38
Twyford Cl. NG11: Clftn..............1C 66
Twyford Rd. NG10: Long E 3B 72
Tyburn Cl. NG5: Arn 4E 21
Tyne Cl. NG8: Aspl.....................5A 32
Tynedale Cl. NG10: Long E 1C 72
Tynedale Cl. NG8: Aspl 6B 32
Tyne Gdns. NG15: Huck..............2D 18
Tyrian Cl. NG16: Gilt 5D 16

U

Ulgham Cl. NG5: Arn..................3B 22
Ulldale Ct. NG9: Chil..................1B 64
Ullscarf Cl. NG2: West Br............6E 59
Ullswater Cl. NG2: Gam..............5F 59
Ullswater Cl. NG4: Ged...............5H 35
Ullswater Cres. NG9: Bram.........2C 54
Ullswater Dr. NG15: Huck...........4H 7
Underwood M. NG8: Stre............6C 30
Union Cl. NG15: Lin 1G 7
Union Rd. DE7: Ilk......................2A 40
Union Rd. NG5: Arn........... 2E 5 (4G 45)
Union Rd. NG3: Nott........ 2F 5 (4H 45)
Union St. NG10: Long E 5G 63
Union St. NG13: Bing..................5E 51
Union St. NG9: Bee.....................5F 55
Unity Cres. NG3: Mapp...............5C 34
University Blvd. NG7: Nott...........3H 55
University Blvd. NG9: Bee 3H 55
University Boulevard
   Stop (NET) 4H 55
University Library Nottingham 4F 45
University of Nottingham
   Jubilee Campus.......................5B 44
University of Nottingham
   King's Meadow Campus...........2D 56
University of Nottingham
   Medical School........................1B 56

University of Nottingham University Pk. Campus – Waterfront Plaza

University of Nottingham
  University Pk. Campus 1A 56
University of Nottingham
  Stop (NET)........................2B 56
University Pk. NG7: Nott........2H 55
Uplands Ct. NG8: Woll 3F 43
Upminster Dr. NG16: Nuth........3D 30
Upminster Dr. NG5: Arn..........4B 22
Up. Barn Cl. DE75: Hea............3D 14
Up. Canaan NG11: Rudd...........5H 67
Up. College St.
  NG1: Nott 3B 4 (4F 45)
Up. Dunstead Rd.
  NG16: Lang M.....................2F 15
Up. Eldon St. NG2: Nott....4H 5 (5A 46)
Up. Orchard St. NG9: Stfrd 4G 53
Up. Parliament St.
  NG1: Nott 3C 4 (4F 45)
Up. Wellington St.
  NG10: Long E.....................4E 63
Uppingham Cres.
  NG2: West Br.....................6H 57
Uppingham Gdns. NG2: Nott 1H 57
Upton Cl. DE75: Hea.............4E 15
Upton Dr. NG5: Sher 2H 33
Upton M. NG3: Nott................1D 46
URGENT CARE CENTRE (CITY LINK)
  NOTTINGHAM 6G 5 (6H 45)
Utile Gdns. NG6: Bulw 6G 19

V

Vale, The DE7: Ilk.................4A 28
Valebrook Rd. NG5: Sher...........2G 33
Vale Cl. NG16: Eastw 3D 16
Vale Cres. Nth. NG8: Aspl 3B 44
Vale Cres. Sth. NG8: Aspl 3B 44
Vale Gdns. NG4: Colw 4F 47
Valerian Gro. NG15: Huck..........3A 8
Valerian Way NG13: Bing 5C 50
Vale Rd. NG4: Colw................4G 47
Valeside Gdns. NG4: Colw 4G 47
Valetta Rd. NG5: Arn..............6D 22
Valeview Ho. NG12: Cotg..........2F 71
Valley Ct. NG4: Car 6D 34
Valley Ct. NG5: Sher 2H 33
Valley Dr. NG16: Newth 3D 16
Valley Farm Ct. NG5: Top V 5E 21
Valley Gdns. NG2: West Br 6E 59
Valley Ho. NG1: Nott.......5C 4 (5F 45)
  ....(off Park Valley)
Valley Rd. DE7: Kirk H...........4A 40
Valley Rd. NG12: Rad T 4G 49
Valley Rd. NG16: Kimb............6F 17
Valley Rd. NG2: West Br..........6C 58
Valley Rd. NG4: Car 6D 34
Valley Rd. NG5: Bas..............5D 32
Valley Rd. NG5: Sher 5D 32
Valley Rd. NG9: Chil.............6A 54
Valley Vw. DE7: Kirk H...........4A 40
Valmont Rd. NG5: Sher............4E 33
Valmont Rd. NG9: Bram...........3A 54
Vancouver Av. NG12: Rad T 1E 61
Vanguard Rd. NG10: Long E........2F 73
Vantage, The NG7: Hys G 1F 45
Varden Av. NG9: Lent A 2G 55
Varley Cl. DE75: Hea.............3E 15
Varney Rd. NG11: Clftn 2D 66
Vaughan Av. NG15: Huck............2A 8
Vaughan Rd. NG9: Chil...........1A 64
Vedonis Ho. NG15: Huck...........6G 7
Venn Ct. NG9: Bee...............5F 55
Ventnor Ri. NG5: Sher 3D 32
Ventura Dr. NG6: Bulw...........4A 20
Venus Cl. NG6: Bas..............2C 32
Verbena Cl. NG3: Nott...........2H 45
Verden Way NG9: Stre............5C 30
Verder Gro. NG5: Top V 5C 20
Vere St. NG6: Bulw 6H 19

Verne Cl. NG4: Car..............2E 47
Vernon Av. NG11: Wilf 3F 57
Vernon Av. NG4: Car 1H 47
Vernon Av. NG6: Bas.............4C 32
Vernon Av. NG9: Bee 5F 55
Vernon Ct. NG12: Rad T..........6F 49
Vernon Ct. NG16: Nuth 4F 31
Vernon Dr. NG16: Nuth 4F 31
Vernon Pk. Dr. NG6: Bas.........4C 32
Vernon Pk. Trad. Est.
  NG6: Bas.....................4C 32
Vernon Pl. NG6: Bas.............3B 32
Vernon Rd. NG6: Bas.............3B 32
Vernon St. DE7: Ilk.............3B 28
Vernon St. NG1: Nott 3B 4 (4F 45)
Vernon Works NG6: Bas...........4C 32
Verona Av. NG4: Colw............3H 47
Veronica Dr. NG16: Gilt.........5E 17
Veronica Dr. NG4: Car...........6F 35
Veronica Wlk. NG11: Clftn.......4A 66
Versailles Gdns. NG15: Huck......6G 7
Vicarage Av. DE7: Ilk...........3H 27
Vicarage Cl. NG5: Sher..........4D 32
Vicarage Dr. NG14: Bur J........3E 37
Vicarage Gdns. DE75: Hea........4D 14
Vicarage Grn. NG12: Edwal.......2D 68
Vicarage La. NG11: Rudd.........6G 67
Vicarage La. NG12: Rad T........6E 49
Vicarage St. DE7: Ilk...........3H 27
Vicarage St. NG9: Bee...........5E 55
Vickers Cl. NG4: Ged............4G 35
Vickers St. NG3: Mapp P.........1H 45
Vickery Way NG9: Chil...........3B 64
Victor, The NG7: Lent...........1C 56
  ....(off Leen Ct.)
Victor Cres. NG10: Sand.........1E 63
Victoria Av. DE75: Hea..........4B 14
Victoria Av. NG2: Nott..........5B 46
Victoria Bus Pk. NG4: Neth......3B 48
Victoria Bus Station....1E 5 (3G 45)
Victoria Centre Clock Tower....3C 44
Victoria Cen. Sth. 3E 5 (4G 45)
  ....(within Victoria Cen.)
Victoria Cl. NG5: Arn...........3B 22
Victoria Cl. DE7: Ilk...........6A 28
Victoria Ct. NG10: Long E.......5G 63
Victoria Ct. NG7: Lent..........5D 44
Victoria Cres. NG5: Sher........5H 33
Victoria Emb. NG2: Nott.........2G 57
Victoria Gdns. NG16: Want......4A 18
Victoria Gro. NG15: Lin.........1H 7
Victoria Hall NG3: Nott 2F 5 (4H 45)
  ....(not continuous)
Victoria Leisure Cen. 3G 5 (4H 45)
Victoria Mkt. NG1: Nott 3E 5 (4G 45)
Victoria Pk. NG11: Rudd........6G 67
Victoria Pk. Leisure Cen.......6A 28
Victoria Pk. Way NG4: Neth.....3B 48
Victoria Rd. NG10: Sand.........6D 52
Victoria Rd. NG11: Bunny.......6A 78
Victoria Rd. NG13: Bing.........4G 51
Victoria Rd. NG2: West Br.......4A 58
Victoria Rd. NG4: Neth..........2H 47
Victoria Rd. NG5: Sher..........4F 33
Victoria St. DE7: Ilk...........4B 28
Victoria St. NG1: Nott ...4E 5 (5G 45)
Victoria St. NG10: Long E.......2D 72
Victoria St. NG12: Rad T........6F 49
Victoria St. NG15: Huck.........3F 7
Victoria St. NG16: Eastw........2B 16
Victoria St. NG16: Kimb.........1A 30
Victoria St. NG16: Lang M.......2G 15
Victoria St. NG4: Ged...........6H 35
Victoria St. NG9: Stfrd.........4F 53
Victoria Ter. NG2: Nott.........5A 46
Victoria Way NG15: Huck.........1A 20
Victor Ter. NG5: Sher...........5G 33
Victory Cl. NG10: Long E........2F 73
Victory Rd. NG9: Bee............1G 65

View, The NG9: Bram.............4B 54
Village, The DE7: D Ab..........6D 38
Village, The DE7: West H........2C 38
Village Cl. NG12: Edwal.........2D 68
Village Rd. NG11: Clftn.........3A 66
Village St. NG12: Edwal.........2C 68
Villa Rd. NG5: Sher.............3H 79
Villa Rd. NG3: Mapp P...........2G 45
Villa St. NG9: Bee..............4F 55
Villiers Rd. NG2: West Br.......5C 58
Villiers Rd. NG5: Woodt.........3H 33
Vincent Av. DE7: Ilk...........1B 40
Vincent Av. NG9: Bee...........6F 55
Vincent Cl. NG15: Huck..........2A 8
Vincent Gdns. NG7: Hys G.......2C 44
Vine Cres. NG10: Sand..........5D 52
Vine Farm Cl. DE7: Kirk H.......3H 39
Vine Farm Cl. NG12: Cotg.......2E 71
Vines Cross NG8: Woll...........1E 55
Vine Ter. NG15: Huck...........4H 7
Violet Av. NG16: Newth.........5D 16
Violet Cl. NG6: Bas............4B 32
Violet Gro. NG15: Huck..........4A 8
Violet Rd. NG2: West Br.........3C 58
Violet Rd. NG4: Car............5F 35
Virgin Active
  Nottingham 6G 5 (6H 45)
Vision Bus. Pk. NG6: Bulw......4G 19
Vista, The NG9: Stfrd..........6G 53
Vivian Av. NG5: Sher...........1F 45
Vivian Ct. NG5: Sher...........1F 45
Viyella Gdns. NG15: Huck........6G 7
Viyella M. NG15: Huck...........5G 7
Voce Gdns. NG15: Huck..........5A 8
Vulcan Cl. NG6: Bas............3C 32
Vyse Dr. NG10: Long E..........1D 72

W

Waddington Dr. NG2: West Br ...1H 67
Wade Av. DE7: Ilk..............2C 40
Wades Av. NG7: Hys G..........1C 44
Wades Way NG13: Bing..........6G 51
Wadham Rd. NG5: Woodt.........2A 34
Wadhurst Gdns.
  NG3: Nott...............1G 5 (3H 45)
Wadhurst Gro. NG8: Woll........1D 54
Wadsworth Rd. NG9: Stfrd.......3H 53
Wainfleet Cl. DE7: Ilk.........4G 27
Wainfleet Ct. NG5: Arn.........3C 22
Waingrove NG11: Wilf...........2E 67
Wainwright Ho. NG3: Nott.......3A 46
Wakefield Av. NG12: Rad T......5G 49
Wakefield Cl. NG11: Wilf.......6E 57
Wakefield Cft. DE7: Ilk........4G 27
Walbrook Cl. NG8: Cin..........4G 31
Walcote Dr. NG2: West Br.......6E 57
Walcott Grn. NG11: Clftn.......4B 66
Waldeck Rd. NG5: Sher..........6F 33
Waldemar Gro. NG9: Bee........5G 55
Waldron Rd. NG4: Ged..........4G 35
Walesby Cres. NG8: Aspl........3A 44
Walgrave Wlk. NG5: Bestw.......6F 21
Walker Cl. DE7: Ilk............5C 40
Walker Gro. NG9: Stfrd.........5G 53
Walkers Cl. NG13: Bing.........5E 51
Walker St. NG16: Eastw.........3C 16
Walker St. NG2: Nott ...3H 5 (4A 46)
Walker's Yd. NG12: Rad T.......6F 49
Walk Mill Dr. NG15: Huck.......2H 7
Wallace Av. NG4: Car...........2H 47
Wallace Gdns. NG9: Toton.......3H 63
Wallace St. NG11: Goth.........5H 75
Wallan St. NG7: Radf...........3C 44
Wallet St. NG4: Neth...........2A 48
Wallett Av. NG9: Bee...........3F 55
Wallett St. NG9: Chil..........1H 57
Wallis St. NG6: Bas............3C 32

Wallsend Cl. DE7: Ilk...........3B 28
Walnut Cl. DE7: Ilk............2C 40
Walnut Cl. NG2: West Br........2E 59
Walnut Cl. NG12: Rad T.........6F 49
  ....(off Walnut Gro.)
Walnut Cft. NG11: Rudd.........1H 77
Walnut Dr. NG9: Bram...........3B 54
Walnut Gro. NG12: Cotg.........2F 71
Walnut Gro. NG12: Rad T........6F 49
Walnut Gro. NG14: Calv.........3H 11
Walnut Tree Gdns. NG6: Bulw....6F 19
Walsham Cl. NG9: Chil..........3C 64
Walsingham Rd. NG5: Woodt......2C 34
Walter St. NG7: Radf......1A 4 (3E 45)
Waltham Cl. NG2: West Br.......5D 58
Walton Av. NG3: Nott...........4B 46
Walton Cl. DE7: West H.........1B 38
Walton Ct. NG12: Key...........4H 79
Walton Ct. NG4: Car............2G 47
Walton Cres. NG4: Car..........2G 47
Walton Dr. NG12: Key...........4H 79
Walton M. NG3: Nott............2B 46
Walton Rd. NG5: Arn............4C 22
Walton St. NG10: Long E........5F 63
Walton Ter. NG3: Nott..........4B 46
Wansbeck Cl. NG5: Arn..........3B 22
Wansbeck Cl. NG7: Radf.........4E 45
Wansford Av. NG5: Arn..........3B 22
Wanstead Way NG5: Top V.......4C 20
Warburton Ct. NG15: Huck.......5H 7
Ward Av. NG15: Huck............2F 7
Ward Av. NG3: Mapp.............4D 34
Wardle Gro. NG5: Arn...........5C 22
Wardlow Rd. DE7: Ilk...........4A 28
Ward's La. DE72: Brea..........5A 62
Ward St. NG7: Bas..............1D 44
Wareham Cl. NG2: West Br.......6G 57
Wareham Cl. NG8: Cin...........4G 31
Warehouse, The
  NG1: Nott..................5F 5 (5H 45)
  ....(off Plumptre St.)
Warkton Cl. NG9: Chil..........6C 54
Warner St. NG7: Radf...........4C 44
Warren, The NG12: Cotg.........3F 71
Warren Av. NG5: Sher...........5E 33
Warren Av. NG9: Stfrd..........4F 53
Warren Ct. NG9: Stfrd..........4F 53
Warrender Cl. NG9: Bram........2C 54
Warrener Gro. NG5: Top V.......5C 20
Warren Hill Cl. NG5: Arn.......6G 21
Warren La. NG10: Long E........5C 72
Warren Rd. NG15: Huck..........6D 6
Warrington Rd. NG6: Bulw.......6A 20
Warser Ga. NG1: Nott 4F 5 (5H 45)
Warsop Cl. NG8: Stre...........5D 30
Warton Av. NG3: Nott...........1B 46
Warwick Av. NG5: Woodt.........2A 34
Warwick Av. NG9: Bee...........3F 55
Warwick Dr. DE7: Ilk...........4G 27
Warwick Gdns. NG12: Cotg.......4F 71
Warwick Rd. NG10: Long E.......6H 63
Warwick Rd. NG3: Mapp P........5H 33
Warwick St. NG7: Lent..........1C 56
Wasdale Cl. NG2: West Br.......6E 59
Washdyke La. NG15: Huck........2E 7
Washington Ct. NG5: Arn........6B 22
Washington Dr. NG9: Stfrd......2H 53
Wasnidge Cl. NG3: Nott...2G 5 (4H 45)
Wasnidge Wlk.
  NG3: Nott..................1G 5 (3H 45)
  ....(off Wasnidge Cl.)
Watchwood Gro. NG14: Calv......3H 11
Watcombe Cir. NG5: Sher........5F 33
Watcombe Rd. NG5: Sher.........6G 33
Watendlath Cl. NG7: Bas........6E 59
Waterdown Rd. NG11: Clftn......4B 66
Waterford St. NG6: Bas.........4C 32
Waterfront Plaza
  NG2: Nott..................6G 5 (6H 45)

124 A-Z Nottingham

Waterhouse La. – Whitely Av.

Waterhouse La. NG4: Ged 5A 36
Water La. NG12: Rad T 6E 49
Water La. NG25: Oxton 1B 12
Waterloo Cres. NG7: Radf.............3E 45
Waterloo La. NG9: Trow 3G 41
Waterloo Prom. NG7: Radf 3E 45
.... (not continuous)
Waterloo Rd. NG15: Lin................ 1G 7
Waterloo Rd. NG7: Radf...............3E 45
Waterloo Rd. NG9: Bee............... 6G 55
Watermark Cl. NG5: Sher 5F 33
Watermark Ho. NG5: Sher 5F 33
Watermeadows, The
NG10: Long E..............................5C 62
Water Orton Cl. NG9: Toton......... 2G 63
Waters Edge NG11: Wilf 4F 57
Waterside Cl. NG10: Sand 2D 62
Waterside Cl. NG2: Gam...............5E 59
Waterside Gdns. NG7: Lent..........2C 56
Waterside Retail Pk.
Ilkeston Junction.......................6C 28
Waterside Way NG2: Colw............1C 58
Waterside Way NG2: Nott.............1C 58
Waterway, The NG10: Sand.........1E 63
Waterway St. NG2: Nott
Newthorpe St. 1H 57
Waterway St. NG2: Nott
Wallet St.................................... 1H 57
Waterway St. W. NG2: Nott.......... 1G 57
Watford Rd. NG8: Aspl................. 5H 31
Watkinson St. DE75: Hea 3B 14
Watkin St. NG3: Nott 1E 5 (3G 45)
WATNALL.......................................5A 18
WATNALL CANTELUPE 5H 17
WATNALL CHAWORTH..................4A 18
Watnall Rd. NG15: Huck.............. 3D 18
Watnall Rd. NG16: Nuth...............1C 30
Watnall Rd. Factory Units
NG15: Huck..................................6F 7
Watson Av. DE75: Hea................ 3D 14
Watson Av. NG3: Nott 3D 46
Watson Rd. DE7: Ilk..................... 5G 27
Waveney Cl. NG5: Arn 1C 34
Waverley Av. NG4: Ged................6A 36
Waverley Av. NG9: Bee................ 5G 55
Waverley Mt. NG7: Nott................3E 45
Waverley St. NG1: Nott...... 1B 4 (3F 45)
Waverley St. NG10: Long E.......... 5G 63
Waverley St. NG7: Nott.................3E 45
Waverley Ter. NG1: Nott..... 2C 4 (4F 45)
Wayford Wlk. NG6: Bulw 5H 19
Wayne Cl. NG11: Clftn 4C 66
Wayte Ct. NG11: Rudd 4A 68
Weardale Rd. NG5: Sher..............5E 33
Wearmouth Gdns.
NG5: Top V..................................4E 21
Weave Cl. NG6: Bas.....................3C 32
Weaver Row DE7: Ilk....................1B 40
Weaverthorpe Rd. NG5: Woodt.....2C 34
Weaving Gdns. NG5: Bestw......... 2G 33
Webb Rd. NG8: Bilb 2H 43
Webster Av. NG16: Eastw 4B 16
Webster Cl. NG15: Huck 1A 8
Weedon Cl. NG3: Nott..................3C 46
Weekday Cross
NG1: Nott 5E 5 (5G 45)
Weetman Gdns. NG5: Top V 5E 21
Weightman Av. NG4: Ged 4G 35
Weightman Dr. NG16: Gilt 6D 16
Welbeck Av. DE7: Kirk H.............. 4H 39
Welbeck Av. NG4: Ged..................5F 35
Welbeck Ct. NG5: Woodt 3C 34
Welbeck Gdns. NG5: Woodt..........3C 34
Welbeck Gdns. NG9: Toton.......... 2H 63
Welbeck Gro. NG13: Bing.............5C 50
Welbeck Rd. NG10: Long E.......... 2D 62
Welbeck Rd. NG12: Rad T 5G 49
Welbeck Rd. NG2: West Br 3A 58
Welbeck Wlk. NG3: Nott.............. 3G 45
Welbeck Workshops
NG3: Nott 3G 45
....(off Alfred Cl.)
Welby Av. NG7: Lent 5D 44
Welch Av. NG9: Stfrd 3H 53
Weldbank Cl. NG9: Chil 1B 64
Welham Cres. NG5: Arn...............6C 22
Welland Ct. NG3: Nott..................3B 46
Welland Gdns. NG13: Bing 6D 50
Wellesley Cres. NG8: Stre 5D 30
Wellin Cl. NG12: Edwal 2D 68
Wellin Ct. NG12: Edwal................ 2D 68
Wellington Cir.
NG1: Nott 4B 4 (5F 45)
Wellington Ct.
NG1: Nott 4C 4 (5F 45)
.....................................(off E. Circus St.)
Wellington Ct. NG16: Eastw 3B 16
Wellington Cres. NG2: West Br.....4B 58
Wellingtonia Cres.
NG12: Edwal 3D 68
Wellington Pl. NG16: Eastw..........3B 16
Wellington Rd. NG14: Bur J.......... 2G 37
Wellington Sq.
NG7: Nott 3A 4 (4E 45)
Wellington St. DE75: Hea 3B 14
Wellington St. NG10: Long E........2E 63
Wellington St. NG16: Eastw 2B 16
Wellington St. NG3: Nott ... 1E 5 (3G 45)
Wellington St. NG9: Stfrd 5E 53
Wellington Ter. NG7: Radf 4E 45
Wellington Vs. NG7: Lent 4E 45
Wellin La. NG12: Edwal 2D 68
Wells Gdns. NG3: Nott..................1B 46
Wellspring Dale NG9: Stfrd 6G 53
Wells Rd., The NG3: Mapp............5A 34
Wells Rd., The NG3: Nott..............5A 34
WELLS ROAD CEN., THE 5B 34
Welstead Av. NG8: Aspl 5G 31
Welton Gdns. NG6: Bulw 5G 19
Welwyn Rd. NG8: Woll..................4E 43
Wembley Gdns. NG9: Bram...........1B 54
Wembley Rd. NG5: Arn 1D 34
Wemyss Gdns. NG8: Woll.............6B 44
Wendling Gdns. NG5: Bestw 6F 21
Wendover Dr. NG8: Aspl 5H 31
Wenlock Cl. NG16: Gilt 5E 17
Wenlock Dr. NG15: Huck 4A 8
Wenlock Dr. NG2: West Br............6B 58
Wensleydale Cl. NG8: Aspl 6B 32
Wensleydale Rd. NG10: Long E... 1D 72
Wensley Rd. NG5: Woodt..............2A 34
Wensor Av. NG9: Lent A................3F 55
Wentworth Ct. NG16: Kimb 1G 29
Wentworth Cft. DE75: Hea 2E 15
Wentworth Rd. NG5: Sher 5F 33
Wentworth Rd. NG9: Chil 5C 54
Wentworth St. DE7: Ilk.................5C 28
Wentworth Way NG12: Edwal 2D 68
Wesleyan Chapel Wlk.
NG9: Stfrd 4F 53
Wesley Av. NG9: Bee 5F 55
Wesley Ct. NG5: Sher 5G 33
...................................(off Drayton St.)
Wesley Gro. NG5: Sher 6F 33
Wesley Pl. NG9: Stfrd 3G 53
Wesley St. DE7: Ilk 3A 28
Wesley St. NG16: Lang M 2F 15
Wesley St. NG5: Sher....................6F 33
Wesley Way NG11: Rudd 1H 77
Wessex Dr. NG16: Gilt..................5C 16
Wessex Dr. NG16: Newth..............5C 16
West Av. NG10: Sand....................5C 52
West Av. NG2: West Br.................4A 58
West Av. NG9: Stfrd 3G 53
Westbourne Ct. NG9: Bram 2H 53
WEST BRIDGFORD........................5A 58
Westbury Cl. NG9: Chil 1C 64
Westbury Rd. NG5: Sher.............. 5D 32
Westby La. NG16: Babb................3E 29
Westby La. NG16: Coss 3E 29
Westcliffe Av. NG12: Rad T 5G 49
Westcliffe Av. NG4: Ged 4F 35
Westcliffe Ct. NG12: Rad T.......... 5G 49
West Cl. NG12: Key...................... 5G 79
West Cres. NG9: Bee 1H 65
West Cross Av. NG9: Stfrd........... 3G 53
Westdale Cl. NG10: Long E...........2C 72
Westdale Ct. NG4: Car..................5F 35
Westdale Cres. NG4: Car............. 6G 35
Westdale La. E. NG4: Car 5E 35
Westdale La. W. NG3: Mapp 4C 34
West Dr. NG7: Nott....................... 3H 55
West End NG14: Calv....................3E 11
West End NG9: Bee.......................6F 55
West End Arc. NG1: Nott ... 4C 4 (5F 45)
West End Cres. DE7: Ilk............... 1H 39
West End Dr. DE7: Ilk................... 1H 39
West End St. NG9: Stfrd 5E 53
West End Vs. NG12: Rad T 6E 49
....(off Main Rd.)
West End Vs. NG14: Lowd........... 2H 25
Westerfield Way NG11: Wilf 1E 67
Westerham Cl. NG8: Bilb 2D 42
Westerham Rd. NG11: Rudd.........1F 77
Westerhope Cl. NG12: Edwal........1E 69
Westerlands NG9: Stfrd................ 5G 53
Western Av. NG13: Bing 4D 50
Western Blvd. NG8: Aspl 1A 44
Western Blvd. NG8: Bas 1A 44
Western Dr. DE75: Hea................ 5D 14
Western Flds. NG11: Rudd 1F 77
Western Gdns. NG8: Aspl 1B 44
Western St. NG1: Nott 3F 5 (4H 45)
Western Ter. NG7: Nott..................5E 45
Westfield Av. DE75: Hea.............. 5D 14
Westfield Cl. DE7: Kirk H 3G 39
Westfield Dr. DE7: Ilk................... 5H 27
Westfield La. NG14: Woodbo 1A 24
Westfield Rd. NG13: Bing............. 5D 50
West Furlong NG12: Cotg............. 3G 71
West Ga. NG10: Long E................ 6G 63
Westgate Ct. NG9: Chil 6E 55
Westgate St. NG3: Nott.................3A 46
WEST HALLAM 1B 38
WEST HALLAM COMMON.............1A 38
West Hallam Storage Dpt.
DE7: West H 3C 38
Westhay Ct. NG8: Woll..................4A 44
Westholme Gdns. NG8: Aspl 3A 44
Westhorpe Av. NG3: Nott..............4B 46
Westhorpe Dr. NG10: Long E........5E 63
Westland Av. NG15: Huck............ 1D 18
West Leake La. NG11: King..........6C 74
Westleigh Rd. NG8: Brox 5E 31
Westmaner Ct. NG9: Chil............. 6D 54
West Mnr. Pk. NG14: Epp 5F 13
Westminster Av. NG10: Sand 6E 53
Westminster Cl. NG3: Nott 2A 46
West Moor NG2: Colw...................5F 47
Westmoore Cl. NG3: Mapp 4D 34
Westmoore Ct. NG3: Mapp.......... 4D 34
Westmoreland Ct. NG5: Sher 6F 33
....(off Ebury Rd.)
Weston Av. NG7: Radf...................3E 45
Weston Cl. NG5: Woodt.................3A 34
Weston Cotts. NG7: Radf..............3C 44
Weston Cres. NG10: Long E 3B 72
Weston St. DE75: Hea 5E 15
Weston Ter. NG5: Sher................. 4G 33
West Pk. Ct. NG10: Long E 6F 63
West Pk. Leisure Cen....................6D 62
Westpoint NG2: West Br 4H 57
Westray Cl. NG9: Bram 6B 42
West Rd. NG7: Nott.......................1B 56
West St. DE7: Ilk...........................2A 40
West St. DE75: Hea.......................3B 14
West St. NG12: S'frd..................... 6H 37
West St. NG15: Huck 4G 7
West St. NG16: Kimb 3A 30
West St. NG16: Lang M..................2F 15
West St. NG2: Nott............ 4H 5 (5A 46)
West St. NG5: Arn.........................6A 22
West Ter. DE7: Ilk..........................6B 28
West Ter. NG15: Huck.................... 4G 7
West Vw. NG2: West Br 6H 57
Westview Ct. NG4: Car 1H 47
West Vw. Rd. NG4: Car 1H 47
WESTVILLE 1D 18
Westville NG2: West Br.................5A 58
Westville Dr. NG15: Huck..............2E 19
Westville Gdns. NG3: Nott 2H 45
West Wlk. NG2: Nott......... 4H 5 (5A 46)
Westward Av. NG9: Bee 5G 55
Westway NG12: Cotg.....................3F 71
Westwick Rd. NG8: Bilb 3C 42
Westwick St. DE7: Ilk 3C 40
Westwood Rd. NG2: Nott..............5B 46
Wetherby Cl. NG16: Kimb............ 6G 17
Wetherby Cl. NG8: Aspl 6H 31
Wetherlam Cl. NG2: Nott 1G 57
Weybridge Cl. DE7: West H 1B 38
Wharfedale NG8: Woll 6B 42
Wharfedale Rd. NG10: Long E......1C 72
Wharf Gdns. NG13: Bing...............6C 50
Wharf La. NG12: Rad T..................6E 49
Wharf Rd. NG7: Nott 6C 4 (6F 45)
Wharncliffe Rd. DE7: Ilk 1A 40
Wharton Cres. NG9: Bee 1F 65
Whatton Dr. NG2: West Br............2F 67
Whatton Ri. NG5: Sher 3F 33
Wheatacre Rd. NG11: Clftn 4D 66
Wheat Cl. NG8: Bilb 4D 42
Wheatcroft Business Cen.
NG12: Edwal 4B 68
Wheatcroft Dr. NG12: Edwal.........3C 68
Wheatcroft Vw. NG2: West Br 2G 67
Wheatfields Rd. NG3: Nott 2C 46
Wheatgrass Rd. NG9: Chil............6B 54
Wheatley Cl. NG11: Rudd 2G 77
Wheatley Dr. NG4: Car..................2E 47
Wheatley Gro. NG9: Chil 1F 65
Wheatsheaf Ct. NG14: Bur J 3F 37
Wheeldale Cl. NG8: Woll...............5B 42
Wheeldon Cl. DE7: Ilk...................1B 28
Wheeldon Ct. NG7: Bas 6D 32
Wheeler Av. NG16: Eastw 4D 16
Wheeler Ga. NG1: Nott....... 4D 4 (5G 45)
Wheldon Av. NG4: Car 5E 35
Whernside Rd. NG5: Woodt..........2A 34
Whetstone Cl. NG16: Nuth........... 5D 30
Whickham Ct. NG2: Nott 2H 57
Whilton Cres. DE7: West H 1B 38
Whimsey Pk. NG4: Car 3H 47
Whinfell Cl. NG11: Clftn 3D 66
Whinlatter Dr. NG2: West Br 5E 59
Whiston Cl. NG5: Bestw.................1E 33
Whitbread St. NG7: Bas................ 1D 44
Whitburn Rd. NG9: Toton 2G 63
Whitby Cl. NG8: Woll 5B 42
Whitby Cres. NG5: Woodt..............2C 34
Whitby Rd. NG16: Newth...............2C 16
Whitchurch Cl. NG5: Top V.......... 5D 20
Whitcliffe Gdns. NG2: West Br 6B 58
Whitcombe Gdns. NG5: Top V 5E 21
Whiteacre NG14: Bur J 2E 37
Whitebeam Cl. NG12: Edwal.........4C 68
Whitebeam Gdns. NG6: Bulw 6F 19
Whitechapel St. NG6: Bas 5B 32
White City Trad. Est. NG2: Nott 6C 46
Whitedale Rd. NG14: Calv 3E 11
White Furrows NG12: Cotg............3E 71
Whitegate Va. NG11: Clftn.............4B 66
Whitehead Cl. DE7: Ilk.................. 5H 27
Whitelands NG12: Cotg 3G 71
White Lodge Gdns. NG8: Bilb 2D 42
Whitely Av. DE7: Ilk 2B 28

Whitely Cl. NG9: Stfrd................3G 53
WHITEMOOR 1B 44
Whitemoor Av. NG8: Aspl 1B 44
Whitemoor Av. NG8: Bas 1B 44
Whitemoor Ct. NG8: Aspl............1B 44
Whitemoor Ct. Ind. Est.
 NG8: Aspl 1B 44
Whitemoor Rd. NG6: Bas............5B 32
Whitemoss Cl. NG8: Woll............6E 43
White Rd. NG5: Bas 4C 32
White's Av. NG3: Nott 3D 46
Whites Cft. NG14: Woodbo.........1B 24
Whiteways Ct. NG11: Clftn..........4C 66
Whitfield Cl. NG11: Wilf..............5F 57
Whiting Av. NG9: Toton 3H 63
Whiting Cl. NG15: Huck.................1A 8
Whittaker Rd. NG9: Chil 2A 64
Whittier Rd. NG2: Nott 6C 46
Whittingham Ct. NG5: Bas 4C 34
Whittingham Rd. NG3: Mapp 4C 34
Whitton Cl. NG5: Top V 4F 21
Whitton Cl. NG9: Chil...................3C 64
Whitwell Cl. DE7: Ilk 1A 28
Whitwell Cl. NG8: Brox 6F 31
Whitwell Rd. NG8: Brox 6E 31
Whitworth Dr. NG12: Rad T 1E 61
Whitworth Dr. NG14: Bur J 5C 36
Whitworth Ri. NG5: Top V 5D 20
Whitworth Rd. DE7: Ilk................3B 40
Whyatt Ct. NG5: Arn 1H 33
Whyburn Cl. NG15: Huck.............1A 20
Whyburn La. NG15: Huck..............4C 6
Whyburn Pct. NG15: Huck..............6E 7
Whyburn St. NG15: Huck..............5A 8
Whysall Rd. NG10: Long E...........6D 62
Whysall St. DE75: Hea.................3C 14
Whyston Ct. NG15: Huck................6C 6
Whytehall Rd. NG10: Long E 2E 73
Wibberley Dr. NG11: Rudd...........6F 67
Wichal Cl. NG5: Bestw.................2G 33
Wichnor Cl. NG11: Clftn...............1C 66
Wickens Wlk. NG3: Nott 3A 46
Wicker Cl. NG6: Bas 3C 32
Wicket Gro. NG7: Lent 5C 44
Wickets, The NG2: West Br 2B 58
Wickstead Cl. NG5: Woodt 4B 34
Widdington Cl. NG5: Arn 3B 22
Widdowson Cl. NG6: Bulw............5F 19
Widdowson Rd. NG10: Long E 2D 72
Widdowson's Row
 NG11: Rudd 6G 67
 ....(off Easthorpe St.)
Widecombe La. NG11: Clftn 5B 66
Widmerpool La. NG12: Key 5A 80
Widmerpool La. NG12: Widm 5A 80
WIGHAY 2F 7
Wighay Rd. NG15: Huck 2F 7
Wighay Rd. NG15: Lin 2F 7
Wigley Cl. NG3: Nott 3A 46
Wigman Ct. NG15: Huck................5B 8
Wigman Rd. NG8: Bilb 1D 42
Wigwam Gro. NG15: Huck............4A 8
Wigwam La. NG15: Huck...............4A 8
Wilberforce Rd. NG11: Wilf.........6E 57
Wilcocksons Yd. NG15: Huck.........4G 7
 ....(off Baker St.)
Wilden Cres. NG11: Clftn.............2C 66
Wildman St. NG7: Radf... 1A 4 (3E 45)
WILFORD 5F 57
Wilford Bri. NG2: Nott................2F 57
Wilford Cres. NG11: Rudd 5G 67
Wilford Cres. E. NG2: Nott 2H 57
Wilford Cres. W. NG2: Nott 1G 57
Wilford Gro. NG2: Nott................1G 57
 ....(not continuous)
WILFORD HILL 1A 68
Wilford Hill Crematorium 2H 67
Wilford La. NG11: West Br...........5F 57
Wilford La. NG11: Wilf.................5F 57

Wilford La. NG2: West Br 5F 57
Wilford Rd. NG11: Rudd 2F 67
Wilford Rd. NG2: Nott 1F 57
 ....(not continuous)
Wilford St. NG2: Nott........6D 4 (6G 45)
Wilford Village Stop (NET) 3F 57
Wilfrid Gro. NG2: West Br 2A 68
Wilkins Gdns. NG11: Clftn 4A 66
Wilkinson Av. NG9: Bee...............5F 55
Wilkinson Cl. NG9: Chil 3B 64
Wilkinson St. NG7: Bas 1C 44
Wilkinson St. NG8: Bas 6B 32
Wilkinson Street Park & Ride....1C 44
Wilkinson Street Stop (NET) 1C 44
Willaston Cl. NG6: Cin 3A 32
Willbert Rd. NG5: Arn 5C 22
Willerby Rd. NG5: Woodt 2C 34
Willersley Dr. NG2: Nott............... 1G 57
Willesden Grn. NG16: Nuth 4D 30
Willett Av. NG16: Eastw 3B 16
William Bancroft Bldg.
 NG3: Nott 2H 5 (4A 46)
 ....(off Roden St.)
William Booth
 Birthplace Mus. 5A 46
William Booth Rd. NG2: Nott.......5C 46
William Cl. NG4: Ged 1B 48
William Gregg VC
 Leisure Cen. 4D 14
William Lee Bldgs. NG7: Nott....3B 56
William Olds Ct. NG8: Woll..........4G 43
William Rd. NG2: West Br............3A 58
William Rd. NG9: Stfrd................4F 53
Williams Dr. NG14: Calv 2G 11
Williamson Gdns.
 NG16: Lang M 2E 15
Williamson Row NG5: Bestw......2E 33
 ....(off Arnold Rd.)
Williams Rd. NG9: Chil 2A 64
Williams Ter. NG10: Long E 3E 63
William St. NG15: Huck................4G 7
Willoughby Av. NG10: Long E 3E 63
Willoughby Av. NG7: Lent 5D 44
Willoughby Cl. DE72: Brea..........5B 62
Willoughby Cl. NG7: Nott............3H 55
Willoughby Rd. NG2: West Br......5B 58
Willoughby St. NG7: Lent 6D 44
Willoughby St. NG9: Bee.............4F 55
Willow Av. NG10: Long E 4F 63
Willow Av. NG15: Huck................1D 18
Willow Av. NG4: Car 1A 48
Willow Av. NG9: Stfrd..................5F 53
Willow Brook NG12: Key 5A 80
Willowbrook Ct. NG2: Nott 2G 57
Willow Cl. NG12: Rad T 1F 61
Willow Cl. NG14: Bur J 2F 37
Willow Cl. NG14: Calv..................5C 12
Willow Cl. NG16: Lang M.............2F 15
Willow Cl. NG2: West Br 2F 59
Willow Cotts. NG8: Bilb 2G 43
Willow Cres. NG4: Ged................5A 36
Willow Cres. NG4: Lamb..............6B 24
Willowdene NG12: Cotg..............2G 71
Willow Hill Cl. NG6: Bulw............1G 31
Willow La. NG4: Car 5H 35
Willow Ri. NG10: Sand 6D 52
Willow Rd. NG12: Cotg 6G 61
Willow Rd. NG13: Bing 5G 51
Willow Rd. NG2: West Br 1A 68
Willow Rd. NG4: Car 1A 48
Willow Rd. NG7: Lent 2C 56
Willows, The NG8: Bilb 2G 43
Willows, The NG9: Bee................5F 55
Willow Vw. NG7: Radf..................3D 44
Willow Wong NG14: Bur J 2F 37
Willow Wong Cotts. NG14: Bur J .2F 37
Willwell Dr. NG2: West Br............2G 67
Wilmington Gdns. NG5: Arn 1H 33

Wilmore Cl. NG9: Chil 1D 64
Wilmot La. NG9: Bee...................6F 55
Wilmot St. DE7: Ilk 6A 28
Wilmot St. DE75: Hea..................4C 14
Wilmot St. NG10: Long E 2C 72
Wilne Av. NG10: Long E...............3C 72
Wilne Cl. NG10: Long E................3B 72
Wilne La. NG10: Long E 3A 72
Wilne Rd. NG10: Long E 3B 72
Wilson Av. DE75: Los...................1A 14
Wilson Cl. NG5: Arn 1D 34
Wilson Rd. NG16: Eastw..............4B 16
Wilsons Cl. NG11: Rudd 6G 67
WILSTHORPE 5D 62
Wilsthorpe Rd. DE72: Brea..........5A 62
Wilsthorpe Rd. NG10: Long E 5D 62
Wilton Pl. DE7: Ilk.......................6B 28
Wilton Rd. NG7: Radf 3C 44
Wilton St. DE7: Ilk.......................6B 28
Wilton St. NG6: Bas 3C 32
Wilton Ter. NG6: Bas 3C 32
Wimbledon Dr. NG16: Nuth 4E 31
Wimbledon Rd. NG5: Sher...........4E 33
Wimborne Cl. NG2: West Br 6G 57
Wimbourne Rd. NG7: Radf 3D 44
Wimpole Rd. NG9: Bram...............2D 54
Winchester Av. NG9: Bee............3E 55
Winchester Cl. NG5: Sher 4A 34
Winchester Cres. DE7: Ilk 1C 40
Winchester Rd. NG5: Sher...........4G 33
Winchester St. NG5: Sher............4G 33
Winchester Ter. NG5: Sher...........4G 33
Windermere Av. DE7: Kirk H........4G 39
Windermere Cl. NG2: Gam 4F 59
Windermere Cl. NG4: Ged 5H 35
Windermere Gdns.
 NG10: Long E 3D 62
Windermere Rd. NG10: Long E.....3C 62
Windermere Rd. NG15: Huck.........4F 7
Windermere Rd. NG7: Hys G 1E 45
Windermere Rd. NG9: Bram.........2D 54
Windings, The NG4: Car 2F 47
Windley Dr. DE7: Ilk....................4H 27
Windmill Av. NG15: Huck.............5G 7
Windmill Cl. NG11: Goth 6H 75
Windmill Cl. NG3: Nott................4B 46
Windmill Ct. NG12: Key 5F 79
Windmill Gro. NG15: Huck...........4G 7
Windmill La. NG2: Nott 5A 46
Windmill La. NG3: Nott................5A 46
Windmill Vw. NG2: Nott 5C 46
Windrush Cl. NG9: Bram 2D 54
Windsor Cl. DE75: Hea................2C 14
Windsor Cl. NG15: Huck..............3H 7
Windsor Cl. NG8: Aspl 2B 44
Windsor Cl. NG9: Trow................4D 40
Windsor Ct. DE7: West H............1B 38
Windsor Ct. NG10: Long E 6G 63
Windsor Ct. NG10: Sand..............1D 62
Windsor Ct. NG13: Bing 5C 50
Windsor Cres. DE7: Kirk H 4H 39
Windsor Cres. NG5: Woodt..........1C 34
Windsor Cres. NG9: Stfrd 4G 53
Windsor Ho. NG3: Mapp P 1G 45
Windsor St. NG9: Bee.................5G 55
Windsor St. NG9: Stfrd 4G 53
Wing All. NG1: Nott 4F 5 (5H 45)
Wingate Cl. NG8: Bilb 3F 43
Wingbourne Wlk. NG6: Bulw.......4A 20
 ....(not continuous)
Wingfield Dr. DE7: Ilk 4H 27
Wingfield Dr. NG9: Lent A...........2G 55
Wings Dr. NG15: Huck 1D 18
Winifred Cl. NG11: Wilf................5E 57
Winifred Cres. NG14: Bur J 3F 37
Winifred St. NG15: Huck...............5H 7
Winrow Gdns. NG6: Bas 4A 32
Winscale Av. NG5: Top V 5E 21

Winscale Gdns. NG5: Top V........5E 21
Winscombe Mt. NG11: Clftn.........5B 66
Winsford Cl. NG8: Aspl 5H 31
Winster Av. NG4: Car...................6F 35
Winster Cl. NG9: Lent A...............2F 55
Winster Pk. DE7: Ilk....................4C 40
Winster Way NG10: Long E 2B 72
Winston Cl. NG3: Mapp 2E 35
Winston Cl. NG9: Stfrd................3G 53
Winterbourne Dr. NG9: Stfrd 2G 53
Winterton Cl. NG5: Arn 1B 34
Winterton Gdns. NG5: Bestw.......6F 21
Winterton Ri. NG5: Bestw............6F 21
Winthorpe Rd. NG5: Arn 6C 22
Wintringham Cres.
 NG5: Woodt 2C 34
Wirksworth Rd. DE7: Kirk H 4F 39
Wisa Ter. NG5: Sher....................4H 33
Wishford Av. NG7: Lent...............6C 44
Wisley Cl. NG2: West Br 2G 67
Wisteria Dr. NG12: Edwal 3B 68
Wisteria Rd. NG4: Neth................2C 48
Wisteria Rd. NG4: Stoke B 2C 48
Wistow Cl. NG8: Bas...................1C 44
Withern Rd. NG8: Brox 6F 31
Witney Cl. NG5: Top V 5C 20
Wittering Cl. NG10: Long E.........2G 73
Wiverton Rd. NG13: Bing.............5E 51
Wiverton Rd. NG7: Hys G............1E 45
Woburn Cl. NG12: Edwal 1E 69
Woburn Cft. NG10: Sand 1C 62
Woburn Rd. NG5: Woodt 2D 34
Wodehouse Av. NG11: Goth.........5H 75
Wolds Dr. NG12: Key 5H 79
Wolds Farm Cotts.
 NG12: Stant W..........................2D 80
Wolds La. NG12: C'ton.................5D 70
Wolds La. NG12: Key 5D 70
Wolds La. NG12: Norm W 6B 70
Wolds Ri. NG12: Key....................4H 79
Woldsview Ho. NG12: Cotg..........2F 71
WOLLATON 6D 42
Wollaton Av. NG4: Ged 4F 35
Wollaton Ct. NG6: Bulw 1C 32
Wollaton Cres. NG9: Bee 3E 55
Wollaton Hall 6G 43
Wollaton Hall Dr. NG8: Woll........6B 44
Wollaton Paddocks NG8: Woll.....5C 42
Wollaton Pk. Golf Course...........6H 43
Wollaton Rd. NG8: Woll 1E 55
Wollaton Rd. NG8: Radf...............5E 43
Wollaton Rd. NG8: Woll 5E 43
Wollaton Rd. NG9: Bee.................2E 55
Wollaton St. NG1: Nott.... 3B 4 (4F 45)
Wollaton St. NG15: Huck..............4H 7
 ....(not continuous)
Wollaton Va. NG8: Woll................5B 42
Wolsey Av. NG7: Radf 4D 44
Wood Av. NG10: Sand..................5C 52
Woodbank Cl. NG8: Woll 1D 54
Woodborough 1C 24
Woodborough La. NG3: Mapp 2E 23
Woodborough La. NG5: Arn.........2D 22
Woodborough Rd.
 NG1: Nott 1E 5 (3G 45)
Woodborough Rd.
 NG3: Mapp 1E 5 (1H 45)
Woodborough Rd.
 NG3: Nott 1E 5 (1H 45)
Woodbridge Av. NG11: Clftn........2C 66
Woodbridge Cl. DE75: Hea...........4F 15
Woodbridge Ct. NG7: Hys G 2D 44
 ....(off St Paul's Av.)
Woodchurch Rd. NG5: Arn 4F 21
Wood Cl. NG11: Rudd 1F 77
Wood End Rd. DE75: Hea.............3C 14
Wood Farm Ct. NG11: Thru 5C 74
Woodfield Rd. NG8: Brox 6E 31
Woodford Cl. NG5: Top V 4C 20

Woodford Rd. NG15: Huck............. 5H 7
Woodford Rd. NG5: Woodt........2C 34
Woodgate Cl. NG12: Cotg............2E 71
Woodgate Ct.
  NG7: Radf....................... 3A 4 (4E 45)
Woodgate La. NG12: Cotg 1D 70
Wood Gro. NG14: Calv 3H 11
Woodhall Rd. NG8: Woll 4H 43
Woodhedge Dr. NG3: Nott............1C 46
Woodhorn Cl. NG5: Arn 3B 22
Woodhouse Gdns. NG11: Rudd 5F 67
Woodhouse St. NG3: Nott............4B 46
Woodhouse Way NG16: Nuth 4D 30
Woodhouse Way NG8: Stre 6D 30
Woodkirk Rd. NG11: Clftn 3D 66
Woodland Av. DE7: Ilk 3H 27
Woodland Av. DE72: Brea...........5B 62
Woodland Av. NG6: Bulw............2A 32
Woodland Cl. NG12: Cotg 3F 71
Woodland Cl. NG12: Rad T........... 6H 49
Woodland Cl. NG16: Want 6A 18
Woodland Dr. NG16: Nuth............3F 31
Woodland Dr. NG3: Mapp P 6H 33
Woodland Gro. NG4: Colw 3H 47
Woodland Gro. NG5: Sher............. 3H 33
Woodland Gro. NG9: Chil............. 6D 54
Woodland Rd. NG2: West Br........2B 58
Woodlands, The NG12: Rad T.....6E 49
Woodlands Farm Cl.
  NG15: Huck........................... 1D 18
Woodlands Gro. NG15: Huck....... 1D 18
Woodland Way NG16: Eastw........3A 16
Wood La. NG15: Huck....................4E 7
Wood La. NG4: Ged......................6A 36
Woodlane Gdns. NG3: Nott...........2B 46
Woodlark Ho. NG3: Nott 2B 46
Woodleigh NG12: Key................. 5G 79
Woodleigh Gdns. NG3: Mapp 5D 34
Wood Leys NG3: Nott..................2C 46
Woodley Sq. NG6: Bulw...............3A 20
Woodley St. NG11: Rudd 6G 67
Wood Link NG6: Bulw...................6E 19
Woodpecker Cl. NG13: Bing........6F 51
Woodpecker Hill DE7: D Ab.........6E 39
Woodrow Av. NG8: Bilb 1G 43
Woodsend Cl. NG14: Bur J 3F 37
Woodsend Wharf
  NG7: Nott 6C 4 (6F 45)
Woodsford Gro. NG11: Clftn 3C 66
Woodside NG16: Eastw 3A 16
Woodside Av. NG12: Rad T........ 6H 49
Woodside Av. NG16: Nuth 1B 30
Woodside Cres. DE7: Ilk 2H 27

Woodside Cres.
  NG10: Long E 5D 62
Woodside Dr. NG5: Arn 5H 21
Woodside Rd. NG10: Sand 6C 52
Woodside Rd. NG12: Rad T 6H 49
Woodside Rd. NG14: Bur J........... 4D 36
Woodside Rd. NG9: Bee 2F 55
Woodside Rd. NG9: Chil 1A 64
Woodside Rd. NG9: Lent A 2F 55
Woods La. NG14: Calv 4G 11
Woodstock Av. NG7: Radf 3C 44
Woodstock Rd. NG9: Toton 2G 63
Woodstock St. NG15: Huck 5H 7
Woodstock St. W. NG15: Huck 4H 7
Woodston Wlk. NG5: Arn.............3C 22
Wood St. DE7: Ilk.........................6B 28
Wood St. NG16: Eastw................3B 16
Wood St. NG5: Arn......................5B 22
Wood St. NG7: Radf 3A 4 (4E 45)
WOODTHORPE 2B 34
Woodthorpe Av. NG5: Woodt 3A 34
Woodthorpe Ct. NG5: Sher 4A 34
Woodthorpe Dr. NG3: Mapp.......4B 34
Woodthorpe Dr. NG5: Woodt...... 3H 33
Woodthorpe Gdns. NG5: Sher 4B 34
Woodthorpe Grange
  NG5: Woodt..............................4A 34
WOODTHORPE HOSPITAL
  Nottingham 2H 33
Woodthorpe M. NG5: Woodt...... 3H 33
Woodthorpe Rd. NG3: Mapp.......4B 34
Woodvale NG8: Woll 5B 42
Woodview NG12: Cotg................. 2G 71
Woodview NG12: Edwal.............. 2D 68
Woodview Bus. Cen.
  NG5: Top V 4E 21
Woodview Ct. NG3: Nott.............4E 47
Woodville Cl. NG9: Chil................5C 54
Woodville Dr. NG5: Sher 4A 34
Woodville Rd. NG5: Sher 5G 33
Woodward Av. NG9: Chil 3B 64
Woodyard La. NG3: Nott 2H 57
Woodyard La. NG8: Woll
  Coachmans Cft....................... 4G 43
Woodyard La. NG8: Woll
  Tom Blower Cl......................... 4G 43
Woolacombe Cl. NG3: Mapp.......2F 35
Wooliscroft Cl. DE7: Ilk 5G 27
Woolmer Rd. NG2: Nott.............. 2G 57
Woolpack La.
  NG1: Nott 4F 5 (5H 45)
Woolsington Cl. NG8: Stre...........5D 30
Woolsthorpe Cl. NG8: Bilb...........3F 43

Woolsthorpe Cres.
  DE7: Kirk H............................. 5H 39
Wootton Cl. NG8: Bilb 2D 42
Worcester Gdns. NG5: Woodt......1A 34
Worcester Rd. NG5: Woodt.........2A 34
Wordsworth Av. NG15: Huck........ 5D 6
Wordsworth Rd. NG16: Aws........2E 29
Wordsworth Rd. NG2: West Br 5A 58
Wordsworth Rd. NG5: Arn 6H 21
Wordsworth Rd. NG7: Radf 3C 44
Worksop Rd. NG3: Nott 4B 46
Worrall Av. NG10: Long E 4G 63
Worrall Av. NG5: Arn...................6B 22
Worth St. NG4: Car 1G 47
Worthy Row NG5: Bestw 2E 33
Wortley Av. NG9: Trow................6F 41
Wortley Cl. DE7: Ilk.....................1C 40
Wortley Hall Cl. NG7: Nott 1A 56
Worwood Dr. NG2: West Br......... 1G 67
Woulds Rd. NG12: Cotg...............4F 71
Wragby Rd. NG7: Lent.................4C 44
Wray Cl. NG3: Nott......................4A 46
Wren Cl. NG10: Long E 3C 72
Wren Dr. NG6: Bestw V 2C 20
Wrenthorpe Va. NG11: Clftn 4C 66
Wrights Orchard NG12: Key........ 5G 79
Wright St. NG4: Neth 2A 48
Wroughton Ct. NG16: Eastw........3C 16
Wroxham Dr. NG8: Woll............... 6D 42
Wychwood Dr. NG9: Trow 1F 53
Wychwood Rd. NG13: Bing 5C 50
Wycliffe Gro. NG3: Mapp............5A 34
Wycliffe St. NG7: Bas 6D 32
Wycombe Cl. NG11: Clftn 5B 66
Wye Gdns. NG7: Radf 3B 44
Wykeham Rd. NG5: Woodt 2C 34
Wykes Cl. NG4: Ged 5H 35
Wymondham Cl. NG5: Arn............1C 34
Wynbreck Dr. NG12: Key.............4H 79
Wyndale Dr. DE7: Kirk H 3G 39
Wyndham Cl. NG9: Chil...............1B 64
Wyndham M. NG3: Mapp P 2F 45
Wyndings, The NG5: Woodt.........3B 34
Wynhill Cl. NG13: Bing.................4C 50
Wynndale Dr. NG5: Sher..............4E 33
Wynwood Cl. NG9: Toton.............3B 64
Wynwood Rd. NG9: Toton 3B 64
Wynyard Cl. DE7: Ilk...................4G 27
Wyrale Dr. NG8: Stre....................6E 31
Wysall La. NG11: Bunny 6D 78
Wyton Cl. NG5: Bestw..................2E 33
Wyvern Av. NG10: Long E............1F 73

Wyvern Cl. NG16: Newth 5C 16
Wyville Cl. NG7: Radf...................4C 44

Y

Yalding Dr. NG8: Woll...................5C 42
Yalding Gdns. NG8: Woll..............5C 42
Yard, The NG7: Hys G................... 3D 44
  .... (off Sophie Rd.)
Yard Gallery, The.........................6G 43
Yarwell Cl. NG3: Nott....................2E 47
Yatesbury Cres. NG8: Stre...........1E 43
Yates Gdns. NG5: Top V................5E 21
Ye Olde Trip to
  Jerusalem Inn....................6D 4 (6G 45)
  .... (off Castle Rd.)
Yeoman Av. NG6: Bestw V 1D 20
Yeomans Pde. NG4: Car 2H 47
Yewbarrow Cl. NG2: West Br........6E 59
Yew Cl. NG5: Sher....................... 5H 33
Yewdale Cl. NG11: Clftn...............5B 66
Yewdale Cl. NG2: West Br............6E 59
Yew Tree Av. NG5: Sher 6G 33
Yew Tree Cl. DE75: Hea...............4A 14
Yew Tree Cl. NG12: Rad T............ 6D 48
Yew Tree Ct. NG5: Sher 6G 33
Yew Tree Ct. NG9: Bee.................5G 55
Yew Tree La. NG11: Clftn.............3A 66
Yew Tree La. NG4: Ged................5A 36
Yew Tree Rd. NG15: Huck............6H 7
Yewtree Rd. NG12: Cotg.............. 6G 61
Yonge Cl. NG12: Rad T.................1E 61
York Av. NG10: Sand....................6C 52
York Av. NG9: Bee........................1F 65
York Cl. NG4: Ged 5H 35
York Dr. NG8: Stre....................... 5D 30
Yorke St. NG15: Huck.................... 4G 7
York M. NG5: Arn.........................5B 22
York Rd. NG10: Long E 4E 63
York St. NG1: Nott.............. 1E 5 (3G 45)
York St. NG4: Neth......................2A 48
Young Cl. NG6: Bulw.....................2F 31
Yvonne Cres. NG4: Car................ 2H 47

Z

Zone, The NG1: Nott 3F 5 (4H 45)
  .... (off Cranbrook St.)
Zouche Cl. DE75: Los 3A 14
Zulla Rd. NG3: Mapp P 1G 45
Zulu Rd. NG7: Bas 5D 32

Published by Geographers' A-Z Map Company Limited
An imprint of HarperCollins Publishers
Westerhill Road
Bishopbriggs
Glasgow
G64 2QT

www.az.co.uk
a-z.maps@harpercollins.co.uk

9th edition 2021

© Collins Bartholomew Ltd 2021

This product uses map data licenced from Ordnance Survey
© Crown copyright and database rights 2020 OS 100018598

AZ, A-Z and AtoZ are registered trademarks of Geographers' A-Z Map Company Limited

A catalogue record for this book is available from the British Library.

ISBN 978-0-00-844518-8

10 9 8 7 6 5 4 3 2 1

Printed and bound in China by RR Donnelley APS Co Ltd.